# United States–
# East European
# Relations in the 1990s

WITHDRAWN

## Edited by Richard F. Staar

**CRANE RUSSAK**
A Member of the Taylor & Francis Group
New York · Philadelphia · Washington, DC · London

AIG 4400-0/2

**USA** Publishing Office:    Taylor & Francis New York Inc.
79 Madison Ave., New York, NY 10016–7892

Sales Office:    Taylor & Francis Inc.
1900 Frost Road, Bristol, PA 19007

**UK**    Taylor & Francis Ltd.
4 John St., London WC1N 2ET

**United States-East European Relations in the 1990s**

First published 1989
Printed in the United States of America


**Library of Congress Cataloging in Publication Data**

United States-East European Relations in the 1990s/Richard F. Staar, editor.
    p. cm.
    Includes index.
    ISBN 0-8448-1612-4.  —ISBN 0-8448-1613-2 (pbk.)
    1. Europe, Eastern—Foreign relations—United States. 2. United
States—Foreign relations—Europe, Eastern. 3. United States—
-Foreign—1989-    4. Europe, Eastern—Foreign
Relations—1945-    I. Staar, Richard Felix, 1923-    II. Title: United States
-eastern European relations in the 1990s.
DJK45.U5U2   1989
327.73047—dc19

89–1506
CIP

# Contents

# INTRODUCTION

*Richard F. Staar*

In 1988 the U.S. Department of State published a booklet on American foreign policy that devotes only half a page to Eastern Europe out of a total of 97 printed pages. Recognizing the fact that the USSR exercises hegemony over the region, the United States government seeks to exercise "a moderating influence on Soviet policy toward those nations. [It] deals with East European governments on an individual basis to promote:

- Increased awareness of and respect for human rights.
- Domestic political and economic reform.
- Greater autonomy in their foreign policy.
- Security for all European nations."[1]

The Hoover Institution on War, Revolution and Peace at Stanford University (Stanford, California) sponsored a workshop after the November 1988 national elections on this subject, as a contribution to the foreign policy debate about future relations between the United States and each of the regimes in Eastern Europe.

Participants had been requested to focus on trends that might be important during the 1990s. The political, economic, and military area surveys as well as country background papers were prepared by recognized academic specialists, most of whom are teaching at American colleges or universities. For the projections, current or former U.S. foreign service officers (deputy chiefs of mission and ambassadors) and senior National Security Council staff members were invited to present their views at the workshop.*

*We wish to thank the John M. Olin program on Soviet and East European Studies at the Hoover Institution for its generous support, which made the conference possible.

## POLITICAL OVERVIEW

The sessions commenced with an overview of changing relations after 1985 between the USSR and its client regimes. Robert L. Hutchings suggests in the opening chapter that this transformation may be more fundamental than any since Stalin's death.[2] The call for a "common European home" by Mikhail S. Gorbachev may result in an even stronger drive for closer contacts between the two Europes after political and economic integration in 1992 by the western part of the continent.

The main obstacle, of course, involves Soviet domination over most of the countries in Eastern Europe. If the peoples in the latter accept less than full independence and sovereignty by the year 2000, there may be a chance for relaxation of Moscow control. Dr. Hutchings cites the director of the USSR Institute of Economics for the World Socialist System as concluding at a conference with American scholars that the East European states allegedly now already have "broad opportunities to realize unhindered their national interests."[3]

This statement obviously should be qualified by the limits to change. As a minimum, all allied governments must remain as members of the Warsaw Treaty Organization and continue the leading role of their respective communist parties. However, two other challenges might arise, according to Dr. Hutchings: (1) a regime-supported movement toward political autonomy, qualified by alignment with USSR foreign policy, i.e., "Finlandization," or (2) a revolt against the ruling party within the context of empire decay, which has been called "Ottomanization."

The second challenge would be met by a Soviet invasion, should a political compromise be impossible.[4] Peaceful change, of course, is preferable for all parties concerned. This may already be taking place in such countries as Hungary and Poland. If so, then perhaps Gorbachev will realize that he cannot expect genuine economic reform and prosperity throughout Eastern Europe with simultaneous domination by Moscow over the region's political life.

## CMEA AND THE ECONOMIES

The economic factor is discussed by John P. Hardt in Chapter 2, who spells out Western policies most likely to result in growth and stability. Nevertheless, a comprehensive reform may take 10 years or longer to complete. The West could postpone loans until this process is in place.

The Soviet Union, by pressuring the Council for Mutual Economic Assistance (CMEA) members in Eastern Europe toward reforms, would be supporting this stance.

Other than rendering bilateral aid, the United States in due time might positively influence the international organizations to offer credits. Joint ventures and relaxed technology transfer would follow. Differentiation should favor earlier help for Hungary, Poland, and Yugoslavia where reforms are more advanced than those in other East European countries.

The potential for growth throughout the region is predicted upon the assumption that both the United States and the Soviet Union will find it in their respective national interests to support the economic recovery in the East European part of the world. Dr. Hardt suggests the following possible developments.

An American policy that facilitates commercial exchange, perhaps by easing export and credit restrictions, would align itself with Western Europe if a breakthrough has been made by a specific country (e.g., recognition by the communist regime of Solidarity as a partner in the reconstruction of Poland). Otherwise, our NATO allies may decide to proceed without the United States.

The Soviet Union could expand intra-CMEA exchange of goods and restructure that organization. The announcement Gorbachev made in his 7 December 1988 address before the United Nations about a 10 percent reduction in Soviet armed forces over the next two years[5] could be emulated by other Warsaw Pact members. If so, the overall military burden would also be reduced by those East European governments, if Moscow permits them to do so.

Closer ties among the USSR, Western Europe, Japan, and the United States in terms of joint ventures and other mechanisms might impact Eastern Europe on a trilateral basis. The key to all of this could affect the Soviet's near monopoly control over energy supplies, primarily natural gas and petroleum.[6] How this leverage is used will influence the outcome of reform in the region.

Dr. Hardt suggests that the response to Western policies involves both benefits and risks for the USSR. He develops several scenarios, the most detrimental of which would lead to a loss of Soviet leadership over Eastern Europe. Another envisages a split between the [West] European Economic Community (EC) after 1992 and the United States, with the former continuing to trade and the latter engaging in economic warfare against the Soviet Union.

The emerging relationship between the EC and the CMEA is treated

by Josef C. Brada in the second part of Chapter 2. He traces the protracted talks between the two economic blocs, which commenced in 1973
although there had been country-to-country agreements long before that.
A joint declaration, signed in June 1988, recognized the right of the EC
to negotiate trade agreements with individual CMEA members. The first
was agreed upon three months later with Hungary.

During 1987 only 7 percent of the EC trade involved Eastern Europe
and the Soviet Union. However, Western Europe sends to the CMEA
some 60 percent of the latter's legal high technology imports. The East
also willingly accepts subsidized agricultural commodities from the West.
In return, the EC receives one-third of all East European exports. It is
doubtful that this ratio will increase substantially, according to Professor
Brada.

One interpretation suggests that by making Eastern Europe dependent
upon EC technology and manufactured products, the non-USSR members
of the CMEA[7] might become detached from their metropole. Other observers argue the reverse, namely, that better East-West relations will
mean a break between the United States and the EC, with Western Europe
becoming dependent on Soviet energy/raw materials and ultimately "Fin-
landized."

After 1992 the West European common market may divert its trade
away from the CMEA, although increased production output could have
the opposite effect. The surge of interest by EC members (and Japan),
with 12 billion dollars in loans given to the USSR or being considered
during October-December 1988 could be looked upon as preliminary to
a "Marshall Plan" for the Soviet-dominated region.[8] Or it could simply
result in a new credit war, according to Professor Brada.


# THE WARSAW TREATY ORGANIZATION

Apart from politico-economic factors, there still exists the military dimension, which is addressed by Christopher D. Jones in Chapter 3. He
identifies the unchanging objectives of the Warsaw Pact and mechanisms
through which they may be achieved. This military alliance is faced with
three sets of adversaries: (1) domestic opposition to each East European
regime, (2) those persons in both Germanys who believe in political unification, and (3) the Federal Republic of Germany's military allies.

Professor Jones does not believe that any of Gorbachev's arms control
initiatives would require either Warsaw Treaty Organization (WTO) re-

structuring or a reduction in its military capabilities.[9] The same missions will endure; they are the following:

- Preemption of independent WTO member capability for defense by national means.
- Designation of elite military units from member states for intervention against other states.
- Combining these elite units into bilateral formations and then into a "greater socialist army" to face NATO.
- Assignment of first-line responsibility for internal repression to indigenous national armed forces.
- Defense of home territory against NATO disruption of Soviet logistics and against domestic antiwar protests.
- Providing occupation troops for areas captured by Warsaw Pact forces.

To achieve these six objectives, the USSR has used several principles vis-à-vis its allies: (1) fragmentation of national control over indigenous armed forces, (2) the use of WTO multinational agencies to legitimize bilateral Soviet-East European links, and (3) the pursuit of cohesion through functional integration, resulting in the absence of any choice other than to accept USSR domination.

These three principles are applied by means of military doctrine, the WTO political directorate, joint maneuvers (both bilateral and multilateral), central agencies of the alliance, the officer education system, and defense production, which makes war materiel interoperable.

All of the foregoing have survived the mismanagement of the Brezhnev-Andropov-Chernenko era. Professor Jones identifies the new arms control proposals, including the one for a set of conventional force reduction talks that would cover the area from the Atlantic to the Urals and supersede the 15-year-old Mutual and Balanced Force Reduction (MBFR) negotiations. Gorbachev already announced in his speech on 7 December 1988 before the United Nations in New York that the Soviet armed forces would be cut unilaterally by 500,000 men over the next two years. However, even the foregoing will not affect the status quo in Eastern Europe or between the two Germanys, according to Professor Jones.

## THE NORTHERN TIER

The discussions center in Part II on the three countries comprising the largest units within the so-called socialist commonwealth of nations. Ar-

thur R. Rachwald (Chapter 4) suggests that the political dynamics of Poland will be affected by USSR domination through the end of this century, unless Soviet power unexpectedly were to decline. The stalemate
between regime and opposition continues.[10] Despite this fact, the Polish
model of socialist pluralism ultimately will include the ruling party, Solidarity, and the Roman Catholic Church.

This should result in freedom to determine the domestic system, although as a member of the Warsaw Pact and with communists in control
of internal security. The choice for the Polish regime in the 1990s will
be either to continue its socioeconomic decline to the point of civil war
or to allow representative government and a free economy. In any event
this road to pluralism is likely to be slow, frustrating, and expensive,
according to Professor Rachwald.

In his projections, also in Chapter 4, Nicholas G. Andrews discusses
the basic objectives of U.S. policy vis-à-vis Poland in the 1990s as supporting de-Stalinization, decentralization, and democratization. He lists
seven principles upon which the foregoing could be based and then de-
lineates three ways in which American goals can be achieved: encouraging political pluralism, offering economic assistance, and expanding
contacts with the Polish population. The success of this policy will depend, of course, upon the regime's attitude and its readiness to compromise. For that to materialize, one may have to wait until a successor
replaces General Wojciech Jaruzelski.

In contrast with those of Poland, the political stability and economic
growth rate of East Germany are the most impressive throughout the region. The alternate model across the border to the West, uncertainty regarding Erich Honecker's successor (which may not be settled until the
next party congress in May 1990), and the lack of full popular support
are mentioned by Robert Gerald Livingston in Chapter 5.

Dr. Livingston does not consider political stability to be a problem,
since both Germanys and the USSR have a shared interest here. Apart
from incremental economic reform, the German Democratic Republic
(GDR) may be moving toward more legality based on pre-1933 traditions.
West German influence is increasing,[11] with the GDR becoming more
attracted to its prosperous neighbor. The possibility of this relationship
developing into a de facto FRG protectorate over East Germany is not
inconceivable, according to Dr. Livingston.

Nelson C. Ledsky (also in Chapter 5) recognizes that the two Germanys
have a special relationship that the United States will not undermine. In
effect, our NATO ally has been given the lead to pursue its own objec-

tives. American concerns center on development of political pluralism, respect for human rights, and more responsible international behavior by the GDR. Progress has been slow. Mr. Ledsky suggests that Moscow is and will be more important for East Berlin than Bonn. If the reform effort fails in the USSR, no intra-German dialogue can prevent a spill-over effect.[12]

Czechoslovakia is also of prime geopolitical importance for the Soviet Union. Zdenek Suda (Chapter 6) develops three possible scenarios, all aimed at preserving dominance of the ruling communist group: (1) continuity through cooperation, with only moderate and controlled reform, (2) an indigenous reform to gain popularity, which might develop a momentum of its own, or (3) ignoring the Soviet changes, which would be a most dangerous course of action. Which one has been selected will be known at the next party congress opening on 10 May 1990, or perhaps earlier.[13]

Professor Suda concludes with a discussion of international communism, now coming to an end. The phenomenon might pose a danger only if directed from a single center that has the power to intervene. To render such intervention impossible by promoting the independence of small countries should become the axiom of U.S. policy in the 1990s, according to Professor Suda.

American relations with Czechoslovakia are surveyed (also in Chapter 6) by Carl W. Schmidt, who contends that modest progress has been made over the past six years, and he provides the evidence for this. He also discusses fundamental differences between the two governments, especially regarding human rights. A possible course of future action is delineated, based on realistic expectations, as follows: encouragement of East-West regional cooperation, pressure for observance of human rights, welcoming genuine economic and political reform with most favored nation status, and expansion of exchanges (including views and information), among others.

## THE SOUTHERN TIER

The three countries remaining as members in both the Warsaw Pact and the CMEA are discussed in Part III, beginning with Romania (Chapter 7). Mary Ellen Fischer stresses that the longevity of current leader Nicolae Ceauşescu would affect trends in the 1990s. Conditions will change only after his removal or death. Until that time, personalized power, nationalism, rapid industrialization, and centralized control should continue.[14]

Professor Fischer concludes that Ceauşescu's resignation is highly unlikely, with forced removal at almost the same low level of probability. A transition managed by the highest ranking communist leaders might not result in a dynastic succession, however. Emil Bobu would seem to be the one most likely to emerge at the top from a collective leadership, unless he is removed earlier by his current mentor. Commitments to Marxism and the Soviet alliance, nationalism that enhances legitimacy, and personalized power as a tradition in politics should remain.

In his projections (also Chapter 7), Robert R. King offers two scenarios: (1) with Ceauşescu and (2) without Ceauşescu. The former would suggest little, if any, change in U.S.-Romanian relations. The limits of Soviet tolerance have been reached. Should the leadership change in Bucharest, Dr. King does not believe that it will alter the strategy of foreign policy. On the tactical side, greater flexibility will lead to improvements, especially if Gorbachev remains in power.

The communist leader in Bulgaria is the oldest (born 1911) in all of Eastern Europe. Todor Zhivkov had conscientiously emulated Soviet policies until his national party conference in January 1987, at which the announcement was made that fundamental reforms would be postponed until the next communist party congress (1991). The mid-1988 Central Committee plenum purged two leading communists, rejected automatic application of USSR experience, and ordered a crackdown on dissent.[15]

However, as John D. Bell (Chapter 8) points out, important factors favor resumption of reform. Society has changed significantly since Zhivkov became party boss in 1954. Members of the generation born after World War II are more sophisticated than their predecessors. Neither disloyal nor antiregime, they find the fundamentalist Marxism of aging leaders irrelevant and an obstacle to progress, according to Professor Bell.

Jack R. Perry (also Chapter 8) agrees that Bulgarians look forward to an economic future with some hope. He suggests that the United States encourage the people to work toward true independence. Normalization of relations with Sofia is well worth pursuing by Washington and is attainable, as Eastern Europe emerges from under the Soviet shadow, according to Ambassador Perry.

Despite the impression that Hungary had become the showplace of Eastern Europe, the national communist party conference in May 1988 revealed a different picture: complacency, delays in reform, a growing hard currency debt, inflation, a declining standard of living, and social tension. Also discussed were political mistakes, which are to be rectified by working groups, appointed at the conference. The new leader, Károly Grósz, however, has indicated that a multiparty system is out of the question during his lifetime.[16]

According to Peter A. Toma (Chapter 9), at least five major independent groups have been harrassed by the authorities. Draft legislation, if approved, supposedly will protect them in the future. Only after a new constitution is adopted in early 1990 (to replace the 1949 Stalinist document) will it be theoretically possible to pass a law allowing other political parties to operate. Unless these economic and political reforms are pursued vigorously, Professor Toma predicts that mass demonstrations will trigger the use of force by the regime. Some 20 peaceful ones took place during the 1988 calendar year in Budapest.[17]

Martin J. Hillenbrand, also in Chapter 9, suggests that the United States alone no longer can play a decisive role in Eastern Europe. Allowing our NATO allies, especially the Federal Republic of Germany, to take the lead would be a wise policy. The United States itself should encourage all Hungarian moves toward economic and political liberalization, perhaps even relaxing controls over the export of dual-use products by the Economic Community in Western Europe. American foreign policy options must be formulated within the broad context of the East European region, including the Soviet Union, according to Ambassador Hillenbrand.

## NON-WARSAW PACT MEMBERS

The larger of the two non-Warsaw Pact countries is Yugoslavia (associate CMEA member), which has experienced inflation, unemployment, strikes, and ethnic disruption during the 1980s. Even this domestic political upheaval has not affected renewed financing by the West, however.[18] Whether conditions can be stabilized depends upon the international environment, according to Susan L. Woodward (Chapter 10). Several domestic Yugoslav policy compromises have been reached to prevent political disintegration, and these are not under serious challenge.

The first is based upon a strong and independent defense to protect national sovereignty. The second compromise, between centralization for defense and development on the one hand and regional self-sufficiency on the other, means a weak center. The third involves free enterprise in commodity production and the market at the micro level, contrasted with

socialist ownership and distribution at the macro level. Professor Woodward suggests that political stability has been bought by Belgrade with a
persistent suboptimal economic policy.

In his considerations of future U.S. foreign policy, Richard E. Johnson
(also Chapter 10) suggests that it would be a mistake to become involved
with these domestic Yugoslav problems. The ferment has brought openness to political life and, to date, has been devoid of violence. It is in
the interest of the United States to preserve an independent and strong
Yugoslavia. The "three liberalizations" concerning prices, imports, and
foreign exchange were introduced in May 1988 without friction. The same
applied to a consensus reached during October of that year on constitutional amendments. However, Mr. Johnson does not recommend that the
West extend more credits tied to economic reform at this time. The International Monetary Fund and World Bank, among others, contributed
$1.4 billion during calendar year 1988 to Yugoslavia.

Albania, neither a member of the Warsaw Pact nor of the CMEA, seems
least prepared to enter the twenty-first century. Decades of economic mismanagement, stagnation, and repression were the legacy of Enver Hoxha,
inherited in April 1985 by Ramiz Alia, who has moved cautiously and
with moderation to reverse these trends.[19] Reinvigoration of the economy
would require that the Albanian regime abolish central planning and overcome resistance of the entrenched bureaucracy.

Elez Biberaj (Chapter 11) contends that radical reform appears unlikely. Since this alternative is unacceptable, Alia has chosen superficial
reforms without touching the fundamental features of the system. None
of these will succeed if unaccompanied by political change and more responsible use of power by the elite. However, reform in the political
system will be difficult, risky, and contentious, according to Dr. Biberaj.

In his commentary, also in Chapter 11, Nathaniel Davis examines the
signs of thaw that have appeared in Albania. These include some flexibility in agriculture, the easing of repression by Alia, slightly more tolerance of religion, and some economic reforms faintly similar to Gorbachev's *perestroika*. In foreign affairs, Professor Davis examines the
continuing obstacles and impediments to the establishment of U.S.-Al-
banian diplomatic relations and discusses the prospects for overcoming
them.

Stanford, California
February 1989

## Notes to Introduction

1. U.S. Department of State, *Fundamentals of U.S. Foreign Policy* (Washington, DC: Bureau of Public Affairs, March 1988), p. 53.

2. See his new preface, "Gorbachev and Eastern Europe," in *Soviet-East European Relations: Consolidation and Conflict* (Madison: University of Wisconsin Press, 1987), paper, pp. xv–xxvii.

3. Oleg T. Bogomolev, "The United States and Eastern Europe," *Problems of Communism*, 37, no. 3–4 (May–August 1988), 65–67. The meeting took place during July 1988 in the United States.

4. This is the assessment also of Zbigniew K. Brzezinski, the dean among contemporary sovietologists. See his Special Address, *ibid.*, p. 69.

5. "Vystuplenie M. S. Gorbacheva v OON," *Pravda,* 8 December 1988, pp. 1–2.

6. A new CMEA Committee for Cooperation on Fuel and Raw Materials held its first meeting in Moscow. "Priniat plan raboty," *Pravda,* 19 November 1988, p. 4.

7. See Steven W. Popper, *Conflicts in CMEA Science and Technology Integration Policy* (Santa Monica, CA: October 1988), RAND Corp., P-7491, for a recent study of this organization.

8. Ronald Bailey, "Let Them Make the Loans," *Forbes* (12 December 1988), p. 102; *U.S. News & World Report* (19 December 1988), p. 20. The USSR owed the West $43 billion at this time, with American banks holding less than half of 1 percent of the outstanding Soviet debt.

9. On these capabilities, see Jeffrey Simon (ed.), *NATO-Warsaw Pact Force Mobilization* (Washington, DC: National Defense University Press, 1988), pp. 563.

10. Evidence comes from a Central Committee plenum that dismissed six members of the ruling Politburo and added eight new ones. John Tagliabue in the *New York Times,* 22 and 23 December 1988, pp. A-8 and A-4, respectively.

11. Serge Schmemann, "2 Germanies' Political Divide Is Being Blurred by Glasnost," *New York Times,* 18 December 1988, pp. 1, 14.

12. In the discussion, the use of National Endowment for Democracy (NED) funding was suggested. For successes achieved, e.g., in Poland by NED, see George F. Will, "Seed Money for Democracy," *The Washington Post,* 18 December 1988, p. C-7.

13. "Razrabotka programmy KPČ," *Pravda,* 17 December 1988, p. 4. See also the *New York Times,* 16 December 1988, p. A-11, for the retirement of two known hard-liners.

14. See, e.g., "Ceauşescu Opposes Reform," *Soviet East European Report,* 6, no. 8 (10 December 1988), 6.

15. Sofia radio, 20 July 1988.

16. For the reasons, see Tagliabue, "Independents a Problem in Budapest," *New York Times,* 19 December 1988, p. A-3.

17. V. Gerasimov, "Perestroika v Vengrii," *Pravda,* 12 December 1988, p. 5.

18. For details, see Richard F. Staar, *Communist Regimes in Eastern Europe,* 5th rev. ed. (Stanford, CA: Hoover Institution Press, 1988), pp. 221–259.

19. For a Soviet assessment, see the article by N. Iurchenko on Albania in *Pravda,* 28 November 1988, p. 6.

# Part I

# The Setting

# Chapter 1

# POLITICAL OVERVIEW*

*Robert L. Hutchings†*

## SOVIET DILEMMAS IN EASTERN EUROPE

The image of Polish opposition figures avidly reading *Pravda,* or of demonstrators in Prague shouting "Gorbachev" and *"glasnost'"* at a rally marking the twentieth anniversary of the Soviet invasion, would have been hard to conjure up a few years earlier. Under Mikhail Gorbachev, it was the Soviet leadership that represented a dynamic, fresh approach to the challenges of the day—in stark contrast to the grey gerontocracies in power in most of Eastern Europe. The winds of change were blowing from Moscow and Leningrad; Budapest and Warsaw were only belatedly moving toward renewal and reform.

After an initial period of domestic consolidation, Gorbachev launched a series of sweeping reform proposals under the rubrics of *glasnost'* and *perestroika.* But for all of his innovation at home and in relations with the West, his early approaches to Eastern Europe were tentative and conservative. Gorbachev sought closed ranks and improved coordination in foreign policy, stressed Leninist discipline in party policies, and largely followed the lead of his predecessors in intrabloc affairs. At least initially,

---

*This chapter concerns Soviet relations with the "Warsaw Pact six": Bulgaria, Romania, Hungary, Czechoslovakia, Poland, and the German Democratic Republic (GDR). It is based, in part, on "Gorbachev and Eastern Europe," preface to the paperback edition of the author's *Soviet-East European Relations: Consolidation and Conflict* (Madison: University of Wisconsin Press, 1984; rev. pb. ed., 1987).

†The views expressed here are the author's, and do not necessarily reflect those of the United States government.

*15*

changes in style did not yield changes in substance—reflecting, perhaps, the intractability of Eastern Europe's economic and political dilemmas.

The demonstration effect of Soviet internal changes, however, was profoundly unsettling, reminding many East European officials of Khrushchev's de-Stalinization campaign and the subsequent upheavals in Hungary and Poland in October 1956. *Glasnost'*, meaning in the Soviet lexicon a controlled "openness" designed to attack bureaucratic inertia and infuse dynamism into the domestic economy, was viewed with particular alarm. For one thing, *glasnost'* in the Hungarian, East German, or Czechoslovak contexts would certainly entail a far deeper process of public examination and unleash potentially uncontrollable expectations for rapid change. For another, Gorbachev's assault on the mismanagement of the Brezhnev leadership in the USSR could only be construed as a critique of the many Brezhnev era holdovers in Eastern Europe, who sought continuity and stability, not change and self-recrimination. Thus *glasnost'* had few adherents among the East European leaders, but it infused a new dynamic into incipient succession struggles, as various heirs presumptive sought to align themselves with Moscow to support their own ambitions.

In this way, the advent of the Gorbachev leadership in Moscow heightened uncertainties and created new divisions in Eastern Europe. More than that, it heralded the end of an era in Eastern Europe and created a mix of hopes and fears that an entirely new era, already begun in the USSR, was about to be ushered in.

The very boldness of Gorbachev's vision dramatized some of the fundamental contradictions of communist rule in Eastern Europe: how to legitimize systems that are widely regarded as alien, how to embrace nationalist aspirations while maintaining internationalist solidarity, how to open certain segments of political life while leaving others closed, and how to "restructure" the political and economic system without fundamentally altering it. For the Soviet leadership, the task was to make the East European states secure, stable, and free-standing while keeping them fully obedient client states. Squaring that circle has been the dilemma of every Soviet leader since Stalin.

## EAST EUROPEAN DILEMMAS

In 1985 when Mikhail Gorbachev took power in Moscow, Eastern Europe had endured more than a decade of stagnation and immobility. Except for General Wojciech Jaruzelski in Poland, who became party first secretary in 1981, the same top party leaders had been in office for years, with two of them (Todor Zhivkov in Bulgaria and János Kádár in Hungary) into their fourth decade in power. Reform ideas were mooted but not implemented, leadership changes were rumored but not realized, and intrabloc relations were held largely in abeyance. Beneath the surface, economic, political, and social deterioration had become more acute, the sense of impending change more pronounced.

Even in Poland, despite the many ups and downs of the internal scene since the imposition of martial law in December 1981, the fundamental impasse remained between the Jaruzelski regime and the population at large. The former had demonstrated its capacity to suppress but not to govern; its policies had succeeded in dividing and disorienting the opposition but not in "normalizing" the internal situation. And neither half-hearted reform attempts nor the good fortune of five successive bounty harvests had arrested the prolonged economic crisis.

## Economic Decline

As in the late 1970s, the Polish economic decline of the 1980s was but the extreme variant of a more general pattern affecting all of Eastern Europe. Most obviously, the regionwide financial crisis of the early 1980s spelled the end of an era of East-West economic detente. Trade with the West collapsed, new credits dried up, and the Soviet financial "umbrella" proved an illusion. By 1982 all the East European countries save Bulgaria and Czechoslovakia had been compelled to enter into refinancing negotiations with Western creditors. Despite massive rescheduling, Poland's debt continued to escalate, as the Jaruzelski regime failed to repay even the interest on outstanding loans. At the other extreme, Nicolae Ceauşescu's aversion to IMF (International Monetary Fund) conditionally prompted him to break off negotiations in 1983 and begin liquidating Romania's foreign debt by draining the domestic economy. Elsewhere, the Hungarians and, outside the bloc, the Yugoslavs managed to avert bankruptcy through periodic refinancing and short-term loans. Only the German Democratic Republic (GDR), buoyed by generous West German loans, managed to survive the financial squeeze and move toward a modest economic recovery.

Economic relations with the USSR fared little better. The price of Soviet oil deliveries to Eastern Europe reached a new peak in the early 1980s, as the CMEA (Council for Mutual Economic Assistance) five-year averaging mechanism belatedly reflected the full brunt of the 1978–1979 increase in world oil prices. Beset with economic dilemmas of its own, the Soviet leadership cut oil deliveries by 10 percent and heightened pressure on the East Europeans for higher quality goods in return.[1] Thus the double economic bind of the late 1970s had grown considerably more acute in the following decade.

External economic pressures took a heavy toll on material living standards, with all that implied for political stability throughout the region. In Romania, shortages of energy supplies and basic foodstuffs reached critical proportions, triggering a series of isolated strikes and demonstrations and raising the prospect of a brushfire of popular unrest. Poland's downward economic spiral transformed the relative prosperity of the early 1970s into a dim memory and further undercut regime efforts toward "normalization." Elsewhere the decline was less catastrophic but still severe, and the dangers of economically-induced political crises were on the rise. More immediately, failure to deliver the promised improvements in material living standards—linchpin for the tacit social contract of the 1970s—had undermined political authority and deepened societal withdrawal and alienation. Even Hungary, once the showcase of socialist stability and prosperity, was experiencing a prolonged economic decline that threatened the very essence of Kadarism.

This prolonged period of economic stagnation had effected the East European economies in more fundamental ways. Sharply reduced investments had perpetuated the aging smokestack industries, further undermining East European competitiveness in world markets and contributing to the environmental devastation that had already made some parts of Eastern Europe virtually uninhabitable. And the failure to keep pace with the newly industrialized countries, much less the advanced industrial democracies, in the scientific-technological revolution had further mortgaged Eastern Europe's economic future. By the mid-1980s, some Hungarian reform economists were arguing that closing the scientific-technological gap was critical to Hungary's national survival. They seemed to mean that literally.

## Political Malaise

Adding to Eastern Europe's economic decline in the 1980s was the stagnation and immobility of its aging party leaderships. In 1987 the average age of the six party first secretaries was well over 70, their average tenure in office more than two decades. Only Jaruzelski, a relative youngster among these gerontocrats, and the GDR's Erich Honecker, still spry at

75, seemed reasonably fit and energetic; the others were all in poor health, presiding over leaderships in manifest decline. In Czechoslovakia, virtually the entire post-1968 leadership remained in power, presided over (but not led) by the increasingly enfeebled Gustáv Husák. These were hardly the leaders to grapple with the difficult policy dilemmas of the late 1980s.

Political malaise in Eastern Europe had been accentuated by a prolonged period of drift in Moscow, stretching from the latter years of the Leonid Brezhnev era through the brief interregna of Iuri Andropov and Konstantin Chernenko. Not only did uncertainties in the Kremlin further complicate succession dilemmas in Eastern Europe, but the absence of clear and decisive Soviet leadership left those regimes largely to their own devices in coping with the challenges of the 1980s.[2]

Under these conditions—economic stagnation, political malaise, and diminished Soviet authority—the natural proclivities of the several East European leaderships were accentuated. The Prague regime's instinctive conservatism turned into obsessive orthodoxy; Ceauşescu's personality cult became a bizarre self-caricature; the GDR's cultivation of better relations with the Federal Republic of Germany (FRG) began to look like an exclusive inter-German "security partnership." As the leaderships sought to establish some new modus vivendi with a disillusioned populace, or at least some self-proclaimed *raison d'état*, their idiosyncracies became more pronounced, their ideological affinity more ritualistic.

The process of ideological erosion, already evident to rulers and ruled alike, was greatly accelerated by the crushing of Solidarity and the imposition of martial law in Poland. If Solidarity had exposed the corruption and incompetence of People's Poland, the martial law regime of General Jaruzelski symbolized the coercive power underlying the entire communist enterprise in Eastern Europe. The liquidation of the Prague Spring, the false promises of "goulash communism," and then the crushing of the first authentic workers' movement in postwar Eastern Europe: all these had irretrievably undermined the ideological premises of communist rule.

Within East European societies the processes of economic, political, and ideological degeneration prompted a kind of regionwide existential crisis, a search for alternate value structures and collective identity. These phenomena, too disparate and abstract to define more precisely, entailed a growing conception of civil society distinct from—and, almost by definition, in opposition to—the ruling political systems. They were variously manifested in a broad-based religious revival, particularly among Roman Catholics; the development of new forms of autonomous social activity, including pacifist and environmental movements; renewed interest among Czech and Hungarian intellectuals in a (highly idealized) "Central European" identity; and, above all, a resurgence of national consciousness throughout Eastern Europe.[3]

In Hungary particularly, there was a tremendous revival of interest in that country's history (popularized by, among others, the rock opera *Istvan the King*), growing concern over the plight of Hungarian minorities in Romania and Slovakia, a resurgence of romantic-chauvinistic populism in Hungarian dissident and writers' circles, and intense discussion of the role of small states in helping overcome the postwar division of Europe. In Bulgaria, the late Liudmila Zhivkova, daughter of the party first secretary, tapped an unsuspected vein of nationalist sentiment in her glorification of Bulgarian history and culture during her brief tenure as culture minister.[4] Underground publishing houses and independent social groups in Czechoslovakia, Poland, and even Romania similarly reflected this growing national resurgence.

The extent to which these sentiments motivated official policy is more difficult to pin down. Certainly there was a great deal of cooptation and manipulation: the Jaruzelski regime's appropriation of national symbols; Ceauşescu's extravagant self-glorification as the embodiment of Romania's historical achievements; and the Honecker regime's expropriation of Martin Luther, Frederick the Great, and others as "objectively progressive" precursors of the East German state. In other cases, official policy played on chauvinistic, exclusivist nationalism, as in Bulgaria's brutal assimilation campaign against its Turkish minority, Romanian repression of the Hungarian minority in Transylvania, and an ugly resurgence of regime anti-Semitism in Poland, Romania, and elsewhere. But even this sham nationalism reflected a new effort on the part of the East European leaders to tap the national theme as an agent of political legitimacy at a time of economic and political decline.

## National Self-Assertiveness

More worrying from Moscow's perspective was the growing tendency toward national self-assertiveness among its allies, particularly in the aftermath of INF (intermediate-range nuclear force) deployments in Western Europe in late 1983 and 1984. East European concern over the Soviet walkout from the Geneva disarmament talks and the threatened Soviet counterdeployment of tactical nuclear weapons in Eastern Europe betrayed deeper anxieties over the erosion of European detente. In response, Ceauşescu refused to join the Soviet-led boycott of the 1984 summer Olympic games, the Kádár regime undertook a diplomatic offensive to shore up relations with Western governments, and the East Germans expressed their determination to "limit the damage" to inter-German relations and announced that Honecker would visit West Germany in the fall of 1984. In the period leading up to that planned visit, these grievances gave rise to an unprecedented, semipublic display of Warsaw Pact disunity, with the Soviets and Czechoslovaks calling for a tougher line and closed ranks, whereas the Hungarians, East Germans, and Romanians were pressing for improved East-West relations and affirming the special role of small states in promoting detente. And although Honecker eventually succumbed to strong Soviet pressure in agreeing to postpone the visit, his open defiance up to the last moment revealed the depth of the dispute.[5]

Beneath the immediate issues of contention lay the more fundamental conflict over the extent to which the East European junior allies should be able to pursue their own interests in relations with the West. Thus various East European exponents of the "role of small states" presented what amounted to a repudiation of the Brezhnev Doctrine, asserting the primacy of the national interests of their states over international obligations to the entire "socialist community." For most of the East European regimes, the preservation of East-West detente was no longer negotiable; it had become an essential ingredient of economic and political stability. More than that, it corresponded to rising pressures from below for national self-expression and self-assertion and, ultimately, for overcoming the Yalta division by affirming the "Europeanness" of the East European states.[6]

Prompted also by continued economic and political erosion, these expressions of national self-assertiveness reflected a new attempt by the East European regimes to build some sort of modus vivendi with their growingly restive populations. Unlike the upheavals of 1956, 1968, and 1980–1981, they did not involve a frontal assault on Soviet primacy in the region but rather aimed at achieving greater scope for diversity in the interest of political stability. And Moscow, having so recently faced in Poland a popular revolt of unprecedented dimensions, was now confronted with a new and more subtle set of challenges led by the East European regimes themselves.

## THE GORBACHEV PHENOMENON

Such was the East European situation that confronted Mikhail Gorbachev when he assumed power in early 1985. It is difficult to know just how he perceived Eastern Europe and how his perceptions differed from those of his predecessors, but it is evident that the assessment was an extension of his internal agenda for the USSR.

Clearly, Gorbachev proceeded from certain fundamental preconceptions: that economic failures had undermined Soviet power and prestige, that the scientific and technological revolution threatened to leave the socialist system behind and consign it to second-rank global status, and that radical restructuring was required to modernize the domestic economy and revitalize Soviet power. This latter aim demanded a controlled process of *glasnost'* to overcome bureaucratic resistance and breathe new life into society at large. Externally, it required an easing of East-West tension, abatement of the debilitating arms race with the United States, and curtailment of some of Moscow's costly adventures in the Third World.

Gorbachev was also reacting against an ideological world view in which Soviet interests were seen through the prism of rigid bipolar confrontation with the United States. This orientation, personified in such figures as the late Mikhail Suslov, Andrei Gromyko, and lesser lights like Boris Ponomarev, gave way to a more pragmatic pursuit of Soviet regional interests under Gorbachev's new foreign policy team headed by Eduard Shevardnadze, Aleksandr Iakovlev, and Anatolii Dobrynin. In relations with Western Europe and China particularly, Gorbachev saw new opportunities for improving the Soviet position through a more activist and innovative foreign policy.

As for Eastern Europe, Gorbachev probably did not have a fully developed conception of its problems and certainly lacked a clear and coherent plan of action.[7] He viewed with obvious disdain the hidebound leaderships in Sofia and Prague, which epitomized the corruption, inefficiency, and dogmatism of Brezhnev's latter years. Improved economic performance was also a high priority—to transform Eastern Europe from a drain on Soviet resources to an asset in the Soviet modernization drive, as well as to diminish Western economic leverage in the region. And given Gorbachev's ambitious foreign policy program, he also required greater discipline and coordination among the East Europeans. This, then, was the early agenda: to assure innovative party leaderships, improved economic performance, and closed ranks behind Soviet foreign policy initiatives. But how to go about it?

## Foreign Policy Coordination

Gorbachev's first task was to reassert Soviet authority over Warsaw Pact foreign policy and end the ad-libbing that had characterized East European initiatives toward the West during the early 1980s. This he achieved through a series of Warsaw Pact summits—four in the first eight months—and the adoption of something approaching a conciliar system, whereby East European leaders were briefed before and after major Soviet policy departures. Evidently a compromise was struck in which the East Germans, Hungarians, and others were put on notice that future initiatives were to be carefully coordinated with Moscow but were assured of a more forthcoming Soviet approach toward the West that would allow the East Europeans greater room for maneuver.

This new Soviet approach was not long in coming, as Gorbachev returned his negotiators to the arms talks in Geneva and mounted a diplomatic offensive toward improved relations with the United States, Western Europe, China, and even Israel. These efforts also involved a much more active role for the East Europeans. Jaruzelski and Honecker paid early visits to China aimed at restoring normal interstate and interparty relations, and several East European governments began exploring the prospects for normalizing relations with Israel. They were particularly active in the arms control field: the Poles and East Germans announced proposals for nuclear and chemical weapons-free zones; and the Prague regime later chimed in with a proposed "corridor of peace" in Central Europe.

Such deployment of allies in support of Soviet objectives was not without its risks. Most obviously, these initiatives threatened to evolve into separate East European interests in regions formerly off limits to them. And the abrupt and unexplained change of heart concerning two former ideological foes like Israel and China—especially China, whose policies had become more heretical than ever—must have shaken the foundations of party orthodoxy in Eastern Europe. (One can only imagine the labored justifications at party gatherings in Prague or Sofia.) Indeed, Chinese overtures toward Eastern Europe seemed designed, in part, to sow discord in the Soviet camp.

In light of these dangers, it should not be surprising that Gorbachev laid great stress on coordination and discipline within Warsaw Pact councils. The renewal of the pact itself was instructive. With its original term (20 years plus an automatic 10-year extension) due to expire in May 1985, the Romanians and others had dropped hints that they favored certain changes in the text—a watering down of mutual defense obligations and more precise provisions for the pact's eventual dissolution—and that they wanted only a 10-year renewal. In the event, the pact was renewed for another 20 years without a single change; and Gorbachev, then only two months in office, had achieved an impressive show of authority. Ceauşescu's

acquiescence, by contrast, demonstrated his narrowing room for maneuver: not only had economic pressures forced him to turn increasingly to
Soviet markets, but Soviet overtures toward China and Israel—two external pillars of Romania's independent-minded line—had undermined
his maverick status within the alliance.

Gorbachev also moved to strengthen coordination on arms control policy, particularly after the U.S.-Soviet INF agreement and movement in
Vienna toward a new forum for the talks on conventional force reductions. Not only was regular bilateral and multilateral coordination expanded, but two new Warsaw Pact bodies were created: a Special Commission on Disarmament Questions and a Multilateral Group for Current
Information Exchange.

Another case in point concerned East German party leader Honecker's
plans to attend the West Berlin ceremonies commemorating the 750th
anniversary of that city in the spring of 1987. As he had three years
earlier, Honecker saw the visit to the "other" Germany as a symbol of
his own diplomatic status and of the GDR's coming of age. Unlike the
open polemics surrounding Honecker's planned visit to West Germany
in the fall of 1984, however, Soviet-East German differences were quietly
resolved in the spring of 1987, with Honecker declining the West Berlin
invitation but accepting (evidently with Soviet blessings) a widely publicized visit to West Germany in the fall of that year.

## Economic Pressure

The second major item on Gorbachev's agenda was to harness the East
European economies to the Soviet modernization drive. Having run up
large trade deficits with Moscow in the 1970s, the East Europeans were
put on notice that the USSR expected more and better goods in return for
energy deliveries. The heavily indebted Hungarians, Romanians, and Poles
were enjoined to reduce their economic dependence on the West; the Bulgarian and Czechoslovak regimes were instructed to revive their stagnant
economies and upgrade performance. And all were pressed to join the
Soviet-led Comprehensive Program for Scientific-Technical Cooperation
through the year 2000—"CMEA 2000," for short—through joint ventures and coordinated production in key high technology sectors.[8] These
measures seemed to herald a new era of economic imperialism—or perhaps a Gorbachev corollary to the Brezhnev Doctrine, whereby the economic interests of the East European states were to be subordinated to

the interests of the entire "socialist community" (as defined by Moscow).

The actual conduct of Soviet-East European economic relations during Gorbachev's first two years revealed less change than the early rhetoric seemed to promise. Trade figures for 1986 showed undiminished imbalances in Eastern Europe's favor; and the improved trade balances thereafter were due almost entirely to falling Soviet energy prices (and not to increased East European exports).[9] Domestically, for all the lip service paid to "restructuring," there was scant evidence of any serious move toward economic reform. Survivors of many a prior Soviet campaign, the veteran East European leaders temporized, as yet unpersuaded of the staying power of the new Soviet leader.

The East Europeans were particularly wary of being drawn into Soviet-sponsored joint ventures in high technology areas, and resistance was evident in the elaboration of the CMEA 2000 program. Owing to its unique access to the Western technology via inner-German trade, the GDR was the key East European participant; and the East Germans were as determined to protect their position as the Soviets were to exploit it. Elsewhere, the Hungarians, Romanians, and others were similarly reluctant to jeopardize their own carefully cultivated trade relations with the West in support of Gorbachev's domestic agenda. These differences came to a head in early November 1986, when the East European party leaders were summoned abruptly to Moscow—just two weeks after their prime ministers, meeting in Bucharest, had failed to reach agreement on the next stage of scientific-technological collaboration. Gorbachev's intervention helped advance the CMEA 2000 program, and it certainly demonstrated his dynamic, activist personal style, but it also revealed the determined obstructionism of the entrenched and cautious East European party leaders.

Gorbachev also came to understand that simply pressing for improved East European trade performance was not enough: the goals he had set for high technology cooperation demanded fundamental restructuring of the conduct of Soviet-East European economic relations. Hence at the 1987 CMEA Council session, Moscow reopened some of the basic problems that had frustrated regional integration from the start: lack of a convertible currency, inadequacy of pricing mechanisms, and low mobility of capital and labor across state boundaries. Correcting these deficiencies, moreover, demanded deep structural reforms in the Soviet and East European domestic economies. Thus just as Gorbachev's domestic economic focus shifted from a limited modernizaiton drive to a more fundamental push toward systemic reform, his approach to CMEA trade increasingly aimed at pushing reform on his still reluctant East European counterparts.

## Succession Dilemmas

These frustrations pointed to Gorbachev's more basic dilemma: how to impart some of his own dynamism to Eastern Europe without first engineering a wholesale shakeup of the ossified party leaderships in Prague, Sofia, and elsewhere. Indeed, Gorbachev's early assaults on economic mismanagement, along with calculated snubs of several allied leaders, suggested that he was bent on securing the removal of Zhivkov, Husák, and perhaps Honecker from their top party posts in Bulgaria, Czechoslovakia, and the GDR. If such was his intent, Gorbachev apparently learned that it would be no easy task to unseat leaders enjoying solid support within their own party/state bureaucracies. (His inability to secure the early ouster of Vladimir Shcherbitskii from his own politburo may have been instructive.)

Thus Gorbachev appeared to entertain second thoughts about imminent leadership successions in Eastern Europe. Given the longevity of most of the top party leaders, any direct Soviet effort to instigate a succession struggle would entail great risks, particularly if it meant reaching down to the second levels of the party hierarchies for a hand-picked successor. Even if Gorbachev were to identify among these cadres reasonable facsimiles of himself, they would probably lack the bureaucratic support needed to consolidate their rule. Such a surprise selection would threaten serious instability within the top leadership and generate dangerously high public pressure for rapid change. Conversely, to weigh in only to choose from among the three or four most senior party officials, themselves creatures of the existing establishment, would hardly seem worth the attendant disruptions. To influence the succession processes indirectly and less abruptly would seem a safer course for Moscow.

Gorbachev also must have figured that most of the East European leaders did not have long to go anyway and that he would be faced soon enough with the task of managing several successions, perhaps simultaneously. In most cases, this would involve not just the replacement of the top party leader but the overhaul of an entire politburo; the Soviet task was to assure that preferred, or at least acceptable, successors were named and that stability be preserved in the process. The Hungarian pre-succession process of June 1987 seemed to fit that general pattern of gradualism, with Károly Grósz, one of the younger and more dynamic figures in the Hungarian leadership, taking over as prime minister, and Károly Németh, Kádár's lackluster party deputy, moving up to the honorific post of state president—thus clearing the path for the eventual successor to Kádár himself.

Whatever his motivations, Gorbachev's initial assaults on the party leaderships in Bulgaria, Czechoslovakia, and East Germany gave way to less direct efforts to shake up the ruling establishments by projecting reformist ideas and the example of his own domestic innovations. (Ceauşescu posed a different sort of problem, in that his firm grip over the Romanian leadership made it less amenable to Soviet influence.) These efforts also aimed at shifting the internal party debates in those countries toward the preferred Gorbachev agenda, and in so doing to alter the context and accelerate the pace of presuccession maneuvering.

Even without direct Soviet calls for reform in Eastern Europe, the demonstration effect of Gorbachev's domestic departures proved profoundly unsettling. The very existence of a reform-minded Soviet leader, coupled with his critique of Brezhnev era mismanagement, served to undermine the authority and cohesion of the more orthodox East European regimes. Apart from that, the winds of change blowing from Moscow gave fresh impetus to reform sentiment and awakened popular expectations of impending change, as did Gorbachev's highly charged visits to several East European capitals.

Nowhere were these trends more evident than in Czechoslovakia, where political life became interesting again for the first time since the Prague Spring of 1968. The human rights group Charter 77 wrote to Gorbachev welcoming his reformist ideas; from abroad, Zdeněk Mlynář, advisor to Alexander Dubček during the Prague Spring, reminisced about his law school classmate Mikhail Gorbachev and proclaimed his policies a vindication of the Czechoslovak reform movement. There were even rumors that Dubček himself had corresponded with Gorbachev. And in February 1987, the long-anticipated trial of leaders of the dissident "Jazz Section" (of the Czech Musicians' Association) ended in a partial victory for the defendants: the sentences handed down were much lighter than expected, and the presiding judge felt constrained to embrace the spirit of *glasnost'* by praising the Jazz Section's artistic contributions.

The seeming vindication of reformist and even dissident ideas sent shock waves through the Czechoslovak party leadership, precariously balanced since 1968 between a hardline faction led by chief ideologist Vasil Bil'ák and a moderate reformist grouping around Prime Minister Lubomír Štrougal. So great did the pressures become that Bil'ák issued a sharp attack in

February 1987 against those who allegedly were attempting to use the Soviet reform debate to import "anti-socialist" ideas. Although Bil'ák stopped short of directly condemning the Soviet reform program, his message was clearly that such ideas had no place in Czechoslovakia. It amounted to a repudiation of Soviet authority and a direct challenge to Gorbachev himself.

Thus Gorbachev's planned visit to Prague in April 1987 emerged as a major test case of his East European policy. Several basic issues were in question. To what extent were the East European regimes obliged to emulate Soviet practices? How much diversity would Moscow permit in Eastern Europe? What were the limits of Soviet tolerance?

That these questions provoked controversy in the Kremlin is suggested by the last-minute postponement of Gorbachev's visit to Prague. (The ostensible reason for the delay, his sudden head cold, gave rise to the latest version of an old saw: "When Gorbachev sneezes, does Husák catch cold?") One can only assume that veteran East European hands in Moscow counseled the Soviet leader that his policies threatened to introduce serious instability into a reliable, albeit inefficient, allied state.

When he arrived in Prague a few days later, Gorbachev tried to perform a balancing act. Denying that the Soviet party claimed a "monopoly on truth" or a "special position in the socialist world," he affirmed the right of each party to seek its own solutions in light of specific national conditions. At the same time, though, he reminded the East Europeans that the USSR, the country "in which socialism was built," was pursuing policies that "corresponded to the essence of socialism." In short, the East Europeans were free to craft their own approaches but not to ignore the Soviet reform drive. Perhaps more importantly, the atmospherics of the visit—Gorbachev's dramatic walking tour of Prague and the stark contrast between the dynamic Soviet leader and his Czechoslovak counterparts—left behind a palpable sense of impending change. Asked during the visit to explain the difference between Gorbachev's reforms and those of the Prague Spring, the Soviet spokesman Gennadii Gerassimov put it succinctly: "nineteen years."

## Rejuvenation and Reform

Moscow's obvious dissatisfaction with the Husák team heightened internal pressure for change in Prague, culminating in December 1987 with Husák's replacement as party leader by Miloš Jakeš. The latter was a long way from being a reformer in the Gorbachev mold: among the anti-

Dubček conspirators in 1968, he directed the post-1968 party purge of those associated with the Prague Spring. But he also seemed an eminently malleable politician—an East European man for all seasons (except spring, perhaps)—capable of adapting as readily to Gorbachev's reform agenda as he had to the antireform orthodoxy of the Brezhnev era.

For Prague as well as Moscow, Jakeš was a compromise choice between change and stability, a transitional figure who would oversee a gradual process of rejuvenation and change. And indeed there were changes under Jakeš: the Prague leadership began adopting the vocabulary of reform, if not yet its substance; implemented a modest *přestavba* (the Czechoslovak version of economic "restructuring"); and undertook a substantial rejuvenation of the party and state bureaucracies, followed in late 1988 by the removal of Štrougal and Bil'ák from the top leadership. These changes did little to alter the basic conservatism of the Czechoslovak regime, but they did encourage dissident and religious activists more openly to test the limits of protest in the Gorbachev era.

If the Husák to Jakeš transition represented incremental movement toward political regeneration in a still-conservative East European leadership, the Hungarian succession of a few months later raised the prospect of truly radical economic and political reform. Kádár's removal came as no particular surprise, nor did his replacement by Károly Grósz, long considered the likely successor. But the dramatic party conference of May 1988 went well beyond the expected transfer of power at the top: a virtual revolt of the delegates swept away the entire Kádár team and installed a strongly reformist new leadership pledged to push forward the frontiers of change. Whereas Grósz himself spoke of change in largely conventional terms, others in the new leadership—notably Imre Pozsgay and Rezsö Nyers—went much further, calling for reforms verging on multiparty social democracy.[10] Hungary was still a long way from that, but several measures under active consideration sought to develop "socialist pluralism" through the democratization of party life, expansion of the role of parliament, and the opening of the political process to nonparty groups. And while the leadership was debating these ideas, intellectuals, workers, and students were busy organizing themselves as if Hungary were already a pluralist society.

In Poland meanwhile, a wave of strikes during April–May and again in August 1988 raised the prospect of a resurgence of labor unrest on the scale of 1980–1981, as young workers rallied around the Solidarity banner and imbued it with their own, more radical agenda. In response, the Jaruzelski regime agreed to open a dialogue with Solidarity leader Lech

Wałęsa and other opposition figures. It was a powerful symbolic gesture, vindicating Solidarity and Wałęsa personally while debunking the regime's seven-year campaign of "normalization." Though hardly an offer of full partnership, the effort seemed to aim at a new formula of governance—an "anticrisis pact" or, as the regime preferred to call it, a "proreform alliance." Mieczysław Rakowski, a tough-minded ex-"liberal" and close advisor to Jaruzelski, was named prime minister to oversee the on-again, off-again political dialogue.

Poland in late 1988 included two distinct conceptions of political change in Eastern Europe. As in Hungary, there was sharpening tension between proponents of radical reform measures and those determined to resist change despite rising popular pressures. If the former prevailed, there seemed to be new possibilities for trade union pluralism, sweeping economic reform, and a more democratic socialism through institutional reform and delimitation of the party's role in society. Impediments to dialogue were obvious: a chaotic economic situation, mutual suspicions on both sides, and the risk that the process could be torpedoed by wildcat strikes or regime provocation. If the dialogue failed, the prospect would arise of unrest on a much wider scale, perhaps leading to a popular upheaval that the Polish regime could not contain. Either way, imminent developments in Poland (and perhaps Hungary as well) seemed to portend a new era in Eastern Europe.

## EASTERN EUROPE TOWARD THE YEAR 2000

Eastern Europe is entering a period of flux more profound than at any time since the immediate post-Stalin period. The Gorbachev era may not be so explosive, but it is likely to introduce changes more fundamental and lasting.

And now the stakes are higher, for change in Eastern Europe coincides with important shifts in Europe as a whole. The European Community has embarked on an ambitious drive toward economic and political integration—seen by many in Western Europe as a magnet that ultimately will pull Eastern Europe into its field. NATO's European members are moving toward a distinctly "European" posture on political and defense issues, as in the WEU (Western European Union) "European Security Platform" of October 1987. The FRG, increasingly caught between alliance and autonomy, seeks a stronger role in Central Europe. Arms negotiations hold out the prospect of deep reductions in nuclear, chemical, and even conventional forces. And Gorbachev's call for a "common European home" strikes a responsive chord among increasing numbers of West Europeans, who see in the new Soviet leader a fresh hope for European reconciliation.

But all these conceptions run up against the reality of Soviet domination of Eastern Europe and the continued presence there of some 30 divisions of Soviet troops. A more ambitious West German *Ostpolitik* would be decidedly one-sided so long as Eastern Europe's destiny remains in Moscow's hands, just as the vision of the "Europeanization of Europe" will go unfulfilled without a substantial relaxation of the Soviet grip on its eastern half. It will not be a very habitable "European house" if it continues to have one large and assertive landlord who periodically terrorizes his tenants.

Hence Eastern Europe is likely to be the arena (let us hope not the battleground) in which Europe's future is decided—as it has been twice already in this century. The "Eastern Question" that bedeviled the European powers up to Versailles is once again the key; as before, it concerns the scope for national self-determination in Eastern Europe. The aim, as Polish opposition strategists say, is not full independence, sovereignty and freedom, but a greater measure of each. The obstacles to such an evolution remained the entrenched party-state bureaucracies in Eastern Europe and, ultimately, the limits of Soviet tolerance.

In practice, the USSR under Gorbachev already had permitted a surprising degree of diversity and experimentation in Eastern Europe. Gorbachev and his key advisors seemed to recognize that it was the absence of change that posed the greater threat to East European stability; their concern was directed not at the reform-minded Hungarians and Poles but at those who were resisting change and renewal. Speaking at a July 1988 U.S.-Soviet conference on Eastern Europe, Oleg Bogomolev, director of the USSR Institute of Economics of the World Socialist System, offered a sweeping (if not necessarily representative) interpretation of "new thinking" about Eastern Europe. The Soviet model, he said, "has not withstood the test of time." "Stagnant neo-Stalinism" and the "hegemonic aspirations of the Soviet leadership" were "among the main reasons for the deep political crises in Hungary in 1956; in Czechoslovakia in 1968; and in Poland during 1956, 1970, and 1980." Now, he concluded, the East European countries have "broad opportunities to realize unhindered their national interests."[11]

Gorbachev's further consolidation of power in September–October 1988—succeeding Gromyko as president and elevating several key associates in the party leadership—gave another boost to reform. The promotions of Aleksandr Iakovlev and Vadim Medvedev, two prominent "new thinkers," as Central Committee secretaries for ideological and international affairs, sent a particularly strong signal to Eastern Europe, and this at a time when radical reform proposals in Hungary and Poland threatened to test the limits of change in the Gorbachev era.

What were those limits? Gorbachev himself probably did not know. The minimum requirement for Moscow's East European allies are presumed to be membership in the Warsaw Pact and preservation of the "leading role" of the communist party; and Soviet leaders, including Gorbachev, probably see the two as inseparable (though Romania's participation in the Warsaw Pact has been little more than nominal for more than two decades now). Under Gorbachev, however, the party's "leading role" has been substantially redefined, as he himself has led the campaign for limiting its management functions and for opening the political process to nonparty groups.

It is important to distinguish at least two kinds of challenges Gorbachev might face in Eastern Europe. One would be of the Prague Spring variety: a regime-led reform movement going well beyond Gorbachev's agenda and tending inevitably toward national self-determination. If successful, it might lead to a "Finlandization" scenario of domestic political autonomy tempered by foreign policy alignment with Moscow. The second would be a popular revolt *against* the ruling party, conjuring up Tim Garton Ash's "Ottomanization" scenario of fitful (and probably violent) imperial decay and disintegration.[12] Gorbachev probably fears the latter more than the former.

A frontal challenge to both party and pact in Eastern Europe, via popular upheaval and the Ottoman progression, would constitute an immediate threat to Soviet control in the region and to Gorbachev's domestic position. Like Soviet leaders before him, he would prefer a political to a military solution. If none were found, he and his leadership would face a stark choice: to countenance the erosion of the Soviet position in Eastern Europe or to invade, thereby undermining the entire edifice of Gorbachev's foreign and domestic strategies.

The more hopeful scenario would be one of evolutionary, peaceful reform, led (at least nominally) by the ruling establishment and pushed forward by independent social groups under the moderating influence of religious and opposition leaders. Under such conditions, it is likely that the limits of Soviet tolerance would be much greater than in the past. One can at least imagine—in Hungary or Poland, perhaps—an evolution toward partial or de facto "Finlandization," in which the rules of the game in Soviet-East European relations were fundamentally redrawn.

We have no way of knowing how the Gorbachev leadership would react to such extreme contingencies. And, of course, they may not materialize at all, though it is hard to see Eastern Europe resisting the pressures for change much longer. Whatever transpires, Gorbachev cannot have it both ways: he cannot have stability and viability in Eastern Europe while maintaining Soviet domination over political life in the region. No less than for his predecessors, this is Gorbachev's dilemma in Eastern Europe.

### Notes to Chapter 1

1. Keith Crane, *The Soviet Economic Dilemma of Eastern Europe* (Santa Monica, CA: The RAND Corporation, 1986), pp. 32–33.

2. Charles Gati, "The Soviet Empire: Alive but not Well," *Problems of Communism* (March–April 1985), pp. 73–86; Robert L. Hutchings, "Andropov and Eastern Europe," in Vojtech Mastny, ed., *Soviet-East European Survey, 1983–84* (Durham, NC: Duke University Press, 1985), pp. 133–135.

3. Called the "new ethnicity" in Peter Sugar et al., *The Problem of Nationalism in Eastern Europe: Past and Present* (Washington, DC: Woodrow Wilson International Center for Scholars, 1988).

4. For a fascinating character sketch, see Yordan Kerov (pseud.), "Lyudmila Zhivkova: Fragments of a Portrait," RAD Background Report/253 (Bulgaria), *Radio Free Europe Research,* 27 October 1980.

5. Ronald D. Asmus, "East Berlin and Moscow: The Documentation of a Dispute" (Munich: Radio Free Europe Research, 1985).

6. Such sentiments were echoed in Western Europe, especially the Federal Republic of Germany, in calls for the "Europeanization of Europe," a former Gaullist rallying cry now gaining much wider currency.

7. The early "debate" waged in *Pravda, Kommunist,* and other publications only added to the picture of confusion. See Karen Dawisha, *Eastern Europe, Gorbachev, and Reform* (Cambridge: Cambridge University Press, 1988), pp. 160–162. Nor was Gorbachev himself much help; see his *Perestroika: New Thinking for our Country and the World* (New York: Harper and Row, 1987), pp. 161–170.

8. The program was first agreed to at the 1984 CMEA summit meeting— i.e., under Chernenko—but was given stronger emphasis by Gorbachev.

9. *Economic Survey of Europe* (New York: United Nations, 1987), pp. 177–179.

10. See, e.g., the reform program outlined in *Fordulat és Reform* [Turnabout and Reform] (Budapest; mimeo, 1986), prepared under the auspices of the Pa-

triotic People's Front, and others surveyed in Rudolf L. Tokes, "The Science of Politics in Hungary in the 1980s," *Südosteuropa* 37 (January 1988), pp. 8–32.

11. "East-West Relations and Eastern Europe: The Soviet Perspective," *Problems of Communism,* May–August 1988, pp. 60–67.

12. See, e.g., Timothy Garton Ash, "The Empire in Decay," *New York Review of Books,* 35, no. 14 (29 September 1988), 53–60, and the next two articles (in nos. 15 and 16, 13 and 27 October 1988) of his three-part series on Eastern Europe.

# Chapter 2

# THE ECONOMIC DIMENSIONS

## EAST-WEST POLICIES TOWARD EAST EUROPEAN COMMERCE IN THE 1990s

*John P. Hardt**

### An Overview

In the 1990s many, perhaps a majority of, Western, Soviet, and East European specialists and policymakers appear to expect a continuation of the 1980s: modest growth of hard currency trade and low export-led domestic growth. A swing back to the more dynamic commercial and domestic growth of the 1970s may be possible, however, under markedly different policies: first, that Soviet, West European, and U.S. policies be targeted toward encouraging political and economic liberalization in East Europe and the expansion of East-West commercial relations; second, that the East European nations may pursue policies of comprehensive domestic reform, industrial strategy, and restructuring; and third, that the Soviet and Western policies make preferential commercial relations conditional on domestic and foreign economic reform in East Europe. If one accepts the premise that improved East European economic performance is in the interests of the leading international players, it is useful to outline the policies most likely to bring about medium and long-term growth and stability in East Europe. Whereas East European domestic reform and

---

*The views expressed in the first section of this chapter are those of the author and do not necessarily represent the views of the Congressional Research Service, the Library of Congress, or the U.S. Congress.

competitiveness abroad may take a decade or more of thorough-going economic and political reform in order to succeed, adopting a policy of "muddling through" or, even worse, of regression to old Stalinist formulas may lead both to deteriorating economic conditions and political instability. Clearly, then, comprehensive reform may be the best strategy available to Eastern Europe in the 1990s.

***Potential for commercial expansion in East Europe in the 1990s under the umbrella of reform: International actor analysis.*** The current easing of East-West tensions and the impetus for social, political, and economic reform based on *glasnost'*, democratization, and *perestroika* have created a more favorable environment for trade. The new trading environment will not be similar to the 1970s period during which the West concentrated loanable funds on Eastern Europe in the form of general purpose or untied credits. On the other hand, the trading environment of the 1990s will not simply be an easing of the more restrictive policies enacted during the 1980s. New commercial relations and loans are likely to be tied to specific programs geared to encourage structural and institutional reform.

In the upcoming decade, the East European nations may, for different reasons, be pressured by both the Soviet Union and the West to proceed with economic and political reform. The Soviet Union could decide in the short run to exercise its full political leverage on the CMEA nations to assure that all future exports to Moscow meet the standards of exports to the West, at once enhancing East European competitiveness in world markets and increasing East European economic contributions to the USSR. The Soviet Union may even opt for restraint on pressing its own demands in view of the adverse effect such a policy could have on the short-term economic conditions in and political stability of Eastern Europe by a delay in the full impact of a shift to "hard goods"[1] trade to the mid-1990s. Moreover, Moscow may encourage the East European nations to act within the current parameters of "democratization" and market-orientation, both to ensure East European conformity to the Soviet Union's present policies and to open opportunities to loanable funds from the West.

At the same time, the West seems likely to support the reform agenda and could continue to withhold loanable funds until such political and economic reform takes place. This seems to be especially true for Poland. These developments place the East European older, Brezhnev-era leaders in a most precarious position, making East Europe dependent on reform policies generated in the East and West, yet at the same time allowing the East European nations considerably more maneuverability for individualized reform and growth than they have enjoyed since the 1970s. Although able to pursue independent reform courses, the political liberalization and renewal may serve to repudiate the policies they have been so directly associated with in the past.

The major international actors, at the very least, have plausible reasons for following policies conducive to increased trade and domestic reform in Eastern Europe.

The United States may provide conditional bilateral support based on further political and economic reform and exert positive influence on the IMF, World Bank, and other interested agencies to step up reform and development programs. The U.S. policy would be pivotal as it has tended to be either a leader in facilitating or restricting commerce with the East. Policies on Western credit, joint ventures, and technology transfer might be central parts of debate. U.S. policies may turn on a differentiation policy toward Hungary, Yugoslavia, and Poland, where comprehensive restructuring, economic reform, political pluralism, and an effective foreign commercial strategy may be synergistic, and if fully implemented could produce results that now might be considered quite optimistic.

Western Europe may extend to East Europe more of the benefits that accrue to the Common Market countries in 1992 with increasingly special, preferential economic relations such as those between the two Germanys. European community normalization of commercial relations with Hungary in 1988 suggests a trend toward East European preferential trade to develop as an economic basis of increased European ties.

Japan and the newly industrialized Asian countries may establish more cooperative relations with East European countries for political and economic relations in Europe as a whole with special debt relief from Japan through its LDC/World Bank funding. Increased Asian-East European trade has political as well as economic benefit. Joint ventures would provide a European base for Asian competition in the Common Market area.

The Soviet Union may consider the success of *perestroika* and interdependence in Eastern Europe as an important element in creating a potentially more productive CMEA alliance. Soviet pressure on Eastern Europe (through moral suasion and a more particular import strategy) to produce high quality consumer and agricultural products for export to Soviet as well as to Western markets, may "encourage" East European reform by essentially giving the bloc "fair warning" that the Soviet market for noncompetitive East European "soft goods" is being phased out. In other words, at current levels of factor productivity and output quality, most East European producers would have to reform in order to produce the volume of "hard goods" sufficient to maintain or expand current levels of exports to the East and West.

For Eastern Europe, these pressures to restructure and modernize their obsolete industrial bases; to apply market forces and hard budget constraints in their reformed economic system; to institutionalize political pluralism and participation; and to develop an effective foreign commercial strategy with the West are all positive and reinforce prospects for long-term growth. Indeed, the convergence of interest in comprehensive East European reform is the new and notable common denominator in the global arena. A sound argument may, in fact, be made that the interests of all players may be served by an economically expanding Eastern Europe. In a sense, therefore, hope for reform in Eastern Europe may even be justified: each of the international actors appears to have a strong motivation to encourage comprehensive reform and, based on the lessons of the 1970s, seem likely to condition their cooperation on East European progress toward effective reform.

## Historical Background: Eastern Europe in the 1970s and 1980s

In the 1970s global economic and political conditions under the umbrellas of progress on arms control, regional security, and human rights formed the background for expanded East-West trade. East Europe, attempting to solve the problems of declining productivity and output based on a by-then obsolete framework of extensive growth, sought expanded trade both within the CMEA and with the West.

The East European nations moved, during the detente environment of the 1970s, into the global trading environment at an opportune time: the Soviet Union sold oil at below world market prices and offered favorable market conditions for East European goods—some suggested the existence of a substantial implicit subsidy from the USSR to East Europe; Western banks, eager to lend the burgeoning supply of petrodollars, offered large credit facilities at favorable rates; private commercial interests seeking to open new markets and Western governments hoping to encourage a greater degree of autonomy for the East European nations promoted policies to increase East-West trade; and the East European nations enjoyed favorable trade vis-à-vis the Soviet Union and the Western industrialized nations. The East European nations, therefore, adopted a strategy of import-led growth. That is to say, the "reform-oriented" East European governments hoped that through import substitution, they could raise living standards, modernize their industries, and become competitive in Western markets. Hard currency revenue was to enable the countries to buy more Western technology and to continue on a path of rapid development. Trade of manufactured goods was to increase both in the East and West.

Rapid economic growth took place throughout Eastern Europe in the 1970s. Long-term investment decisions were based on the three major assumptions: first, that easy lending practices in the West and effectively subsidized energy costs in the East would continue indefinitely; second, the traditionally low capacity for producing goods that could compete in Western markets and the comparatively low standard of living was due to a remedial lag in technology, which could be solved through increased imports of Western technology and import substitution; and third, if the governments allowed for a period of "incubation" whereby they could shield their domestic economies from world price shocks, domestic industry would develop more effectively and the East European nations would eventually emerge as Newly Industrializing Countries (NICs).

Given the prevailing assumptions, East European growth plans did not account for future potential scarcities of critical inputs such as credits and energy. Since Western credits were not treated as a scarce input, finished products often required intermediate goods and raw materials imported from the West—more often than not with Western credits. As most East European economies had a characteristically negative institutional bias toward export promotion, a low capacity to produce goods competitive in Western markets, and dependence on Western imports and credits for production, many accumulated large, hard currency debts. By the end of the decade, the East European countries were highly dependent on and, therefore, subject to negative shifts in the world economy.

By the early 1980s, the global economic and political environment changed dramatically: oil prices increased sharply, Western economies became depressed, and the free flow of credits began to dry up in the wake of the burgeoning Third World debt crisis. As a renewed "Cold War" environment set in, the political sphere took priority over trade policy. Therefore, even as trade decreased due to world recession, a hostile East-West political environment quickened the pace and broadened the scope of restrictive Western trade policies. Both the pipeline dispute and the imposition of Western sanctions following the establishment of martial law in Poland illustrate the negative Western mood toward the East. When in 1981 Poland was unable to service its external debt, Western creditors and governments came to the clear realization that East Eu-

ropean governments would not necessarily guarantee repayment of outstanding loans nor would the USSR be the debtor of last resort.
Reassessment of East European creditworthiness in the changed context
of the debt crises in Latin American led Western banks to stop lending
and start demanding that outstanding loans be serviced. In effect the net
flow of hard currency was reversed.

At the same time, intra-CMEA terms of trade shifted away from Eastern Europe—in favor of the Soviet Union. The Soviet Union, chaffing
under costs of empire, had begun reducing net transfers to East Europe.
When the world market price of oil dropped, the Soviet Union did not
drop its prices accordingly but continued to sell oil to East European nations at artificially high prices. That is to say, the Soviets chose to maintain the five-year moving price average rather than help East Europe by
selling at the lower world market prices. Furthermore, the Cold War atmosphere resulted in continued Warsaw Pact military expenditures and
more restrictive CMEA trade policies toward the East.

Notwithstanding the sudden shift from a favorable to a restrictive external trading environment, the absence of effective domestic reform exacerbated economic difficulties: investment resources continued to be allocated inefficiently, often going in the direction of subsidies to unprofitable
firms and to keep consumer goods prices below costs; hard-currency exports were reduced despite growing hard-currency debts because vital intermediate goods routinely purchased from the West in the 1970s could
no longer be purchased; and export promotion, never fully developed when
credit was flowing, became even more difficult in the 1980s. Throughout
the 1980s, many debts have been rescheduled by the West, Moscow has
intervened to help some of the East European nations, and the halting
and painful process of reform under bleak growth conditions began in
several of the East European countries.

## Eastern Europe in the 1990s

Whereas many of the growth-retarding factors that emerged in the 1980s
remain, it does not necessarily follow that the widely accepted pessimistic
forecast for slow or negative growth in Eastern Europe, both familiar and
substantiated by recent performance, will continue to be valid. In this
section, I am, therefore, examining the potential for East European growth
based on the assumption that it is in the broad interests of both the Soviet
Union and the West to foster a favorable environment for reform-led commercial and domestic growth in Eastern Europe. A bill of particulars un-

derlying the optimistic scenario that advanced industrialized nations will condition their commercial policies on progress toward reform and that the Soviet Union will not exercise its full political leverage in Eastern Europe by squeezing its allies for their best export products to facilitate short-term Soviet success in *perestroika* and interdependence but will instead facilitate reform in East Europe. That is, the Soviet Union may formulate its policies as if successful East European interdependence and *perestroika* were as much in the interest of the Soviet Union as it would be for Gorbachev's supporters in the leadership of East European countries. Moreover, Western governments and commercial interest may differentiate their policy toward facilitating commerce and reform in East Europe. These specific statements represent a point of departure from which a more detailed analysis of East European growth and reform in a favorable trading environment could take place.

***Western policy facilitation of commercial expansion, conditioned on domestic economic restructuring and reform, could facilitate improved commercial and economic performance.*** International institutions, such as the World Bank and IMF, may facilitate more effectively the flow of funds providing an opportunity for commercial expansion conditioned on modernization and restructuring of the obsolete and unproductive capital stock and infrastructure. Countries such as Poland, Hungary, Romania, and Yugoslavia as members of these organizations might be increasingly affected.

The development of a more cohesive integrated West European Common Market in 1992 with inclinations to expand commerce with East Europe may adopt more facilitating trade policies than the United States for the following reasons:

- West European trade-surplus countries may seek to expand present markets and commitments through loanable funds and investments.
- Political umbrellas, such as the EC-CMEA accords, may create new opportunities for expanded East-West European trade, as have similar, albeit broader inter-German and Austro-Hungarian trade arrangements. The political benefits from a commercial differentiation policy may override economic disadvantages of East European trading partners vis-à-vis cooperation with NICs and others.
- A unified Common Market may be better able to differentiate its policy from that of the United States, particularly if differences such as the earlier pipeline and credit disputes should arise.

The United States may follow a commercial facilitation policy if bilateral relations with the Soviet Union on arms, regional issues, and human rights are favorable and the United States determines that competition for the Eastern market is beneficial to security, diplomatic and commercial interests, and that an enhanced differentiation policy is in the U.S. reform supporting policy interest, e.g., U.S. favorable reaction to a Polish round table setting a course toward political and economic reform based on sharing of power would be an example of an occasion that the United States might put in front of its European allies. Even if the United States does not become a leader in this area, it may choose to ease restrictive export and credit policies in order to avoid potentially damaging tensions with the allies. The current U.S. stance regarding technology sales and credit policies toward East Europe and the Soviet Union have the potential for developing into a new "pipeline dispute." By now, West Europe may have both the power and inclination to resist the "extraterritorial reach" of the United States. (In 1981 President Reagan attempted to block the sale of goods by European manufacturers for completion of the Urengoi gas pipeline to the Soviet Union by extending extraterritorial legal control from U.S. firms to those of U.S. allies.)

***Soviet policy may facilitate intra-CMEA commerce and CMEA-wide perestroika.*** A reduced burden of Warsaw Pact commitments might release East European capacity and manpower for domestic civilian restructuring. Implementation of Soviet new doctrine on "reasonable sufficiency," highlighted in Gorbachev's announced troop cuts in his UN speech of December 7, 1988, successful Conventional Arms for Europe (CAFE), and reduced military burdens for Warsaw Pact activities outside of Europe could provide an environment for reduced military burden. East Europeans have now publicly linked the success of their domestic reform and restructuring to reduced military claims, e.g., the president of the Hungarian Academy of Science, Iván Berends, at the Hungarian party meeting that elected Grósz.

Gorbachev may not only provide a policy umbrella for beneficial economic and political reform, but may not use his full leverage to extract high quality resources from East Europe, especially those exportable to the West. This policy of forbearance might be in Gorbachev's short-term political interest in supporting like-minded East European leaders and in his long-term economic interests in ensuring a stronger economic alliance.

East Europe may indirectly benefit from closer Soviet ties with West

Europe, Japan, and the United States through favorable joint venture, credit, and other trade facilitating mechanisms. In particular, beneficial intra-CMEA trade based on comparative advantage and collateral benefits of increased Soviet trade with the West may be advantageous. Trilateral joint ventures involving East European partners with special expertise in dealing in both the Soviet and Western market could be beneficial.

Availability of Soviet oil and gas may be sufficient for East European needs and at lower cost in hard goods, such as consumer goods and food. Moreover, East Europe may be in a stronger commercial bargaining position due to the fall in OPEC energy prices. Whereas the USSR has a strong monopoly position on energy supplies to East Europeans and provides the captive market that shelters CMEA trade, more extensive use of these economic levers for political conformity may be less desirable and less effective for the USSR in the future; increased trade of Soviet energy for East European "hard goods" may be economically attractive.

*Response to Western commercial facilitation and interaction and Soviet perestroika, interdependence, and democratization, if successful, might create opportunities to moderate the Leninist framework of party dominance and central planning austerity and improve commercial exchange and its effect on domestic economic performance.* Success may well be measured in expanding, balanced, hard-goods trade and export-led domestic growth in East Europe. The Soviet Union, Western Europe, and the United States can facilitate these successes. In doing so, however, the international players face a shifting constellation of potential short- and long-term risks and benefits. In the short term, all the international players could, on balance, assume more benefits than risks by implementing initiatives that foster economic, social, and political restructuring in East Europe.

Western players may gain access to new markets and renewed opportunities to form closer political ties. These outcomes could be further reinforced by coordination or converging Western interests concerning East Europe.

Changes in East European leadership either due to policy changes or other reasons pose risks to the external powers in that new leaders may replace the "devil one knows" with a greater devil rather than an enlightened reformer. If, however, Soviet and East European restructuring, reform, renewal, and interdependence fail to take hold in the East, a return to a status quo environment prior to that which existed in the 1960s or even the 1970s would be very difficult to implement. The result seems more likely to be extreme instability and discord. On balance, an Eastern Europe in turmoil, without prospects for economic improvement and political pluralism, would present a risky environment for all the major actors and international players.

The Soviet Union and, in particular, Gorbachev could potentially enjoy benefits from several sources based on short-term successes concerning restructuring and liberalization in East Europe.

- Gorbachev has gained and will most likely continue to maintain great personal popularity and leadership authority among the East European reformers because he has responded to East European concerns on two fronts. First, he has been willing to supply a certain amount of public information and engage in discussions on critical historical issues such as the execution of Polish military officers during World War II and the invasion of Prague in 1968. Second, he is responsible for prodding their leaders to pursue progressive reform based on the model Gorbachev himself is exposing in the Soviet Union. Whereas East European peoples previously may have looked to the West for ideas, increasingly they now may look to the Soviet Union.
- Gorbachev's restructuring effectively requires the old guard in East Europe to update their policies or, more likely, to turn power over to new leaders—leaders who believe in the necessity for reform and who will be loyal to or dependent on Gorbachev.
- The Soviet Union indirectly benefits from expanded East European trade with the West to the extent that it allows the East European governments to simultaneously implement reform measures, decrease debt burdens, and increase the availability of consumer goods. If this were to be accomplished, the political stability of East Europe could, in the medium term, be secured.
- The Soviet Union might also benefit to the extent that the East European nations upgrade the quality of their manufactured goods to world market standards and that the better quality goods go not only to Western markets but to the Soviet Union as well.
- The Soviet Union also would gain increased access to Western credits based both on internal progress and also on Western perceptions of a Soviet Union that allows, in fact encourages, the East European nations freedom to reform.

In the short- and long-term, therefore, it is probably the East European elite and government bureaucrats who presently hold power that risk the greatest losses. Whereas all actors may suffer through the short-term "growing pains" period of comprehensive reform, it may be that East European and Soviet reformers may find the long term not to their political liking. A long-term context depends very much on one's assumption concerning the ability of the Soviet Union and the individual East European governments to find a "reform equilibrium" at the Leninist stability position. In other words, the answer to the question "Can reformers stop the reform before it gravitates too far from an acceptable Leninist and CMEA framework?" will determine the composition of long-term risks and benefits for the Eastern leadership and international players.

All of the international players may benefit, as outlined above, if East Europe carries out reform in a fashion that accomplishes further interdependence with the West, broader political representation, and greater scope for social activism without overstepping the implicit bounds of the one-party framework and central Soviet-type policymaking role. On the other hand, if reform goes beyond the "acceptable," all international players may be faced with a different calculus on risks and costs.

The potential for Soviet risks in "unacceptable" outcomes in successful East European restructuring, reform, renewal, and interdependence:

—The Leninist economic and political framework might eventually be challenged and the dominant role of the party eliminated in one or all of the East European nations.

—Interdependence with the West could set in motion a process whereby the dominant role of the USSR in foreign, security, and ideological affairs might be challenged within East European nations.

• At the extreme, if certain East European nations were to become very dependent on Western economic and political facilities, separatist tendencies could emerge—and perhaps even in a broad East-West European context. Gorbachev's "European House" might be for only East and West Europeans.

If one or all of the above scenarios developed, the Soviet leadership may be reluctant to act overtly to constrain the country in question. If, however, Soviet intervention did take place—either through direct external imposition of martial law or in a manner perceived to require a reinstitution of the Brezhnev Doctrine—then all of the international players could potentially be exposed to the following high costs.

—The Soviet Union could lose its leadership role as a progressive force favoring reform both in the East and in the West.

- The reaction to intervention in East Europe could weaken *perestroika*, *glasnost'*, and democratization in the Soviet Union itself.
- Extreme instability could result in East Europe, as those who believed and heeded Gorbachev's encouragement to reform reacting to Soviet-imposed constraints.
- Negative Western response could result in a rapid decline in Western commercial facilitation with the Soviet Union.

Western interests and policy responses may diverge markedly and a divisive split could occur along EC-US lines. In this context, by 1992 the EC would already be a unified and powerful voice with stronger relative commercial and political interests in the East than that of the United States. If traditional responses to a Soviet intervention emerged whereby the EC chose to continue to lend and trade both with East European countries and the Soviet Union while the United States chose economic warfare, the immediate costs and long-term politico-economic fallout could be very damaging to the cohesion of the Western alliance.

## EC AND CMEA: ECONOMIC RELATIONS BETWEEN INTERNATIONAL ORGANIZATIONS

*Josef C. Brada*

The expansion of the European [Economic] Community (EC) in Western Europe and the growing unification of its members suggests that, with a few exceptions, the countries of Europe will be divided into two economic blocs, the EC and the Council for Mutual Economic Assistance (CMEA). To the extent that each of these blocs increasingly strengthens the economic integration among its member countries, it simultaneously influences the conditions under which its members can carry out trade and other forms of commercial intercourse with members of the other bloc. Because each bloc disposes of vast resources and productive power, because each is an important market for the other, and because their proximity suggests a large and unrealized potential for economic intercourse, the relations between the blocs are of vital importance, the more so because the member countries of the two espouse competing economic and political systems. The purpose of this essay is to examine the history of relations between the EC and CMEA, to set out the political and economic factors that have influenced these relations, and to offer some observations on their future relations.

## Evolution of EC-CMEA

The road leading to establishment of formal relations between the CMEA and the EC has taken many wrong turns, with economic factors impelling the participants sometimes forward and sometimes backward, whereas the self-interests of the two international bureaucracies have generally acted as stumbling blocks to rapprochement, not only out of the natural caution born of the unprecedented establishment of formal relations between two international organizations, but also because the establishment of relations between the two had important implications for the balance of power between these organizations and their members and also among the members of the two blocs.

The CMEA was founded in 1949, largely in response to the Marshall Plan, but it remained dormant until the late 1950s since Stalin preferred more direct and informal means for influencing the trade and economic development of the East European countries.[2] The EC, when formed in 1957 as the European Economic Community, was accorded a negative reception in CMEA circles. The new organization was seen as a tool of monopoly capital designed to exploit its weaker members, to suppress the West European labor movement, and to promote the internationalization of European capital.[3] Given this view and the EC's relatively minor role as an actor on the international scene, the CMEA countries could well afford to ignore it.

This position of hostility and neglect changed rather rapidly. By the early 1960s, the experience of the EC in promoting integration among its member states and the outstanding results achieved by these states in terms of economic restructuring and a macroeconomic performance that seemed to combine the rapid growth of production and living standards with price stability and low levels of unemployment clearly attracted international attention.[4] At the same time, Khrushchev began to try to revive the moribund CMEA. The slowdown in investment programs following the end of the Korean War and Stalin's death created strains and disproportions in Eastern Europe. Since Khrushchev was neither desirous nor capable of maintaining the direct control over East European regimes that Stalin had employed, economic integration brought about by reviving the CMEA appeared to be a feasible way for dealing with the disproportions created by extensive development and a duplication of the Soviet industrialization strategy in Eastern Europe. Khrushchev, of course, did not go so far as to admit that the EC was a viable and useful international organization, but he did suggest that its success should be studied in order to show what integration among socialist countries, unfettered by the contradictions of capitalism, could achieve.[5]

Unfortunately for Khrushchev's intentions, the moment for harnessing the East European regimes to the will of a supranational organization had passed, and the intransigence of the less-developed CMEA countries, most notably Romania, which saw its dreams of industrialization thwarted by a supranational CMEA, meant that the latter would be a weak organization with no power to impose policies on members and hamstrung by the need for unanimity on all questions of substance. Neither the CMEA's charter nor the first effort to implement socialist economic integration, the "Basic Principles of Socialist Economic Integration" (signed in 1962), was able to impose serious limits on the behavior of member states or to serve as a mechanism for integration.

Such an integrating force might have emerged from the centripetal effects of the Soviet Union's predominance in the trade and, thus, economies of the smaller CMEA members. In the 1960s, however, this was not to be because the beginning of the decade saw a rapid upsurge in commercial exchange between East and West, fueled by trade-promoting policies on the part of EC members and by a growing interest in the potential that such trade had to speed the growth and further industrialization of the smaller CMEA members.[6] This trade served to ameliorate the structural tensions that existed within CMEA and turned the attention of the East European leaderships away from issues of integration and toward those of East-West trade.

At this time, a number of tendencies and problems surfaced that were to play a long-standing role in EC-CMEA relations. Due to the limited foreign exchange earnings of the East European countries and their desire to import machinery, equipment, and technology from the West, the provision of export credits by Western Europe became of critical importance in determining the competitiveness of individual Western suppliers. In part as a reaction against heavy-handed United States policies toward East-West trade, but no doubt more for commercial objectives, EC countries in rapid order breached the Berne Union limits on the duration and terms of government-guaranteed credits to CMEA countries, creating a credit war in their trade with the East. In most cases, these concessionary credit terms were embodied in bilateral treaties of trade and economic cooperation between the creditor and the lender.

Another element unique to East-West trade that emerged at this time was the concept of industrial cooperation between Western firms and their counterparts in Eastern Europe.[7] Industrial cooperation involved the transfer of technology and capital from the West to the East through long-term interfirm relations that financed such transfers through the resale to Western Europe of the goods produced in the CMEA by means of the imported know-how and equipment. In the East it was viewed as a superior mode for technology transfer and as a means of overcoming limitations on trade imposed by the lack of hard currencies. Western firms, on the other hand, perceived it mainly as a marketing tool to aid them in selling their technology and equipment and as a way of getting "inside" the CMEA in much the same way that U.S. multinationals had established European affiliates in order to get "inside" the common external tariff of the EC.

These innovations, although facilitating the rapid expansion of economic relations between East and West Europe, created a conflict between the EC and its members. The main mechanism of EC integration was the creation of a common external tariff against nonmembers and the abolition of tariffs and, more gradually, of other barriers to the movement of goods and of factors of production among members. At the same time it was envisioned that other aspects of trade policy of the member countries would be regularized by the early 1970s in the form of a common commercial policy (CCP) for the Community. Clearly the area in which policies differed most among EC members was in the area of East-West trade, where individual members maintained a variety of tariff, quota, and other nontariff barriers against imports from Eastern Europe. Similarly, arrangements for trade flows resulting from industrial cooperation agreements differed from country to country, as did policies for financing export credits.[8] Because the import restrictions were largely intended to protect domestic markets against disruption and because their removal was viewed as a means of improving trade relations with individual East European countries, members of the Community viewed these policy instruments and their manipulation as a useful means of improving the competitiveness of their exports to CMEA countries.[9] Credit policies as well as policies toward industrial cooperation and the flow of goods and resources associated with it were also obvious means of promoting exports, particularly of machinery equipment and technology to the CMEA.

Because these nontraditional elements of trade policy were somewhat outside the integration mechanism of the EC, individual members of the Community could manipulate them to make their goods more competitive in East-West trade. The unique character of these trade measures made it difficult for the Community to bring them under its purview; their efficacy in the competition for East-West trade made individual EC members reluctant to permit the Community to do so. Thus members of the EC tended to maintain policy independence in East-West trade by arguing that such policies, often embodied in bilateral agreements on cooperation, represented instruments of foreign policy rather than trade policies, and therefore remained outside EC competence.[10]

In the 1960s the EC had little leverage to force members to accept its supremacy over these aspects of East-West trade; they were peripheral to the main issues and means of integrating the EC countries, but they were seen as valuable prerogatives of economic policy by the member states. This situation began to change during the late 1960s with the entry of the United States and Japan into the East European market. Hitherto, the United States had followed a policy that tended to minimize the volume of its trade with CMEA, and Japan followed suit, playing the role of loyal ally. Changes in U.S. policy included adopting a more differentiated trade strategy toward Eastern Europe, rewarding states that seemed more independent of the Soviet Union by providing credits, reducing export restrictions, and granting most favored nation (MFN) tariff treatment. The culmination of this policy was the Nixon-Brezhnev summit of 1972, which opened the USSR market to the United States and, by extension, to Japan as well. The competition for CMEA markets was exacerbated by the oil-price shock of 1973, as Soviet terms of trade improved sharply, giving Moscow planners more money to spend and expectations of even higher foreign exchange earnings in the future. These expectations, coupled with the West's need to recycle petrodollars, set off intense competition to finance both capital and consumption goods exports to the CMEA countries.

In the face of such competition, there was recognition in Western Europe that some coordination of credit policies was necessary. Nevertheless, the issue was too important for national interests to permit individual EC members to leave it to the EC to resolve the matter. Thus the question of Western credit policy toward the CMEA was taken up not solely by the EC but rather during talks held in 1974 where the EC commission participated jointly with the West European countries, Japan, and the United States. Nevertheless, subsequent agreements between the large EC countries, France, Germany, Italy, and the UK, and the United States and Japan, were negotiated without EC participation, in part at the Rambouillet summit meeting. The EC reacted to this by seeking a judgment against the summit participants from the International Court of Justice. Despite a favorable ruling from the Court in 1975 affirming the Commission's right to control a common credit policy, the ultimate resolution to the contest of wills came about only in 1977 when the smaller members agreed to the credit limitations negotiated among the four large members of the EC and the United States and Japan. At this point the Commission simply chose to accept these terms and incorporate them into its own policy. Thus, vis-à-vis major Western nations and over issues that touched on broader issues of cooperation among the Western powers, the EC was neither a major factor in the negotiations nor was it able to force its members to abide by the CCP.

The CMEA had no more success than did the EC in influencing its members' behavior during this period. In part this was due to the limitations imposed on the CMEA, which could make no decisions on matters of substance such as plan coordination, trade, or specialization in production that would be binding on all members. It could only make recommendations on these issues and then only with the unanimous consent of its members.[11] This powerlessness was further exacerbated by the reforms that were implemented in a number of CMEA countries during the 1960s, which tended to make the possibility of plan coordination more difficult to carry through than it had been previously. Moreover, with detailed central planning discredited at the national level, it hardly seemed reasonable to attempt to establish the same economic mechanism at the supranational level.

The CMEA, hamstrung by its own rules of operation and thwarted by reforms within its member countries, turned to the EC model in the late 1960s, with the drafting of the Complex Program "for developing socialist economic integration," which was approved in 1971. The CMEA thus accepted the language and objectives of the EC, opting for integration, albeit of a socialist variety, as its ultimate objective. The road to integration was to be a long one, to be traversed by means of a variety of market mechanisms including an increase in "unplanned" trade and a limited convertibility for national currencies. There were, of course, plan elements as well, with long-term programs meant to coordinate investment programs in member countries and to promote specialization. In any event, market elements were never implemented and long-term programs had little force behind them; whatever coordination of investment and specialization that took place occurred largely through the agency of bilateral agreements between the smaller CMEA members and the Soviet Union, whose size and consequent import demands were a much more tangible and powerful force for altering the production and investment programs of its partners than were the needs of the remainder of the CMEA market.

Thus both the EC and the CMEA began their relationship in circumstances where each organization was attempting to achieve integration among its members and where the members, although paying lip service to the goals of integration, were reluctant to part with any or all of their de facto or de jure rights to act as sovereign states. What is interesting is that the institutional symmetry between the two blocs enabled or, better, aided the two international organizations in establishing themselves as legitimate actors in international relations, though, as we shall see, the two organizations were not able to exploit this opportunity to an equal degree.

Although the large West European countries resisted the intrusion of the EC into their relations with the United States and Japan, they were more amenable to EC involvement in their trade with East Europe, in part because the stakes were lower and in part because the EC's mandate was clearer. In 1970 the EC Council of Ministers agreed to the Commission's proposal that all member country trade agreements with East European countries of more than one year in duration contain a clause permitting the modification of the treaty to account for the provisions of the as yet undeveloped CCP. Moreover, the EC had gained rights vis-à-vis its members that were not directly related to East-West issues but that forced the CMEA countries to deal with the EC. One of these issues was the Commission's control over the EC's Generalized System of Preferences (GSP). Romania applied for GSP treatment in 1972, and the EC granted it the following year. EC's control over agricultural policy in the form of the Common Agricultural Policy (CAP) also forced some of the East European countries, notably Bulgaria, Hungary, and Poland, to deal with the Community regarding the effects of the CAP on their agricultural exports to the West. These contracts, however, were on an informal basis.

The CMEA countries recognized that the Commission would continue to gain power over its members' trade with the East, but in the late 1960s and early 1970s they clearly believed that, with some effort on their part, East-West trade could be conducted on the basis of binational agreements. To this end in 1973, N. V. Faddeev, CMEA secretary general, approached the EC to explore the possibility of achieving some form of agreement between the two organizations. This approach came through the diplomatic missions of EC member states. The EC countries thus contacted refused to rise to the bait, directing Faddeev to the EC Commission. Consequently, in 1974 an EC delegation was invited to Moscow to discuss issues of common interest. These talks, held in 1975, were unsuccessful and the parties could not even agree on a joint communiqúe.

The CMEA objective, which represented something of a reversal of past policies and a vindication of the EC's insistence that it, rather than the individual member countries, would control trade with the East, was that some form of coordination between the two organizations would be worthwhile, but that the concrete issues of trade, credits, and cooperation should continue to be determined through bilateral government-to-government agreements. To this the EC could not agree for two reasons. The first was that the EC was determined that policy in this field was to be governed by agreements between the EC and individual CMEA member countries, not between the EC and the CMEA. The second reason was that the EC was not willing to treat the CMEA as an equal partner because of the fundamental differences between the two organizations. The EC viewed itself as a supranational organization that through the process of integration had and was acquiring the power to act in matters of international trade, finance, and cooperation on behalf of its members and to impose its decisions on them. As we have seen, this view was only in part true; as late as 1974 France was challenging the EC's competence over East-West economic cooperation and the issue of East-West credits was de facto decided outside the framework of the EC and largely without the participation of the EC bureaucracy. In contrast, the CMEA, despite a charter revision in 1974 giving it the right to sign agreements with other international organizations and despite its explicit goal of fostering socialist integration, had no supranational powers.

Despite the breakdown in negotiations, the EC continued to apply pressure on the CMEA countries to compel their recognition of the EC as an autonomous international actor. One means of applying pressure was by persevering with the implementation of the CCP. The bilateral agreements between the EC members and CMEA governments were scheduled to expire during 1974–1975 and the EC was determined that subsequent agreements be negotiated within the framework of the CCP. To this end in 1974, the EC drew up and sent to each CMEA member country a draft agreement on EC trade with that country. The agreement called nonpreferential trade relations embodying MFN, and GSP where applicable, as well as mechanisms for resolving trade and market disruption disputes. Interestingly, the EC did not attempt to assert its control over member countries' quotas on imports from the East or over credits or cooperation. Thus the trade objectives of the EC appeared to be minimal; rather the principal objectives were to achieve recognition for the EC as an autonomous international actor and for the principle that the EC would sign trade agreements only with individual CMEA countries.

None of the individual CMEA countries responded to the draft agreement. Instead, in 1976 CMEA made a counterproposal calling for an eight-point agreement, which included:

1. Reciprocal MFN treatment.
2. Nondiscrimination in trade, a point aimed mainly at the remaining West European quotas against East European exports.
3. A mechanism for dealing with market disruption.
4. Development of long-term trade in agriculture.
5. Discussion of currency and payments issues.
6. A recognition of each country's right to sign agreements with any organization *or* country of the other side.
7. A joint commission to oversee the implementation of the agreement.
8. Cooperation on issues of standardization, statistics, the environment, etc.

This proposal was unacceptable to the EC for several reasons. At the broadest level, it appeared to place the EC and the CMEA on an equal footing as autonomous international actors, a position that the EC viewed as incompatible with its de jure and increasingly de facto supranational powers and the CMEA's lack thereof, as well as with the EC's insistence on having individual CMEA members deal exclusively with it on substantive issues of trade. On the first and second points the EC was concerned that a broad interpretation of MFN and the abolition of quotas were both one-sided, since there were no reciprocal measures that CMEA members could take. Moreover, they would be difficult to implement. On the CMEA side, there was no power to enforce compliance, whereas on the EC's side the interference with national quotas was likely viewed as a thorny issue. The third point no doubt was viewed by the EC as directed toward an effort to breach the CAP. The seventh point was also problematic in that, if EC agreements with CMEA members were to be viewed as those between co-equal sovereign entities, then no supranational organization should have the right to intervene in the negotiation or execution of such agreements.

The CMEA position was confused at best. With the exception of Romania, which signed trade agreements with the EC in 1976 and 1980, the other East European countries continued to resist signing agreements with the EC.[12] At the same time, its draft proposal to the EC seemed to offer both de facto and de jure recognition of the EC and of its supranational powers, if the EC would agree to a de facto recognition of similar power on the part of the CMEA.

The two parties continued to hold to these positions at both high-level and expert-level meetings held during 1977–1980. The EC, in principle, was willing to sign a skeleton agreement with the CMEA that would officially recognize the existence of the EC and its right to negotiate with CMEA members on a bilateral basis; the CMEA clearly wanted better terms of entry into EC markets and a trading framework where the two international organizations would play a more equal and more comprehensive role. Lack of progress then led to a hiatus in negotiations until 1984.

The meeting that year of party leaders of the CMEA countries declared itself in favor of signing an agreement with the EC, and the CMEA initiated contacts with the EC in late 1984 with the objective of resuming negotiations toward that end. The signing of a joint declaration that recognizes the right of the EC to negotiate trade treaties with CMEA members was held up until June 1988 by a dispute over the specific inclusion of West Berlin in the EC. Subsequent to the signing of the declaration, the EC began negotiating trade agreements with the individual CMEA members. The first such agreement, with Hungary, was signed in September 1988. In return for reciprocal preferences, the EC agreed to remove all quotas on Hungarian goods by 1995.

## Economic and Political Issues in EC–CMEA Relations

*Economic Issues.* In 1987 the volume of trade, exports plus imports, between the EC and CMEA was about $58 billion, with the Soviet Union accounting for almost half ($26 billion) and the East European countries for the rest. For the EC, this is approximately 7 percent of its total trade. Nevertheless, it is important to recognize that EC businessmen and hopefully also officials make their decisions on the margin, and the marginal increase in exports that can be obtained in the CMEA market looks attractive to the EC for several reasons. First, a large proportion of EC exports consists of products from industries that, in the EC, are facing difficult times on domestic and international markets; thus exports to the East ameliorate the need for subsidies, restructuring, and serve to reduce unemployment. Other exports take the form of high technology products; the EC provides over 60 percent of CMEA imports of high technology items. To the extent that these are produced by firms that benefit from economies of scale and serial production and are the object of EC members' industrial policies, the export markets of the East must be viewed quite favorably. Finally, the CMEA has been a willing market for the EC's highly subsidized exports of agricultural products, thus enabling the EC to reduce the embarrassing agricultural surplus that results from the CAP. In recent years, the EC's exports of agricultural goods to the CMEA have been surpassed only by those of the United States and Canada. Finally, EC banks and governments hold a good deal of the CMEA's external debt. Thus EC members no doubt place greater importance on trade relations with the CMEA than the CMEA's share in EC trade might imply.

Trade with the EC accounts for about one-third of CMEA's external trade, but there is much less homogeneity in CMEA exports. The Soviet Union exports largely fuels and raw materials, the East European members of CMEA must rely more on exports of manufactured and agricultural products. The import structure is more homogeneous. Thus for the CMEA the EC is the major supplier of advanced technology, a major outlet for fuels and raw materials, an important source of agricultural products, but a very competitive and problematic market for the CMEA's exports of manufactured goods and food products.

The EC-CMEA agreement and the bilateral EC trade agreements that will follow from it would appear to have a limited impact on the trading conditions between the two blocs. It is important to bear in mind that no such umbrella or national agreements existed in the 1970s or for much of the 1980s, yet EC-CMEA trade did not appear much hampered by this situation. Surely economic forces, both within and outside Europe, played a much more important role. From the West European standpoint, preferential treatment on CMEA markets probably counts for little. East European import organizations, strapped for hard currency, will continue to seek out the lowest prices, the greatest willingness to cover sales with buyback arrangement, and the best credit terms. On the Soviet side, exports of fuels and raw materials have not been seriously affected by West

European trade restrictions in the past. In the case of East Europe, the removal of quotas on industrial products is unlikely to have a great effect on East European export competitiveness. The quotas cover a relatively small range of goods, in past years some East European countries have not fulfilled their quotas, and in any case it is more the lack of competitiveness of these goods and the growing competition from the newly industrialized countries that represent the main obstacle to East European manufactured exports to the EC.

***Political Issues.*** As is to be expected, the political aspects of EC-CMEA relations involve somewhat more far-reaching issues than do the economic ones. The EC has projected both an official and a public relations view of its stance vis-à-vis the CMEA. The latter is that the Soviet Union is a hegemonic power and that its control over the East European countries would be strengthened and legitimized if the CMEA were to be recognized as a co-equal of the EC. Thus by refusing to deal with the CMEA as a co-equal and by insisting that the members of CMEA sign bilateral treaties with the EC, East Europe is given greater scope for independent foreign and economic policy action than it would have under a comprehensive EC-CMEA agreement.

Although this view has a certain surface plausibility, it does not stand close scrutiny. First of all, the CMEA's ability to project Soviet hegemony is sharply constrained by its charter and mode of operation. There is nothing in the CMEA framework that would be changed by a comprehensive agreement with the EC. Indeed, if the Soviet Union wanted a different CMEA structure, there surely must be other more effective ways to bring it about than by attempting to reach an agreement with the EC. Moreover, the EC's view is in sharp contrast with the manifest feelings toward the agreement within the CMEA. There it was the Soviet Union that tended to resist recognition of the EC and the smaller East European countries who campaigned for greater flexibility in the CMEA position and for some form of relations between the two organizations.

The lack of East European appreciation for the ECs view of the Soviet-East European relationship within CMEA suggests another interpretation of the EC's stance toward the CMEA. This interpretation suggests that the EC wishes to prevent a meaningful agreement with the CMEA so that the full leverage of the EC could be brought to bear, in turn, on each small East European nation in bilateral negotiations. This divide-and-conquer strategy would permit the EC to extract maximum benefits from each East European country while denying it the countervailing economic and political support of the Soviet Union that would be available in bloc to bloc negotiations. In this way the EC would not only extract maximum economic benefits from its East European trade, it would also open the way to a long-term goal of establishing itself as a legitimate superpower. By making East Europe dependent upon itself for technology and as a market for its manufacturers, the EC would extend its power into East Europe and increasingly detach it from the Soviet Union, at first economically and perhaps later even politically.

The official position of the EC, that it could not sign more than a framework agreement with the CMEA because the latter is not a supranational organization, also leaves some doubts. The EC has signed agreements with other international organizations such as the League of Arab Nations, ASEAN, and the participants in the Lomé Convention. It is not evident that these organizations have any greater supernational power than does the CMEA.

On the CMEA side, the political issues touch mainly the Soviet Union. Some observers argue that the Soviet Union views better relations with the EC as a means of detaching the EC from the United States and its East-West trade policy. The EC, thus, would become an alternate source of technology and agricultural products that would be less vulnerable to disruptions than the United States. At the same time, the EC would become more dependent on Soviet energy and raw materials' supplies, leading to an eventual economic and political "Finlandization" of Western Europe.

## Toward 1992

In 1992 the expanded EC will create a true common market. What are the implications of this for the CMEA? On the trade front, the expansion of the EC and the intensification of integration should be a source of trade diversion away from the CMEA, particularly in the production of textiles and standard manufactured goods. On the other hand, if increased integration leads to more rapid growth of output in EC countries, the trade opportunities for the CMEA may expand correspondingly.

It is important, however, to keep in mind that neither the supranationality of the EC nor the issues surrounding EC-CMEA trade have been settled for all time by the agreement between the two blocs or by the measures that will be adopted in 1992. It is worth noting that there has been an upsurge of interest in East-West relations among West European states. Business leaders and government functionaries have visited the capitals of East Europe, numerous contracts have been signed, and new credits have been offered. Some have suggested that this activity amounts to a "European Marshall Plan" for the Soviet bloc, meant to restore the flagging East European economies and to ensure the success of *perestroika* and *glasnost'* in the Soviet Union. An alternative explanation is that the competition among EC members for the East European market is now intensifying, with evidence of a new credit war. Thus the EC may again be facing a test of its power over member countries' credit policies that may replicate the events of the 1970s.

## Notes to Chapter 2

1. "Hard goods" are those with quality sufficient to compete in the convertible (hard) currency markets of the advanced industrial economies.

2. For a history of the CMEA, see Jozef M. van Brabant, *Socialist Economic Integration* (Cambridge: Cambridge University Press, 1980), Chapter 1.

3. Ernest Mandel, *Die EWG und die Konkurrenz Europa-Amerika* (Frankfurt: Europäische Verlagsanstalt, 1968) presents a good summary of these views.

4. Indeed, not only among the members of CMEA. President Kennedy proposed sending the chairman of his Council of Economic Advisors, Walter Heller, to find out the secret of Western Europe's economic success.

5. Nikita S. Khrushchev, "Vital Questions of the Development of the World Socialist System," *Kommunist*, No. 12 (August 1962), pp. 1–8.

6. For a survey of West European trade strategies and an estimate of their effectiveness, see Larry Wipf and Josef Brada, "The Impact of West European Trade Strategies on Exports to East Europe," *European Economic Review*, 6, no. 2 (April 1975), 155–171.

7. United Nations, *Analytical Report on Industrial Cooperation among EC Countries* (Geneva: United Nations, 1973), Chapter III.

8. A good survey and analysis of West European export financing policies is provided by Thomas A. Wolf, "East-West Trade Credit Policy: A Comparative Analysis," in Paul Marer (ed.), *U.S. Financing of East-West Trade* (Bloomington, Ind.: International Development Research Center, 1975), pp. 149–198.

9. Wipf and Brada, "Impact."

10. France was particularly, but not uniquely, adamant on this distinction. See Peter Marsh, "The Development of Relations between the EC and the CMEA," in Avi Shlaim and G. N. Yannopoulos (eds.), *The EC and Eastern Europe* (Cambridge: Cambridge University Press, 1978), pp. 25–70.

11. In 1967 this was modified by limiting the need for unanimity to "interested" members, but this clearly did not strengthen the supranational power of the CMEA in any significant way.

12. A serious problem arose in 1977 when the EC demanded that the USSR

and the GDR sign a fisheries agreement with it. The Soviet representative de-
murred, arguing that he was empowered only to sign agreements with the member
countries of the EC. Romania signed a favorable agreement with the EC on textile
trade in 1976 an a more comprehensive agreement in 1980. Poland explored the
possibility of a textile agreement also, but the discussions foundered because of
the limited concessions the Community was willing to make.

# Chapter 3

# THE MILITARY ALLIANCE

*Christopher D. Jones*

## THE WARSAW PACT IN THE ERA OF "REASONABLE SUFFICIENCY"

By concluding an INF agreement with the United States in December of 1987 and by announcing a series of unilateral force cuts at the United Nations one year later, Mikhail Gorbachev is defining reasonable sufficiency in the European theater as the minimum military power necessary to maintain communist regimes in Eastern Europe and to guarantee the permanent division of Germany. In eliminating Soviet intermediate-range nuclear forces and in reducing the size and capabilities of the Soviet ground forces, Gorbachev is also emphasizing the role of the Warsaw Pact in securing Soviet objectives in Europe.

Gorbachev's spokesmen are now criticizing the Brezhnev regime for a policy of unreasonable sufficiency—maintaining a military force sufficient not only for pursuing Soviet objectives in Eastern and Central Europe but sufficient for threatening NATO at any level of conflict—conventional, chemical, or nuclear. The Gorbachev critique goes on to argue that the Brezhnev posture was worse than unreasonable; it was self-defeating. In wartime, Brezhnev's policy for the European theater closely coupled the possible limited use of Soviet conventional power in Eastern and Central Europe with a larger Warsaw Pact-NATO conflict likely to end in a global nuclear war in which all combatants would perish. In peacetime, Brezhnev's military policies locked the Soviet Union into an arms race that increasingly emphasized economic strength and technological sophistication, two areas in which the West was much stronger.

By reducing Soviet threats to NATO in the categories of INF, chemical weapons and "offensive" elements of ground forces, Gorbachev is refocusing Soviet/Warsaw Pact forces on the primary Soviet objective in Europe: preserving the status quo that had crystallized by 1955. This status quo first took shape in 1949 with the formation of separate German states and the establishment of NATO. In the Soviet view, it became permanent in 1955 when the Federal Republic of Germany (FRG) joined NATO and when the East bloc states, including the German Democratic Republic (GDR), signed the Warsaw Treaty. For the Soviets, these two events irrevocably linked the preservation of communist regimes in East Europe with the permanent division of Germany. The reason is obvious enough: the GDR is both a German state and a socialist state.

In the period from 1944 to the first systematic formulation of Soviet military doctrine under Khrushchev in the late 1950s several related security problems also crystallized. The FRG committed itself to reliance on a U.S. nuclear guarantee to deter a Soviet attack. The FRG adamantly rejected the finality of the division of Germany. The GDR faced a perpetual crisis of survival as hundreds of thousands of its citizens fled each year, mainly through the Western zones of the city of Berlin. Other East European states—Hungary, Poland, Albania and Romania—presented the Soviets with challenges that required maintenance of a capability for rapid military intervention.

For Khrushchev's generals, Soviet military policy had to meet the requirements of repressing East European upheavals, keeping East Germany under permanent occupation, deterring any West German political or military response to revolts in East Germany, and dissuading the FRG's allies from honoring their commitments to the conventional and nuclear defense of the West German border.

The Khrushchev solution was to configure large enough conventional forces, even after the cuts of the late 1950s and early 1960s, to mount offensive actions against East Europe, the two Germanys and Western Europe. The Soviets counterposed their superior conventional capability to the superior U.S. nuclear forces committed to the European theater and added a daring bluff: the Soviet Union was prepared to fight and win a nuclear war, by preemption if necessary.

The Brezhnev regime witnessed potential solutions to the linked problems of West Germany's rejection of the post-war status quo and the American nuclear guarantee to the FRG. The Soviets achieved parity at the theater and strategic levels, and, thus, called into question the credibility of a U.S. nuclear guarantee in the event of a limited war in Central

Europe over the reconstitution of Germany. Brandt and Brezhnev together greatly reduced the likelihood of such a conflict through a series of treaties: The 1970 USSR-FRG treaty and subsequent West German treaties with Poland and Czechoslovakia which recognized the transfer of former German territories to these three states; the 1971 four-power treaty which in effect acknowledged the fact of the Berlin Wall and de facto FRG sovereignty over West Berlin; the 1972 Basic Agreement between the GDR and FRG which allowed the resumption of economic, cultural and family ties between the two states, without giving FRG de jure recognition to the GDR.

In 1975, the Helsinki Agreement in effect committed every member of NATO to the terms of the agreements worked out between the FRG and the Soviet bloc. But rather than adjusting Khrushchev's military policies to recognize the reinforcement of the status quo by nuclear parity and the diplomacy of *Ostpolitik*, Brezhnev's generals continued to plan for the worst possible case. They achieved the worst possible result: a tighter linkage among upheavals in East Europe, reemergence of the "German Question," NATO's commitment of defense at the inner German border, and the U.S. nuclear guarantee to the FRG. The tighter linkage came as a consequence of the following Western responses to the Brezhnev military buildup: the 1978 NATO Long-Term Defense Program with its various follow-ons (Air-Land Battle, the Rogers Plan, Deep Strike, Emerging Technologies etc.); the 1979 NATO decision to deploy U.S. INF, and the French and British decisions to expand greatly the capabilities of their nuclear arsenals; and the Reagan defense build up, especially its commitment to the Strategic Defense Initiative.

Gorbachev cut through the Gordian knot of Brezhnev's defense policy by rejecting the military strategy developed by Khrushchev and refocusing on Khrushchev's original objectives. Where Khrushchev and Brezhnev had tried to undercut the American nuclear guarantee by matching or surpassing U.S. nuclear forces, Gorbachev seeks to undercut the guarantee by removing U.S. nuclear forces from Europe—at the price of removing Soviet nuclear forces as well. Where Khrushchev and Brezhnev sought to undercut Western Europe's commitment to the conventional defense of the FRG by overawing NATO with greater numbers of troops and tanks, Gorbachev is seeking the same objective by cutting conventional force levels on both sides.

But Gorbachev, like Khrushchev and Brezhnev, requires unquestioned military superiority over the *Bundeswehr* as an insurance policy on *Ostpolitik*-detente. But unlike Brezhnev, Gorbachev wants reasonably superiority. As the Soviet general secretary told the U.N. on 7 December, 1988:

> "We shall maintain our country's defense capability at a level of reasonable and reliable sufficiency so that no one might be tempted to encroach on the security of the Soviet Union and our allies."[1]

Gorbachev is seeking a less costly way of maintaining the status quo on the internal and external fronts of the Warsaw Pact. Lowering the gross numbers on both sides, as Gorbachev has proposed, will not affect the Soviet capability to intervene in Eastern Europe or to devastate West Germany. Reducing the size of conventional forces and eliminating long-range Soviet theater nuclear missiles may significantly change the Western perception of the Soviet threat to the non-German members of NATO. This in turn may greatly complicate Bonn's relations with its NATO allies. None of the arms control proposals advanced by Gorbachev will require a restructuring of the Warsaw Pact or reduce its capabilities to act in East Europe or immediately across the inner German border. Rather than calling for a restructuring of the Warsaw Pact, Gorbachev has in fact identified it as a model for interbloc relations. The structure of the Warsaw Pact will endure under Gorbachev because this structure focuses on a series of missions still critical for the pursuit of Soviet military-political objectives in Europe.

## MISSIONS OF THE WTO

The first mission of the Warsaw Pact has been to preempt any independent national capability for defense of national territory by national means. In practice, this means preventing any other signatory of the Warsaw Treaty from following the examples of Romania, still a nominal member of the WTO, and Albania, which formally withdrew from the pact in 1968. By refusing to sign codicils that have been attached to the Warsaw Treaty,[2] Romania has adopted a territorial defense strategy directed against a Soviet intervention, as has Albania and Yugoslavia. These three states have each demonstrated that an independent defense capability is a prerequisite for the exercise of national sovereignty in either external or internal policies. They have also demonstrated that deploying national troops for defense of national territory also denies to the USSR the use of these troops for offensive actions against NATO.

The second mission of the WTO has been detaching designated elite units from pseudo-sovereign WTO states. Detaching these elite units from national control first of all preempts organized national resistance to Soviet intervention, but also places these units at the disposal of the Soviet Ministry of Defense for joint Warsaw Pact interventions against fellow WTO members. Such elite units from Poland, the GDR, Hungary, and Bulgaria participated in the 1968 intervention against Czechoslovakia. Though their significance was entirely political, their political role was extremely important. Colonel Ryszard Kukliński, formerly an officer on the Polish General Staff in charge of planning for martial law in the post-1980 period, reports that the Soviets planned to use Czech and GDR units for intervention in Poland. Kukliński also reports the direct supervision of Polish planning for martial law by then WTO commander-in-chief, Marshal V. G. Kulikov, who also organized plans for a back-up intervention by Warsaw Pact forces.[3]

The third mission of the WTO is that of combining the detached elite units from all service branches into bilateral formations and then in turn combining these formations into a greater socialist army configured for war against the Bundeswehr and other allied NATO forces. Within the bilateral formations the Soviets appear to seek a 2:1 ratio of Soviet to East European personnel. In the combined WTO superformations each East European contingent will find itself surrounded by an even higher ratio of nonnative forces. This greater socialist army will enjoy at last a 1.5:1 ratio against the Bundeswehr, offset by other NATO troops on West German soil and the American nuclear guarantee to the FRG. Additional Soviet forces based in the USSR could alter the WTO-NATO ratio in favor of the Soviets, but these additional Soviet troops will almost certainly not be paired with East European forces. The Soviets will almost certainly not call upon the nonelite East Europeans to perform any significant combat role against NATO except for defensive actions on native East European territory.

The 2:1 pairing Soviet forces based in East Europe and elite East European units is a goal rather than a reality. At present the northern tier strength of the greater Socialist army consists of some 26 Soviet divisions—19 in the GDR, 2 in Poland, and 5 in Czechoslovakia. Four additional Soviet divisions are based in Hungary, but it is not clear what their wartime mission would be. The present contribution of the northern tier states is six solid East German divisions, probably two–three Czechoslovak divisions, and perhaps three–four Polish divisions, of which one is a brigade-size marine "division" and another a brigade-size airborne "division." The East Germans maintain four well-equipped reserve divisions that the Soviets may well prefer to Polish or Czechoslovak forces, for reasons of geography, readiness, and political reliability. The Czechoslovak People's Army maintains a nominal force of ten divisions, of which four are credited with category I status.[4] The Poles maintain another 10–11 standing divisions, but these appear to be poorly equipped and evidently suffer severe morale problems connected with the general demoralization of Polish society in the postmartial law period. However, the *Military Balance* lists eight of these divisions as category I, in addition to category I airborne and marine brigades.[5]

By reducing the number of Soviet divisions by six, Gorbachev has also reduced the required contributions of WTO states by three divisions. More than likely the bulk of the Soviet reductions will come from Hungary and Czechoslovakia, where the local resources have been insufficient for meeting the 1:2 (East European-to-Soviet) ratio at current force levels. Taking the bulk of Soviet reductions in these two states would also emphasize the message that while Gorbachev wishes to reduce the threat to NATO but maintain the threat to Germany. Despite the socio-political pathologies that rule out the full mobilization of military manpower in Poland and Czechoslovakia, the greater socialist army will probably attain a high degree of combat reliability. This reliability is based on a 2:1 "ratio of distrust" within bilateral Soviet-East European formations,[6] reinforced by a complex overlapping system of control mechanisms discussed below.

A fourth mission for the Warsaw Pact, evident in the reforms that followed the WTO intervention in Czechoslovakia, is the assignment of the first-line responsibility for internal repression to the entire complex of national armed forces. The national forces specifically assigned to the internal front consist of the nonelite regular armed forces not included in the greater socialist army, internal security troops, border troops, police, and various "militia" paramilitary forces. At the far end of this scale are the elite national forces, which are in turn linked to the Soviet forces based throughout the region. The 2:1 ratio of distrust maintained on the external front appears to have an equivalent 2:1 ratio on the internal front.[7] The internal ratio consist of the ratio of cadre in one uniform or another who have a stake in the existing system to the conscripts in the regular armed forces and security forces. Such a ratio on the internal front makes it possible to field highly specialized, highly reliable units like the ZOMO forces in Poland to carry out direct repression, whereas the regular forces, dependent on conscripts, play an important psychological-political role in the background.

A fifth mission of East European forces is that of defending home territory against NATO efforts to disrupt Soviet supply lines and/or incite East European protests against the WTO war effort.

A sixth possible mission is that of providing occupation troops for any areas captured by the greater Socialist army and Soviet follow-on forces.

# PRINCIPLES OF THE WARSAW PACT

To achieve the objectives discussed above, the Soviets have consistently applied three basic principles to the national forces of the WTO. The first principle is a fragmentation of national control over the separate components of national armed forces. In practice, this principle converts national defense ministries into the equivalents of Soviet military districts—that is, large housekeeping organizations that train and maintain units available for assignment to operational commands. National units may do service on either the external or internal fronts, but ultimately these forces are not under independent national authority, even on the internal front. The second principle is using the multinational agencies of the WTO to legitimize bilateral Soviet-East European links. On the national level, these links produce activities that appear national in form but are bilateral in content. On the alliance level, these bilateral links produce an entity that is multinational without being multilateral. The third principle is that of pursuing cohesion and reliability, not by attitudinal integration (voluntary obedience) but by functional integration (leaving military personnel with no rational choice other than to go along with Soviet domination). Functional integration is dependent on maintaining the proper "ratios of distrust" that counterbalance the disaffection of the rank-and-file in both military and civilian spheres. These ratios of distrust also control the privileged elites by giving them reason to fear the collapse of the system that protects them from the disenfranchised.

In fact, the command cadres dependent on the survival of the system and their privileged comrades in the party and state hierarchies endorse the three principles identified above because the application of these principles assures an unopposed Soviet capability of intervention on behalf of the existing East European elites. Though the local elites may occasionally quarrel with the Soviet patrons over the fine points of bloc pol-

icy, they share with the Soviet leadership a deep interest in the perpetuation of the military mechanisms that deny sovereignty to East European
governments.

# CONTROL MECHANISMS OF THE WTO

The three principles identified above have their specific applications in
the following control mechanisms of the Warsaw Pact. These control
mechanisms are mutually reinforcing and mutually dependent. Their end
product—military power—is in turn used to guarantee the perpetuation
of the control mechanisms that produce military power.

## Military Doctrine

In Soviet/WTO systems military doctrine defines and justifies virtually
all aspects of a nation's defense system. Soviet/WTO military doctrine
consists of two principal components—the military-political and the military-technical. The Soviets argue that although the two components interact, the military-political component is the more decisive. In the case
of the WTO, this claim is entirely true. For it is in ruling out military-
political formulas like those of Yugoslavia or Romania that the Soviets
are able to fragment national control over national armed forces.

The constant theme of WTO military-political statements is the necessity for joint defense of the gains of socialism against internal and external
reaction. This phrase, written into the bilateral treaties of the USSR with
every WTO state except Romania, achieves the following objectives: (1)
ruling out independent national defense capabilities, (2) justifying the integration of East European units into a large alliance mechanism, and (3)
the use of military force against changes in the political status quo, either
in East Europe or between the two Germanys.

The shared military-political axioms of the WTO states have the practical effect of imposing on East European states Soviet norms for the four
"theories" of the military-technical component of doctrine. These are:
"military art" (strategy, operations, and tactics), which in effect gives the
Soviets a monopoly in defining the missions and capabilities of national
WTO forces; "military administration," a theory that in practice means
making the structure of a national defense ministry analogous to that of
the USSR (similar organizations facilitate the linking of corresponding
Soviet and East European components); "military economics," which

provides an economic plan for leaving East European militaries thoroughly dependent on external suppliers, mainly Soviet; and "military education and troop training," which in practice gives the Soviets control over both officer education and the types of training acquired by conscripts.

For the independent defense ministries in Bucharest, Belgrade, and Tirana, national military doctrine is sharply different on the basic questions of military art (strategy, operation, and tactics), the structure of national military organizations, the organization of defense production, and the type of education and training provided to officers and enlisted personnel. Each of these states has deployed a territorial defense system. All the pronounced differences in the military-technical sphere derive from a sharply different military-political component of doctrine: defense of national territory by national means.

The combined effect of the military-political and military-technical components of WTO doctrine are: (1) to keep Soviet forces in an offensive posture against both East Europe and West Germany, (2) to preempt East European defensive capabilities against the USSR, and (3) to mobilize elite East European forces for use on either the internal or external front. The formulation of the military-political content of Soviet/WTO doctrine has remained constant from the early 1960s to the present, including the rhetoric about the "defensive nature" of Soviet doctrine. The current rhetoric still specifically allows for the use of military force to reverse changes in the political status quo in either East Europe or in the two Germanys. For instance, the 1987 Political Consultative Council (PCC) communiqué, which declares,

> The combat readiness of the armed forces of the allied states is maintained at a sufficient level so as not to be caught unaware. In the event of an attack, they will give a devastating rebuff to the aggressor. The Warsaw Treaty member states never had, nor have an aspiration to possess, armed forces and armaments in excess of what is necessary for these purposes. Thus they strictly comply with the units of sufficiency for defense, for rebutting possible aggression.[8]

WTO Commander V. G. Kulikov reaffirmed this implicit commitment to maintain a military capability to reverse political changes in a radio interview following the July 1988 meeting of the PCC. Marshal Kulikov declared,

> We do realize, however, that it is impossible to defeat an enemy and destroy an aggressor through defensive actions alone. We are working out

such active forms of action as offensive action, counterstrikes, and other kinds of combat action which are in the context of the new defense doctrine.[9]

In the early 1960s the military-technical discussions of waging nuclear war have the same purpose of the late 1980s discussions of avoiding nuclear war: the goal is to dissuade the United States from relying on nuclear forces to offset WTO conventional advantages against Germany. The deployment of nuclear weapons also has the objective of binding East European militaries to the nuclear arsenal of the USSR and preempting their examination of nonnuclear options like those of Romania or Yugoslavia.

## The Political Directorate of the Warsaw Pact

The military-political axioms of the WTO provide the texts and justification for a de facto functioning agency of the pact, its political directorate, which has not been publicly identified because Romania refuses to participate in its activities. The Romanian refusal testifies to the importance of the directorate's activities. The directorate links corresponding agencies of national political administrations. The WTO agency coordinates the drawing up of formal, annual programs of joint political activities, from the level of the unit to the level of the Main Political Administration (MPA) of Soviet force groups and national MPAs. Chiefs of national MPAs regularly meet, though without the Romanians. Military historians and military journalists provide common texts for political education programs at every level. The utility of MPA work was evident in the occupation of Czechoslovakia, where allied political officers could draw upon a wealth of previous experience in conducting civil-military exercises in Czechoslovakia. In combat with NATO, MPA officers might well play critical roles in assuring combat reliability.

Though couched in soporific phraseology, the basic message of WTO political officers is blatantly offensive to East European national sensibilities: the leading role of the Soviet army in all aspects of alliance affairs. This message is often delivered by the analogy of the elder brother. Within the Soviet units stationed in East Europe, the Russian soldier is identified as the elder brother within the fraternal Soviet Army, by virtue of big brother's selfless past services to his siblings. The analogy is then extended to the Warsaw Pact: the Soviet soldier serves as the elder brother of WTO soldiers whose kin have likewise been the recipients of selfless Soviet support.

This analogy not only justifies the de facto chain of command within the greater socialist army, it also identifies the dynamics of political reliability in the context of the proper ratios of distrust. That is, the cohesion of the greater Socialist army depends on the cohesion of the Soviet Army, which in turn depends on the cohesion of its ethnic Russians and Russified Slavs.

Under the guise of pursuing the attitudinal integration of the WTO on the basis of common attitudes, the Warsaw Pact MPA system is in fact mainly concerned with functional integration, that is, communicating to all WTO personnel that the only alternative to accepting Soviet/Russian domination is engaging in a solitary and hopeless struggle against the system as a whole. The special expertise of alliance political officers is the use of national symbols to deliver a message that is "international," that is, antinational. The most visible and most extensive of the joint MPA activities take place during the regular joint exercises of the Warsaw Pact, which serve as both the symbol and substance of Soviet domination.

## Joint Military Exercises

The principal activity of the Warsaw Pact is the conduct of joint training programs and joint military exercises. These are the programs that translate military doctrine into military power. The annual joint military exercises encompass three levels of activity: basic training in purely national units, bilateral Soviet-East European joint training, and large, complex multilateral military maneuvers. The bilateral exercises preempt independent national capabilities of East European forces and bond the elite units of East Europe to their Soviet counterparts for service on either the external or internal fronts.

The larger multilateral exercises permit the Soviets to accomplish several tasks: (1) the practice of large-scale invasions of East European states; this opportunity was critical to the successful conduct of the 1968 intervention in Czechoslovakia and was just as important in providing the Soviets with political leverage during the Polish crisis of 1980–1981; (2) preemption of the capabilities of East European militaries for large-scale independent action on their own territories; any large-scale action in the loyal WTO states is invariably a multilateral exercise in which the host country integrates its forces and command-and-control systems into the larger WTO operation; (3) preparation of elite East European forces for action as part of a greater Socialist army operating on foreign soil; these exercises also play critical roles in the career advancement of East European officers because Soviet officers on the WTO staff evaluate the performance of alliance personnel in performing alliance missions; (4) occasional participation of paramilitary forces in joint WTO exercises. This practice, particulary evident in the GDR and Czechoslovakia, is an effort to integrate the entire spectrum of armed forces missions, ranging from the internal to external fronts; and (5) by maintaining the system of joint exercises, Gorbachev can cut the Soviet force levels in Eastern Europe which alarm NATO but retain the capability of massive Soviet interventions. The exercise system should thus allow substantial reductions of the Soviet garrisons in Czechoslovakia and Hungary without degrading the Soviet capability for the rapid reintroduction of Soviet forces.

## The Central Agencies of the Warsaw Pact

The central agencies of the WTO preside over the joint exercises and all other joint activities of the WTO. The primary purpose of the central agencies is to compete with corresponding national agencies for operational control over the key components of national defense systems. By playing legitimate roles of liaison with national defense establishments, the central agencies legitimize the transfer of real power to the corresponding agencies of the Soviet general staff. The question of whether the WTO staff has any real power in its own right as a multilateral agency is a moot question, since the key personnel are Soviet officers with dual responsibilities to the WTO and the Soviet Ministry of Defense.

Colonel Ryszard Kukliński testified to this dynamic when he noted that in 1979–1980, Defense Minister Jaruzelski accepted a WTO document that provided for the wartime transfer of command authority over virtually the entire Polish defense ministry to Soviet officers without even the courtesy of establishing Polish liaison officers. According to Kukliński,

> In the event of a war peril or war, as much as 90 percent of the Polish Army will find itself directly under the orders of Soviet commanders. Left within the purview of the national military-political leadership will be, properly speaking, only domestic logistic units, engineer maintenance units for safeguarding the transit of Soviet troops across Polish territory, and units expected to train reserves for complementing war losses.
>
> All orders and directives of the Soviet commanders will be addressed directly to their subordinate Polish troops, bypassing the Polish high command. In practice, this means an unbounded right of the USSR to dispose of the people's Polish Army without any prior consultation with PRL authorities.

The role of the Polish high command will be confined solely to that of supplying all material to the Polish troops fighting under Soviet command, training reserves, and compensating for human and material war losses.[10]

The central agencies of the WTO preside over the Soviet and East European units assigned to the combined armed forces, that is, the greater socialist army. The United Command of the WTO consists of major service functions (ground forces, navies, rear services, etc.), each headed by a Soviet officer also responsible for the corresponding Soviet service branch or special service. For the operation of this system, the uniformity of structure among the WTO militaries is crucial. Below the level of the United Command, the Warsaw Pact commander-in-chief has two overlapping bureaucracies. One is that of his direct liaison representatives to each national army. The other bureaucracy consists of the multiple agencies subsumed in the staff of the combined armed forces; the staff is headed by a Soviet officer who is the deputy commander of the WTO. The WTO staff officially serves as the executive agency of the pact's two highest bodies, the Council of Defense (CDM) and the Military Council (MC). The CDM is nominally in charge of all major policy issues; the MC is in charge of annual training and exercise programs. Three Soviet officers serve on the CDM: the defense minister, the Warsaw Pact commander, and the WTO chief of staff. By international treaty, the representatives of the WTO staff have extraterritorial privileges on East European soil. Within the WTO staff are de facto (although not de jure) agencies for military doctrine, political administrations, and officer education. Several de jure bodies have been established for various aspects of military technology: the Technical Committee (responsible for the introduction and integration of new weapons systems), the Military-Scientific Technical Committee (responsible for the organization of military research), and the Military-Industrial Commission (responsible for weapons production).[11] The main point here is that for every key function in an East European military, there is a de jure or de facto multilateral body that can legitimize transfer of real authority to the corresponding Soviet agency.

This multilateral façade is remarkably effective at camouflaging the real mechanisms of power. Colonel Kukliński noted that the regulations concerning these mechanisms,

All the foregoing decisions are, in view of the exceptionally sensitive nature, classified top secret and no one in the Polish Army apart from a

handful of heads of the defense ministry has the least notion of them. Even
the commanders of arms of service and military districts are familiar with
that part of the decisions which concerns them directly.[12]

## The WTO Officer Education System

An elite segment of East European officers plays a critical role in enabling
the national, multilateral, and Soviet components of the WTO system to
mesh together. These are the East European graduates of Soviet military
academies. The vast majority of East European officers begin their careers in national officer candidate schools, although a small group enrolls
in equivalent Soviet institutions. The WTO officer network is a two-track
system designed to train both the officers who command the entire units
assigned to the combined armed forces and the officers assigned to the
larger number of less important units that function as support systems for
both internal and external fronts. The critical decision point for most East
European officers comes in midcareer during their late twenties when
further advancement requires enrolling in a domestic midcareer service
academy or one of the 16 Soviet service academies that train East European officers for command positions in the elite East European units
that participate in multilateral exercises.

The East European graduates of these Soviet midcareer academies constitute a greater socialist officer corps trained to execute the WTO missions defined by Soviet doctrine. These officers combine technical military skills with the political skill of taking orders in Russian and reissuing
them in their native languages. Such officers are largely self-selected, for
they have voluntarily chosen to go through the admission process for Soviet academies, to meet the academic and political standards of their Soviet alma mater, and to meet the standards of the WTO staff in their
postacademy assignments, particulary in the joint military exercises. What
binds the greater Socialist officer corps together is not attitudinal integration (common ideological commitments) but functional integration—
that is, the expectation of Soviet patronage combined with an awareness
of the resentment of fellow officers without Soviet degrees. What is at
stake for the East European members of the greater socialist officer corps
is caste privileges for the elite officers and the temptation of appointment
to the handful of top-level national commands.

The Voroshilov General Staff Academy is the exclusive gateway to
these top-level commands. Virtually all the defense ministers, chiefs of

national general staffs, heads of MPAs, and national service branch commanders are alumni of the Voroshilov Academy. An East German general noted in 1986 that the National People's Army had a total of 170 graduates of the Voroshilov Academy, an elite among the 2,400 East German officers with Soviet degrees, themselves an elite.[13]

A former Polish ambassador claims that the senior Polish commanders receive corresponding rank—and salary—in the Soviet military,[14] an apparent continuation of a policy that existed in the immediate postwar period for Soviet officers of Polish descent who served in the Polish military. There is at least a hint of a similar system in Bulgarian practice of listing both the Bulgarian and Soviet decorations held by ranking Bulgarian officers, with the Soviet decorations first in the order of protocol.[15]

For Soviets, the care and feeding of a greater Socialist officer corps is not without precedent. In the interwar period non-Russians were sent to native-language officer schools to train them for command and political posts in the ethnic divisions of Soviet republics. Promotion past mid-career levels required further education in Russian-language military academies as preparation for command of larger multinational formations. In the Warsaw Pact, as in the Soviet army from 1924–1938 and during the first years of World War II, "ethnic" officers play a critical role in the political and combat reliability of multinational military forces. The WTO officer education system is sufficiently well developed to supply a full complement of the officers necessary to command the elite units assigned to the combined armed forces and to reliably fulfill the alliance obligations at the top level of national defense ministries.

## Defense Production

According to the military-political axioms of the WTO, the ideologically appropriate system of defense production for the Socialist coalition is an international division of labor. This is carried out under the auspices of three agencies mentioned earlier, the Military-Industrial Commission of the CMEA, the WTO's Military Scientific Committee, and the Technical Committee. In practice, the Warsaw Pact's division of labor leaves each WTO military (except Romania's) absolutely dependent on the Soviet Union and other external suppliers for all but the most basic military equipment. The consequences for national sovereignty are obvious, as are the advantages for the Soviet Union of the interoperability of WTO materiel.

# GORBACHEV AND THE NATO-WTO BALANCE

The Warsaw Pact has been so well designed for the pursuit of its internal and external missions that it has survived structurally intact despite the upheavals occasioned by the overall mismanagement of Soviet-East European and Soviet-West European policies during the Brezhnev-Andropov-Chernenko period. The fundamental soundness of Warsaw Pact mechanisms have also provided Gorbachev with a secure strategic basis for launching the initiatives of "new thinking" and "reasonable sufficiency."

Gorbachev reversed the theater nuclear weapons policy that began with Khrushchev and continued through the tenures of the next three general secretaries of the CPSU. He has signed agreements removing nuclear missiles in the 1,000–5,000 km range and the 500–1,000 km range and has opened the possibility of a "third zero" as well in the category of missiles with ranges under 500 km. He has also proposed the creation of a 300 km-wide nuclear-free zone along the West German border—150 kms on each side. He further proposed linking this zone to nuclear-free zones in Northern Europe and the Balkans. These proposals are radical in at least two respects—they are reversals of previous Soviet policies and they were originally put forward by public officials either in the United States or Western Europe. The Soviet leader has also advanced a series of his own proposals, the most important of which are calls for large cuts in U.S. and Soviet air power in Europe, prohibition of defense technology transfer among the Western allies, and prohibition of joint Western military research.

Prior to Gorbachev's 1988 speech to the UN, the WTO had proposed mutual NATO/WTO cuts of 500,000 troops in an area extending from the Atlantic to the Urals. In his UN speech Gorbachev announced a unilateral cut of 500,000 personnel by 1991 along with the reduction of the Soviet tank inventory by 10,000, elimination of 8,500 artillery pieces and 800 combat aircraft. These reductions will limit the soviet capability for a general continent-wide war with NATO while preserving Soviet superiority in Eastern and Central Europe.

As part of these reductions Gorbachev announced the removal from the GDR, Czechoslovakia and Hungary of 6 tank divisions, 5,000 tanks and 50,000 personnel. The 50,000 personnel are to include "offensive" troops—marine landing forces, paratroop formations and bridge-building units.

In addition, Gorbachev promised to reconfigure the remaining troops into a "clearly defensive" posture. The removal of 5,000 tanks from Eastern Europe exceeds by 2,500–3,000 the number of tanks usually attributed to Soviet tank divisions in this region. The removal of 50,000 troops is probably less than the total number of personnel assigned to man and support 6 tank divisions of 8,000–10,000 personnel each.

The remaining Soviet forces in Eastern Europe and the European theater as a whole will have fewer assets for conducting a transcontinental campaign against Western Europe. But they will also be able to focus their power on a much more limited set of targets in Eastern and Central Europe. If most of the Soviet divisions are withdrawn from Czechoslovakia and Hungary (2 to 5 divisions altogether), then these two states will find it much easier to meet the 1:2 pairing requirement of elite East European and Soviet units. Even if all 50,000 troops and all 6 divisions were to come from the group of Soviet forces in Germany, the GSFG would still constitute a very serious threat to the FRG. Unlike a Soviet capability to overrun Western Europe, which would require large numbers of troops, naval and air forces to occupy a very large area, a Soviet capability to seize and/or devastate West Germany would not depend so much on absolute numbers as on the ratio of NATO-WTO troops on the central front. Preservation of the existing ratio at a lower level might enable the Soviets to maintain their threat to the FRG without creating as much alarm in the states west of the Rhine.

The Soviet capability to intervene in Eastern Europe depends not so much on raw numbers as on the preemption of East European capabilities for sustained resistance organized by a professional officer corps. The agencies and programs of the Warsaw Pact deliberately and systematically deny such capabilities to the loyal members of the WTO. Warsaw Pact troop reductions would not affect these agencies or programs; they might even reduce residual East European capabilities for self-defense.

The Soviets already extended such an offer to NATO in the January 1983 declaration of the Warsaw Pact PCC. This document put forward earlier versions of many of the European security proposals currently advocated by Gorbachev. In its proposal for "practical measures for the prevention of surprise attack," the 1983 PCC statement included an escape clause—or rather, a nonescape clause for East European states facing the prospect of a surprise Soviet military intervention. The PCC insisted that a WTO-NATO treaty on the nonuse of armed force

> would not, of course, limit the inalienable right of its participants to individual and collective self-defense in accordance with Article 51 of the United Nations Charter.[16]

Soviet discussions of Article 51 of the UN charter have specifically in-
voked this article as the basis in international law for exercise of joint
defense of the gains of socialism against internal and external threats.[17]
The text of the 1983 PCC statement, immediately after referring to Article
51 of the charter, continues with this sentence:

> At the same time, it [a WTO-NATO nonaggression treaty] would free the
> members of both alliances from the fear that allied obligations, which are
> effective within each alliance, could be intended for aggressive actions against
> the member states of the other alliance, and that, consequently, these ob-
> ligations could create a threat to their security.[18]

In other words, NATO should not regard "allied obligations" for the collective defense of socialism in East Europe as "intended for aggressive
actions against the member states of the other alliance." NATO should
recognize that the carrying out of such allied obligations against fellow
allies is simply the Warsaw Pact's way of honoring Article 51 of the UN
charter.

## CONCLUSION

The present structure of the Warsaw Pact, inherited from the "period of
stagnation," should emerge fully intact from the consequences of the nuclear and conventional arms control policies advanced by Gorbachev. These
proposals in fact rest upon a redefinition of Soviet theater nuclear policy
and general East-West policy to fit better with the basic missions embed-
ded in the structure of the Warsaw Pact: preservation of the political status
quo in Eastern Europe and preservation of the status quo between the two
Germanys.

### Notes to Chapter 3

1. "Address by Mr. Mikhail Gorbachev" in *Provisional Verbatim Record of
the Seventy-Second Meeting of the General Assembly* (43rd Session, December
7, 1988), p. 28.

2. Col. Ryszard J. Kukliński, "Wojna z narodem widziana od środka" [The
War Against the Nation seen from the Inside], *Kultura*, no. 4/475, 1987, Paris.
Selections translated in *Orbis*, Winter 1988, p. 16.

3. Kukliński, in *Orbis*, p. 16.

4. International Institute for Strategic Studies, *The Military Balance 1987–88* (London, 1987), p. 49.

5. *Ibid.*, p. 52.

6. This concept is presented by Teresa Rakowska-Harmstone in *The Warsaw Pact: The Question of Cohesion* (Ottawa: Department of National Defence, 1984), pp. 322–329.

7. *Ibid.*, p. 52.

8. "On the Military Doctrine of the Warsaw Pact Member States," PCC Declaration, *Pravda*, May 31, 1987, in FBIS-Sov 87-104, June 1987, p. BB 20.

9. Quoted in Gloria Duffy and Jennifer Lee, "Reasonable Sufficiency," *Arms Control Today*, October 1988, p. 22.

10. Kukliński, in *Orbis*, p. 29.

11. Christopher D. Jones, "Agencies of the Alliance: Multinational in Form, Bilateral in Content," in Jeffrey Simon and Trond Gilberg, eds., *Security Implications of Nationalism in Eastern Europe* (Boulder, CO: Westview, 1986).

12. Kukliński, in *Orbis*, p. 29.

13. See the speech by General Horst Bruenner in FBIS-DR-EEU, February 12, 1986, pp. E2, E3, cited in Douglass A. MacGregor, "The GDR: A Model Mobilization," in Jeffrey Simon, ed., *NATO-Warsaw Pact Force Mobilization* (Washington, DC: National Defense University Press, 1988), p. 194.

14. Zdzisław Rurarz, "Komuniści polscy czy polscy komuniści," *Pomost* 2(26), July 1983, cited in Andrew A. Michta, *Red Eagle: The Politics of the Polish Army 1944-1986*, unpublished manuscript (forthcoming from Hoover Institution Press), p. 6.

15. Daniel N. Nelson, "The Bulgarian People's Army," in Jeffrey Simon, ed., *NATO-Warsaw Pact Force Mobilization*, p. 463.

16. "Politicheskaia deklaratsiia gosudarstv-uchastnikov Varshavskogo dogovora" (Political Declaration of the Member States of the Warsaw Pact)", *Krasnaia zvezda*, January 7, 1983, p. 2.

17. For example, see V. F. Samoilenko, *Osnova boevogo soiuza: internatsionalizm kak faktor oboronnoi moshchi sotsialisticheskogo sodruzhestva* (The Basis of Combat Alliance: Internationalism as a Factor of the Defensive Might of the Socialist Confederation) (Moscow: Voenizdat, 1981), pp. 245–46.

18. "Politicheskaia deklaratsiia . . ." (1983 PCC statement), p. 2.

# Part II

# The Northern Tier

# Chapter 4

# POLAND

## TOWARD THE YEAR 2000
*Arthur R. Rachwald*

Short of an unexpected decline in Soviet power, politics in Poland toward the end of this century will continue to operate within the same international framework of USSR domination as in the previous four and a half decades. Geostrategic continuity will include the Eastern international orientation of the Polish regime guaranteed by its ruling communist party, which is firmly in control of internal and external security affairs as well as the military-industrial complex. Poland stresses allegiance to the Warsaw Pact, and this foreign policy orientation will be maintained in the name of friendship with the USSR. Also, the Soviets regard their domination over Eastern Europe as a geostrategic necessity mandated by the Yalta agreement; USSR control over this part of Europe has not been questioned by the de-Stalinization policies of present leaders. The most constant political variable in the region will be the maintenance of close political, military, and economic relations between the Soviet Union and the key northern tier states—Poland, East Germany, and Czechoslovakia.

The critical dilemma between socioeconomic stability in Eastern Europe and survivability of a communist state now faces the party leadership in Moscow. An evolution away from the Stalinist version of Marxism has characterized political processes in this region, and has received official sanction as a legitimate trend at least in economic matters. Reluctant to subsidize inefficient allies, which are draining rather than contributing to Soviet resources, Moscow is promoting decentralization of economic management and limited political openness. The countries of Eastern Europe have been allowed to work out their own models of socialism, as long as the indigenous communist party stays in power and vital Soviet strategic interests are secured.

Located in the strategic corridor between the western and eastern parts of Europe, Poland is the second largest contributor to the military might of the Warsaw Pact. However, at the same time, the country has been the most unstable, unruly, and nationalistic member of the Soviet bloc. The October 1956 revolt in Poland gave credence to the concept of a national road to socialism, breaking the Stalinist notion of the monolithic communist system. The December 1970 revolt shattered the image of harmony between the working class and the communist elite. Finally, the events of 1980–1981 suspended for the first time in history the principle of the leading role of the party.

The ensuing martial law resulted in a lengthy political stalemate between society and the regime. Unable to challenge the military power of the communist state, Polish society refused to cooperate with the authorities. The military attack on Solidarity was a Pyrrhic victory, because the restored communist power has been unable to lead the country out of an unprecedented economic catastrophe. It is evident that the communists in Poland can no longer rule alone. The emergence of Solidarity has permanently changed the political expectations of the people; nothing short of institutionalized pluralism can inspire them. General Wojciech Jaruzelski's war against his own nation has discredited the communist system to the point of no return.

## Politics

The search for a political model that would result in a compromise between the traditional one-party system of communist and the growing demand for a broad coalition that would encompass Solidarity and the church is likely to dominate the next decade in Poland. In Warsaw, authorities have already acknowledged the pluralistic essence of society; however, they have been unwilling to allow grass-roots political movements to operate legitimately. The opposition may articulate political demands but is not allowed to make decisions. Political changes in Poland have a more liberalizing than democratizing character. Several steps toward pluralism have been taken, such as the recognition of "debating clubs"; establishment of a consultative council, a chief administrative court, a constitutional tribunal, and a spokesman for civil rights; and legalization of other institutions designated to protect the rights and privileges of citizens. Under consideration is the restoration of the second chamber of parliament and the office of president.

However, only a decisive move toward political partnership will restore public confidence in government and enhance popular support for economic reforms that would require considerable sacrifice of the living standard. The authorities have learned that the likelihood of overcoming the crisis with Stalinist administrative-command methods is very remote. The only alternative available is to release the initiative and activeness of the people. In the 1990s Poland can either continue its socioeconomic decline to the point that a mass, desperate social explosion will bring a civil war that could open the gates for a Soviet invasion, or the country will institutionalize a representative system and free the economy from close party oversight. The relatively liberal policies of Jaruzelski's government are no substitute for political pluralism. The public's refusal to endorse economic reforms offered by the regime during the 1987 referendum and the wave of strikes in the summer of 1988 demonstrate the Polish nation's will to resist official policies until a meaningful share of political power is delegated to autonomous social organizations. Mieczysław F. Rakowski, the new premier, wrote recently that communist-ruled countries are at a "historic turning point." Poland will either "find in itself creative powers, courage, and imagination to free itself of [outmoded] concepts or it will condemn itself to dry out slowly." The country, in his assessment, is facing the immediate threat of "disruptions and revolutionary explosions."[1] Without political reforms, Poland will soon become ungovernable.

A violent confrontation in Poland can be avoided if the political arena is opened in part to grass-roots forces. The party has to reconcile itself to the fact that it is unable to provide leadership for a modern society strongly committed to its democratic-liberal tradition. A drift away from the one-party system has become a trend: "Poland is already undergoing a process that could constitute an epochal evolution in the history of Marxism-Leninism with unpredictable consequences elsewhere in the communist world."[2]

Political concessions made by the communist authorities in Poland during the 1980s were unprecedented and unthinkable in the 1970s, yet they fall short of current social aspirations. A relatively uncensored media, a large domestic free market economy, freedom of travel to the West, and the right to associate in "debating clubs" are not enough in the age of *glasnost'*. The regime is expected to share power, in addition to such concessions as the right to travel or speak freely. The Polish model of socialist pluralism is likely to begin with a trilateral contract among the ruling party, Solidarity, and the church. These three power centers must agree on basic aspects of political competition as well as on the exact limits allowed for the free play of political forces, in order to comply with geostrategic constraints. Alliance with the Soviet Union, through membership in the Warsaw Pact, remains an unavoidable ingredient of the future contract; furthermore, the communist party must retain final authority in all matters pertaining to international security.

Two immediate steps on Poland's future political agenda include legal recognition of Solidarity and granting constitutional status to the Roman Catholic Church. Such a democratic-totalitarian hybrid also requires a fundamental revision of the election law that now gives preference to communist candidates. So far, the authorities have promised to change the law to permit an opposition in local elections. The authorities have been willing to grant legal status to the church if it would accept the principle of communist leadership and, thus, agree to become an instrument in the hands of the ruling party.

Communist hegemony has produced a "parallel society" or a deep social division of one ethnic group into two nations, each following different values and lifestyles, and a protracted economic crisis. Only pluralism can bring back the sense of belonging and mobilize the nation to focus on social and economic issues. The relationship between politics and economics in Poland was clearly formulated by Bronisław Gieremek, an adviser to Solidarity leader Lech Wałęsa: "The government does not want to accept dialogue with an independent partner, but without that guarantee, society will not believe in government reforms."[3] The success of Poland's "renewal" is contingent on mutually acceptable political arrangements. Pluralism is the key to the future of Poland, as one observer noted, and "Jaruzelski has to give in on this issue, or his successor will."[4] So far, the Jaruzelski-Rakowski team has made no tangible progress in search for a compromise with the union. The "round-table" talks between the government and Solidarity originally scheduled for November 1988 had to be cancelled after the authorities unilaterally made procedural changes and refused to include two members of the union among the delegates. Instead, the regime decided to risk a provocative step by declaring its intention to close or to "reorganize" the Lenin shipyard in Gdańsk. Another round of confrontation between the authorities and the union is imminent, since "Solidarity will defend the enterprise, which is, for the union and the whole nation, a symbol of the struggle for a new and better Poland," declared Lech Wałęsa.[5] Failure to relegalize Solidarity in a reasonable period of time will undoubtedly bring about national catastrophe. Solidarity's return to the official public life, however, would be just the first step on the very long road to normalization.

Transition to democratic institutions will result in a partial reverse "Finlandization" of Poland. The country will ask not for international neutrality, but for the freedom to determine its domestic system. Improving East-West relations creates favorable conditions for emancipation from democratic-centralism without threatening the security interest of the USSR. The main features of "Finlandization" were discussed in *Polityka,* in which its reporter recognized that by taking "advantage of both worlds" Finland became politically stable, economically prosperous, and an internationally respected state.[6] Also, the pattern of international equality established by Moscow-Helsinki relations is more beneficial to Moscow than the vassal system of the Eastern bloc. As one Finnish official observed, his country is "a liberal, democratic, capitalist state that can offer the Soviet Union a reliable good neighbor and a mutually profitable economic partnership."[7]

Political developments currently taking place in Poland suggest progressive separation of government and party. "The party," stated First Secretary Jaruzelski, "is not going to be a political insurance policy for the government." As a dominant and leading force in the country, the communist party would like to distance itself from an excessive entanglement in daily decision making and escape responsibility for political and economic failures. The government, no longer a direct extension and representative of the party, is free to select its own political course, including, eventually, a coalition with independent political forces. Speaking of party-government relations, Premier Rakowski stated that as

> a Politburo member, I am accountable to the Politburo on how I and other PZPR [communist party] ministers are pursuing the party's social and economic objectives. I am obliged to take the party's view into consideration in economic and social policy. Of course, that does not mean that those relations have to be stiff. In addition, one has to remember that the government consists of a tripartite coalition, and I am considering how to establish these relations, hear this coalition's wishes, and be answerable to this coalition. This zenith of goverment independence is being implemented every day. As head of the government, the ministers I have proposed are my own choice."[8]

Politics in Warsaw are influenced also by international developments, particularly those occurring in Moscow, Bonn, and Washington. Soviet leader Mikhail Gorbachev's success or failure will determine the future course of evolution in Poland more directly than any other international factor. The success of *glasnost'* and *perestroika* would secure Gorbachev's tenure as the Soviet leader, ending the wait-and-see attitude in Eastern Europe. Although relations between Gorbachev and Jaruzelski have been friendly and mutually supportive, the Polish leader appears to be hesitant to identify himself entirely with the Soviet program of socio-economic reforms. Apparently, Jaruzelski is uncertain about the political future of his mentor. Should Gorbachev's program be terminated in the same manner as Khrushchev's experiment in modernizing the Soviet Union (which resulted in his disgrace and dismissal), the Polish leadership has prepared for a backlash by keeping a comfortable distance from Moscow. A return to ideological orthodoxy and discipline as a cure for the communist system would end all progress toward democracy in Poland.

On the other hand, the Polish leadership must be prepared to deal with a less-interventionist USSR. Although there are reasons to doubt Soviet sincerity, the new doctrine, first formulated in March 1988 at the conclusion of Gorbachev's official visit in Yugoslavia, stated that "the threat or the use of force in any form and the interference in internal affairs of other countries under any pretext whatsoever" is incompatible with socialism.[9] Also, Soviet officials recently concluded that "everyone has to follow very silently the principles of sovereignty, noninterference and mutual respect. The Brezhnev Doctrine is completely unacceptable and unthinkable. . . . It's time to keep our advice to ourselves."[10] Moscow recognized that the destructive character of the Brezhnev Doctrine is harmful to their neighbors as well as to the USSR society.

The East European governments, including that in Warsaw, must be prepared to accept greater responsibility for the outcome of their political and economic actions, knowing that they can no longer expect Soviet tanks to rescue them from troubles. The Gorbachev Doctrine does not entirely supersede that of Brezhnev. Moscow will not permit the neutralization of Eastern Europe, but the new USSR leadership will not be as "trigger happy" as its predecessors. According to a semiofficial Soviet view:

> New thinking, free of outlived stereotypes and dogma, underlies the policy of the Soviet Union with respect to the countries of Eastern Europe. The policy is directed toward a harmonious development of true good-neighborliness with these countries; toward a relationship free from dictate, pressure, and interference in each other's internal affairs; and toward strict ob-

servance of the principles of equal partnership, independence, and attentive respect for the national interests and the national forms of socialist development of each country. The countries of Eastern Europe now have broad opportunities to realize unhindered their national interests both within the framework of the socialist community and in relations with the West.[11]

However, Soviet flexibility with respect to Eastern Europe is based on the assumption that the region is an integral part of the "socialist community." It is important to note that the USSR made similar promises of noninterference on a number of occasions, including two previous joint Soviet-Yugoslav declarations in 1955 and 1956, and in the 1975 Final Act of Helsinki.

West Germany is both a friend and a foe of Poland. Generous with economic assistance in the 1970s and sympathetic to Warsaw's problems in the 1980s, the Federal Republic of Germany (FRG) is also a source for the most anti-Polish sentiments in all of Western Europe. Various organizations of German refugees from Eastern Europe persistently question the finality of the Polish western border, exerting effective political pressure on Bonn to incorporate a statement on territorial claims in the country's foreign policy.

Understandably, the entire Polish nation is ultrasensitive to any of these revisionist trends in West Germany. They bring back painful memories of World War II and provide justification for hardline policies at home. The "German menace" is used to divert attention from domestic to foreign matters, because containment of German nationalism is an overriding priority for all Poles, regardless of their political orientation or social background. The legal fiction of "Germany" within its 1937 borders, perpetuated by the West German constitution and kept alive by rightist politicians, has become a historical barrier against relaxation in Poland and may have an adverse effect on the current political evolution. Without *Ostpolitik* to guide West German policies toward Poland, political assertiveness and militarism in the FRG would undoubtedly halt or even reverse the liberal trend in Poland, as the ruling communist party could consolidate its power around foreign policy and portray its domestic opposition as willing to sacrifice the national existence for a partisan interest. Hopes for pluralism may materialize only in an atmosphere of stability and relaxation in Europe that includes full and unqualified respect for the territorial status quo.

The American contribution to the direction of Poland's internal processes over the next decade will depend on the reconstruction of mutual ties between Washington and Warsaw. Lacking a positive foreign policy instrument, the United States has no leverage to effect changes in Poland. The policy of economic sanctions imposed by the Reagan administration as a reprisal against martial law and delegalization of Solidarity has forced the Jaruzelski regime to pay a very heavy price, but it also contributed to a deepening of the economic crisis and impoverishment of the Polish nation. In the long run, the main weakness of sanctions was that they could be applied only once, and now the United States has few tangible means to promote democratization except for vague promises of new loans.

Another obstacle to American relations with Poland is that they are subordinate to the U.S.-Soviet state of affairs. Although it might be impossible to isolate the former from the latter, there is an urgent need for the United States to formulate a bipartisan, long-term policy tailored exclusively for this important member of the Eastern bloc. For decades Moscow has pursued its own West German policy, whereas a symmetrical American effort to build independent ties with Poland is long overdue. The so-called policy of differentiation, adopted by Washington in the 1980s, sanctioned U.S. disengagement from Eastern Europe.

Only a comprehensive, realistic American policy could have a lasting effect on internal developments in Poland. It must avoid a simplistic and mechanical tit-for-tat response to the abuse of human rights inherent in any totalitarian system. Adoption of such a policy by the Bush administration and its consistent implementation, regardless of ups and downs in East-West relations, would greatly encourage pluralism in Poland. The policy of building and burning bridges is inherently counterproductive, and the overemphasis on economic sanctions damaged America's standing in Poland. The regime cannot be isolated without simultaneously isolating the Polish people. And when Poles feel abandoned, sovietization has a better chance of succeeding. Consequently, membership in the broadened international community of nations is conducive to politically restrained behavior.

Finally, to be effective, American policy toward Poland should avoid excessive reliance on economic means, inasmuch as fluctuation in economic trends adversely affects the realization of long-term political objectives. Only through the network of political, economic, scientific, and cultural cooperation can the United States reach a large number of Polish citizens and encourage political restraint by the authorities. Under no circumstance should Washington try to promote U.S.-Polish relations at the expense of Polish-USSR ties. Destablization of Poland is counter productive.

Obviously, what the West—or, more correctly, certain Western circles—should not do (or should cease doing) is to regard Eastern Europe's plight in the zero-sum terms of East-West rivalry—as a welcome development weakening international communism in general and the Soviet Union in particular. East Europeans are justifiably suspicious of being treated as the objects of international relations.[12]

The idea of economic assistance for Eastern Europe has strong support among the Western states interested in political stability on the European continent. However, to avoid past mistakes, Western economists advocate an à la carte approach tailored to the requirements of the recipient country. In particular, the West is opposed to a Marshall Plan for Eastern Europe, since membership in the Warsaw Pact is the only "element common to all those countries. Even their status as CMEA members does not confer on them any "community" virtue, because the tensions and differences prevailing within that organization are so great . . . "[13]

An additional precondition to Western economic assistance to the countries of Eastern Europe was pointed out by a former national security advisor. Our help

should be based on clear indications that they [the countries of Eastern Europe] are pursuing serious institutionalized economic and political reforms. The former without the latter simply will not work. Indeed, that has been tried, and these efforts have produced indebtedness and continued non-productivity, waste, and economic failure. Unless institutionalized political changes unleash social creativity, and lose the productive, creative potential within the respective societies, economic reforms by themselves will not work and large-scale Western investment will not be money well spend and probably will be money non-repayable—a fact which should not escape the attention of those who might be advancing it.[14]

In conclusion, Warsaw is facing a critical period of transition to a national and pluralistic political system. In general, external and internal conditions are favorable, as the Soviet Union is moving away from the orthodox form of communism and the new American administration will have an opportunity to initiate a fresh approach to Poland. On the domestic scene, pluralism is already a way of life, and both major opposition groups are showing enormous self-restraint to assure the rulers that a pluralistic system would not jeopardize Poland's security or threaten the survival of the communist party as an arbiter of the state. The road to pluralism, however, will involve lengthy bargaining, with the communists determined to pay only a minimal price for social peace. The dawn of democracy in Poland is yet to come.

## The Economy

The Polish economy suffers from numerous problems, among them stagnation, low productivity, a low technological level, deprivation of national assets, a very low degree of integration with foreign markets, high consumption of energy and raw materials, and inflation. In addition, it is incorrect to look at the economy as one coherent system. Rather, it is a mosaic of several economies, each governed by its own rules and each catering to a different social group. Poland's economic pluralism involves the simultaneous operation of four parts of the economy: a centrally controlled industrial sector, a private entrepreneur agricultural system, privately operated light industries and services, and the underground economy. Finally, Poland has three monetary systems: the distorted system of value used by centrally controlled enterprises, the domestic currency used by the less affluent to purchase less expensive goods provided by the state, and the hard currency market available for wealthy people. The net result of this conglomeration is the lack of an effective means for solving one set of problems without damaging another. A zero-based economic reform could be the only effective method of restructuring the Polish economy, but such a solution is socially and politically unfeasible.

Since the introduction of martial law in December 1981, the regime of General Jaruzelski has identified itself with a program of economic reform. Successfully dealing with economic problems became a substitute for trade union pluralism and the implementation of the August 1980 agreement between Solidarity and the regime that pledged an improvement in the standard of living. The first stage of Jaruzelski's reforms was intended to overcome centralization, command planning, managerial and fiscal inflexibility, and substantially increase the quality of production. This attempt failed, because the managers of publicly owned enterprises adopted the most risk-free approach and used newly granted autonomy to raise prices rather than productivity. Managerial flexibility in setting the size of the work force and selecting products to be manufactured has not materialized. The package of economic reforms was balanced with antireform legislation that increased the government's power of intervention in the economy. Mandatory contracts between economic enterprises and the government, the so-called operational program (a new label for old central planning), and militarization of key industries preserved the priority of politically defined objectives. One may argue that the first stage of reform has introduced uncertainty and confusion in the public sector, substantially contributing to the failure of Polish *perestroika*.

The second stage of reform attacked inflation and the lack of equilibrium between supply and demand. A national referendum in the fall of 1987 invited all citizens to express support for the regime's economic policies and to accept up to a 110 percent price increase for basic goods and services. The majority of the population voted against the government program and, in 1988, the country experienced several waves of strikes. Over a brief period of time, the regime suffered two major setbacks in its economic policies. Momentum toward reform had been lost, whereas popular attention shifted to politics.

Moreover, economic reforms designed by the regime failed to address the fundamental structural problem of the economy. A Polish economist explained as follows:

> We are concentrating our attention on changing the methods of economic functioning; replacing administrative methods with economic ones. This, of course, is necessary but it does not suffice. We must also change the objectives of management; economic priorities—in other words, the structure of the economy. This structure took shape in our country during the 1950s during the 6-year plan period. From that time on, heavy industry, which is energy intensive, and quite unproductive, has been a priority. It consumes two-thirds of energy while giving one-third of the value of the national income. And it does not produce consumer goods for the market. This structure continues to be maintained; adequate social awareness and social pressure, which could secure a change in this economic structure into a more modern one, have not developed yet.[15]

In addition to structural problems, the economy will be handicapped by runaway indebtedness to Western states and other members of the Soviet bloc. The increase in Poland's hard currency trade surplus recorded in recent years is insufficient to reverse the persistent growth of its Western debt, which is now close to $40 billion, or about $1,000 per capita. During 1987 and 1988, for example, Poland's trade surplus with Western countries was about $1.6 billion per annum, yet a minimum of $3 billion was needed each year to pay for the debt service charges. It is estimated that the Polish economy has the potential to increase exports by 4 percent per year, which is 50 percent below the level of growth required to achieve a balance of payments equilibrium. The country will be at least $1 billion per year short of the level of earning necessary to service the debt. A radical improvement in Poland's export capabilities is most unlikely because of "an ill-adopted and out-of-date product pattern, even as compared with other East European countries. To this must be added problems of quality, for example, in the case of engineering goals such as vehicles and machinery, poor energy efficiency."[16] By the end of the 1990s, the country may face a foreign debt well over $50 billion, or almost three times more than the amount originally borrowed during 1971–1981.

Poland's intrabloc economic situation is hardly better, as the nonhard currency debt already has exceeded six billion transferable rubles. Because economic relations between Poland and the Soviet Union are among the most sensitive national secrets, it is unknown how the authorities plan to repay this obligation. However, the USSR reluctance to subsidize the Polish economy is well documented, and new economic agreements within CMEA stress balanced trade relations in the future.

Poland's economic outlook for the next decade is gloomy. As yet, the country has no effective mechanism to reverse the stagnation and low per capita productivity that is now only one-sixth of a Swedish worker. The lopsided character of the Polish economy, which favors an unproductive heavy industry, cannot be changed suddenly without threatening job security. More than four million people derive their income from this sector of the economy. Political conditions will necessitate subsidies for heavy industry, now exceeding $8 billion annually. In the opinion of some specialists, the Polish economy is already beyond repair, and 10 years from now the country may find itself "outside the European economy," as a "raw material-pig iron backup facility of developed countries . . . "[17]

In contrast, Poland's private economic sector has performed reasonably well. Employment in private agriculture is estimated to match employment in industry and account for almost 30 percent, or about four million persons of the labor force. Other nonagricultural private enterprises employ an additional 5 percent of the labor force and contribute 5 percent to the national income, in addition to slightly more than 16 percent generated by private farmers. In sum, about 35 percent of Poland's labor force is employed by the private sector, producing close to 22 percent of national income. This data, however, does not reflect employment and income produced by the underground economy, which may increase privately generated national income by up to 5 percent.

The good performance of Polish agriculture in the 1980s is hardly a reason for optimism. Recent studies indicate that only 44 percent of Poland's rural roads are hard surfaced; only one-fifth of all villages have water mains; and only 27 percent of the rural communities are accessible by paved road. Despite 13 percent higher productivity, the private farmers are discriminated against by the regime, which favors collective and state agricultural farms by supplying them with a disproportionally high amount of financial resources, machinery, and spare parts. Agriculture is one of the government's lower priorities, directing about one-fifth of its investments for food production. The regime is not serious about supporting agriculture.

Many economists see the expansion of the private economy as an avenue leading out of the crisis. Several years ago the church proposed to establish a private agricultural foundation with $2 billion in assets to stimulate modernization of agricultural production, but lengthy negotiations with the authorities have produced only limited results. The original project has been scaled down to assistance for purchasing farm equipment from Western countries and support for export of high-quality ham to the United States. The Foundation for Development of Polish Agriculture was granted legal status at the beginning of 1988, once the Rockefeller Brothers Fund designated $350,000 to initiate help for Polish farmers.[18]

Whether 10 years from now Poland is a Third World economy or will manage to preserve its status as a modern state will be answered soon in the form of either a national agreement or an "Afganistan of Europe." Solidarity leader Lech Wałęsa warned the government against "going from a crisis to a catastrophe. People aren't dying on the streets or starving, but we are threatened with going backward. It is hard for someone who is used to a car to switch back to a scythe. We call it Mongolization."[19]

## Society

The living standard in Poland is already one of the lowest in Europe, and it continues to deteriorate. The average monthly wage reported by government sources qualifies approximately 60 percent of the population as living below the poverty level. The housing shortage is so catastrophic that a young couple is expected to wait up to 20 years for an apartment. During 1981–1985 only five new apartments per 100 individuals were made available, whereas more than two million people are on waiting lists. Currently there are 113 households per 100 dwellings, and the rapid population growth in recent years has magnified the housing crisis. Available plans indicate that no solution is expected during the next decade.

Alcoholism has become the most visible evidence of social degeneration in communist Poland. The annual per capita consumption of alcohol is set officially at 8.5 liters, but most likely approaches 12 liters once illicit production is added. Official sources indicate that there are more than 150,000 drug addicts and that close to one million children suffer from emotional problems. Opposition groups estimate that Poland has close to half a million homeless, and that during the last six years the crime rate has increased annually by 20 percent. These and numerous other indicators testify to the extent of social decay. Most people feel trapped in a hopeless system, protected by the military might of the Soviet Union. Emigration from Poland to the countries of Western Europe, the United States, and Canada has reached mass proportions; it is estimated that close to half a million Poles have left their country since 1980. A very liberal passport policy, adopted by the authorities, indicates that the mass exodus has de facto support as an economic and political safety valve.

For those young people who do not consider living in the West an alternative, political radicalism is seen as the only option. The Solidarity organization of 1980–1981 has become for the new generation a symbol of the failure of peaceful resistance. Lech Wałęsa's simple philosophy, that "no stones and no clubs, we must win with wisdom," has its psychological limits. A new attitude became fully visible during the 1988 summer strikes when, despite his enormous popularity and respect among the workers, Wałęsa encountered strong opposition from strike committees to ending the occupation of shipyards and coal mines before reaching a settlement with the authorities. Whereas Wałęsa counsels mediation and caution, the younger generation is impatient and demands immediate improvements. Participation in clandestine political organizations like Fighting Solidarity, the pacifist Freedom and Peace Movement, and radical underground parties like the Confederation for an Independent Poland is prevailing among the younger generation. A trend toward radicalism may proliferate in the near future. A Polish youth has no fear of the authorities and nothing to lose, because his economic situation and prospects are bleak. A pluralistic government in Poland could preempt the radicalization of the masses, but persistent economic crisis only fuels discontent and a search for immediate solutions.

The Roman Catholic Church may find it increasingly difficult to play its stabilizing role in Polish politics. In the past the political prestige of the church has saved the country from many potential disasters, but the atomization of the opposition has decreased its effectiveness as a broker between society and the state. Stability in Poland will depend on the ability of the church and of Solidarity to consolidate their power and unite groups that tend to drift away. This task is complicated by the official encouragement of fragmentation into various smaller and less influential "clubs" representing different professions, social groups, and regions, because the cumulative bargaining weight of all these organizations is much lighter than that of a single union backed by more than 10 million members.

Poland's sensitivity toward human rights is likely to grow in the near future. Its standing in the international arena and relations between the state and society are determined by the government's willingness to refrain from oppressive activities. The vulnerability of the Polish regime on the human rights issue was brought to light during recent years, when Western economic sanctions suffocated the economy and isolated Poland in the international arena. The need to respect human rights and the price for violating these basic rules of official conduct are serious constraints on the Polish authorities. This weakness of communism was recognized by the church, and the policy of stressing human rights was adopted by its representatives. The third pilgrimage by Pope John Paul II to Poland in the summer of 1987 focused on human rights as the most urgent problem facing the Polish state and one of the most effective political weapons against the regime in Warsaw. The pope linked human rights to peace and prosperity by calling on the regime to pay close attention to such "inalienable" rights as freedom of organization, freedom to conduct economic activities, freedom of religion, and the right of the people to develop their own cultural life.

## Foreign Policy

The diplomatic activities of Poland will be confined to the limits imposed by its membership in the Warsaw Pact, but the Polish regime has always been able to advance some of its own foreign policy objectives. Although the economic dependence of Poland on the Soviet Union has continued to increase, the country is expected to gain greater opportunity to pursue its national interests. Improvements in East-West relations and the reorientation of Soviet priorities from international expansion to domestic issues provides favorable conditions for an active foreign policy. Poland's intention to stimulate exports and encourage foreign investments will require a visible political presence abroad.

One of the constant factors in Warsaw's foreign policy is its strong emphasis on good relations with Moscow as a precondition for independence and a mechanism to influence Soviet relations with the West, particularly with the FRG. The USSR must feel confident that Poland would not attempt to weaken its hold over Eastern Europe. Soviet doubts about the future strategic usefulness of Poland may lead to several undesirable developments, among them displacement by East Germany as the first ally of Moscow and a "Rapallo"-like arrangement of Soviet-West German relations at the expense of Poland.

The key to good relations between Poland and the USSR is the same as it was in 1947, namely that the country would not allow free elections. Internal changes must be certified by Moscow as strategically safe. Domestic policy in Poland is subordinated to the requirements of friendship with the USSR. It is understood that this partnership will be dissolved and the Soviets have a free hand in Poland, when a movement such as Solidarity is allowed to compete for power. For the Poles, the necessity of good relations with Moscow is not an ideological issue, but rather a dictate of *Realpolitik*. The USSR is the strongest state in Europe and Poland's neighbor.

The maintenance of friendly relations with Moscow is no longer as simple a matter as it was two or three decades ago, owing to the rapidly changing internal situation in the USSR. The Poles have to monitor developments in the Kremlin, avoiding excessive association with any of the groups competing for power. The regime in Warsaw probably would prefer to invest heavily in the military dimension of the Soviet alliance as it appears to be the best guarantee of a high rating in Moscow, while trying to maintain a distance from its political and ideological turmoil.

Besides their military contribution to the Warsaw Pact, the Poles have learned to take advantage of their strategically critical geographic location—in the center of Europe and between two powerful neighbors. On one hand, it has contributed to the nation's historical misfortunes; on the other, it is the main reason why Poland cannot be by-passed or ignored. This strategic asset has already been incorporated into Poland's foreign policy. Warsaw will seek involvement in numerous diplomatic activities to focus international attention on its good services and the importance of the country for the European balance of power. Every chance to construct a network of bilateral political and economic ties between foreign states and Poland will be welcomed as a safety net against another attempt to isolate the country in the international arena.

In the next decade, Poland will search for strong and viable ties with the West. Besides expected economic benefits, relations with such countries as the United States, West Germany, Great Britain, and France represent a yardstick of independence and proof of legitimacy for an unpopular regime. Europeanization of NATO will undoubtly become a great magnet attracting Poland and other East European states to the economically united Western Europe. The socialist system performs visibly better, having unobstructed access to Western currency and markets. Poland's Westpolitik is comprehensive, well orchestrated, and focused on enhancing the national interest. In matters of international security, however, the regime will act on behalf of the entire bloc, carefully guarding its privilege to address issues on the conventional balance of power in Europe. The 1987 proposal, known as the Jaruzelski Plan, to trade Warsaw Pact tanks for NATO bombers, is a good example of Poland's aspiration to become a key conventionally armed power in Europe.

Polish foreign policy will also reflect the pluralistic character of the state. Although the communist party would never relinquish its exclusive control over national security affairs, forming a partnership with the church and Solidarity will give these organizations a role to play in international affairs. Both groups, and especially the church, have extensive connections in Western societies. These contacts already have been tapped by the authorities to keep in touch with Poles living abroad or to solicit funds for charitable projects in Poland. The international prestige of these organizations is higher than that of the ruling regime, and it is not unusual for foreign governments to consult with representatives of the church and of Solidarity. It is a well-established practice for foreign guests visiting Poland to meet with Józef Cardinal Glemp, the head of the Polish episcopate, and with Lech Wałęsa chairman of the outlawed Solidarity. The Western states have adopted a policy of dualism toward Poland by maintaining formal diplomatic ties with Warsaw and active but informal contacts with the opposition. Premier Rakowski protested against the "impertinence" of Western politicians requesting equal time with leaders of the opposition. "Indeed, this has become such a prevalent practice," according to Rakowski, "that there might seem to be not one, not two, but three competing government entities in Poland: one headed by Jaruzelski, one by Wałęsa and one by the Catholic Church."[20] But this dualism will continue; Western humanitarian aid and the proposed agricultural foundation are examples of this trend. By assuming greater responsibility for social and political issues, the opposition will expand its foreign contacts and in effect build its own foreign policy.

Poland will search for access to hard currency, high technology, and new materials. The nation's readmission to the International Monetary Fund (IMF) in 1986 formally entitled the government to borrow as much as $480 million and, under special circumstances, up to $4 billion for specific industrial projects supervised by the creditor. It is expected that Warsaw will soon be authorized to take advantage of its IMF membership and to use its creditworthiness to approach West European countries for hard currency. Poland already has established favorable economic ties with Greece and Italy, and in early 1987 the United States removed all economic sanctions and restored most-favored-nation trade status to Poland. Economic expectations are driving the Polish pursuit of good relations with Western governments. As a high-ranking official admitted following his visit to Washington in 1987, the purpose of Polish-American relations is to "create instruments that enable us to obtain trade loans instead of paying cash for purchases . . . "[21]

## Conclusion

Poland seems to be on the road to a socioeconomic reality never before experienced by a Soviet client state. Communist authorities have realized how overextended their political resources are, and they might be inclined to tamper with democracy. Past experience indicates, however, that the party has been moving too slowly on the road to reconciliation, provoking social unrest. The immediate question for Poland is whether this time the internally divided party will mobilize enough wisdom and courage to preempt the next political upheaval.

A nonviolent form of struggle against communist authoritarianism has succeeded in developing a high level of social awareness among the Polish people, who are determined to challenge the regime until a satisfactory political compromise is achieved. Solidarity survived martial law and Jaruzelski's "renewal"; it is again a partner in the bargaining between the state and society. These are irreversible processes confined to the strategic interests of the Soviet Union. A second martial law would be fatal to *glasnost'* and *perestroika* in Poland as well as in the USSR.

The Polish road to pluralism is slow, frustrating, and costly. It is now a one-step-at-a-time motion, fueled by the self-confidence of the people and opposed by authorities with a long record of failure and mistakes. The appointment of Rakowski as Poland's new premier may signal a preference for liberalization without significant institutional adjustments. The new government may search for ways and means to outmaneuver Solidarity through cooperation with the so-called constructive elements of the opposition and by obtaining new loans in the West prior to implementation of political reforms. But this strategy of divide and conquer combined with verbal democratization may postpone rather than prevent disaster. The opposition is determined to achieve: "pluralism in Poland without adjectives . . . "[22]

## PROJECTIONS

*Nicholas G. Andrews*

### U.S. Policy Toward Poland in the 1990s

Eastern Europe has never been an area of high priority for U.S. policy-makers. More often, it has been regarded as an adjunct to American policy toward the Soviet Union, i.e., relations with Eastern Europe were seen through the prism of the superpower relationship. Only during the period of détente in the 1970s did the United States pay increased attention to Eastern Europe itself. This attention included attempts to resolve outstanding bilateral problems, efforts to promote bilateral ties, initiatives in commercial, economic, and financial relations, human rights issues, and, in some cases, political discussions at high levels.

With the conclusion of the INF Treaty, the new leadership of the Soviet Union under Mikhail Gorbachev appears to have brought about a notable relaxation of tensions between East and West in a remarkably short time. Furthermore, the Soviet leader has made it clear that the process of change that he is inaugurating in the USSR and that is embodied in the terms *glasnost'* (openness) and *perestroika* (restructuring) is necessary not only for the Soviet Union but also for Eastern Europe. As a result of these changes in Soviet policy internationally and domestically, a review of U.S. policy toward Eastern Europe is timely.

### The Soviet Attitude Toward Eastern Europe

The USSR's role in Eastern Europe, including Poland, cannot be insulated from the effects of *glasnost'* and *perestroika*. But after taking account of Soviet policy changes since Gorbachev's accession to power, it still appears likely that the relationship between the USSR and the Eastern

European states will remain approximately the same as it has been for the past 40 years. When considering the attitude of the Soviet leadership toward Eastern Europe, certain key elements define Soviet policy. These may be summarized as follows:

1. The USSR continues to regard Eastern Europe as part of its defense perimeter and the Warsaw Pact as an essential component of its security shield. It will, therefore, not tolerate any attempt by any Eastern European state to leave the Warsaw Pact under present circumstances.
2. In addition to its insistence on the continuity of its military alliance with Eastern Europe, the Soviet Union will demand coordination of broad foreign affairs policy, particularly toward Western Europe and North America.
3. The Soviet Union will continue to demand that the communist parties must control the key posts in Eastern European governments, in order to ensure the satisfactory adherence to the two points noted above.
4. The Brezhnev Doctrine, which provides for the use of Soviet military force to prevent any feared defection of an Eastern European country from the Warsaw Pact or from socialism, remains the ultimate weapon for enforcing Soviet control over Eastern Europe.
5. The USSR will work hard to promote growing economic ties with Eastern Europe, both bilaterally and through the integrative mechanism of the Council for Mutual Economic Assistance (CMEA).

Two additional observations appear appropriate. First, Soviet power will seem to decline less in Eastern Europe (because of geographic propinquity and the presence of Soviet troops stationed in several states) than in other parts of the world.

Second, although Soviet domination of Eastern Europe is still a paramount fact despite an apparent decline in relative USSR power and in the desire to impose it abroad, the Eastern European states appear to have more room to maneuver in their relations with Moscow than at any time since World War II. Soviet tolerance of economic restructuring and reform and of political and media openness gives the East European leaderships the opportunity to make significant and far-reaching changes in the management of their economies and their political style.

# Aims of U.S. Policy Toward Eastern Europe

Within this framework, the United States and its allies have an opening to attack Soviet vulnerabilities. The points of attack, obviously enough, are: (1) the communist economic system, based on Marxist ideology, which is floundering in its ability to provide an improved standard of living for the peoples of the Soviet Union and Eastern Europe, (2) the Stalinist methods of rule, based on totalitarian controls, which have not yielded communist discipline, ideological conformity, or political loyalty, and (3) the Marxist-Leninist emphasis on a one-party system, which has not prevented inefficiency, corruption, nepotism, careerism, and other political sins.

Turning to the general aims of U.S. toward Eastern Europe in the 1990s, these may be summarized as further de-Stalinization of their prevailing political systems, decentralization of their economies, and democratization of their societies. By "further de-Stalinization" is meant reducing the powers of the police and security establishments, strengthening the rule of law, granting the judiciary independence from the ruling party, making government ministers subject to the legislative branch, increasing the authority of the legislature to develop national policy, and so forth.

Decentralization of the economy in this context is not only what is understood by *perestroika* but includes denationalization or privatization of small industry and services, the opening of the economy to foreign investment, the enhancement of the profit motive, the flexible use of incentives for workers and managers, the sharing of economic information and objectives, and the building of an economic consensus with trade unions, nonparty organizations, and other interest groups. In fact, decentralization should be merely one important aspect of comprehensive economic reform.

Democratization of society signifies the abandonment of the system whereby only party-approved organizations or associations are permitted to funciton. Such democratization should include freedom of association for interest groups, including political organizations, independence of the media (and reasonable access to state-run radio and television), multi-candidate elections, and so on—all of which may be subsumed under the term pluralism or competition. Other aspects of democratization, no less significant, are the freedom to demonstrate, freedom of speech, freedom to travel, and other generally recognized human rights.

## Past U.S. Policy Toward Poland

During the last 40 years, U.S. policy has not challenged Soviet domination of Eastern Europe. At the time of crises in East Germany (1953),
Hungary (1956), and Czechoslovakia (1968), the United States, as Zbigniew Brzezinski put it in a *Foreign Affairs* article, "adopted a passive
posture masked by anti-Soviet rhetoric."

Yet, U.S. policy was not entirely inactive, especially as far as Poland
was concerned. In the aftermath of workers' demonstrations at Poznań
(1956) and the upheaval in party ranks, which brought Władysław Gomułka to power, the United States recognized an opportunity to increase
its presence in Poland and to play a helpful role. Seeing in Gomułka a
symbol of Polish nationalism and anti-Stalinism, it responded to Polish
needs by providing agricultural products under Public Law 480. It also
restored most-favored-nation tariff treatment for Polish goods imported
into the United States and initiated exchange-of-persons programs, which
brought many Polish intellectuals to the United States for the first time.

Later, after Gomułka's overthrow in the wake of strikes, demonstrations, and riots in the Baltic Coast cities (1970), his successor, Edward
Gierek, turned to the West for increased trade and credits. Western governments and commercial banks happily obliged. The United States government provided Commodity Credit Corporation (CCC) credits for the
purchase of agricultural commodities and Export-Import Bank credits for
industrial projects. The political climate was also propitious for the expansion of educational and cultural exchanges, for example, the Fulbright
program and seminars to promote the teaching of English. Political contacts were developed up to and including the presidential level. It can
also be asserted that the Gierek regime's relatively mild attitude toward
the appearance of dissident groups in the late 1970s was connected, as
least in part, to Polish dependence on Western economic assistance to
sustain the standard of living that Gierek had made the hallmark of his
policy.

During the confrontation between the Polish party and the independent
Solidarity trade union movement in the 1980–1981 period, U.S. policy
was cautious and geared primarily to the prevention of Soviet military
interference. Policymakers were not entirely sympathetic to the aims of
Solidarity, some of whose leaders demanded a too rapid evolution away
from the Polish communist system, if not its complete removal.

In any event, the declaration of martial law by General Wojciech Jaruzelski and the economic and other sanctions imposed by the United

States and other Western powers had the effect of reducing American involvement in Poland itself and leaving the field for a while to the Soviets. But the developments of the 1960s and 1970s had brought Poland to a position in which it could not meet its own political or economic agenda by relying predominantly on the support of the Soviet Union and the other CMEA members. Gradually, out of necessity, Polish leaders struggled to restore relations with the West, including the United States.

Among the factors certainly involved in the Polish regime's decisions to release political prisoners in 1984 and 1986 and present a milder, more tolerant human rights face to the world were the following: the desire to see the United States completely remove its economic sanctions; the problem of expandinng Polish exports to the West in order to service the hard currency debt; the question of obtaining spare parts and equipment for the Western-oriented portion of its industrial plant, the need to regain stature in international affairs; the matter of winning popular support for government policies; and the issue of achieving a degree of reconciliation with the working class and with Polish society at large.

## Principles Underlying U.S. Policy Toward Poland

The principles that lie at the foundation of U.S. policy toward Poland are often taken for granted. Nevertheless, they are worth setting forth both to ensure that a consensus on them continues to exist and that they may be expressed with conviction in the U.S.-Polish dialogue.

These principles may be stated as follows:

1. Poland is an important member of the European family of nations. With its Western-oriented, Catholic population, it is an integral part of Western civilization.
2. Poland is an important geostrategic factor, as seen from both the Soviet Union and Western Europe. Poland faces both worlds: the East, which demands its military and foreign policy allegiance and provides assurance against German revanchism, and the West with which it shares fundamental cultural and human values.
3. Existing Polish frontiers are permanent. The United States will not support any revision of the territorial borders. We reaffirm the provisions of the Helsinki Final Act relating to territorial borders.
4. The United States treats Poland as an independent, sovereign nation with its own personality and outlook, not as a pawn in U.S.-Soviet relations.

5. The United States recognizes that the Yalta agreement with respect to Poland was not faithfully adhered to. The provision for free elections was ignored by the Soviet and Polish leaderships in order to achieve a predetermined result. The United States continues to pursue peacefully the cause that is symbolized by the inclusion of the provision for free elections in the Yalta agreement.

6. The promotion of human rights is and will be a constant theme of U.S. foreign policy. We reaffirm the central importance of increasing adherence to the provisions of the Helsinki Final Act and other international documents on the part of the East European states, including Poland.

7. The United States considers that Western Europe has a large contribution to make to overall Western policy toward Poland and must participate actively in building a Western consensus both in policy formulation and implementation.

## A Three-Prong Policy Toward Poland in the 1990s

Based on these broad principles, U.S. policy must address the situation in Poland today and the likely trends that Professor Arthur Rachwald has so ably laid out earlier in this chapter. Of course, there is the alternative of doing nothing. But this option has been widely rejected during the past 30 years as ineffectual and unworthy of a great power. The real question, then, is what to do in order to advance U.S. interests in Poland during the next decade and assist the Polish people to develop a political and economic system that will better promote their welfare.

A three-prong policy of encouraging political pluralism, providing economic assistance, and developing ties to Polish society would meet the criteria of improving bilateral relations, helping Poland's recovery, and encouraging private interests and initiatives between American and Polish citizens and organizations.

Ever since Jaruzelski's imposition of martial law in December 1981, the United States, as part of its economic sanctions, espoused the concept of pluralism in Poland in the form of trade union pluralism. It demanded the restoration of Solidarity as an independent trade union with all the attributes of an organization devoted to protecting the interests of its worker-members. Although in 1987 the United States largely lifted its sanctions in recognition of Jaruzelski's release of all political prisoners, it had not achieved its demand that the Polish regime engage in a dialogue with Solidarity and the Catholic Church. After a series of debilitating strikes in 1988, however, the Polish authorities agreed to "roundtable" meetings with the opposition. The party delegation, headed by General Czesław Kiszczak, minister of internal affairs, and the opposition group, led by Solidarity leader Lech Wałęsa, are to negotiate the relegalization of Solidarity, political reforms, and economic programs and policies. Joint working groups have been set up to narrow differences.

The U.S. Congress' initiative in fiscal 1987 in appropriating $1 million for Solidarity is probably a counterproductive way of encouraging either trade union or political pluralism. The Polish authorities immediately called Solidarity, which had not asked for such assistance, a "paid agent" of the U.S. government. In thanking for the funds, Wałęsa extricated the union from an embarrassing situation by explaining that the funds would not be used for its own purposes but for the nation's medical needs.

For the United States, it appears evident that an effective Polish government policy in the economic and labor field requires the conclusion of an understanding with Solidarity, including its official recognition as a legal trade union. The longer the government delays in reaching an agreement with Solidarity, the more arduous will be its task of organizing Poland's economic and social recovery. In fact, if current Polish tactics to split the Solidarity movement are successful, they may produce several Solidarity offshoots, which will also demand recognition as legitimate trade unions. This result is likely to make the government's task of salvaging the economy more rather than less difficult.

Trade union pluralism is only the most urgent aspect of political pluralism. In the ensuing 10 years, U.S. policy should encourage Polish acceptance of an honest multiparty system, one that would include not only the Polish United Workers' Party's (PUWP) rather subservient allies (the United Peasant and the Democratic parties) but also newly formed political organizations. It may be necessary for these political organizations (parties, clubs, movements, or whatever) to accept Poland's membership in the Warsaw Pact and the preeminent role of the PUWP for the time being. At a later stage it is realistically possible to envisage a situation in which the PUWP would not dominate the Polish political scene by Soviet fiat.

Economic assistance is an essential obligation of U.S. policy if the United States wishes to have Poland repay its hard currency debts and restore its credit rating. No agreement between the communist PUWP and Solidarity will signify anything if practical financial and economic assistance is not an integral part of U.S. policy. Past financial mismanagement, however, has discouraged American government officials (as well as many observers) from trusting in Polish assurances as to its future financial competence. In addition, the United States has few budgetary resources available for communist-ruled countries. Thus the best solution is reliance on the resources and advice of the International Monetary Fund (IMF) and World Bank (which Poland rejoined in 1986) for its economic recovery. Although the U.S. role would primarily be facilitative in seeing to it that the IMF and World Bank adequately met Poland's basic needs, it still would play a central part in such international assistance.

There is no doubt that Poland would have to undertake a demanding program of economic restructuring and reform in order to convince IMF and World Bank officials of its serious intentions and commitment. The U.S. administration would expect no less. For that reason, it appears essential that Polish Leaders gather maximum popular support for what are, inevitably, unpopular measures. Popular support for, or at least acquiescence in, the Polish government's economic reform measures presupposes a degree of cooperation, trust, and mutual respect among representatives of the party/government apparatus, the working class, the church, and the rest of society. Thus far, Polish communists have firmly held on to the notion that, since they are in responsible positions, they must take the hard decisions and the people must accept that those decisions are necessary. The idea of building up a broad consensus of support outside the ruling party in favor of a given policy or decision is not one that appeals to the communist leadership. It appears to believe that this approach smacks of a loss of communist decisiveness and authority.

The hard facts nevertheless remain: the ruling party cannot achieve economic success in the absence of the cooperation and sympathetic understanding of the Polish people. An important task of U.S. policy is to explain American thinking as to the interrelationship between international economic assistance to Poland, the Polish leadership's program of economic reform, and the Polish people's attitude toward that reform program.

People-to-people contacts must play a significant role in U.S. policy toward Poland. Much progress has been made since the 1960s when private American foundations financed the travel abroad of many Polish intellectuals. U.S. official efforts to broaden the scope of exchanges in the educational and cultural fields have also been useful contributions to mutual understanding. Despite interruptions, the programs of joint U.S.-Polish scientific research sponsored by the Marie Curie-Skłodowska Fund have been mutually beneficial and should be broadened into various additional areas of research cooperation. To these efforts must be added numerous existing connections, often entirely private, between research-ers, universities, institutes, and other organizations that may or may not have benefited at one time from official sponsorship or financial support.

More needs to be done, especially in areas that have barely been touched thus far. Some areas that come to mind are agriculture (where a church-sponsored foundation and a Rockefeller Foundation program are barely underway), the environment, public health and medicine, business administration, labor-management relations, personnel management, housing, market research, and civic responsibility. In each area, assuming Warsaw's interest, joint U.S.-Polish teams should meet to determine the desires, needs, and possibilities of both sides and ways of meeting their objectives. Private as well as public and foundation support should be sought to initiate programs that might later become self-financing. Private citizens and organizations should be invited to contribute their expert knowledge to these joint efforts.

The United States is not the only Western power interested in pro-moting institutional and organizational ties between itself and Poland. Certainly, other Western countries have their particular interests to pursue that should be largely compatible with ours. Multilateral programs may also advance the general aim of developing contacts between Poland and the West. The only limitation is on the part of the Polish side in terms of its ability to absorb and handle efficiently a variety of international programs. The multiplicity of exchanges, contacts, and joint programs devoted to mutually useful projects should serve to persuade the Poles of Western interest in Poland's future and to link them more intimately to Western civilization.

This U.S. policy would, as now, be directed toward both the ruling communist party and government and toward Polish society. Such a pol-icy cannot be judged effective if the American government deals only with its counterpart in Warsaw. Nor would it be successful if it focused only on Polish society and bypassed governmental ministries, institutions and organizations. U.S. policy, therefore, must be broad-gauged and multidirectional, although limited inevitably by the resources available to promote it.

An essential dimension of the effectiveness of this or any U.S. policy toward Poland will be its stamina. Will it endure from one American administration to another, during good economic times and bad? Will Washington be patient and persistent in pursuing the objectives of such a policy? To what extent can the United States (and the West in general) persuade the Polish leadership that it must find a way of addressing the hopes and aspirations of the Polish people if it expects to obtain their cooperation, commitment, and self-sacrifice?

In the last analysis, American policy toward Poland must find some resonance in Polish willingness to respond in areas of mutual interest and in its readiness to negotiate and compromise on issues where differing views prevail. Experience during the last 30 years and longer suggests that the United States has maintained a steadfast interest and concern in the welfare of the Polish people and in the policies of their leaders. There is ample reason to believe, therefore, that U.S. policy will continue to convey an attitude of involvement rather than standoffishness, of a desire to help rather than indifference.

## Notes to Chapter 4

1. Quoted by Rowland Evans and Robert Novak, "A Polish Communist's Warning," *Washington Post*, 5 October 1988, p. A16.

2. Tad Szulc, "Poland's Path," *Foreign Policy*, No. 12 (Fall 1988), p. 210.

3. Quoted by Jackson Diehl, "Polish Party Adopts Package of Reforms," *Washington Post*, 9 October 1987, p. A32.

4. Jan Vanous in *Newsweek*, 5 September 1988, p. 32.

5. Quoted by Jackson Diehl, "Poland to Close Shipyard Where Solidarity Was Born," *Washington Post*, 1 November 1988, pp. A1, A27.

6. Krzysztof Teodor Toeplitz, "Dobrze jest być Finem," *Polityka*, 8 October 1988, pp. 1, 13.

7. Quoted in Dimitri Simes, "Finland—Role Model for Eastern Europe," *Washington Post*, 16 October 1988, p. C2.

8. "Mieczysław F. Rakowski's Press Conference," *Trybuna ludu* 15–16 October 1988; in FBIS-EEU-88-202, 19 October 1988, p. 35.

9. Quoted in the *New York Times*, 19 March 1988, p. 28L.

10. Quoted by Simes, "Finland—Role model."

11. "East-West Relations and Eastern Europe," *Problems of Communism*, 37, No. 3–4 (May–August 1988), p. 62.

12. James F. Brown in "East-West Relations and Eastern Europe," p. 59.

13. Jean-Claude Renauld, "East-West Economic Relations in the Context of Perestroika," *NATO Review*, 36, No. 4 (August 1988), pp. 17–19.

14. Zbigniew Brzezinski, "Sustaining a Consensus on East-West Foreign Policy," *Atlantic Community Quarterly* (July 1988), special issue, pp. 43–44.

15. "Economist Blasts 'Incomplete' Reforms, 'Platonic' Attitude Toward Democracy," *Reporter*, Warsaw (May 1988), No. 5, pp. 6–7, in JPRS-EER-88-073, 2 September 1988, pp. 14–15.

16. George Blazyca, *Poland to the 1990s: Retreat or Reform?* (London: Economist Publications Limited, 1986), EIU, Special Report No. 1061, p. 100.

17. Leszek Zieńkowski, "Przyśpieszyc-zmienić" *Polityka* (26 July 1986), p. 4; "Economist Blasts," p. 16.

18. Kathleen Teltsch, "Western Fund Set Up to Aid Polish Farmers," *New York Times*, 21 February 1988, p. A-1.

19. Quoted in the *Washington Post*, 11 August 1985, p. A14.

20. Quoted by Evans and Novak, "A Polish Communist's Warning," *Washington Post*, 5 October 1988, p. A14.

21. Karol Szyndziełosz, "Jesteśmy gotowi do szerokiego dialogu," *Życie Warszawy*, 11 March 1987, p. 1.

22. Lech Wałęsa quoted in Jackson Diehl, "Polish Opposition Balks at Government Demand," *Washington Post*, 26 October 1988, p. A18.

# Chapter 5

# GERMAN DEMOCRATIC REPUBLIC

## HOW GERMAN? HOW DEMOCRATIC?

*Robert Gerald Livingston*

Zbigniew Brzezinski believes that five Warsaw Pact countries are "ripe for revolutionary explosion" and that this may occur in more than one simultaneously.[1] That is "an exaggeration," thinks Britain's foremost expert on the northern tier of those countries.[2] Brzezinski may not, but Timothy Garton Ash does include the German Democratic Republic (GDR) among the five.

Can the German Democratic Republic, accustomed as it has been to modeling itself on the Soviet Union and closely tied economically and politically to Moscow, resist *perestroika, glasnost'*, and *demokratizatsiia?* Suffering itself from lags in its economy, can it resist reforms such as those that Poland and Hungary have been introducing? Most leading Western experts on the GDR are now wrestling with these questions.[3]

So far the East German leaders have rejected the kind of reforms instituted or planned by Mikhail S. Gorbachev and the leaders of Poland and Hungary. In an era when Western observers have pronounced Marxist-Leninist ideology dead as a guide to political action and when it has been widely replaced in Eastern Europe by cynical pragmatism, the East German ruling Socialist Unity Party (SED-*Sozialistische Einheitspartei Deutschlands*) remains devoted to Marxism-Leninism with a seriousness endemic perhaps only to Germans. "The idea surely remains a dangerous illusion," wrote a leading ideologist "that the introduction of market and competitive mechanisms of the capitalist system could abolish or overturn

*113*

the dialectic of the forces and conditions of production as explained by Marx."[4]

Determined as Erich Honecker, general secretary of the SED, appears to resist Soviet-, Polish-, or Hungarian-type reforms, uncertainties are nevertheless quite palpable in the GDR today. The end of the era of Honecker's rule is in sight. He is 76 and many of his politburo colleagues are also well over 70. Directives from Moscow, on which for better or worse East Berlin could always rely in the past, are absent today. An ever more self-confident, assertive, and strong West Germany presses upon the GDR. In the past few years, intellectuals, peace movement members, environmentalists, and Protestant pastors and bishops have lost their fears and are challenging the authorities openly and frequently on a range of issues. The uncertainties combine to rattle a leadership that attaches a high value to hierarchy, calculability, loyalty, and stability.

Thus far no example seems to be inducing East Germany's leaders to institute economic reforms. No "logic" therefore, nor other force, is moving them toward political reform either. What encourages—and also enables—them to stick to their present course, and what may move away from it? Those are issues to be examined here.

## The Road to Success: 1971–1985

Since the early 1970s, East Germany has been the most successful communist-ruled country politically as well as economically, judged by most criteria except those of democracy and individual liberties. American observers sometimes are reluctant to concede this, partly because the latter criteria are decisive for us and partly because the instruments of the GDR's success, an authoritarian political system and a centralized and planned command economy, are ones we dislike.

What constitutes success in the East German regime's own evaluation?

First, political stability. The GDR has had the most stable government, not only in Eastern Europe. Since the brief workers' uprising of 1953, there has been no significant unrest. No spillovers were felt from the Prague Spring of 1968 or the Solidarity-led opposition in Poland of the early 1980s. In the leadership, there has been but one change—from Walter Ulbricht to Erich Honecker in 1971. Career stability has been remarkable, too, at the key party level, that of district (*Bezirk*) secretaries. Only 19 men have held these 16 positions since Honecker assumed power.

Stability has been maintained by a classically centralized, strictly hierarchical, highly ideological, and somewhat Stalinist communist party.

If Prussia was said to be a state owned by an army, the GDR is a country owned by a party. The SED continues to monopolize power, relegating so-called bloc parties dating back to the early years of the republic (Christian Democrats, Liberals, National Democrats, and Democratic Farmers) to political insignificance.

Communism has deep roots in German history, going back some 150 years. The SED gains at least historical legitimacy from its links with this tradition and also from its direct descent from the KPD, the strong communist party of the Weimar Republic, which rivaled the Nazis in size and whose leaders were Hitler's first victims in 1933. It can justifiably claim for itself a large share of the anti-fascist tradition. It is proud to have implanted "socialism" in at least part of Germany, the homeland of communism's founders, Karl Marx and Friedrich Engels.

This legacy counts for less in today's ideological age than during the 1940s, 1950s, and 1960s, when the party was consolidating its power and memories of the years of "anti-fascist struggle" and of the anti-Hitler coalition were still fresh. It does lend the party legitimacy, however, at least in the eyes of the elite who lived through those years. Perhaps it still may give Honecker and his colleagues confidence today, when they argue against Gorbachev for the correctness of a "German road to socialism."

The separateness of the GDR, too, is fully within German political tradition. The unitary Bismarckian state lasted only 74 years (1871–1945); and they were years that brought disasters upon Germans and Europeans, as SED spokesmen never hesitate to remind us. Perhaps no other factor works as much in favor of maintenance of the GDR as a state than the contribution that its very existence makes to keeping the Germans divided—a situation that neighbors in the West no less than the East have found eminently comforting over the past 40 years.

Economic growth and efficiency during the past decade have been an impressive hallmark of success, too. "Produced national income" growth in the first half of the 1980s averaged close to 5 percent each year in real terms.[5] Rapid growth has been accompanied by a decline in population,[6] a trend that (students of the GDR sometimes forget) facilitates distributing to each East German a share of the national output that is bound to increase. Honecker has consequently been able since 1971 to expand East Germany's consumer communism, its generously subsidized welfare and housing programs, and its general standard of living, which is the highest of any communist-ruled state.[7]

Under Honecker, too, the GDR has successfully increased its foreign trade, so that today the country is almost as export-oriented as West Germany. From statistics deliberately kept imprecise, the degree of foreign trade intensity cannot be specified. West German specialists estimate it at about 35 percent of "produced national income."[8] Although about two-thirds of that external trade is with the CMEA countries (and about 40 percent of the total with the Soviet Union alone), the GDR has since 1974 increased the share with developed market economies to 30 percent (and about 10 of the total with West Germany, by far the most important Western trading partner)[9]—an indication that some East German products are competitive on world markets.

As early as the 1960s, the GDR tried to introduce reforms that through some decentralization techniques were designed to enhance economic efficiency. In the early 1980s restructuring took the form of establishing 127 combines, each with considerable management decision-making powers below the central government ministries.[10] Much about the exact locus of decision-making authority remains unclear, but the combines have been vital in the country's priority switch to a policy of intensive economic growth based on microelectronics and other high technologies[11]—an effort in which it is well ahead of its CMEA partners.

Honecker's third and greatest achievement has been to establish his state on the international scene. Following its Basic Treaty of 1972 with West Germany, the GDR could join the United Nations. It was subsequently recognized by all the major countries of the West. A. James McAdams has shown[12] how Honecker, who was initially wary of closeness with the Federal Republic of Germany (FRG) and adopted a policy of limiting contact with it (*Abgrenzungspolitik*), soon came to understand how he could utilize the GDR's dealings with Bonn to strengthen his authority at home. Since the 1980s the GDR has gradually emerged as a full-fledged international actor. Honecker has been received in most Western capitals (in September 1987 at Bonn but not yet at London or Washington). An East German diplomat was elected president of the U.N. General Assembly also in 1987.

The GDR began to project itself five years earlier as initiator and promoter of European arms control and disarmament proposals, taking over the role once played by Poland. To the astonishment of those who always thought it Moscow's most loyal ally, the GDR began to show signs of defying the USSR in this important area. At the time of the tense American-Soviet struggle over deployment of intermediate-range nuclear missiles in Europe, the SS-20s and the Pershing IIs, Honecker voiced objections to stationing yet more Soviet missiles on GDR soil. He announced his hope that such deployments would not damage relations with West Germany. He advocated a "coalition of reason" in Central Europe, plainly indicating that the reasonable ones were only those who were against more nuclear weapons in the region. He has continued to pursue this "peace policy," falling in with the overwhelming support for more arms control by West and East Germans alike. After the West German social democrats lost power in 1982, they started intensive exchanges with the SED, which led to widely publicized draft agreements between the two parties on chemical and nuclear weapons-free zones in Europe. The GDR has perhaps been able to devote so much attention to profiling itself internationally in this way, because it has been less preoccupied with domestic problems than, for example, Poland or Hungary.

Compared to other Warsaw Pact countries, advantages and successes of the GDR are many: a productive and highly educated labor force, a relatively modern and technologically advanced economy, and an army that is the finest in the Warsaw Pact man for man.[13] It used to claim it was the tenth-ranking industrial country in the world. Although it may have dropped on the scale since 1985, the GDR certainly still ranks high by world standards. It has even made collectivized agriculture work reasonably well.[14]

## Existential Burdens

Like that of Israel, the GDR's existence has been overwhelmingly influenced by a single factor: a sense of vulnerability. The GDR finds itself caught between an immensely powerful Soviet Union and an immensely attractive West Germany, the two strongest states in Europe. They not only influence the GDR from without, they penetrate its system in many important ways as well.

With a large military presence on the ground, integrative links through the Warsaw Pact and CMEA, the USSR is the GDR's largest foreign trade partner (about 9 percent of its total) and has a political leverage that becomes clear at crucial moments.[15] The Soviet Union dominates the GDR today as it has for more than four decades. The years of slavishly emulating USSR models or of automatically submitting to CPSU dictates are long gone. Still, for the present aging leadership, the old concepts remain strong of an international "socialist system" headed by Moscow and of mutual loyalty among communist parties. East German citizens, of course, feel little affection for the Soviet Union, whom they wryly refer to as "big brother." (If asked, they explain that one can choose a *friend* but not a brother.)

Behind the close relationship lurks an existential threat—that Moscow might one day make a deal with West Germany and sacrifice the GDR. Soviet diplomats like to float hints to West Germans about reunification from time to time. The geopolitical disadvantages to the Soviet Union of any kind of reunited Germany seem overwhelming. Yet SED politburo members must certainly worry that the bold and innovative Gorbachev might one day sell them out. Some of his predecessors, they recall, have considered it.

Just as fundamental is the challenge posed by the Federal Republic. Unlike any other Eastern European country, the GDR must deal with the reality of an alternative model to its communist system, one that is strong, magnetic, and right next door. It shares a common language, history, and (most East Germans would agree) a common culture. As long as national feeling remains alive (and although nationalism has been declining within the European Community, it has been increasing in communities to which the GDR belongs), the tug exercised by West Germany and the theoretical option of resurrecting the Bismarckian state will remain alive also. Personal, family, government, institutional, and other links between the two Germanys are far greater than between any other pair of states in Eastern and Western Europe.

Not only is the West German challenge fundamental, it is immediate. The Federal Republic is democratic, liberal, open, economically dynamic, technologically advanced, and unapologetically consumerist. West Germany sets the standard for the GDR in almost every field. The SED leaders spend their first office hours each morning reading up on what Frankfurt or Bonn newspapers are writing about them. Ordinary East Germans come home each evening to West German television, which reaches almost every corner of the country. It is the second (West) German TV channel at Mainz and the first channel at Cologne that determine what East Germans talk about around the supper table. They make West German politicians and their stands better known than are the SED leaders, and they play back to East Germans happenings in their own country that have gone unreported in the tightly controlled GDR media.

The rapidly growing number of Germans visiting in both directions (see below) is bringing about a greater familiarization with West German life and achievements. Connections, between the churches most notably but also between sister cities and professional associations, are growing. These personal and institutional connections proliferate completely outside of regime control. They penetrate the system in countless ways. Whereas the precise political impact is difficult to assess, intensifying German-German closeness without any doubt compounds and reinforces that essential challenge to the GDR's system that emanates from the existence of the Federal Republic.

Economically also West Germany has an enormous impact on the GDR. Bonn has quietly employed its considerable economic leverage to extend East Germany's rights, notably since 1983, to increase opportunities for travel to the West. Basic in the economic relationship, as in the case of the Soviet Union but even more so, is that the GDR needs the partner far more than it is itself needed. Trade with the other Germany accounts for less than 2 percent of the West German total.

The Honecker era has witnessed a striking expansion and diversification of inner German economic relations.[16] Trade increased from 6.9 billion DM in 1974 to 14.1 in 1987, with the FRG accumulating in each of the past three years substantial surpluses, which are financed by a generous "swing" arrangement. The GDR derives many other advantages from this economic relationship, some of which cannot really be calculated. Unique among Eastern European countries, it has since 1958 enjoyed privileged access to the West German market. Direct payments from the Federal Republic's national budget, mainly for transportation, telecommunication, highway, waterway, rail, and postal services to West Berlin and revenues earned from private transfers probably total about 2.5 billion DM annually.[17] When during 1982 the GDR ran into difficulties in repaying the Western loans taken in the 1970s, Bonn stepped in to guarantee two untied credits of about one billion DM each during 1983.

It is difficult to assess the economic effect of the many advantages accruing to the GDR from this relationship. Officials elsewhere in Eastern Europe enviously attribute the GDR's success mainly to this special inner German relationship. Certainly it is true that such trade and Bonn's payments and credit guarantees have stabilized the GDR economy, enabled it to consolidate its foreign debt position, helped it overcome bottlenecks in the supply of materials for essential production, and prepared a favorable basis for its 1986–1990 five-year plan.

Fully conscious of the possible political consequences of economic dependency on Bonn, East Berlin has tried since 1980 to diversify its trade with the West, concentrating on countries such as Austria and Switzerland. The overwhelming predominance of the Federal Republic remains, however. Motivations on the West German side are political: to maintain links between states that, according to official West German theory, are but parts of one single "Germany," to work against further integration of the GDR into the Soviet sphere, to protect the position of West Berlin from eventual GDR pressures, and to improve the living conditions of fellow Germans and advance their rights and liberties. Bonn inevitably prefers the carrot of advance concessions to the stick of sanctions. It has since 1962 regarded inner German trade not as an instrument of economic warfare against a communist regime, but as an instrument of political rapprochement with a German state. This approach has been common to conservative as well as to social democratic administrations in Bonn. The long-term aim is entanglement of the GDR in an ever-proliferating network of relationships with the Federal Republic.

The final existential burden that Honecker must bear is the absence of complete loyalty from his people. Legitimate as the SED may be due to German history and anti-fascist tradition, it still lacks full legitimacy in the hearts and minds of East Germans. Such matters are difficult to assess in any authoritarian-ruled country. The SED has unquestionably succeeded in creating a state consciousness. East Germans take pride from their own achievements in building an economy against great odds, one "arisen out of ruins," as the official anthem begins. They identify with the Olympic achievements of their swimmers, runners, and figure skaters. As Honecker well knows, they take some pride, too, in his acceptance by Western political leaders. Their young men generally serve loyally in the National People's Army. And the SED is a mass party of 2.2 million members, to which about half of all East German men over 18 belong. Of the several million private travelers to West Germany in 1987, fewer than 1 percent defected. These are all signs of a certain degree of support.

On the other hand, the SED does not seem confident of that support. Restrictions on individual liberties, especially, and most irritatingly on freedom to travel abroad, continue. The Berlin Wall still stands as the most ugly symbol of this kind of repression. Dissidents are harassed, arrested, expelled to West Germany, or sentenced to prison. Censorship of the media and of writers continues. The regime vacillates between harassment, toleration, and cooperation with the Protestant churches. The surest sign of East German discontent with the system and rulers is the large and possibly increasing number of applications for emigration, estimated to total between 200,000 and 500,000.[18] East Germans are still willing to risk their lives to escape, swimming the Elbe or scaling the Wall.

To generate a sense of support, the regime always has given priority to economic and social benefits. It has supported a policy to subsidize liberally basic necessities, food, housing, and public transportation. The SED's effort to raise living standards can never cease, because East Germans always are comparing their gains with those of the West Germans and not with the living standards of Poles or Russians. For about a decade now, the SED has sought to link the GDR to great figures of German history as a way of further legitimizing itself. Martin Luther, Frederick the Great, and most recently Otto von Bismarck, the founder of the unified Reich, have assumed their places in the pantheon of approved East German heroes. Whatever risks might arise from a revisionist arrogation of such conservative nationalists seem to be outweighed by the anticipation of gains in creating a sense of common East German identity, whose absence has constituted the greatest handicap of all for Honecker and his men.

## Current Uncertainties

The SED leaders could and did congratulate themselves on continuing economic success in 1986, with public claims that the year was the best ever economically and behind-the-hand observations that it was poor in most other communist countries, including the Soviet Union. By that time, East Germany had reduced drastically its heavy foreign debt burden to the West of the early 1980s, had accumulated at least $4 billion in hard currency assets in Western banks, and was able to point to highly satisfying results in agricultural production and housing. What amounts to a crash program to introduce and assimilate modern technologies, including industrial robots, was in full swing. However, 1987 was a less successful year, with underlying uncertainties evident. Foreign trade had begun to stagnate. Given the centrality of continuing high economic performance for the country's competitiveness, prestige, identity, and support of its citizens, these uncertainties must trouble the regime.

It is becoming worrisomely obvious, too, that the technology and productivity gap with Western countries is widening, as innovations and their application surge in the First World but lag in the GDR. Total investment fell throughout the early 1980s, as East Germany battled to repay its foreign debt by focusing on exports. As a consequence of that policy, delays in modernization, rationalization, and the introduction of new technologies are now becoming evident. Endemic problems such as energy shortages (lignite coal, the GDR's one plentiful natural resource, covers 90 percent of energy demand) and an inadequate rail network can hit the economy hard, especially during severe winters such as that of 1986–1987. And probably the gap in living standards with West Germany is widening also. The requirement is two-fold: both to maintain export competitiveness, which requires increased and costly investment, and to keep raising living standards as well. Personal consumption seemed to be growing more slowly than productiion during 1986 and the first half of 1987.[19] Quite possibly the economy is in far worse shape than it appears from the limited and often distorted data and from the leadership's own assertions.[20]

It is uncertain whether the leadership can cope with these new economic problems as well as it has with past ones. Indeed the greatest uncertainty of all is whose leadership will follow. Time is running out on Honecker and his generation in the politburo. Five members (Honecker; Stoph, the prime minister; Sindermann, chairman of parliament; Hager, chief ideologist since the 1950s; and Axen, in charge of foreign relations) are all well over 70, and the man in charge of security, Erich Mielke, is over 80. Although much younger, Günter Mittag (62), the politburo member who directs industry and planning for the economy, is seriously ill. Change is inevitable soon, and the contrast with the new, youthful look in Moscow is obvious.

Signs are multiplying that Honecker no longer has full control, with vacillation in dealing with the churches and dissidents the best evidence. He had been dubbed crown prince as early as 1958, some 13 years before he took over, but his eventual successor is yet to be tapped.[21] Rivalries abound on the politburo, with a transfer of power to a younger leadership actually near. Until it has been accomplished, East German policies to deal with both existential burdens and with crucial economic problems will remain unprecedentedly subject to change.

## New Challenges for an Old Leadership

Honecker and whoever succeeds him face three new challenges: the incalculability of developments in the Soviet Union, from which the SED is used to receiving at least a sense of direction; the new nature of the world economy; and a heightened self-assertiveness by a new generation of East Germans. Let us consider each of these challenges of the late 1980s and 1990s.

*Soviet reforms.* Unlike the other two challenges, *perestroika, glasnost'*, and *demokratizatsiia* are not subject to influence from the GDR.

Their outcome depends on the internal dynamics of the USSR. It is not clear to what degree Gorbachev expects the East German regime to take his reforms as a model. He has several times stressed that each communist-ruled country should follow its own course. On the other hand, he reminded Honecker during his visit in Moscow in September 1988 that information about the reforms was important for the "German comrades," that the Soviet Union and its allies had a "common fate," and that changes in each country had an effect "one way or the other" on friends and allies.[22]

The SED probably does not wish the Soviet reforms well. As a popular and sarcastic saying in East Berlin has it: the party's motto today must be like that Weimar KPD warning to imperialist would-be interventionists against the Bolsheviks—"Hands off the Soviet Union" (*Hände weg von der Sowjetunion*). Honecker's calculation must be to wait in the expectation that *perestroika* will fail, *glasnost'* be reversed, and Gorbachev disappear. Honecker knows that, as Andrei Sakharov told a Boston press conference, Moscow's liberalization policies are in "a very acute phase" and may not survive.[23]

The SED has given all-out support to Gorbachev's "new thinking" in foreign policies, his lessening of confrontation with the West, withdrawal from fruitless involvement in Afghanistan and elsewhere in the Third World, and promotion of closer relations with Western Europe and the United States. The SED has followed suit by increasing exchanges of all kinds with the capitalist West.

Ideological chief Kurt Hager repeatedly has made clear that the GDR has no intention of copying Gorbachev's domestic reforms, however. In a speech published by *Neues Deutschland* on 29 October 1988, he stressed again that Soviet restructuring resulted from internal USSR developments and was "not transferable to other socialist countries."

Above all the powerful and monopolistic SED regards with wariness any transfer of authority away from the communist party, as Gorbachev plans. The standard SED rationale for its rejection of *perestroika* is that East Germany has been reforming its economy for more than 15 years, most recently with its industrial *Kombinats*. It needs no more *glasnost'* since, thanks to West German television and liberalized travel to the West, the GDR is already the most open of communist-ruled states. East Germany has been extraordinarily sensitive to the effect that news of liberal Soviet cultural policies might have in the GDR, even going so far in February 1988 as to stop circulation of the Moscow journal *New Times* with the text of the new anti-Lenin, anti-Stalin play. The SED's rationale is not without merit, although one may reflect mischievously on the irony that the party's favorite slogan until recently was that "to learn from the Soviet Union means to learn to win."

Whereas few East Germans will be urging Honecker to copy Gorbachev's reforms, *perestroika* has made the Soviet leader immensely popular in the GDR. He and his liberalization serve those dissatisfied with the system as a symbol of general reform that is useful, because it is irreproachable. Young rock concert audiences chant "Gorbachev, Gorbachev" as policemen try to disperse them. The importance of *perestroika* and *glasnost'* for East Germany is to be found in the atmosphere of anticipation that they have generated.

On the economic side, of course, the GDR success story has made it relatively easy for the SED to resist reforms being tried in the Soviet Union, Poland, or Hungary. Indeed, what East Germany is *not* doing so far is striking. To list a few instances: no retreat from central economic planning or control; no reduction in the number of central economic ministries; no increase in exporting firms' rights to dispose of foreign exchange earned; no willingness to move toward ruble convertibility; no joint ventures—at least not yet; no announced plans to expand the private sector; no countenancing of unemployment, attendant on restructuring; no moves toward realistic pricing; no added competition among banks; no discussion of worker participation in selecting factory managers; and no talk about the GDR joining GATT or the International Monetary Fund— all ideas instituted, planned, or at least bruited elsewhere in CMEA countries.

Resistance on some of these scores may result from the views of a leadership schooled in an ideology that rejects free market solutions on principle. Honecker and his comrades can claim that there can be no argument with the fact of their country's economic success under its present planned system, that the price in political instability that might have to be paid is not worth the uncertain economic gains, and that those countries that have experimented with such ideas have not fared well.

***The new nature of the world economy.*** Whereas the GDR may not be required to adopt, certainly not to copy, Gorbachev's reforms, it must respond to the fast-moving changes in the world economy. Export-dependent, it has no choice. The SED leaders learned some time ago that their economy is now involved in a world system that is being transformed by the expansion of instantaneous communication, high technologies, information, and services of all kinds. It is becoming a system of great complexity and places a high premium on speedy, innovative, and even spontaneous response to changes in the marketplace. These are attributes for which the East Germans are not known but which they may have to learn, if they are to remain competitive. Autarky has never been possible for the GDR. Greater openness and more international integration have now become absolutely unavoidable.

A particular concern over the next few years will be the likely effects of the European Community's (EC) move toward a single unified market in 1992. Situated right next to the EC and marketing over three-quarters of its exports going to Western industrial countries to those within the Community, the GDR like Austria fears being excluded. Unlike Austria, however, it cannot join the EC. Working out a satisfactory arrangement, perhaps with support from Bonn, will be among the most difficult economic problems facing Honecker and his successor.

Adapting to the international economy and in particular to an integrated EC will certainly compel changes in the GDR's internal economic system, at an absolute minimum requiring more autonomy for enterprises and industrial *Kombinats* capable of competing abroad. It is questionable whether a highly centralized command economy can carry off the necessary adaptations quickly enough and whether the political system can tolerate the unemployment that structural adjustments may bring. According to a leading East German economist who defected in 1986,[24] Günter Mittag, the politburo secretary responsible for economic planning and industry remains stubbornly devoted to the command system he has personally installed.

***The successor generation and dissenters.*** Almost two-thirds of all East Germans have grown to adulthood in the GDR and have no memories of Nazism, the war, or the years of struggle to build the country afterward. As is the case in West Germany also, the regime has to deal with a "successor generation" now moving into positions of responsibility that is better educated, more competent to make decisions, and less inclined to accept party discipline, even if for career reasons some are SED members. The younger among them, like their West German counterparts, are willing to challenge authority on new issues such as the environment, peace, disarmament, nuclear power, and the need for compulsory military service in an era of detente.

The regime has been slow to enter into dialogue with dissenters. During the 1970s, the unhappy East German's reaction was simply to withdraw into a private world of family and personal interests and concerns. The keenest West German observer of the GDR for the period characterized the GDR then as a "society of niches."[25] It was the Soviet/NATO missile deployments and the Chernobyl disaster of the early 1980s that brought young dissenters out to demonstrate in churches and sometimes even on the street, first for peace, later for the environment, and most recently for individual freedoms. Finding the state unresponsive and occasionally repressive, many of the discontented found refuge and support in the Protestant churches (see the next section).

The authorities have handled dissenters adroitly for the most part,[26] having learned well before the Soviet Union that the best way to deal with troublemakers is to permit them (or force them) to go West. Emigration or expulsion to West Germany of the critical and discontented is one important reason why a strong, united opposition movement has never crystallized. Since 1963 the Federal Republic has been buying the freedom of between 1,000 and 2,000 East German annually, among whom are many the West considers to be political prisoners.

Since 1983 the SED and its state security have adopted a fairly sophisticated policy that mixes measured toleration of dissent within the sheltered framework offered by the Protestant churches, with a greatly liberalized policy for private and professional travel to the West, and when necessary a crackdown on public demonstrations. In July 1987 the GDR announced a general amnesty and, as the first communist-ruled country, abolition of the death penalty. Amnesty International believes that all known "prisoners of conscience" were amnestied but considers that during 1987 at least 150 such persons were arrested.[27]

The most noteworthy element in the policy mix have been the strikingly increased travel opportunities. In obvious response to a large bank credit, arranged by the Bavarian leader Franz Josef Strauss in 1983, the regime during the following year permitted 40,000 East Germans to emigrate permanently to West Germany. Chancelor Helmut Kohl claimed that his government's credit guarantees had led to the new GDR policy of permitting many more private visits to the Federal Republic. In 1987 at least three million and perhaps even four million (including 1.2 million under pensionable age) East Germans crossed the border on such trips.[28] The figures for 1988 look similar. Counting repeat visits, almost one-fifth of the GDR's entire population visited the FRG last year. The authorities originally hoped that these visits would serve as a safety valve to relieve pressures, at least on the one human rights issue that East Germans deem most important: the right to travel. The policy has not, however, led to a diminution but rather to an increase in applications to emigrate,[29] a situation that the Protestant bishop of East Berlin compared to "an infectious disease like an epidemic, like a plague."[30]

## The Church in Socialism

It is somewhat surprising, given Lutheran Protestantism's long tradition of political subservience, to hear East German churchmen underline expressly that theirs is the only organization in the GDR not controlled by the SED. One observer considers that, except for the Polish Catholic Church, it has become, politically, the most important religious institution in Eastern Europe.[31] Since the time Honecker worked out a modus vivendi with the church leadership a decade ago, the eight reform (Calvinist) and Lutheran churches in the coordinating league (*Bund Evangelischer Kirchen in der DDR*) have gained in self-confidence. Many leaders and pastors have given open support to dissenters on a wide range of issues—environmentalists, peace movement members, opponents of nuclear weapons and nuclear power, advocates of human rights and of arms control, conscientious objectors to military service and, particularly controversial within the church itself, to would-be emigrants from the GDR.

The church does not conceive of itself as a power against the state, as the Polish Catholic Church possibly does. Its leaders are divided, some adhering closely to the Lutheran teaching of "two kingdoms" and others insisting that the church has a responsiblity to raise its voice on behalf of and as a surrogate for those whom the state does not want to hear. There are divisions also on which issues to challenge the state openly, although religious education, conscientious objection, equal opportunities in schools and careers for practicing Christians, and the right to an uncensored church press seem ones on which there is widespread agreement. "The church is there for *everyone* but not for *everything*"[32] is the general approach. Although active membership in a secularized East German society remains very low, the church has emerged for oppositionists in the last five years as a rallying point with which the SED leadership must deal.

Following Honecker's 1978 meeting with the church leadership, the SED has worked well in a spirit of mutual tolerance with an organization that conceived of itself as a "church *in* [not *against* or *outside* but, of course, not *for*] socialism." For that reason and, as a church of the majority of Christians in the GDR, the Protestant church has come to enjoy "a significantly greater autonomy and freedom than Protestant communities and churches in other Eastern bloc countries."[33] It has in recent years even organized grass-roots activity in the form of large public as-semblies (*Kirchentage*) or church-supported public peace forums or peace marches.

Since the church has started offering shelter and comfort to dissenters and challenging the state on important political issues, relations have grown tense at times. During the winter of 1987–1988, the police raided a parish office and arrested environmentalists and human rights advocates. Not since the 1960s, when the churches were still organizationally linked to their West German counterparts, has the relationship between church and state been so difficult and sensitive. In no other areas have the authorities recently vacillated more than in church policy, censoring church news-papers and then permitting large church regional assemblies, at which prominent West German politicians such as Helmut Schmidt or Egon Bahr were permitted to speak.

## What Future for the GDR in the 1990s—Projections

Predictions about any future are difficult, especially owing to the im-minence of change in leadership. Honecker has been in a top position since the late 1940s. He and his closest colleagues, believing communists all, became politically conscious during the Weimar Republic. They were stamped by their life under Nazism and Stalinism and by the struggle to establish the GDR against a hostile West Germany and its NATO allies during the 1950s and 1960s. The heirs presumptive belong to a new breed, unmarked directly by these cruel and bitter experiences. They have been formed in and by the GDR. Although they have been for the most part schooled in Moscow and doubtless vetted there, they probably are not men of an international communist movement but of East Germany. What they think or how they may act once in power is difficult to foresee. But it may be quite different than in the past.

On the other hand, the same compelling reasons of state that obtain for Honecker will obtain for his successor also. Supreme among them is pres-ervation of the GDR as a state and its political stability. This will be easier than it was for Ulbricht (SED leader, 1950–1971) or for Honecker. The external environment is far more benign.

Today, it is almost unthinkable that the Soviet Union would sacrifice the GDR for any gain that one can imagine. East Germany is a highly important economic partner for Moscow, the more valuable to Gorbachev as he seeks to revitalize his own economy. *"Davai, davai, rabotat'"* (Let's go, let's go, let's get to work), he called out to East Berliners on an early visit, playing on the GDR's German initials. Furthermore, East Germany remains the keystone of a military security structure that the Soviet Union erected in Eastern Europe after World War II. It continues to provide not only a glacis for USSR military forces but the second arm of a vise that could be used one day against Poland, the restive neighbor that poses the greatest threat to Soviet security.

Equally comforting for Honecker's successor, West Germany long ago called off the latent, undeclared civil war against the existence of the GDR, which it had been waging since 1949. At present, it has in virtually every way accepted East Germany as a separate state. It treats the East German leaders and authorities on an equal basis. It accords the GDR economic advantages of all kinds (discussed earlier).

In fact, a community of interest in the maintenance of a stable GDR will continue to exist at Moscow, Bonn, and East Berlin for the projectable future. That is a basic given in today's European political system.

Bonn's long-term objective may be to destabilize the GDR system. Who knows? The West German government and opposition will deny this, usually with vigor. More important, the entire spectrum of policies encompassed by the term *Deutschlandpolitik*—from trade advantages and credit guarantees to asylum and prisoner buyouts—works toward precisely the opposite result. Behind this lies a conviction that the revolution policy, which Brzezinski believes is coming, would be disastrous for further progress toward lowering East-West tensions and overcoming the divisions of Europe. These two accomplishments are essential if unity of the Germans is—in some fashion—to be restored, an aim articulated by West German's constitution and one that no administration in Bonn has yet renounced.

How successful can we expect a post-Honecker leadership to be in dealing with the two other major challenges, modernizing the economy to keep it competitive and dealing with the discontent of a less deferential citizenry?

Initially, untried new leaders may be less flexible and less willing to experiment in economic policy and less tolerant and adept in dealing with dissidents. They will fear that iron "logic" of economic reforms diluting party control. They will worry—unnecessarily—that the West Germans may exploit the opposition against them. To some degree the ways they cope will depend on the external environment—on whether Gorbachev's reforms succeed or whether he decides that the GDR should again "learn from the USSR," and on whether West Germany's is easy, since the social democratic opposition in Bonn is inclined to be ever more willing to make concessions to East Berlin than is Kohl's administration.

East Germany has taken the initiative before in reforming its economy. Today the need to do so is more compelling than ever. Once Honecker and Mittag depart the scene, their successors should find ways to introduce new flexibilities into the economy and open it up still more to the world. These measures will probably be cautious and incremental at first, but the basis for the adjustment is there. The private sector in services, small business, and crafts can be expanded. Some form of joint ventures, perhaps using the old joint stock company law, which is still applicable, seems likely. Revision of the banking system is conceivable. Whatever sensible reforms the GDR undertakes, it can count on the support and advice of West German business firms and government agencies. Thanks to its previous herculean efforts, the GDR is eminently creditworthy again in the eyes of Western financial institutions.

If it can overcome its initial apprehensions, a new leadership seems certain to continue Honecker's policy of raising living standards, with improved housing a priority. It will also continue his internal liberalization course. The right to visit in West Germany once a year is now so firmly established that any attempt to restrict such travel would be foolhardy. Greater tolerance for writers and intellectuals, increased opportunities for them to visit and teach in the West likewise seem probable. To defuse the tensions with the church and those who seek shelter within it politically, a post-Honecker regime might well try to pay more attention to environmental issues and establish a legal alternative to military service. It may well make a determined effort to repair relationships with the church.

Probably the most likely area for liberalization, besides expansion of travel to the West, would be introduction of legal norms that will move the GDR toward the kind of "socialist legality" that Gorbachev has recommended for the Soviet Union.

In East Germany, the legacy of the rule of law (*Rechtstaatlichkeit*) and application of legal norms is far stronger than in the USSR. These traditions also are more firmly based than a concept of human or civil rights vis-à-vis the state. They provide a respected basis upon which the SED can meet its discontented citizens and open a dialogue with them. Some signs indicate that Honecker is already proceeding along these lines. There are reports that a system of administrative courts (*Verwaltungsgerichte*) is soon to be established, a set of institutions similar to those in the Federal Republic, which gave citizens the right to appeal adverse decisions by the state. It is also said to be likely that the regulations governing travel abroad will be codified and published, a step that might meet demands by churchmen and dissidents for more transparency in administrative decision making in this area.

At the moment the discontented are disinclined to push their demands vigorously, anticipating that the SED's gerontocracy will not be around much longer. They are certain to press a new leadership for greater adherence to legal norms, for liberalization of travel, and on some other civil rights. But it is important to remember that traditions of constitutionalism, individual liberties, and opposition are not strong among East Germans, whereas the Prussian virtues of discipline and obedience are. Even a new regime, therefore, probably will be able to cope with likely levels of dissidence.

## How German? How Democratic?—Speculations

Any new leadership will have no choice but to continue expanding relationships with the Federal Republic. East Germans have come to expect this. That policy is set, barring the unlikely return of an aggravated Soviet-American confrontation. Even in that case, it is probably irreversible. The two Germanys made clear during the last Soviet-American disagreement in Europe, over missile deployment in the early 1980s, that they would insulate their mutual relationship as far as they could. Not only do East Germans count on this policy continuing, the GDR is becoming more and more dependent on the Federal Republic economically. It seems condemned by the nature of the world economy to fall victim to West German's policy of entanglement.

Although it may not show up in the published trade figures, economic relations will expand, intensify, and diversify. Banking and firm-to-firm relationships are multiplying. The GDR's commitments to the Soviet Union set quantitative limits on the share of its trade with West Germany, but there is considerable room for expansion qualitatively and in co-production arrangements that are not directly reflected in trade figures.

Politically the penetration of the East German system by the Federal Republic also seems sure to continue, past rivalry, Marxist-Leninist ideology, and mistrust of the "class enemy" notwithstanding. The process will accelerate should the social democrats (SPD) come to power at Bonn in 1990 or 1994. Sympathies for the SPD are widespread in East Germany, since it has already found ways to play directly into GDR politics (through the joint SPD/SED paper of August 1987, on "The Struggle of

Ideologies and Common Security," for instance). Travel, scientific, academic, athletic exchanges, and communications (telephone calls from the Federal Republic have doubled, to over 32 million annually, in the past decade) are expanding. So are new institutional links—between cities, churches, theaters, symphony orchestras, and sports clubs. Official and private visits to East Germany by senior West German politicians of all parties (except the Greens) have become routine. And West German television remains dominant.

The GDR has always been "German" in the sense of its self-definition apart from its Slavic or Hungarian allies in the Warsaw Pact and in its cleaving to traditional German lifestyles, particularly in the provincial cities. It is becoming more "German" now, but in the new sense of reawakening to what it shares with the other German state and through the Federal Republic with the Western world and its values. That the GDR is becoming more German in *this* sense is bound to have political consequences, international as well as inner German.

The German Democratic Republic and the Federal Republic of Germany may be expected to advocate within their respective alliances security policy positions that are common to them but still not alliance policy. Talks should become more frequent between Bonn and East Berlin on arms control and disarmament issues. Whereas the SED proposals for chemical and nuclear weapon-free zones have been with an out-of-power West German party (SPD), they point the way. Chancellor Kohl's government has not condemned them out of hand, knowing the support such ideas enjoy among voters. Its reluctance to agree to modernize NATO short-range nuclear weapons and the proposals advanced by some conservative leaders to get rid of nuclear artillery certainly would meet with approval in the GDR, which would voice similar ideas about Soviet nuclear weapons if it could.

It may be further speculated that the two Germanys will be establishing more joint institutions in a variety of functional fields that relate to economics, business, and the environment. Air and river pollution are common problems to which the East German government by itself cannot afford to devote much attention. Such efforts can help channel West German funding, technology, and know-how to the GDR and pave the way to German-German cooperation verging on the political in a variety of fields. It does not strain the imagination too much to envisage the establishment of elective bodies in the case of organizations such as the Protestant churches, where they existed not too long ago.

In one field in particular, the movement of peoples, a joint regulatory body of some kind seems essential if more freedom for East Germans is to be realized. Were the Wall be removed today, there would still be a massive outflow of East German professionals, capable of finding jobs in the Federal Republic (physicians, engineers, and technicians). West Germany repeatedly has stated that it does not pursue a policy intended to depopulate the GDR. Moreover when 40,000 East Germans were permitted to emigrate in 1984, even liberal West Germans began to wonder aloud if the labor market could absorb them. Bonn continues to contend that its constitution prohibits it from introducing restrictions on German nationals wishing to enter the country and take up West German citizenship. Influential East German churchmen are calling upon the Federal Republic to consider how it can limit emigration from the GDR. They claim—provoking denials in Bonn and East Berlin—that there already exist informal quotas for such emigration.[34]

Assuming that current trends in East-West relations continue, both parts of Europe will come much closer together, no two states more so than West and East Germany. What we may see 10 to 20 years from now is a de facto West German protectorate over the GDR, with a variety of joint institutions, some of them elected, joint approaches to international problems, including those of security, and a drastic demilitarization of both countries. This probably presupposes a withering away of both alliances or a reduction of the Germanys' current active memberships in them to a merely nominal status.

Also, developing closeness between the Germanys will require a gradual lifting of GDR restrictions on individual freedoms, although Bonn has never pushed or openly sought the introduction of democracy or a free market in the GDR and is not likely to start now. If East Berlin eliminates the most repressive features of its system, Bonn in exchange at some early point will have to renounce its aspirations for reunification. Under conditions of enhanced freedom in East Germany, this should be no problem. As nearly as three decades ago, FRG leaders signaled that they would be prepared to accept an "Austrian" solution for an East Germany, which granted its citizens freedom. Such a solution would probably include one overriding limitation on the East German right to self-determination: a ban on reunification of the two Germanys in a single state, much as a new *Anschluss* is prohibited for Austria.

Movement toward constitutional democracy in the GDR is to be expected but at a slower pace. It is quite reasonable to anticipate that, with the establishment of something like a rule of law (*Rechtstaatlichkeit*) soon, West German legal standards and norms might come to prevail also in

East Germany. A more autonomous, quasi-political role for GDR associations and organizations, of which there are many, is conceivable. It is conceivable, too, that the subservient bloc parties, aided in some cases by their counterparts in West Germany, might develop more independence. But the road to pluralist, electoral democracy in East Germany will probably be a long one.

One final conjecture: West Germany's federal structure might one distant day permit the GDR to reassociate itself with the federation as a kind of "Red Bavaria." (It is after all even now not much larger than the *Freistaat* and its economy is much smaller and less productive.) Such a scenario would require profound changes in the East German (and perhaps in the West German) political system. It carries our speculation too far.

Conjectural answers to the two questions posed at the outset of this chapter should be given in conclusion: The GDR is rapidly becoming much more German as its relations with the Federal Republic develop. It is somewhat more liberal in the treatment of its citizens, but it still remains far from being a democracy.

# PROJECTIONS

*Nelson C. Ledsky\**

American policy toward the German Democratic Republic stems in the first instance from the responsibilities in Europe that the United States assumed after World War II. These include our rights and responsibilities for Berlin and Germany as a whole. We also have developed certain broad policies toward Eastern Europe that contribute to those toward the GDR. Finally, we recognize that a special relationship exists between the GDR and the Federal Republic of Germany, which heavily influences our own policy toward the former.

Under our policy of "differentiation" toward the countries of Eastern Europe, we seek to develop U.S.-East German relations as quickly—or

*The views expressed in this section represent the personal views of the author and are not necessarily those of the U.S. government.

as slowly—as our assessment of the GDR's internal and external policies may warrant. At the same time, we recognize that our NATO ally, the FRG, has a special and extensive relationship with East Germany, which we do not wish to undermine and will in all probability never be able to equal. We are thus willing to give Bonn the lead in development of relations with the GDR and to defer to its pursuit of inner German objectives.

This is not to say that we have no objectives of our own. As with other East European countries, our prime objective toward the GDR is to promote a process of peaceful evolution and reform that will increase internal pluralism, respect for human rights, and more responsible GDR international behavior. These objectives generally—but not always perfectly—coincide with West German objectives and, when there are differences of priority, we defer readily and virtually automatically to Bonn.

In general, this has meant that U.S.-East German relations have improved gradually, albeit slowly, since 1974. This slowness is attributed in large part to hesitant GDR progress in areas of special concern to the United States.

In the human rights sphere, East Germany lags behind a number of other East European countries. The GDR government today remains a very rigid and authoritarian regime that has refined to new levels the art of converting elementary human rights into hard currency. The unprecedented level of intra-German travel, which the GDR has allowed in recent years, for example, has been well paid for and rarely permits entire families to visit the West together. We welcome human rights concessions even on this basis, but believe it important to have no illusion about the motivation or inherent nature of the GDR government. Moreover, by whatever criteria one applies, the GDR regime has simply not been successful in gaining the loyalty of its own citizens. Any country that has several hundred thousand pending applications for emigration, as is reported to be the case in the GDR, cannot be termed a success. The most obvious evidence of the East German continued failure in meeting the needs of its own people is the Berlin Wall. As long as this barrier exists, we know that the GDR has not succeeded even in its own eyes in gaining the most basic commitment of support from its own citizens.

In the international sphere, the GDR has traditionally been one of the Soviet Union's most active allies in the export of arms to Third World trouble spots and in providing security assistance and intelligence support to repressive Asian, African, and Latin American regimes that contribute to regional tensions. The United States cannot help but take such factors

into account when evaluating U.S.-East German relations. Our interest
in these relations is peaceful evolution and change, not stagnation and
mischief masquerading as stability.

When looking at the future of the GDR and of U.S.-East German relations, we must look at the broad context which must include U.S. relations with the Soviet Union and West European relations with Eastern
Europe more generally. The division of Europe cannot be viewed from
a German perspective alone—as important as that perspective is. Gerry
Livingston, in the first part of this chapter, takes a close look at internal
development in East Germany and at the FRG-GDR relationship, but both
of these are only parts of the broader East-West relationship that may yet
be the most decisive factor influencing East Germany's evolution. Despite the rapid development of intra-German relations over the last decade, what happens in Moscow is still at least as important to the GDR
than what happens in Bonn, and this is likely to remain so over the foreseeable future. Both the FRG and the GDR are members of opposing
security alliances that will also be around for a long time and that neither
German state will leave. In short, there are much larger questions at play
here than the intra-German relationship and the GDR's success, or lack
of it, in gaining internal legitimacy.

If the German question cannot be objectively viewed outside of the
broader question of a divided Europe and of an adversarial East-West
relationship, the intra-German dialogue can produce only incremental
progress, and will have fairly clearly defined limits. In my view, the
German question can never be resolved until a solution is found to the
much wider divisions that exist between East and West in Europe or in
that continent as a whole. For this reason, I personally think we should
not become mesmerized by the intra-German relationship as holding the
"key" to East Germany's future as a political entity. That key, unfortunately, is held in Moscow and is not likely to be traded to the West
anytime soon.

The United States has long been committed to the support of German
reunification, just as we support reconciliation between the Eastern and
Western halves of the European continent. We believe that there has been
progress made toward such reconciliation over the last 40 years through
Western unity and persistence. A good measure of credit for this clearly
belongs to the imaginative policies pursued by the Federal Republic in
recent decades. And we all may have the prospect of moving still further
in coming years if some of the present trends in East-West relations continue.

Today we can see ever more clearly that the GDR is very much out of step with the reformist pressures exerted by Moscow. If the reformist orientation of the Soviet Union continues into the next decade, it will be very difficult for the East German leadership to continue disregarding substantial political and economic reform. On the other hand, should it move toward political and economic reform, this in itself might have destabilizing results. Finally, if some unforeseen development halts Soviet reform efforts and brings a new winter to the East-West relationship, no level of intra-German dialogue or economic dependence will allow the GDR to escape the consequences. Ironically, the more we become focused only on the intra-German relationship and its dynamics, the more we face the danger of losing sight of the larger issues that will ultimately shape this relationship's fate.

## *Notes to Chapter 5*

1. Zbigniew Brzezinski, *A Year in the Life of Glasnost* (London: Centre for Policy Studies, 1988), Policy Study No. 94, p. 12.

2. Timothy Garton Ash, "The Empire in Decay," *The New York Review of Books*, 35, no. 14 (29 September 1988), 54, fn. 8.

3. See, e.g., David Childs, *East Germany to the 1990s: Can it Resist Glasnost?* (London: The Economist Intelligence Unit, December 1987), Special Report no. 1118.

4. Otto Reinhold, "Dynamik und Komplexität unserer Gesellschaftsentwicklung," *Einheit*, no. 6 (June 1988), p. 500.

5. Ian Jeffries, "The GDR in Historical and International Perspective," in Ian Jeffries and Manfred Melzer, eds., *The East German Economy* (London: Croom Helm, 1987), Table 1.3, p. 10.

6. Childs, *East Germany*, p. 35; Henry Krisch, *The German Democratic Republic: The Search for Identity* (Boulder, CO: Westview Press, 1985), p. 24.

7. Childs, *East Germany*, p. 16.

8. Hanns-Dieter Jacobsen, "The Foreign Trade and Payments of the GDR in a Changing World Economy," in Jeffries and Melzer, *East German Economy*, p. 236.

9. Jacobsen, "Foreign Trade," p. 257; Childs, *East Germany*, p. 65.

10. Phillip J. Bryson and Manfred Melzer, "The *Kombinat* in GDR Economic Organization," in Jeffries and Melzer, *East German Economy*, pp. 51–68.

11. Ian Jeffries and Manfred Melzer, "The Economic Strategy of the 1980s and the Limits to Possible Reforms," in Jeffries and Melzer, *East German Economy*, p. 46.

12. A. James McAdams, *East Germany and Detente: Building Authority After the Wall* (New York: Cambridge University Press, 1985).

13. Bernard E. Trainor, "East German Military: Warsaw Pact's Finest," *New York Times*, 8 November 1988.

14. For a positive view of agriculture, see C. Bradley Scharf, *Politics and Change in East Germany* (Boulder, CO: Westview Press, 1984), pp. 88–89. For a less favorable view, see Childs, *East Germany*, pp. 43–46, and Krisch, *German Democratic Republic*, pp. 105–108.

15. Examples include when Ulbricht was ousted in 1971 or when Honecker was compelled to cancel his planned trip to Bonn in 1984.

16. Hanns-D. Jacobsen and Heinrich Machowski, "Die Wirtschaftsbeziehungen zwischen beiden deutschen Staaten," to appear in *Perspektiven für die Sicherheit und Zusammenarbeit in Europe* (Bonn: Bundeszentrale für politische Bildung, 1988).

17. Jacobsen, "Foreign Trade," p. 241, and Childs, *East Germany*, p. 92. By way of comparison, (1) on 4 May 1988 the *Bundestag* approved appropriations of six billion DM for development and 16.5 billion DM for purchase of the European fighter aircraft, a military plane for the 1990s; or (2) payments from the West German federal budget for unemployment benefits in 1987 came to 14.3 billion DM. *Die Zeit*, 4 November 1988.

18. No official data are published. The author's estimates are based on conversations in June and October 1988 with various leading SED officials and churchmen. *Die Zeit*, 19 August 1988, gave an estimate of 200,000 to 900,000 applicants.

19. Childs, *East Germany*, p. 2.

20. See Harry Maier, "Der grosse Bruder ist kein Vorbild," *Die Zeit*, 28 November 1986, and "Marx würde sich im Grabe umdrehen," *Die Zeit*, 5 December 1986. Maier, a leading GDR economist, defected to West Germany in March 1986.

21. For a discussion of likely candidates to succeed Honecker, see *Der Spiegel*, 8 August 1988, pp. 16–18.

22. Leslie Colitt, "East Europe's Sceptics of Glasnost' Find Ways to Resist Moscow," *Financial Times*, 19 October 1988, p. 2.

23. Celestine Bohlen, "Sakharov Assails," *New York Times*, 8 November 1988.

24. Harry Maier, *Die Zeit*, 5 December 1986.

25. This term was coined by Günter Gaus, who was the Federal Republic's permanent representative in East Berlin from 1974 to 1981. See his book, *Wo Deutschland liegt: Eine Ortsbestimmung* (Hamburg: Hoffmann und Campe, 1983), pp. 156–233.

26. See Krisch, *German Democratic Republic*, pp. 129–133; Scharf, *Politics*, pp. 163–167; and Childs, *East Germany*, pp. 76–77, 94–95.

27. "German Democratic Republic," in *Amnesty International Report 1988* (London: Amnesty International Publications, 1988), p. 201.

28. Dorothee Wilms, *Erfolgreiche Bilanz der Deutschlandpolitik 1987: Zah-*

*len, Daten, Fakten* (Bonn: Bundesministerium für innerdeutsche Beziehungen, 1988), p. 6.

29. Note 17.

30. Interview with Bishop Forck, East Berlin, in *Frankfurter Allgemeine Zeitung*, 23 April 1988.

31. Krisch, *German Democratic Republic*, p. 122.

32. Unpublished manuscript, "Das Verhältnis von Staat und Kirche in der DDR," from a talk delivered by Dr. Folkert Ihmels, chairman of the Lutheran World Federation of the GDR, at the Church of the Reformation, Washington, DC, 13 October 1988, p. 6.

33. *Ibid.*, p. 3.

34. See Note 30.

# Chapter 6

# CZECHOSLOVAKIA

## POSSIBLE DEVELOPMENT OF THE POLITICAL REGIME AND THE SOCIOECONOMIC SYSTEM IN THE 1990s

*Zdenek Suda*

Czechoslovakia belongs to the northwestern tier of the Soviet bloc in Europe, and this fact alone should mark it as one of the key countries of the USSR alliance system. There are undoubtedly additional reasons why controlling Czechoslovakia since World War II appeared essential to the Kremlin. The economic potential of the Czechoslovak Republic (ČSSR) is one of them; apart from East Germany, the ČSSR is the only communist-ruled country that entered the bloc as a developed industrial society. Czechoslovakia also has shared the fate of most satellite nations of this region in that it experienced, some 20 years ago, a severe crisis of the regime. Soviet reaction then indicated, as it had shown in the case of Hungary 12 years earlier, the importance that the Moscow leadership attributed to a close alignment, internal as well as external, of the ČSSR with the Soviet Union.

However, it is not only similarities to other communist party-states in Central and Eastern Europe in the last 40 years that have determined the development of society and politics in the ČSSR. Significant dissimilarities have also played a crucial role in shaping its destiny, among them the unique experience of a genuinely pluralist democratic government in the period preceding World War II. This experience deeply influenced not only social institutions and movements that had espoused democracy without reservation, but also the Czechoslovak communist party itself. As a consequence, the party evolved in quite a specific way and had to adopt strategies not always required from other communist parties in the region, which had operated, for the better part, under conditions of illegality. Even the relations between the Czechoslovak communist party and the Comintern, and later between the ČSSR as a client state and the USSR as the dominant superpower, were marked by this difference.

Both the similarities and the dissimilarities listed here are likely to appear as meaningful factors in the ČSSR's development during the 1990s. Forecasting its course would be risky enough even if these factors remained constant, which evidently is not the case. Among all the elements of uncertainty, those of the Soviet perceptions of ČSSR-USSR relations—of the place of Czechoslovakia in Soviet world politics—and of future USSR policies in this area are at the same time the most important and the most difficult to predict. Being the cornerstone of the whole mechanism of the politics in this area, the Soviet master plan—once it has become subject to the general process of change—inevitably destabilized also the ČSSR domestic situation. This chapter endeavors, despite all these odds, to identify the most probable variants of the future evolution of Czechoslovakia and to assess the probability of their implementation.

## "In Tune" and "Out of Tune"

The ČSSR, in the eyes of many Western observers, has always passed for a "model satellite" whereby the most enthusiastic and faithful emulation of the USSR's example is understood. The brief period of the 1968 Prague Spring is usually viewed as an aberration, however far-reaching and dramatic it may have been. Based on this premise, a fast and smooth falling in line with every change or turn of Soviet politics is anticipated on the part of the Czechoslovak communist leaders. Their contemporary behavior, in the face of the USSR reform drive and especially of its more successful and conspicuous aspect, the "openness," must therefore be difficult to grasp in many Western quarters. It is found to be somewhat "out of tune."

A closer look at the history of Czechoslovak-Soviet relations reveals that the periods of such disharmony were more frequent than is generally assumed. The Alexander Dubček era and the present contrast of "frost in Prague" vs. "thaw in Moscow" are not the only two instances. In fact, starting with the 20th Congress of the Communist Party of the Soviet Union (CPSU) in 1956, the past has seen several occasions in which the policies of the Communist Party of Czechoslovakia (CPCS) were clearly "out of tune" with those of the CPSU (it would be possible to find such occurrences even earlier). These experiences may also have contributed to the present attitude that the CPCS governance takes vis-à-vis the Soviet reform initiative. As we show later on, the theory of "absolute dependence"—or should we perhaps call it the theory of "communicating vessels"?—is too simplistic and has, therefore, little explanatory value.

As early as during the first years of the Soviet "collective leadership" that followed on the death of Stalin and the liquidation of Beria, the Czechoslovak party line considerably deviated from that of Moscow. Political trials continued until 1954, not infrequently meeting out death sentences to defendants. The monstrous oversized Stalin monument in Prague was unveiled as late as May 1955, almost simultaneously with Khrushchev's reconciliation visit in Belgrade. The rehabilitation of the victims of Stalinist justice began much later than anywhere else in the communist bloc. It actually was officially endorsed only at the 12th CPCS Congress in 1962, and carried out the following year. The following year, First Secretary Antonín Novotný finally and reluctantly boarded Khrushchev's bandwagon of overall de-Stalinization.

For a short time, the ČSSR was "in tune" with its "big brother"—but not for long. The ouster of Khrushchev and the beginning of the Brezhnev era in the USSR coincided with an ever increasing momentum of liberalization in Czechoslovakia. Discredited by the revelations about his part in the Stalinist terror and weakened by the expulsion from the party of many of his closest collaborators, Novotný had to more or less passively witness the revolt of Czech intellectuals, economists, and Slovak autonomists. This development culminated in the already famous January 1968 shake-up of the CPCS, which ushered in the reform movement under the leadership of First Secretary Dubček. The dissonance, or the state of being "out of tune" with the Soviet power center, was then complete.

## "Normalization into the Abnormal"

The so-called normalization process that the sponsors of the August 1968 military intervention professed to promote could also be defined as a process, the objective of which was to restore identity, or at least a maximum similarity between the internal conditions in Czechoslovakia and those in the USSR. This notion of what is "normal" and the Brezhnev Doctrine that supported it in terms of international law have thus far been the most forceful articulations of the ideological underpinnings of the Soviet bloc. Even the methods by which the state of "normalcy" was to be brought about—the crowds of Soviet "advisors" at all levels of government—were indicative of what the Kremlin leadership then believed to be the most appropriate principles for relations between the USSR and the smaller party-states within the Soviet orbit.

For the present rulers of Czechoslovakia, who were put into positions of power literally by the brute force of Soviet tanks (in application of the spirit and the letter of the Brezhnev Doctrine), today's situation is confusing, challenging, and threatening at the same time, for two reasons. On the one hand, the definition of what constitutes the "normal" state of things in a communist party-state or "normal" policies of a communist government in such a state was implicitly changed by Mikhail Gorbachev's embarking upon a reform course, not unlike that which the Soviet military intervention of 1968 had for its purpose to stop and reverse. In other words, the USSR's model, which in terms of the unwritten organizational statutes of the Soviet bloc had been so strictly binding for all satellites, was radically transformed. On the other hand, however, these statutes themselves changed, or at least became a subject for reconsideration by Gorbachev's leadership. Not only was the hitherto authoritative blueprint discontinued; it also ceased to be obligatory, and with it any substitute blueprint in the years to come.

Thus the disharmony between Prague and Moscow is now again complete. Owing to a substantial policy shift in the decision-making center of the Soviet bloc after 1985, the "normalization" begun 20 years ago led Czechoslovakia to the most "abnormal" situation it has faced ever since the coup d'état of 1948. The current policy line of the CPSU is an implicit rejection of the line currently pursued by the CPCS in faithful emulation of the previous Soviet model; however, no new explicit advice or instructions may be forthcoming. If we consider this, we will better understand the seeming paradox of a puppet party not dancing to the master party's tune: it is simply because the master is no longer interested in pulling the strings.

This basic change, or the indication of a possible change, in the Soviet perception of the assets and the liabilities of close control over the policies of the client communist parties need not be an unqualified source of grief for the present Czechoslovak leaders. Even though they have started as Brezhnev's puppets, they may have—and some of them undoubtedly have—developed a taste for power during the two decades separating us from the Soviet-led invasion. Theoretically, the thinking and the attitudes of the CPSU under Gorbachev manifested in the sphere of intrabloc relations could provide them with an additional option. They may come to believe that instead of having to choose merely between pursuing a discredited course and adopting the new Soviet course, which they most likely would not politically survive, they could contemplate adopting a policy or a set of policies of their own. It seems plausible to conclude that such policies would be distinctly more conservative than those of Gorbachev. However, as we will argue later, it need not necessarily be so under all circumstances.

Nor are all hopes of the present CPCS establishment pinned to the elbow room that the revision of the authority structure within the Soviet bloc promises to give to the individual party-states. The eventuality that the reform course will not succeed and will be replaced in the near future has certainly also been taken into account by Miloš Jakeš and his associates. It may not be viewed with too much apprehension; on the contrary, it may even be hoped for. In any event, paired with a record of several abrupt reversals of Soviet policies in the relatively recent past, the awareness of the possibility or yet another turnaround will counsel caution.

## Changed Domestic Situation

A nonnegligible resource of the ruling group in its efforts to meet the challenge of the Soviet bloc internal relations undergoing radical change is its ability to point to the specific Czechoslovak situation that may compare favorably with other communist-ruled states in the same area. Of the various aspects of this unique situation, the economic level as perceived by the consumer—but also some macroeconomic indicators, such as a relatively low foreign payments deficit—are often emphasized as arguments in the defense of the continuity of the pre-Gorbachev line. Even some consequences of the "normalization," which in the eyes of external observers may be regrettable, for example, widespread apathy and indifference to politics, are occasionally presented as achievements, in this case as "pacification" of public life after the upheaval of the 1960s.

The strategy of the regime propaganda notwithstanding, the state and the society in Czechoslovakia did change considerably over the past 20 years. Not all these changes work in favor of those now having power. It will be critical in the immediate future whether their impact will induce in the public at large, as well as within the rank-and-file of the communist party, more desire for innovation, greater propensity for change and thus greater willingness to imitate the reform experiments in the neighboring bloc countries, which are likely to abound, or rather greater preference for stability, if not directly fear of change. The team presently in control of the CPCS most probably would welcome a trend toward the second, since the first can only generate new problems.

Of the internal changes that occurred during the time of "normalization," two should be mentioned because they are most likely to play a key role in the future development of Czechoslovakia. In the first place, it is the change, or the changes, that the communist party has undergone as a consequence of the abortive reform and the Soviet intervention. Reform movements, whether successful or not, have always left a deep imprint upon all parties in the USSR's sphere that had experienced them. It would be possible to argue that no communist party remained the same after such an event; that reform could be compared to the phenomenon of "reformation" in the Christian church. Although the nature of the change might have differed from one party to another, the parties—and the party-states that they have been ruling—today form two distinct categories: those that lived the trauma of the reform, and those that did not.

In Czechoslovakia, the so-called liberalization experiment of 1968 represents the culmination of a trend that had run inside the CPCS for a very long time, possibly since the party's constitution in the 1920s, but most certainly since the seizure of power in 1948. The Brezhnevian critique of the spirit of the Prague Spring may not have been too far off the mark when it charged that Dubček and his team had "indulged in social-democratic illusions." The CPCS first secretary and many of his collaborators were too young for this indictment to be taken literally, but there can be little doubt that the idea of a "socialism with a human face" can be traced back to the early years of the Czechoslovak Republic, when the CPCS had seen itself rather as a radical left party, with mass membership, as an underwriter of the great progressive traditions, willing to operate within the democratic system of the country. To the Kremlin masters in 1968, the deviance engaged in by the Czechoslovak communists must among others have appeared also as a sign that the "bolshevization" process to which the CPCS had been subjected in 1929 had not been completed after all.

In any event, the Prague Spring mobilized and made highly visible all individuals and groups in the party who either explicitly subscribed to the principle of the respect of human rights and to democratic methods of government, or at least accepted pluralism of ideas, structures, and policies as the broad framework within which the socialist program should be implemented. This more than any other original initiative of the reformist leadership was perceived as supreme heresy by the USSR's power center. The elements advocating such views became the primary targets of the "normalization." Thus the mass purge of 1970 eliminated with unprecedented consistency precisely those members and leaders who had shared the socialist dream, who believed in the possibility of its realization—in short, it eliminated all idealists. What was left was an empty organizational shell, manned by skillful apparatchiks enamored of power but prepared to carry out the orders of their Soviet sponsors.

This was an essential change that will circumscribe Czechoslovakia's options in the future. It is likely that in its present composition the CPCS will not be particularly anxious to profit from the opportunities that the loosening grip of the Soviet Union on the satellites may offer. It may not even recognize such opportunities. Its domestic position, perceived as insecure because of insufficient legitimacy, will induce it to seek the status quo rather than innovation. To be sure, in the 18 years that elapsed since the great purge, the composition of the party changed again. Considering, however, the image that it had during that time in the public at large, it is doubtful whether among the new recruits those with idealistic motivation prevailed or even formed a significant percentage. More hopeful from this point of view might be the membership contingents that in 1968 had been too young—those between 21 and 30 years of age—to participate in the leadership, and who therefore may have escaped the attention of the "normalizers." There may be found sympathizers with the reform among these circles that probably now would be ready to follow or to support the current Soviet example. Only the years to come will show how important this group is or may become.

## "Life is Elsewhere"

Another important change that the experience of a reform, or of an attempt at a reform, tends to produce in communist-ruled countries is the political mobilization or activation of the society at large. This appears to have happened in all historical cases. Indeed, it would seem that the basic difference between the communist-ruled states that passed through the crucible of the reform and those that did not is the intact monopoly of political activity enjoyed by the parties in the latter. Among them, the axiom still holds that in a totalitarian state anything political takes place in the party, by the party, and through the party. Czechoslovakia, however, belongs to the former category.

As in other party-states of the region, the galvanization of the broad strata of citizens produced by the reform experiment had also in Czechoslovakia some effects that outlived the brief liberalization episode. Rudimentary centers of social activity, independent of direct party control, emerged in several places. Some were splinters of nonpartisan groupings constituted during the reformist rule but banned or dissolved after the military intervention. Some came into existence in the days of the peaceful "national uprising," immediately after the occupation; this climate was particularly favorable to initiatives of all kind, outside the official institutions and structures. Eventually, some were an immediate product of the "normalization" drive itself, as the wave of expulsions from the party and dismissals from employment threw into the public at large a number of elements of the elite used to and experienced in political organization and action.

Although a part of this revival concerned also nonpolitical activities, it generally had strong political overtones, if for no other reason than because of the endeavor to secure or enlarge a shelter from political control. A number of these groups, nevertheless, were outspokenly political. It is not an exaggeration to say that they represented—and wished to represent—a political alternative. In other words, they saw themselves as forms of political opposition. Others again, in spite of their explicit declarations that they were not political parties or movements, assumed clearly political tasks. These were the various human and civil rights groups, such as Charter 77 or the Committee for the Protection of Unjustly Persecuted Persons. They obviously proposed to fill the gap, typical of a communist party-state where separation between political and juridical powers is unknown.

The most active, or the most conspicuous, of these centers were those engaging in publication. This sector, too, experienced the most dramatic growth during the last two decades. Its production is usually subsumed under the Russian term *samizdat,* and it includes virtually all areas of literature: poetry, fiction, arts, art criticism, philosophy, religion, science, and politics. Even the most apolitical of the *samizdat* genre is a stark political act in itself, by the very fact that it is published outside the official system. The less currently used Czech term *nezavisla literatura* (independent literature) underscores this quality. In a certain way, *samizdat* has its roots in the exhilarating experience of uncensored mass media, which had started in March 1968 and continued long after the invasion, until the replacement of Dubček in the function of first party secretary by Gustav Husák in April 1969. Not unlike the current call for *glasnost'* in the USSR, the idea of a free press had then by far the most powerful appeal among all components of the reform program in the entire nation.

True enough, this spontaneous public activity is partly possible thanks to a relative softening—or change—of the repressive methods applied by the regime. Should the latter stiffen again, many a group that today operates in the gray zone between the legal, the merely tolerated, and the illegal would be discouraged. Yet the fact remains that today's CPCS, emasculated of all originally thinking and truly believing elements, faces a population in which it does not any longer possess a monopoly over social activity. Moreover, alternatives to many of the officially professed views are clearly articulated by independent centers of thought, which keep gaining prestige and authority and communicate with the public via their own uncontrolled media. In addition, open opposition to some crucial regime policies—occasionally called "dissidence"—continues to take shape. To paraphrase the exiled writer Milan Kundera, "[Political] Life is Elsewhere" in 1988 than only in the CPCS Presidium and the Central Committee. This is the situation at the threshold of the 1990s, when in addition to serious problems at home the Czechoslovak rulers will have to deal with the impact of systemic changes of unprecedented dimension in the communist neighborhood.

## Three Main Scenarios

These circumstances, too, are the critical variables to be considered in an attempt to forecast the course (or courses) of possible development for Czechoslovakia in the near future. The present establishment will be confronted with forces that it can hope to master, as well as with those that are beyond its control. These factors may, of course, gain or lose in importance, or change, the same as there may be changes effected in the governance of the communist party. Should such occur, they would probably not be imposed from outside and therefore they would be circumscribed by the resources, especially human, currently available within the CPCS. In view of all these givens, three probable scenarios could be envisaged for the end of the 1980s and the start of the 1990s.

If our analysis of the situation in the communist party and in society at large is accurate, the most probable course for internal development of Czechoslovakia in the immediate future would be a reluctant and delayed emulation of the Soviet example. This then would be our first scenario. In view of the past experience of all communist party-states, where the changes in the system or in the major policies have always entailed changes in the governing bodies, the composition of these bodies should in our forecasting represent an important variable—independent as well as dependent, according to the perspective we would take. The adoption of the Soviet model, even if controlled and carefully circumscribed, could, of course, take place under more than one constellation within the power structure. Considering this, it will be to our advantage to subdivide the main scenario into three subscenarios.

The alternative that the present leadership is the most likely to seek, for obvious reasons, is a slow, "minimalist" application of a Czechoslovak version of *perestroika* and *glasnost'* with the current team unchanged, or with cooptations limited only to the pool of those associated with the "normalization" line. This approach—we could call it the tactic of musical chairs—has already been chosen on several occasions, most recently when Husák relinquished the post of general secretary and was replaced by the centrist apparatchik Jakeš in December 1987, and during the reshuffling of the party Presidium and the federal government in October 1988. The changes effected were such that it was difficult to believe that any serious modifications of the political course were contemplated. Some observers even saw these moves as gains for the hardline wing. Should this practice continue, however, nothing could be solved, and the regime would lose what little is left of its credibility.

That is why other alternatives may be chosen. One of them, in our review here representing the second subscenario, would consist in emulating the Soviet model while trying to broaden the support basis by the cooptation of elements outside the "normalization" establishment. The present leaders could draw upon two major reserves. They could either rehabilitate and coopt some of the reformists who had been eliminated after August 1968, or they could recruit from the circle of politically active nonpartisans, which includes the dissidents, or they could do both. Although the second option would be more spectacular than the first, and would probably make headlines in the West, the first would have comparably far-reaching consequences. To rehabilitate the reform leadership of 1968, or even a part of it, would be tantamount to the admission that the current regime lacks legitimacy, and would considerably restrict its future freedom of action. The inclusion of elements from outside the party that had not been directly involved in the reform controversy, even though they disagree with the regime's policies, might prove a less risky choice. In both cases, however, the individuals or the groups to be coopted would probably set a price for their cooperation that would comprise profound changes in the party line. These would soon translate into further concessions to the opposition. The situation according to this scenario would be inherently unstable, but it could continue for some time.

In the third subscenario, the initially slow and controlled reform course, instead of solving the economic and political problems, would exacerbate the crisis. The perception of the cause of this exacerbation being the timidity and the inconsistency of the reform measures would prevail in the party, where also the younger age groups would come to the fore and press for more audacious steps. A major shake-up at the party top would result, which would eliminate all or nearly all the components associated with the "normalization" drive. The change at the highest echelons could be facilitated by the hand of time, too; several of the conservative leaders have by now reached an advanced age. There is little doubt that a vigorous reorganization of the party apparatus could not but give the reformists a near-free hand. A situation similar to that of 1968 would soon be recreated, with the reformists now pursuing even more ambitious goals than 20 years ago. Possibly some of the *oktiabrists,* i.e., the advocates of falling in line with Gorbachev who resigned or lost their positions at the tenth session of the Central Committee in October 1988, would be seen among the new team. Although the team would probably enjoy wide support from the population, its cohesion might not be too great and its position not too stable. Much would depend on its ability to resolve the economic problems, but it could buy time by further enlarging the area of political freedoms and human rights. On the other hand, as in 1968, this approach would probably prove to have its own momentum, concessions calling for new concessions. Thus a point could be reached where the entire political and socioeconomic system would be put in doubt.

## Going It All Alone?

The steps undertaken by the current leadership until now, however, suggest that conscious, planned, and well-mapped opposition to, or avoidance of, the Soviet example cannot be ruled out altogether. Such an option is taken into account in our second main scenario, which again can be divided into three subscenarios, following the impact this choice would have upon the power structure. We aim to show that the "congeniality" of this line with the frame of mind among the party bosses notwithstanding, to embrace it would not be without problems for them. In fact, the present CPCS governance's attempt at "going it all alone" might prove to be an even more perilous course than grudgingly to follow the Soviet lead.

Again, the first subscenario envisages the leaders embarking upon their own course, rejecting or ignoring USSR initiatives, while maintaining the composition of the party apparatus unchanged. This would be increasingly difficult, if for no other reason than that of the advanced age of many top officials. It is probable, therefore, that younger conservatives or centrists would in such cases by coopted. However, the dwindling pool of party members suitable for this purpose would probably not be the most serious problem. Far more difficult to meet might be the necessity of buttressing the apparently independent course by a clearly profiled program, by something more inspiring than "business as usual." It is obvious that mobilizing broad support in the party as well as in the public in general would require a modicum of popular measures. In addition to this need, the CPCS leadership would have to give some thought to its image in other countries of Europe and the world and to the place of Czechoslovakia in the global industrial economy.

Of all the aspects of the ČSSR's international position, the economic one, that is the role of Czechoslovakia in the system of international division of labor, might reveal itself the hardest to work upon or to revise; here, the four decades of deliberately increasing the dependence upon the USSR and the Soviet bloc, but especially the last 20 years of "normalization," would backfire at its erstwhile proponents. A change in this area, of course, would not be impossible. The ČSSR could try to reopen the markets abandoned or lost in the West after 1948. Such a policy would take more than the handful of joint enterprises or production partnerships established with the advanced industrial nations since 1985. The impending complete integration of the economies of the countries of the European Community (EC) is likely to make the task even harder. Czechoslovak communists in the 1990s may be very sorry for what they had started in the 1950s; they may even find that they have already missed the bus.

An "independent Czechoslovak road"—a term that, as a matter of fact, sounds rather strange if it describes a policy of a team put in power by the force of Soviet arms—would also inevitably mean the quest for a new language and new symbols in communication between party and nation. Inexorably, these would have to be found in the pre-communist arsenal, some of them being anathema to communist ideology, such as the name and the political philosophy of the first president of Czechoslovakia, Thomas G. Masaryk. The ostentatious celebration of the seventieth anniversary of the foundation of the Czechoslovak Republic, 28 October 1988, in Prague and at the diplomatic missions all over the world, of an event that for a long time had been passed over in silence, indicates how inescapable is this need. On the same occasion, the first ideologist of the party Jan Fojtik admitted that the interpretation of Czechoslovak modern history by the CPCS had been "one-sided." In the eventuality of a real separation of the paths traveled by the CPSU on the one hand and the CPCS on the other hand, the narrowness of the choice range in this respect would become even more patent.

However, what is perhaps even more significant about the second scenario is the paradox that a conservative CPCS leadership would face if it tried to "go it alone." The very purpose of such a policy would logically be the preservation of the conservative, neo-Stalinist regime, economically centered on the "command economy" at home and on "safe" inflexible markets of the CMEA system abroad, and politically as well as culturally based on neo-Stalinist ideology, hostile to pluralism and all national political traditions. Yet in order to survive, the leadership would have to introduce and espouse the very same policies and symbols that it fears may be reintroduced if the Soviet reform model is adopted.

This hard dilemma would persist also in the remaining two subscenarios. We assume in the former that the party leaders would see an advantage in broadening the power base while keeping the conservative core intact. The elements that in such a case would be coopted could hardly be the expelled reformists of 1968 or the dissidents of today. Cooperation probably would be sought from other groups and parties of the National Front. These components, however, after a brief revival in 1968, were forced back into limbo as part of the "normalization" process and have since then ossified or atrophied. Their use for the CPCS leaders might be only "decorative," as political window dressing, but it might be found sufficient. Nevertheless, here also an irony can be seen. The conservative team would, in courting the partners in the National Front and enhancing their status, imitate the steps undertaken by the Dubček leadership during the Prague Spring.

In the third subscenario we envisage a shake-up in the party, preceding the break with Moscow. Such a shake-up, however, would be sharply to the right, eliminating not only the "moderates" but also the centrists. It is unlikely that the present secretary general could in such a case keep his post. Yet despite its dogmatic character, the new leadership would have to seek domestic and international support equally urgently as any other leadership in this main scenario. This makes the built-in paradox even more obvious, and further reduces the probability that it will materialize.

## Ignoring the Challenge

Among the possibilities given in the contemporary Czechoslovak situation, it is conceivable to imagine yet another scenario, that in which the power structure would decide to ignore the Soviet example, banking iron-ically on one important element in the process of change to which the communist world is currently subject, namely, on the implementation of new principles of intra-bloc relations as advocated by Mikhail Gorbachev. Thus a hope would be entertained by the CPCS leaders that the success of one aspect of the Soviet-sponsored reform may provide an escape for those who reject it. This reasoning is not devoid of logic, but what would be the chances and the consequences of the adoption of such a course?

With police control still effective, the present line—because this part of our third scenario corresponds the most closely to today's reality—could continue for some time, although the situation would progressively deteriorate. Changes in the leadership due to biological imperatives could not be avoided any more than under the previous scenarios. Occasional concessions, symbolic or substantial, to the non-communist majority, such as the reintroduction of Independence Day as a full holiday, would grad-ually undermine the authority of the regime. However, even if no further explicit concessions are made, the activation of the nonpartisan segments of the population is likely to continue. New groups will emerge that will be outside the reach of CPCS cultural and political planners. New un-offical publishing centers will be created, and new uncensored books and periodicals will circulate among the population.

If the contemporary political and cultural scene in Poland can provide some clues as to the potentialities of the development in Czechoslovakia, it would seem that the articulation of distinct political theories and even programs, wholly independent of the communist establishment, is now only a matter of time. Poland and Hungary, by the way, are not only historical examples of trends to which Czechoslovakia is exposed at pres-ent; the developments in these two countries may have direct impact upon the events in Prague and Bratislava, since some of the informal groups in the whole region maintain close relations with one another.

These groups are still only rudimentary, vulnerable to possible system-atic repression. However, if immobility is chosen as the response to change elsewhere in the Soviet bloc, disintegration of the party and the socio-economic order will inevitably set in. In that scenario, when disintegra-tion has progressed far enough, dissidence may take shape as the basis of future pluralism. The judgment of history then would be that what we know as "real socialism" is beyond repair, that what "socialism with a human face" had tried to accomplish in 1968 was indeed "squaring the circle." Instead of "democratizing socialism," the forces now at work would free the captive nations from the fetters of dogmatic illusions and restore their freedom, as well as their responsibility, to deal with their own problems as they best can.

## Looking Beyond the Scenarios

These internal Czechoslovak scenarios have been developed while not taking into account possible changes in the Soviet power center, that is, external conditions have been held constant. In the present situation this means that the scenarios unfold on the assumption that the current reform trend represented by Gorbachev will continue, which, of course, is not absolutely certain. However, considering all possible alternatives would have multiplied the number of conceivable scenarios to an almost unmanageable extent. A variant to the contemporary development within the USSR is nevertheless implicitly contained in main scenario II and some of the subscenarios. The disregard of and possibly even resistance to the Soviet model, as postulated in the scenario, is understood to be based on the hope entertained by the present CPCS leadership that a reversal of the reform course in the USSR is imminent or is going to occur in the not too distant future, and that the good old times of postinvasion identity of views between Moscow and Prague will return.

Yet in terms of a rigorous analysis, this apparently simple reasoning attributed to Jakeš and his associates does not do enough justice to the potential development of the Soviet power structure, which is much more complex. There is no guarantee, namely, that the conditions as they had prevailed under Brezhnev will automatically be reestablished should Gorbachev fall. No doubt this is what the Czechoslovak leaders imposed after the armed Soviet intervention in August 1968 expect to happen. However, in reality at least three different outcomes of such a change could be envisaged: (1) return to the status quo ante, that is, to conditions of 1985, (2) a severe dogmatist backlash, a kind of "neo-Stalinism," wiping out the last vestiges of all previous reforms since Malenkov, including the "immobilist moderation" of the Brezhnev era or, (3) a substantially more vigorous pursuit of *glasnost'* and *perestroika*, in the acknowledgment that the blueprint prepared by Gorbachev had not been radical enough.

However, even this list may not be complete. It does not consider, for example, possible disintegration of the CPSU as a consequence of its failure to resolve the problems besetting Soviet society, especially to contain the centrifugal tendencies of the various ethnic components of the USSR. It is self-evident that any such development would profoundly influence and modify the internal Czechoslovak scenarios presented here.

As already observed, however, there is no room to discuss these issues in this chapter.

## In Lieu of a Conclusion

It is not my task to examine what policies on the part of the United States of America would be the most appropriate in the eventuality that the various scenarios sketched here materialize. This will be more competently handled by the discussant. Nevertheless, I would like to point to one, in my opinion, very important element in this universe of discourse. Any U.S. policy vis-à-vis Czechoslovakia can be but part of the more general policy toward the entire block of communist-ruled states dominated by the Soviet Union and, above all, toward the USSR itself. Such a policy, logically, should always be based on an adequate interpretation of what the Soviet Union and its client states represent in the international arena. During the period of the Cold War, this entity was perceived mainly as a threat, not only to the West but to all nations outside the Soviet orbit. This perception in itself was correct; however, in order to be translated into effective policies, it required also a correct understanding of the nature of the Soviet threat. Before concluding, I would like to observe that this has not always been the case.

The most general misunderstanding—if not misconception—of what came to be called "the peril of communism" occurs where any radical social movement, including the nationalism of the ex-colonial areas of the Third World, is identified with "communism." However, the error becomes much more serious when the threat is seen in the radical movement and ideology—Marxian or other—*as such*. In reality these phenomena are truly dangerous to world freedom and peace only when they become instruments of subversion in the service of a major power bent on expansion, that is, when they are parts of a master plan orchestrated from one single center. This precisely was the case of the Soviet Union under Stalin's rule, and as long as Stalinist policies continued there after his death. If we accept this fact, we will not only cease to consider radical movements that are not under Soviet control as threatening our existence, but the positive side of this acknowledgment will be our ability to better identify the policies that are likely to counteract the real peril. These policies obviously should aim at a reduction or neutralization of the dependence by the smaller communist-ruled states on the USSR. If successful, they in themselves might be sufficient to remove the substance of the Soviet threat. The advantages of such an approach are especially patent in the case of Czechoslovakia.

However, there has been more to the Western error in assessing and interpreting communist danger. Even the communist blueprint for world subversion and domination, where it actually exists or existed, and the working of its mechanism have often been grossly misunderstood by the policymakers of the West. Soviet strategy aiming at broadening the geographical base of what we call communism has put the main emphasis upon the preparation of the ground for a takeover by domestic, autochthonous forces. The goal was to be achieved by "genuine subversion," that is, through political activities, constitutional as well as extraconstitutional, within the confines of the target country. Military support of the intended takeover, especially direct intervention by Soviet troops has always, even in the times of Stalin, been considered the very last resort, which preferably was to be avoided. The case of the Czechoslovak coup d'état of February 1948 well illustrates this point; the takeover then took place in a country where no Soviet troops were present or entered for this purpose.

USSR's strategy, of course, has been different in situations where a communist regime, already established, was threatened or gave grounds for concern over its loyalty to the Soviet power center. This was the case not only of Hungary in 1956 or of Czechoslovakia in 1968, but also, as it appears, of the Berlin blockade of 1948. In these instances, Kremlin leaders did not shun from direct use of military means to avert the danger. The costs of such moves to be paid in other areas, especially in terms of the Soviet image and prestige enjoyed in Western communist parties or in the Third World, have always been very high, and it can be assumed that they have not been decided upon lightly. There may have been different degrees of determination, too, on the part of the USSR to pursue its action in these various contingencies: Stalin discontinued the blockade of Berlin after the Western airlift proved successful, and also limited the campaign against Tito to an economic boycott of Yugoslavia. However, the West only seldom truly tested the strength of Soviet resolve.

American interpretation of the true nature of the specific methods of the Soviet expansionist drive has not been consistent. The launching of the European Recovery Program (ERP, the Marshall Plan) in 1947 would seem to indicate that the United States at that time correctly recognized the rules of Soviet strategy; that they realized the necessity to thwart USSR objectives already in the crucial initial phase of potential internal subversion. The ERP would also have prevented or limited economic dependence of the countries in the Soviet orbit on the USSR. It is not an accident that Stalin used all means at his disposal to stop them from accepting the Marshall Plan. On the other hand, the experience of the Berlin blockade, which provided the last stimulus to the establishment of NATO, seems to have encouraged in the United States an overemphasis on the military component of the Soviet threat. Since then, American perceptions appear to have oscillated between the first and the second view, but on the whole more stress has been put on the military. This could perhaps be partly explained by the momentum of U.S. and West European rearmament after 1948. The huge outlays for military hardware had to be justified, and undoubtedly also generated distinct vested interests (recall President Eisenhower's warning of the emerging "military-industrial complex"). In this climate, the Soviet Union was often thought of as a variant of Hitler's Germany, calling for the same or comparable measures of defense.

Yet an adequate approach to the phenomenon of "international communism," led and inspired by the Soviet Union, requires an objective analysis and interpretation. It also requires the ability to recognize genuine change whenever such should appear in the USSR and other communist party-states, and to distinguish it from the change of mere form or rhetoric. This is of essence, especially today. American thinking in the realm of international politics and the U.S. response to Soviet and other communist initiatives must be flexible. The primary objective has to be to restore the political and economic independence of the countries now called "satellites," and to prevent that their reintegration into the power structure of the USSR should be engineered in any other form. The internal socioeconomic system of these countries constitutes no threat to the free world and can, therefore, be left to the decision of the domestic populations. Only in combination with Soviet control of the national communist parties, does the situation in Central and Eastern Europe give grounds for Western apprehension. The United States and the West must be at all times aware of it. So, and only so, they can contribute to a development that especially in Czechoslovakia will lead from the present profound crisis to the healing of the multiple wounds inflicted upon the societies in this part of Europe during the last 40 years.

# PROJECTIONS

*Carl W. Schmidt\**

## The Historical Context

U.S. relations with Czechoslovakia over the past 70 years have ranged from exceptionally close and friendly to virtually the worst with any of the states in Eastern Europe.

During the decades preceding Czechoslovakia's emergence in 1918 as an independent state, American political and social ideals had been upheld as models by Czech and Slovak nationalists; at the same time the United States—Dvořák's "New World"—became a new homeland for more than a million Czech and Slovak immigrants. Philosopher-statesman Tomáš Masaryk visited the United States several times and his firm belief in democracy and vision of independence were deeply influenced by the American experience. These views were further strengthened by his marriage to an American, whose family name he added to his own.

Although Woodrow Wilson's peace program of January 1918 set forth as one of the Fourteen Points the principle of self-determination and thereby greatly encouraged Central Europeans in their efforts to achieve independence, it was by no means clear at that time that Wilson favored the breakup of the Austro-Hungarian Empire as a consequence. It was not surprising, therefore, that Masaryk spent the last six months of World War I in the United States, developing support for an independent Czechoslovakia among the American public and especially by the U.S. government and President Wilson, who in effect had become the leader of the Allies. In September 1918, the United States became the first to recognize the Czechoslovak National Council as a de facto belligerent government. And in the following month, Masaryk, realizing the time was right, drafted and issued in Washington, D.C., the Declaration of Independence of the Czechoslovak Nation.

At the same time, replying to Emperor Karl's peace overture, Wilson publicly stated his support for full self-determination by the peoples of Austria-Hungary. This led directly to the establishment of the Czechoslovak Republic on 28 October 1918, and the election of Masaryk as its first president. The constitution of the new state, approved in 1920, was

---

\*The views expressed in this section are those of the author, who recently served as Deputy Chief of Mission at the American Embassy in Prague and is now a Research Fellow at the Center for the Study of Foreign Affairs, U.S. Department of State, and do not necessarily reflect those of the United States government.

based on principles contained in the American and French constitutions.

These historical and philosophic bonds, and in particular the crucial role played by the United States and Woodrow Wilson in the independence of Czechoslovakia, fostered harmonious, problem-free ties between the United States and the new, progressive democracy in Central Europe during the interwar period. A reading of the volumes of *Foreign Relations of the United States* for the years 1919–1938 reveals that U.S.-Czechoslovak diplomatic interchanges were notably amicable and straightforward, with work focused chiefly on negotiation of agreements to facilitate relations (MFN trade status, 1923; extradition, 1926; naturalization, 1929; arbitration and conciliation, 1929), and on Czechoslovak import restrictions, the sole bilateral issue that seemed to defy a lasting solution. During the late 1930s, however, consistent with its general policy toward events in Europe, the United States in the face of Nazi Germany's actions was not prepared to play a central role—as it had 20 years before—in support of Czechoslovakia's independence. Instead, as Under Secretary Sumner Welles informed the Czechoslovak minister in March 1938, U.S. policy was "to remain completely aloof from any involvement in European affairs." President Roosevelt's belated appeals in September of that year to all parties in the dispute, ostensibly over Sudeten Germans, had little or no apparent impact on the developments which led to the conclusion of the Munich Agreement. Thus, in March 1939, the U.S. government found it necessary to issue a statement condemning Germany's takeover of the remaining territory of Bohemia and Moravia, while stressing the "specially close and friendly relations" that the United States had maintained with the people of Czechoslovakia.

The United States refused to recognize Nazi Germany's occupation of Bohemia and Moravia and in July 1941 extended formal recognition to the Provisional Government of Czechoslovakia in exile at London. Although on that occasion, Roosevelt assured President Eduard Beneš that "we look forward with eagerness to the day when democratic institutions will again flourish in your beautiful country," in retrospect it seems clear that the United States, occasionally together with Great Britain, did not make full use of opportunities during World War II to help ensure that those institutions would indeed flourish. In 1944, for example, the United States and Britain decided not to accept the Czechoslovak Provisional Government's invitation to conclude agreements concerning the entry of their armies into Czechoslovakia, and termed unfeasible its requests to send military supplies to partisan forces in Slovakia—thereby in both cases leaving the field open for strategic moves by the Soviet Union.

Remarkably, papers prepared on Czechoslovakia by the U.S. Department of State in January 1945 for President Roosevelt's "Yalta Briefing Book" refer to plans for elections and recommend that the United States "accord every facility" for the return of constitutional government, but contain no hint of possible Soviet interest in dominating or subverting the country's postwar government.[1] Also noteworthy in this context is General Eisenhower's controversial decision, approved by President Truman despite Winston Churchill's urgent personal appeal elaborating "highly important political considerations," not to direct General George Patton to send his tanks further eastward to liberate Prague in the closing days of the war.

U.S.-Czechoslovak relations began to deteriorate soon after the end of the war and remained seriously troubled in the period leading up to the communist coup in 1948. Differences focused on delays in opening negotiations to compensate American citizens for property seized and nationalized in October 1945; subsequent suspension of a surplus property credit and negotiations for an Eximbank loan, Lend-Lease debts and other government claims; hostile press coverage; Czechoslovakia's votes with the Soviets at international conferences and reversal of its decision to join the founding Marshall Plan conference; and other problems stemming from the communist party's central position within the coalition government. The impact of the coup in February 1948 was far-reaching. According to Ambassador U. Alexis Johnson, the successful takeover "ended the first postwar effort to work with communists in a democratic framework and disillusioned those who had hoped to find a constructive basis for relations with the Soviets in Europe [and] was the culminating factor in persuading Western Europe and the United States to conclude the North Atlantic Treaty."[2]

As the Cold War intensified in the early 1950s, bilateral relations approached the breaking point. It was a downward spiral of events: Czechoslovakia nationalized additional property owned by Americans, and the United States blocked return of Czechoslovak gold recovered from Germany and the shipment of a steel mill purchased from an American supplier; Czechoslovak employees of the embassy and American citizens were harassed, arrested, and imprisoned on unwarranted charges of espionage; missionaries and other private American citizens were expelled; USIA libraries in Prague and Bratislava were ordered closed (the U.S. response included closing the Czechoslovak consulate in Chicago); 66 American embassy staff members were simultaneously declared personae non grata and the U.S. retaliated by cutting the Czechoslovak embassy staff to 13, closing the remaining consulates in Cleveland and Pittsburgh, and withdrawing the American consulate from Bratislava; Czechoslovakia's MFN tariff status and other trade concessions were suspended; passports of private American citizens were invalidated for travel to Czechoslovakia; and defendants in the "show trial" of top-ranking Czechoslovak officials all pleaded guilty of spying for the United States.

U.S.-Czechoslovak relations remained essentially unchanged through the 1950s and 1960s. In 1965, within the overall context of President Johnson's policy of "building bridges of understanding" to Eastern Europe, bilateral negotiations were resumed on a settlement of nationalization claims and related financial issues, but progress proved very slow. Two years later the mysterious death in Prague of an American citizen and the abduction and trial of another cast new clouds over long-troubled relations. The U.S. maintained a reserved posture toward Alexander Dubček's government during the brief Prague Spring, whereas the ideological tightening and purges that followed the Soviet-led invasion in August 1968 did nothing to break the pattern.

In 1972, however, as part of an emerging U.S. policy approach toward Eastern Europe, which responded to growing diversity in the region and emphasized the principle of dealing with each country "as an independent, sovereign state," senior American and Czechoslovak representatives agreed to attempt to resolve certain outstanding problems. Negotiations were initiated for a consular convention, resolution of financial issues, an agreement concerning educational, cultural, and scientific exchanges, and on reopening consulates in Chicago and Bratislava. Nevertheless, in keeping with the pattern of U.S.-Czechoslovak relations during the postwar period, despite initial progress, none of these initiatives came to fruition during the 1970s. The U.S. congress, for example, passed legislation requiring renegotiation of an ad referendum agreement on nationalized property claims, the Czechoslovak side decided not to ratify the Consular Convention signed in 1973, and the United States chose to suspend negotiations on the exchanges agreement following the arrest and imprisonment of Czechoslovak human rights activists.

## U.S. Policy: The Current Approach

Current U.S. policy toward Czechoslovakia is squarely anchored within the general framework of American policy toward Eastern Europe. U.S. policy toward these countries has gradually evolved over the past 40 years from one that functioned essentially as a corollary of policies toward the

Soviet Union and viewed those countries principally as members of the "Sino-Soviet bloc," to an approach that increasingly has treated each state as individual and separate and that shapes U.S. actions in accordance with its national interests and the specific conditions prevailing in each country.

Overall U.S. efforts in the 1960s at "peaceful engagement," with a special focus on expanding "peaceful" two-way trade, were followed in the 1970s by a heightened emphasis—manifested through the Helsinki process—on respect for human rights. President Ford, for example, on signing the Final Act of the Conference on Security and Cooperation in Europe (CSCE) at Helsinki on 1 August, 1975, stressed to "the countries of the East" the importance of recognizing "the deep devotion of the American people and their government to human rights and fundamental freedoms and thus to the pledges that this Conference has made regarding the freer movement of people, ideas and information."[3] In remarks delivered at London on East-West relations in June 1976, Secretary of State Henry Kissinger made clear that the basic elements of U.S. policy toward Eastern Europe included the pursuit of measures "to improve the lives of the people in Eastern Europe in basic human terms. . . ."[4] This emphasis has since remained central to U.S. concerns regarding the countries of Eastern Europe.

American policy also has demonstrated evolution with regard to what became known as "differentiation," an approach designed to concentrate U.S. bilateral priorities on the degree to which individual Eastern European governments pursued independent foreign policies and/or more liberal domestic policies. This approach, to the extent it was strictly applied, generated certain criticism not only because it served to encourage development, or at least maintenance, of expanded ties with internally rigid Romania along with more liberal Hungary, but also because it was seen as unnecessarily restricting U.S. flexibility to pursue specific national interests and respond to changes taking place in other Eastern European countries as well. And, perhaps most importantly, dramatic change has taken place in the context for this policy approach, that is, differences between individual Eastern European countries and the Soviet Union.

Starting in 1985, far-reaching liberalization moves introduced and pursued by Mikhail Gorbachev within the Soviet Union—in many instances outstripping changes in Eastern Europe—have substantially altered the terms of reference for such an approach. Reflecting these factors, in recent years, U.S. policy statements and practice have both shifted to emphasizing the interest of the United States in expanding and improving relations with all of the countries of Eastern Europe on step-by-step basis. As Deputy Secretary of State John Whitehead stated during a speech in January 1988, the United States seeks "to improve official ties and to develop unofficial ties with each individual country at whatever pace it can stand" on the condition that progress is made on issues that are of priority to the United States, including human rights, "the extent to which each country is moving toward greater pluralism and democracy," improved trade, and the extent to which such countries "show independence on other matters of interest to the United States, from votes in the United Nations to the fight against international terrorism."[5]

As described earlier, U.S.-Czechoslovak relations have been at a low level for more than 40 years. This in large part has been a direct result of the Czechoslovak government's conservative, repressive actions toward its own populace, and its customary close alignment with Soviet foreign policies. In addition, unreceptive and even harsh actions toward American citizens, such as repeated refusal of visas to former Czechoslovak nationals intending to make family visits, have frequently exacerbated the situation. Czechoslovakia has continued to object to its lack of MFN status, and bilateral trade has declined since the levels reached in the middle 1970s. Access for U.S. representatives to Czechoslovak government and communist party officials has generally been tightly restricted; the United States, as a part of its policy response, has limited high-level contacts. Thus whereas most other Eastern European countries have seen visits by American presidents or vice presidents, the highest-level U.S. official visitor to Czechoslovakia thus far in the postwar period was Secretary of State William Rogers in 1973.

During the past six years, in keeping with the overall U.S. policy of continuing to seek ways to resolve problems and expand contacts with individual Eastern European countries on the basis of American interests, it has been possible to achieve modest yet important progress in U.S.-Czechoslovak relations. In 1982 an agreement was finally concluded, after intermittent and troubled negotiations over the course of nearly 37 years, providing for the settlement and subsequent payment of nationalization claims of American citizens, the return to Czechoslovakia of gold seized by Nazi Germany, and the resolution of certain other long-standing financial issues. In 1986, following the successful conclusion of negotiations, the first government-to-government Exchanges Agreement was signed, providing for increased exchanges in the fields of education, culture, science, and technology. In 1987 periodic, bilateral working-level meetings began to be held to discuss and work to resolve specific issues and cases involving humanitarian affairs and business conditions. Later in the same year, a new long-term bilateral Civil Aviation Agreement was signed, the Consular Convention negotiated in the early 1970s was entered into force by both governments, and Czechoslovakia's acting foreign minister visited Washington for official discussions.

However, despite the advances recently made in U.S.-Czechoslovak relations, fundamental differences remain. This is highlighted by the fact that change, including economic and political liberalization, is coming slowly to Czechoslovakia, especially in comparison with certain other Eastern European countries and the efforts underway within the Soviet Union. At the center of U.S. policy concerns is the observance of human rights, as embodied in Czechoslovakia's undertakings under CSCE and in other international commitments. Yet freedom of expression in particular continues to be heavily restricted by Czechoslovak authorities.

In addition to human rights concerns, which also encompass religious freedom and freedom of movement problems, current U.S. policy priorities toward Czechoslovakia include the following elements: an interest in genuine political and economic reform measures; expansion of economic and trade ties in nonstrategic areas, including formation of joint ventures; maintenance and expansion of official dialogue on such issues as arms control, narcotics, and international terrorism; full implementation of the Exchanges Agreement and the encouragement of its application in such areas as health, environment, agriculture, and the creative and performing arts; enhanced access to Czechoslovak officials and maintenance of contacts with segments of Czechoslovak society representative of a broad spectrum of opinions; and the conduct of public ceremonies by American embassy officials to recall the important contribution made by the United States in the establishment of an independent Czechoslovakia in 1918, and to commemorate the role played by U.S. armed forces in the liberation of the country during World War II.

## U.S. Policy in the 1990s: A Possible Course

Forecasting the course that Czechoslovakia will take in the 1990s is indeed a risky undertaking, especially given the uncertainties regarding how developments within the Soviet Union will unfold and their impact on the countries of Eastern Europe. Nevertheless, it is possible to identify a number of factors and make certain assumptions about Czechoslovakia that can help define the likely parameters of change during the next decade and also provide guideposts for the most effective U.S. policy toward that country. These are as follows:

- The Soviet Union and its perception of security interests will continue to be the dominant fact of life for Czechoslovakia, and for other Warsaw Pact members as well. Despite Gorbachev's remarks at Prague in April 1987 allowing for different paths to socialism, and even though the Soviets may no longer be as inclined to involve themselves so directly in the decision making of Eastern European regimes, it is unrealistic to think that there will not be thresholds of Soviet tolerance for actions by and developments within other Warsaw Pact countries. It should be assumed that the "Brezhnev Doctrine" will continue to live, although, when possible, more likely implemented indirectly as with Poland in December 1981 rather than as with Czechoslovakia in August 1968.
- The majority of the population is alienated from the Czechoslovak government and communist party. Cynicism and low labor productivity are widespread. At the same time, Western values and material achievements, including those of the United States, are held in high esteem by many.
- Czechoslovakia's economy, already in need of fundamental reform during the 1960s, faces profound problems. Exports to Western markets, hampered by lagging competitiveness, will encounter added difficulties as the European Community becomes a single market in 1992. Thus despite Czechoslovak efforts to the contrary, trade with the Soviet Union and other CMEA member states can be expected to continue to predominate, but those markets also will demand higher quality products.
- The principal pressures for change, both economic and political, will arise from within Czechoslovakia and, regardless of whether or not fully intended, as a result of changes taking place in the Soviet Union. The ability of the United States and the West as a whole to influence these developments is decidedly limited; however, this does not prescribe a policy of inaction.

Although not excusing it in any way, U.S. policymakers should not be surprised by Prague's reluctance to adopt a course of far-reaching economic and especially political reform. (All the scenarios for the 1990s that Professor Suda has described in the first part of this chapter are properly pessimistic on this score, with what he suggests as most probable

forecasting only a "reluctant, delayed following of the Soviet example.")
Although many of the objective reasons for reform are clearly present,
especially in the economy, the "lessons" of the Prague Spring are still
very fresh in the minds of Czechoslovakia's leaders, who fear instability
and cannot easily "jump over their own shadows" to criticize what they
themselves have created. Moreover, as Professor Suda notes, given the
massive purge of liberals in the early 1970s, it is questionable who within
the next generation of communist party officials would be able to provide
the leadership. Therefore, while welcoming and to the extent possible
encouraging measures leading to economic and political liberalization,
the policy of the United States should be firmly grounded on realistic
expectations. By the same token, should the forecasts prove wrong and
reforms begin to take on a greater dynamic, the United States and the
West in general must take care to act prudently and avoid actions that
could be seen as destabilizing within the region as a whole.

U.S. policy toward Czechoslovakia has achieved some favorable results in recent years. It would seem to make sense, therefore—especially
given the conservative prognosis for change in that country—to continue
to pursue the basic lines of that policy, at the same time extending and
modifying certain elements to encourage further progress on issues of
interest to the United States. This approach must be mindful of the constraints as well as of the new opportunities being created throughout Eastern Europe, as a result of unprecedented changes in the Soviet Union and
the concurrent reduction of East-West tensions. To achieve results, it also
must be mindful, to the extent possible, of Czechoslovak interests and
objectives. The following policy points suggest themselves:

- Continue to deal with Czechoslovakia as a separate, sovereign state,
  while focusing additional attention on its unique location and potential role in the center of Europe. For example, regional cooperation
  with countries from East and West on environmental issues, transportation, and navigation could be encouraged as an outgrowth of
  the "Zones of Confidence" initiative proposed by Czechoslovakia.
- Urge Czechoslovakia to improve its observance of human rights, including its CSCE commitments, and make clear that its repressive
  record in this regard is the most important barrier to further expansion and elevation of bilateral relations. Whereas progress has recently been made, for example, on divided families and visa refus-
  als, Czechoslovak citizens continue to be harassed, detained, and
  imprisoned for attempting to express their own views. Contacts and

exchanges between lawyers, jurists, and those concerned with prison conditions should be encouraged.

- Welcome reform moves in the economic and political spheres, and be prepared to respond positively to genuine liberalizing trends, as opposed to tactical shifts. Contacts with Czechoslovak economists and economic institutions should be expanded, and Western management techniques reintroduced. In part to mobilize human resources long idle and internally exiled, Czechoslovakia should be encouraged to promote pluralism by permitting a real invigoration of its National Front and establishment of organizations and groups with alternative views, and by conducting genuine dialog with them. Elimination of controls over religious activities and the clergy should also be encouraged.
- Recognizing that Czechoslovakia's economic problems will become even more pronounced in the coming decade (e.g., are its current set of piecemeal, halfway reforms under the rubric of *přestavba* an attempt to have economic without political reform?) and that rigors of the market mechanism and Western know-how must play key roles in any successful transformation, open the way for Czechoslovakia to become more closely integrated into the global economy. Currency convertibility and exchange rate rationalization should be encouraged, together with reform of the foreign trade and banking sectors, perhaps as conditionality for membership in the World Bank and International Monetary Fund. Bilateral trade could be promoted more actively by both sides. Joint ventures, such as in hotels and tourism, and bank credits to facilitate purchase of American commercial aircraft, could occur even in the absence of MFN status. However, the importance of the lack of MFN, partly psychological and artificially generated but nevertheless real, should not be minimized. Expanded trade and economic links could bring manifold benefits. Therefore, subject to genuine improvement in Czechoslovakia's human rights performance, a means should be found, either under the Jackson-Vanik amendment or in another way, to extend MFN treatment to Czechoslovakia.
- Expand bilateral exchanges in education, culture, and science, including joint research projects in nonsensitive but priority areas such as environment and health, and open access to archives by scholars and preservation specialists. Encourage institutionalization of exchange activities through direct agreements between universities, re-

search institutions, and public-interest groups, while facilitating open and broad-based participation.

- Continue exchanging views and information with the Czechoslovak government on issues such as arms control and narcotics, and expand discussions on international terrorism while seeking Prague's moderating influence with states such as Libya.

- Be aware of the long-term internal importance of Soviet troop withdrawals from Czechoslovakia whether they occur as a result of unilateral Soviet actions or from successful future multilateral negotiations on reduction of conventional forces in Europe. Develop a failsafe mechanism for defusing and dealing with accidental border crossings by U.S. and Czechoslovak military aircraft along the frontier with the Federal Republic of Germany.

- Encourage the Czechoslovak authorities to rightfully acknowledge their country's own history regarding the bonds between the American and Czechoslovak peoples and governments, such as by providing factual accounts in media reporting and history textbooks of the work of Masaryk and Wilson and of the role played by U.S. armed forces during World War II.

### Notes to Chapter 6

1. The memorandum, prepared by the Division of Central European Affairs, U.S. Department of State, begins with the statement: "The Czechoslovak Government's relations with the British and Soviet Governments are excellent, and present no problems." Later in the summary, the briefing memorandum states: "We have no questions to raise about Czechoslovakia now; nor have Great Britain or the U.S.S.R., as far as we know." (*Foreign Relations of the United States,* 1945, IV, 420–422.) It also should be noted that the Department of State Policy Statement regarding Czechoslovakia, which was drafted less than four years later, reveals a decidedly more realistic understanding of the situation regarding that country. (*Foreign Relations of the United States,* 1949, V, 416–427.)

2. U. Alexis Johnson, with Jef Olivarius McAllister, *The Right Hand of Power* (Englewood Cliffs, NJ: Prentice-Hall, 1984), p. 177.

3. Gerald A. Ford, Address to the Conference on Security and Cooperation in Europe, Helsinki, Finland, 1 August 1975, *The Department of State Bulletin,* LXXIII, No. 1888, 1 September 1975, 304–308.

4. Henry A. Kissinger, "The Western Alliance: Peace and Moral Purpose," *The Department of State Bulletin,* LXXV, No. 1935, 26 July 1976, 105–115.

5. John C. Whitehead, "The U.S. Approach to Eastern Europe: A Fresh Look," *Current Policy,* no. 1044 (19 January 1988).

# Part III

# The Southern Tier

# Chapter 7

# ROMANIA

## THE 1990s, OR, AFTER CEAUȘESCU WHAT?[1]
*Mary Ellen Fischer*

This chapter focuses on political, economic, and military trends in Romania and asks what we can expect to see develop in that country during the 1990s. The single most important factor influencing those trends will be the longevity of the powerful and idiosyncratic Romanian president, Nicolae Ceaușescu, head of the Romanian Communist Party (RCP) since 1965. Born in 1918, he will be 72 in 1990 and could conceivably rule until the turn of the century. In 1985 and 1986 he appeared to be ill, and rumors of his impending death were widespread both inside and outside Romania. However, he then made a remarkable recovery, and in 1987 and 1988 was once again maintaining a busy schedule of public appearances and trips, though not at the hectic pace of the 1970s. His health and strength are crucial in assessing Romania's future for he has centralized decision making around himself, and his personal priorities have formed the basis of Romanian policies for two decades. Following Ceaușescu's death (or his departure—removal or resignation cannot be excluded as possibilities), there will undoubtedly be some continuities in policy and personnel, but Romania after Ceaușescu will not be the same as Romania under Ceaușescu.

As a result, any analysis of potential developments in Romania during the 1990s consider two scenarios: that Ceaușescu will survive the decade in office or that there will be a transition in top leadership from him to a successor or successors. We therefore start by summarizing the major features of the Ceaușescu era—the internal political process under

Ceauşescu, and his economic and military priorities—and the possibility of change while he remains in office. Next we examine the most likely scenario for the 1990s in view of Ceauşescu's age and health: a leadership transition. In doing so, we look closely at the one example we already have of leadership transition in communist Romania, Ceauşescu's consolidation of power after the death of his predecessor, Gheorghe Gheorghiu-Dej. Given this precedent, what is likely to occur during a post-Ceauşescu transition? The concluding section examines prospects for change in Romania by asking which political, economic, and military policies characteristic of Romania under Ceauşescu—the cult, for example, or the autonomous and nationalistic foreign policies—have depended on his personal priorities and which are endemic to Romanian politics or Leninist parties. In other words, which policies and processes of the Ceauşescu era are likely to continue in the 1990s under his successor(s), and which will end with him?

## The Ceauşescu Era

Four features of Romanian policies under Ceauşescu stand out to any observer: (1) personalized power (including nepotism and the leadership cult), (2) nationalism (including autonomy in foreign and military affairs), (3) rapid industrialization of the domestic economy, and (4) centralized political and economic control. Romania has become well known during the 1970s and 1980s for what has been termed a "cult of personality," the extensive praise heaped upon Ceauşescu as the omnipotent and omniscient leader of the Romanian nation, and the tight personal control exercised by him. The worship of Ceauşescu is indeed reminiscent of a religious cult with (1) an iconography, (2) inspired scriptures, (3) an infallible leader, and (4) rituals of mass worship. Icons, or portraits, of Ceauşescu are found in most public places and private offices, though not in most homes. The scriptures of the Romanian Communist Party (RCP)—about 30 volumes of his collected speeches—have been published in Bucharest in many languages, and there is even a "concordance" to his words, not merely an index, but a series of volumes recording his views on specific issues. The Romanian leader is infallible in his own country: successes are attributed to him, failures to organizations or individuals that have not carried out his suggestions correctly. Finally, when Ceauşescu appears in public his speeches are frequently accompanied by rhythmic chanting, many voices in unison repeating "Ceauşescu, PCR" [*Partidul Comunist Român,* the Romanian Communist Party] or "*Ceauşescu şi poporul"* [Ceauşescu and the people], or a variety of other ritualistic slogans.[2] Throughout Romania, he is portrayed as the brilliant interpreter of Marxism-Leninism, the hard-working communist who rose from poverty to party leadership, and the stately symbol of Romanian sovereignty in dealings with foreign heads of state, royal or revolutionary.

In addition, Ceauşescu's personal and often arbitrary decisions and preferences determine policy directives and personnel appointments. By the early 1970s he had consolidated his control over the RCP, and since then he has been the source of all major policy initiatives—announcing them, explaining them, and blaming others if problems develop. The promotion of his supporters, which enabled him to consolidate his power after 1965, turned into a rapid circulation of officials during the 1970s: only rarely did anyone remain in one post more than four years, and shifts usually occurred much more frequently. Power became personalized rather than institutionalized as Ceauşescu with increasing frequency ignored constitutional requirements for legislation and for appointing personnel. He even brought his family to prominence with him: his wife Elena, who holds high offices in the RCP and the government; his son Nicu, formerly head of the Union of Communist Youth and now a county first secretary (the most frequent career path to the top party bodies); and a number of brothers, sisters, cousins, nephews, and in-laws scattered throughout the various ministries, the armed forces, and the police. Ceauşescu has not merely carried on Gheorghiu-Dej's tradition of personalized political power and decision making; he has intensified the personalization of the political process into a leadership cult, and he has made his family a crucial part of his support network.[3]

A second feature of the Ceauşescu era has been a nationalistic foreign policy, a strategy in international relations that, if not totally independent of the USSR, is at least exceptional among members of the Warsaw Pact. Before World War II, nationalism was a prominent feature of Romanian politics. Soviet occupation following the war temporarily substituted "Marxist internationalism," or loyalty to the USSR, as the cornerstone of the Romanian political structure, but after the withdrawal of Soviet troops in 1958 Romanian leaders began to reassert an autonomous and eventually nationalistic line in foreign policy. This new foreign policy was initiated by Gheorghiu-Dej, but it was continued even more vigorously by his successor. In fact, as one student of Romanian politics has observed, "under Ceauşescu there has been an ideological acceptance of the nation as opposed to a simple political manipulation of it."[4]

This nationalistic policy in international affairs has had several components. Most significant have been Ceauşescu's attempts to distance Romanian policies from those of the Soviet Union whenever feasible, usually in arenas of peripheral importance to Moscow such as the United Nations or the Middle East, but also in the Warsaw Treaty Organization (WTO) and the Council for Mutual Economic Assistance (CMEA)—though the country's continued membership in these organizations and its loyalty to Marxism-Leninism have never been at issue. Simultaneously, the Romanian leader has established political and economic relations with as many different states as possible, including Third World countries and NATO members, in order to render bloc boundaries more "permeable"[5] and reduce his dependence on any one state or alliance system. In addition, he has criticized both the Soviet Union and the United States on issues—such as development aid or disarmament—that divide the superpowers from the many less wealthy and less powerful states throughout the world and from their own allies. For example, Ceauşescu has advocated a general reduction in military spending for all states and has unilaterally reduced Romania's military budget, including its contributions to the Warsaw Treaty Organization. Even so, he has carefully asserted his loyalty and determination to join his East European allies in resisting imperialist aggression, presumably from NATO.

Here we see yet another aspect of Ceauşescu's autonomous policies: his military doctrine. Unlike that of the other WTO members, Romanian doctrine is a defensive one of guerrilla warfare carried on against a foreign aggressor within Romanian borders by units of "patriotic guards." Since Romania is surrounded by WTO members (except for neutral Yugoslavia), it is difficult to see how this doctrine could be directed against the NATO imperialists, or how it could make a substantial contribution to WTO military strategy. Indeed, Romania has refused to cooperate in joint maneuvers, except on paper, so its insistence on national autonomy has weakened the Soviet alliance system, albeit on its less vulnerable southern front.[6]

A third feature of politics in the Ceauşescu era is a commitment to rapid industrialization. Ceauşescu defines himself as a Marxist, he speaks and writes in Marxist categories, and he views progress in terms of industrialization.[7] Since a very early age his life has revolved around the collective experience of revolutionary and postrevolutionary activity within the Romanian Communist Party. His only education was in the small circle of Marxist revolutionaries active in Romania in the 1930s, and he has lived his entire life within the borders of Romania. It is no wonder that his policies all reflect one goal: the industrialization of socialist Romania.

More specifically, he insists on the Stalinist model of economic development: the rapid growth of heavy industry, financed largely by internal sources, and requiring the postponement of adequate supplies of consumer goods and services. During the 1970s, for example, the investment rate in Romania averaged one-third of national income, and the country's debt service ratio at the end of 1979 was the lowest in Eastern Europe.[8] Despite these high rates of investment, economic growth was sufficient to provide modest improvements in living standards. Then, as we shall see, economic difficulties in the early 1980s brought a sudden rise in the foreign debt, much lower rates of growth and investment, and a drastic fall in living standards. Even so, Ceauşescu has blamed the problems largely on the international economic environment and has never abandoned his commitment to rapid growth. Instead, he has insisted that high rates of investment be resumed from internal sources—without the help or interference of foreign capitalists.

A final feature of the Ceauşescu era reveals that he is not only a nationalist and a Marxist with Stalinist economic tendencies, but he is also a Leninist: the Romanian political process under him has been characterized by centralized power. For Ceauşescu, as for Lenin, the party must monopolize politics and direct economic and social policy. Like Lenin, Ceauşescu is a first-generation revolutionary, a supremely self-confident activist who dominates his own party and is impatient with slow processes of development. Both men have been willing to speed the course of history by force whenever necessary. Unlike Lenin, however, Ceauşescu is unwilling to compromise with reality. He insists that any change in policy or organization must bring even more rapid economic development. He permits economic reform measures only if they do not interfere with centralized planning, high rates of accumulation, and socialized property and economic activity. He has grudgingly accepted some material incentives directly related to improved production, but in general he prefers to stimulate productivity by increasing requirements and penalties—the stick rather than the carrot. His response to the economic problems of the 1980s has been to tighten central control and impose still heavier penalties on the population.

During the first decade of his rule, Ceauşescu's political priorities were to some extent compatible with economic growth and popular expectations. By the late 1970s, however, all four features of Romanian politics in the Ceauşescu era were becoming less and less appropriate to the country's needs. In a sense, Ceauşescu's successes—Romanian economic growth and his own personal power—contributed to the eventual difficulties. Industrial development should have been accompanied by institutionalized, not personalized, politics, and efficient, flexible economic decision making rather than the centralized system he imposed. To make matters worse, two crucial economic decisions of the 1960s and early 1970s—to minimize cooperation in CMEA and to invest heavily in petroleum-related industries—increased Romania's dependency on hard currency imports of technology and raw materials, including petroleum, just when the cost of these inputs reached unprecedented levels.[9] These economic mistakes brought into question the wisdom of the nationalistic foreign policy. This policy had stemmed initially from the Romanians' rejection of CMEA integration, and later had been the major justification for Ceauşescu's rule in the eyes of many Romanians. As a result, Romania in the early 1980s was facing not only an economic crisis, but also a crisis of political legitimacy. The potentially explosive effects of both crises, however, were smothered by the strength of Ceausescu's personal rule.[10]

By 1981 the previously rather self-sufficient Romanian economy was seriously in debt to Western banks, a debt whose sudden growth was stimulated by the unfavorable balance in oil trade, but whose roots can be traced also to unwise investment decisions made jointly during the 1970s by the Romanians and the foreign investors. In that same year Poland's potential default (for quite different reasons—the Polish government had borrowed quite heavily in the early 1970s) destroyed the confidence of Western bankers with respect to all the East European economies. As it turned out, it was much more difficult for Romania to obtain extensions on its loans than for neighbors such as Hungary or Yugoslavia, since excessive Romanian secrecy, restrictions on contacts with foreigners, and erratic leadership intensified the mistrust of Western bankers and businessmen.[11]

Simultaneously Romanian agriculture, which had in the past been a source of exports and so might have helped the balance of payments, was falling short of its production goals partly as a result of several years of bad weather but also from long-term structural problems that reached crisis proportions only after 1979. Romanian agriculture had been long neglected in favor of industry, but the country's rich soil, favorable climate, and large (though inefficient) agricultural labor force had continued to feed the population and produce a surplus for export. However, the economy was structured to encourage labor to move into industry and left little incentive for the ever-shrinking agricultural work force to raise productivity. Those who remained in villages tended to be old, less qualified, or tied to their homes by children. After 1970, investment in agriculture did increase substantially, but it was so rapid as to be inefficient since productivity of land and labor grew more slowly. By 1979 the combination of bad weather and low productivity in a shrinking labor force brought major shortfalls in planned production for internal and external markets.

The international structure of oil prices improved in 1981 and 1982, and eased the hard currency crisis somewhat for the Romanians. But Ceauşescu decided that the $11 billion foreign debt must be paid off, not just serviced, and he proceeded to even the balance of payments and to repay the loans in the same way that he had found investment funds: by depressing the domestic standard of living and exporting what consumer goods and agricultural products were produced.[12] There have been serious food shortages in Romania throughout the 1980s. Bread, sugar, and oil are rationed, and even the peasant markets are usually empty. Only those with private connections to peasants are able to obtain regular supplies of food, and such private sales are subject to stiff penalties. Limits on electricity and heat have made cities and towns dark, and apartments and workplaces cold. One major symbol of rising living standards in the 1970s was the proliferation of private automobiles, but in the 1980s gasoline has been rationed and the use of cars strictly limited. Ceauşescu has been able to impose such stringent controls that the debt is scheduled to be paid off by the end of the decade.[13]

The severe economic difficulties did not induce Ceauşescu to alter his commitments to heavy industry or to centralized control of the economy. Instead, he continued to rely on regulations and coercion to motivate citizens to produce. For example, a number of decrees and campaigns in the early 1980s to link labor and income more closely stressed penalties rather than incentives, and required tighter labor discipline.[14] Ceauşescu has clung to these policies despite the calls for *perestroika* and *glasnost'* emanating from Moscow under Mikhail Gorbachev. Like Gheorghiu-Dej, who insisted to Khrushchev and the world in 1956 and thereafter that he had ousted the Stalinists from the RCP back in 1952 and had no need to implement further de-Stalinization, Ceauşescu insists that he implemented his own *perestroika* (*perfecţionare* is the term he uses; "perfecting" rather than "restructuring") back in 1978–1979 with a New Economic and Financial Mechanism (NEFM), and he explicitly rejects both *perestroika* and *glasnost'* for Romania.

The NEFM, however, did not try to decentralize decision making in the Romanian economy, nor did it introduce market mechanisms. Rather, the 1978 directives aimed at greater efficiency in production and more accurate fulfillment of the planners' requirements by increasing the number of centrally determined indicators to include some of the desired improvements in efficiency, quality, and productivity. Perhaps the most significant provision required each economic unit henceforth to cover its own costs, and to finance bonuses and social and cultural expenditures out of profits.[15]

The NEFM brought a sense of insecurity to both managers and workers, and engendered considerable passive opposition. As early as May 1980 Ceauşescu was complaining bitterly that the provisions of the NEFM were not understood and were not being implemented.[16] Then the growing economic problems seemed to distract attention from the new procedures and reinforced the centralizatiton of the economy as enterprise officials retreated to a system they knew well.[17] Their quest for security was foiled, however, since Ceauşescu, in another attempt to stimulate productive effort by decree, introduced a new system of renumeration in 1983, the *acord global,* which provided that individuals—managers and workers— would be paid according to output, without lower or upper limits. In effect, therefore, there was no longer a minimum wage, and there was little chance of receiving the normal income, let alone earning extra money, since plan targets were set unrealistically high. The 1983 directives also contained incentives for managers to reduce the number of workers and close entire units, so Romanian workers were faced with the threat of unemployment. Again problems developed during implementation, and by October 1987 Ceauşescu was demanding revisions in the *acord global,* and complaining vigorously that goods were being produced irrationally for plan fulfillment rather than for sale.[18]

Just as the problems of the 1980s have reinforced Ceauşescu's commitment to industrial growth at the expense of consumption, and to centralized economic planning with coercion rather than material incentives as the stimulus for production, so have the other major features of his rule—nationalism and personalized power—been strengthened in this decade. In fact, Ceauşescu's nationalism has turned into xenophobia as he has repeatedly stressed Romania's need to be self-sufficient and to find autarkic methods of continuing developing and growth. His attitudes and Romanian policies continue to be covertly anti-Soviet, but they have become overtly anti-West as well, not only on economic issues but on disarmament and also human rights. In 1981, for example, he staged giant demonstrations against both superpowers for engaging in a nuclear arms race, pointing out his own rejection of military alliances. In 1986 he held a referendum on nuclear disarmament in which over 99 percent of eligible

Romanians voted to support his call for military budget cuts. Such events served Ceauşescu's domestic and foreign goals by demonstrating his ability to elicit obedience from the Romanian population as well as his independence of both military blocs.[19]

Ceauşescu is also firmer than ever in rejecting outside efforts to influence his human rights policies. Friction between the Hungarian government and Romania over the latter's treatment of its Hungarian minority became public during 1987, and Gorbachev's efforts to mediate the dispute during his visit to Bucharest that May were unsuccessful. Relations between the two states continued to deteriorate until the new Hungarian party leader, Károly Grósz, met with Ceauşescu in Arad, Romania, at the end of August 1988. These talks were evidently a humiliating failure for Grósz who was unable to persuade Ceauşescu to compromise on any of the major issues involved. Attempts by the United States to influence Ceauşescu met with similar rebuffs, culminating in Ceauşescu's sudden rejection of most-favored-nation (MFN) trade status from the U.S. Congress in early 1988 because it was conditional on his compliance with emigration and human rights provisions. Ceauşescu has consistently portrayed such efforts by foreign governments as impermissible interference in the internal affairs of Romania.

Just as his nationalism has intensified in the face of adversity, so has his personalization of political power become still more extreme and arbitrary. The leadership cult is flourishing, and his seventieth birthday was celebrated in January 1988 with great pomp and circumstance. He still presides at important meetings, presents the major reports, initiates policy, criticizes those who fail to carry it out, and makes royal appearances throughout Romania and abroad. The arbitrary circulation of officials has increased in recent years, members of his family continue to hold high posts in many ministries, his wife Elena is more prominent than ever, and his son Nicu is clearly being groomed for the succession. Despite serious economic difficulties at home and increasing tension in relations with foreign states, Ceauşescu has not changed his economic policies or his techniques of rule. Yet his political skills are such that he has been able to prevent any successful opposition to his rule.

The single policy that best exemplifies Ceauşescu's goals and methods is known in Romania as "systematization," a plan to "rationalize" land use by reorganizing all villages into agro-industrial complexes, distributing industrial production more equally throughout the country, and maximizing the land area devoted to agriculture.[20] First mentioned in the early 1960s, "systematization" was given a new impetus in 1968 by an administrative-territorial reform of the entire country, and the planning evolved during the 1970s amid promises to improve living standards among peasants, to end the flight of labor from agriculture to industry, and to eliminate the long commute for many workers from villages to industrial jobs. The fears of the smaller nationalities, however, were aroused at the prospect of focusing investments in regions where few minorities resided, thus encouraging internal migration and reducing the concentration of the non-Romanian ethnic groups. In the 1980s systematization promised to raze half of Romania's villages and concentrate the rural population in the remaining "viable" villages, which would be turned into agro-industrial complexes with two-story apartment blocs in place of the traditional peasant houses. Churches, cemeteries, and other remnants of pre-communist Romanian rural life would be destroyed, leading to more efficient utilization of land, which would increase the area devoted to agriculture. Thus Romania would become a laboratory of socialist experimentation, a living example of Ceauşescu's conception of the ideal society. He has already destroyed many of the older sections of Bucharest—mostly homes and churches—in order to "rationalize" land use in the capital and to build a gigantic complex of public buildings as a permanent monument to his rule. Although there are signs that rural systematization has stirred considerable opposition, and is being blocked or slowed in a number of areas, there was no sign of direct resistance in late 1988. Only outside the country—particularly in Hungary and West Germany, where the threat to the ethnic heritage of the Hungarian and German minorities in Romania stirs considerable sympathy—has Ceauşescu aroused open criticism. Yet he shows no signs of rethinking his position.

In fact, as long as Ceauşescu remains president, we can anticipate no major adjustments in political techniques, economic organization, or military doctrine. For almost two decades he has refused to compromise on his goals for Romania. When the foreign debt is paid off, he may allow some improvement in living standards by increasing domestic supplies of food and energy. We can also expect him to continue to maximize his autonomy in foreign policy. But it is highly unlikely that he will deviate from his commitment to Stalinist industrialization techniques, and so he must maintain his own centralized control of political and economic processes at the expense of the Romanian population.

## Leadership Transition

The question remains: what will happen if Ceauşescu leaves the scene? Of course, the way in which he departs—death, resignation, forced removal—will have a considerable impact on the transition. Death seems most likely. It is only a remote possibility that Nicolae Ceauşescu would voluntarily resign from his positions, unless that resignation were merely a formal relinquishing of titles in favor of a chosen successor, such as his son, who would rule in his father's name and with his parents' help behind the scenes. Even so, this possibility seems quite unlikely unless Ceauşescu's health demands it, and in that case resignation would be merely the first act in a prolonged transition due to his impending death.

It is, of course, possible that Ceauşescu will be forcibly removed from office. If so, the instigators of that removal would most likely be members of the top RCP leadership in a coup similar to the ouster of Khrushchev in 1964. Lower party officials are moved around too quickly to form cohesive groupings and threaten the hierarchical lines of control within the highly centralized RCP. Individuals or groups outside the party that might ordinarily be expected to pose a threat to party control have been eliminated, infiltrated, or coopted in the two decades of Ceauşescu's rule. Today, for example, there is no Jaruzelski or Beria in Bucharest, although there do exist Romanian precedents for both military and police threats to civilian control (Ion Antonescu during World War II, for example, and Alexandru Drăghici in the 1960s) and there were rumors of an attempted military coup preempted by Ceauşescu in early 1983.[21] During the past decade Romanian military officers have been given expanded responsibilities in economic production and direct administration of important areas of the country. Constantin Olteanu, for example, defense minister from 1980 to 1985, was put in charge of Bucharest in late 1985, and then made Central Committee secretary for propaganda, culture, and ideology.[22] But Ceauşescu has been careful to maintain personal control over the military and the police through family members, and even Olteanu can be expected to show primary loyalty to the party. A graduate of the military academy in Bucharest, he worked in the Central Committee headquarters from 1973 to 1979 as deputy chief and then chief of the section that controls both the armed forces and security. He served as chief of staff for the "Patriotic Guards" in 1979–1980 before his appointment as defense minister, and has been well known for his vocal support of those citizens' militia units, which have taken personnel and financial support away from the more professional units and have been regarded with considerable resentment by other officers. Thus Olteanu seems an unlikely candidate to mobilize military support against the party, even though he would be an important ally in any move against Ceauşescu by the other RCP leaders.

Nevertheless the longer Ceauşescu remains in power, alienating the population with his policies and weakening the party by the constant circulation of officials, the greater the possibility of an assassination or a military move against him in the name of the party. Moscow would be likely to give tacit approval in either case as the new leaders continued to accept the Soviet alliance and the political monopoly of a restructured and restaffed communist party. Until now Ceauşescu has been too strong and has managed to preempt both assassination and overt opposition. But by the mid-1990s, weakened by age and illness, he would be much more vulnerable to such actions, and they cannot be ruled out.

Mass action to prevent continued party control seems unlikely at present, although Ceauşescu's policies have produced such resentment that episodes of violence are becoming more frequent. There were strikes in Braşov in late 1987 but, like the miners' strikes in the Jiu Valley in 1977, the strikers were isolated and later treated harshly. In communist Romania there has never been the cooperation between workers and intellectuals that occurred in Hungary in 1956 or in Poland after 1970 and that seems to be a prerequisite for popular revolt in Eastern Europe.[23] Political culture, tradition, and social structure all play a role as most Romanians choose individual, indirect, and nonconfrontational methods to avoid rather than oppose the demands of the state. We must also remember that, in the first decade of his rule, Ceauşescu managed to identify himself with Romanian national interests in the eyes of many citizens. They gave him credit for keeping Soviet troops out of Romania and preventing Soviet political interference and economic exploitation. As a result, many Romanians—workers, peasants, intellectuals, party and nonparty—still fear that open opposition to Ceauşescu and RCP control will bring Soviet intervention. This fear contributes to political passivity as individuals and groups, paralyzed by nationalism and fear of the Soviets, fail to challenge the party.

In recent years Romanians have begun to question the high cost of their national autonomy, especially as calls for reform issue from Moscow. Soviet and Romanian communists had attempted in the 1940s and 1950s to reconcile the Romanian population to Soviet control, but were never able to do so. Ceauşescu has accomplished the impossible: he has managed to make many Romanians wish for greater Soviet influence in Bucharest, a truly Herculean feat. Nevertheless, Ceauşescu's departure could again produce hopes in Romania that the RCP would be able simultaneously to keep out the Soviets and to bring higher living standards. Such hopes would undoubtedly be exploited by the new leaders to reinforce the national paralysis.

If, then, the post-Ceauşescu transition will most likely be managed at the highest levels of the RCP, following his death or removal, who will be the major figures in the new leadership? His family members would almost certainly be excluded from the new leadership if he is forcibly removed. Even after his death, however, a dynastic succession would be improbable, except possibly for a brief period. After all, one of the reasons that Ceauşescu promotes family members is that he is assured of their loyalty: they fear that their political power will not long survive him, and they are probably right. The family is extremely unpopular, and new leaders would see their legitimacy considerably enhanced by dissociating themselves from Ceauşescu. Both Elena and Nicu Ceauşescu are attempting to gain positions and allies, but neither seems to have the ability, the personality, or the independent base of power to take control.

If we restrict candidates for succession to the party leadership, and eliminate Ceauşescu's immediate family, what type of individual is likely to emerge as the next leader of Romania? To answer this question we need to remember that during the 1970s Ceauşescu changed his personnel strategy from promotion to circulation of cadres. Individuals moved back and forth between party and state, and they also moved geographically from Bucharest to county posts or the reverse. The horizontal circulation of top officials enabled a relatively stable group to remain on the Political Executive Committee (PEC) of the RCP, whereas the administrative bodies, the Secretariat and Council of Ministers, saw frequent turnover. Meanwhile, the second type of elite circulation—the interchange of cadres between Bucharest and outlying areas—emphasized the importance of certain posts in the party apparatus, especially that of county first secretary. There are over 40 of these officials, and each is a "little Ceauşescu" directly administering both party and state hierarchies at the county level. Ceauşescu has used the post of county first secretary to train and test new people on their way up and also to move more experienced officials away from the center temporarily, sometimes to signal a demotion or sometimes to entrust a crucial region to a competent subordinate.[24] Ceauşescu's successor will most likely have served as a county first secretary, since these individuals have proved themselves competent to rule as general administrators implementing party policy. Other positions are important under Ceauşescu—in the Central Committee apparatus, or as presidential counselor—but it is those who have demonstrated ability as county first secretaries who are most likely to have the political skills to propel them to the very top. The successful contender should also have spent some time on the Political Executive Committee and in a number of high administrative positions but, whoever the successor, election as party leader will only be the first step. Next, he or she must consolidate power, just as Ceauşescu did in the late 1960s. We now turn to that example to see whether it contains any insights for a transition in the 1990s.

## Transitions: The 1965–1969 Example

Leaders of Leninist movements make use of various sources of strength to gain control of their party. Three of the most important sources of power have been prestige as the leader of the revolution, violence or even terror, and foreign support. All three of these power sources were crucial to Gheorghiu-Dej, but none was available to Nicolae Ceauşescu when Gheorghiu-Dej died in 1965. Despite his years of party activity, there were others with greater seniority so he could not claim to be the leader responsible for placing Romania on the path to socialism. Nor could he use violence to establish himself firmly in control of the political system. Despite his influence in the military hierarchy, it was one of Ceauşescu's major rivals within the RCP, Alexandru Drăghici, who controlled the Ministry of Internal Affairs, and hence the secret police. And Ceauşescu certainly could not use Soviet support to implement his policies, for by that time the independent course in Romanian foreign policy was firmly established, and many of Ceauşescu's international priorities would turn out to be anti-Soviet.

Since revolutionary prestige, terror, and foreign support were not available to Ceauşescu in 1965 (nor are they likely sources of power to any Ceauşescu successor), he resorted to a combination of four other strategies to gain internal support for himself and his policies: (1) policy compromise and ambiguity within a collective leadership, that is, promise everything to everyone, (2) personnel manipulation, especially promotions, (3) repeated emphasis on legality and constitutionality in the political process, both party and state, and (4) direct appeals for support to the Romanian masses through political mobilization techniques stressing democracy, participation, and nationalism. The culmination of this transition process began in 1968 with the denunciation of Gheorghiu-Dej and Drăghici, and the time will undoubtedly come when Ceauşescu himself will be criticized by his successors.

*Policy compromise and collective leadership.* A Leninist political system, like any one-party system, must depend on informal bargaining within a small group—the party political bureau or executive committee—to determine the outcome of a succession struggle. The result often is a period of change and uncertainty, and the surviving leaders assure an orderly transition by temporarily emphasizing collective leadership and policy continuity to strengthen group unity. Simultaneously, they promise to satisfy consumer demands, and they reassure the military-industrial complex. In other words, the new leadership makes overtures to all major social groups and uses promises instead of threats. Caution, compromise, and optimism become the projected virtues in the policy process. Romania from 1965 to 1967 followed this pattern. As spokesman for the collective, Ceauşescu simultaneously advocated policy continuity and promised reforms; his own priorities remained submerged until 1969, and so he alienated no major groups while his personal power remained vulnerable.

***Personnel manipulation.*** The pattern of personnel change from 1965 through 1967 was one of promotions, not demotions, and the size of top party bodies increased as a result. Not until 1968 had Ceauşescu promoted enough supporters—many from the lower party apparatus—to begin removing his rivals from high office. Suddenly in 1968–1969 there were a significant number of demotions, and those were the crucial years when Ceauşescu eliminated any rivals and formed a new party leadership around himself.

***Legality and constitutionality.*** New leaders usually promise improvements over the performance of their predecessors, and Ceauşescu was no exception. He began almost immediately to stress the need for strict observance of legality within the party and also in society as a whole. This implied criticism of Drăghici and his security forces, since they would have been the major violators of constitutional norms of behavior. Then in 1968 Ceauşescu even went so far as to criticize Gheorghiu-Dej for "transgressions of legality," to implicate Drăghici in those mistakes, and to remove the latter from the party leadership.[25] Ceauşescu thus promised to initiate a new age of legality in the party and constitutionality in the overall political process, and so party members and all citizens were encouranged to look to Ceauşescu as their protector and hope for the future.

***Popular mobilization.*** Ceauşescu's final strategy for enhancing his political power was aimed mainly at the broad masses of Romanians. He attempted to mobilize them into positive support for regime policies by increasing their participation in the political process and playing on their strong feelings of national loyalty. His techniques for mobilization were essentially populist,[26] for his rhetoric appealed over the heads of local officials to create an image of participation by interested groups and individuals in all sectors. For example, he held mass meetings and created new "consultative" bodies including collective management committees. Such participation, however, did not reflect influence over policy priorities or budgets; such choices remained centralized.

Ceausescu's most successful mass appeal was to Romanian nationalism. He continued and intensified the de-Russification measures of the early 1960s and began to rewrite history.[27] His first efforts attempted to create a place for the RCP and other leftist movements in Romanian history, and as such encouraged historians to do serious research on neglected topics rather than engage in the flights of fantasy that were to become characteristic of Romanian historiography in the late 1970s.[28] But the major cause of Ceauşescu's success in mobilizing Romanian nationalism to support his personal rule was his response to the intervention in Czechoslovakia in August 1968.

When WTO troops entered Czechoslovakia, Ceauşescu was able to establish himself as an authentic national leader and defender of the homeland. He publicly denounced the action as "a great mistake and . . . a shameful moment in the history of the revolutionary movement."[29] The most important consequence of August 1968 for Romania, therefore, was the immediate (and long-term) increase in Ceauşescu's popularity. His defiant stand gained him the personal stature that no amount of economic achievement or diplomatic success could have given him, consolidating and legitimizing his own rule and that of his party. For the next decade, Romanians disillusioned with other aspects of party policy would point to August 1968 as the major reason for supporting the RCP. In 1974, for example, many Romanians could not understand the Watergate crisis. "Why," they asked repeatedly, "should Nixon resign? His foreign policy is good. Look what we put up with at home for a good foreign policy!"[30]

The 10th Party Congress in August 1969 signaled Ceauşescu's complete victory in establishing himself as the dominant political force in Romania. Every speaker felt compelled to begin and end any remarks by praising the party leader and many referred to him in almost every paragraph, crediting him personally with the economic advances made since 1965. Ceauşescu had become the undisputed leader of party and state.

## The Post-Ceauşescu Succession

What does all this mean for the post-Ceauşescu transition? Although predictions in politics are both risky and futile, we can try to assess the probabilities of various scenarios. Most likely would be a post-Ceauşescu transition similar to the post-Gheorghiu-Dej transition in several ways. First, personnel manipulation would be crucial to the new leaders and would probably be characterized first by unity and stability. Demotions would be gradual unless Ceauşescu were forcibly removed, in which case his family would quickly leave political life. Most other officials would remain, at least for a short time, to ensure the stability of party control. Second, the new regime would emphasize legality and return to institutionalized procedures rather than presidential decrees. Third, some populist policies would continue, but a gradual effort would emerge to dissociate the new leadership from the Ceauşescu era. Therefore, the huge rallies and flag-waving parades would be discontinued, and the new regime would seek ways to use Ceauşescu's only truly successful populist appeal, to nationalism.

The major difference between leadership transition in Romania in the 1960s and the 1990s would involve policy; whereas the earlier process stressed continuity with Gheorghiu-Dej's themes of industrialization and independence in order to maximize internal support, the post-Ceauşescu succession would for similar reasons immediately emphasize the need for change in economic policies: slower growth rates and new priorities in industry, for example, higher prices and other incentives for the private sector in agriculture, immediate improvements in living standards, and a halt, temporarily at least, to systematization.

Ceauşescu's successors will need to seek internal acceptance of their rule, as Ceauşescu himself did after Gheorghiu-Dej died, in part because such acceptance is the most effective way to rule an industrial society, but also because those three sources of power unavailable to Ceauşescu—revolutionary prestige, terror, and foreign support—will also be of little use to his successors. There is no individual in contemporary Romania with any prestige apart from the president himself, and his policies in recent years make passing of his mantle—to family members or any other designated heir—highly improbable. Extensive use of terror is also unlikely. Party successors to Ceauşescu would certainly not hesitate to use whatever military or police coercion would be needed to maintain civilian control, and the threat of such force would be constantly in the background. However, party leaders should prefer to try first the less drastic measures outlined above if only to prevent the military and security forces from gaining too much importance on the political scene.

Foreign support would be another possibility, but overt Soviet support would be regarded with considerable suspicion by Romanian leaders who rose to the top under Ceauşescu. Such dependency would weaken their own control of Romanian affairs. In addition, an open rapprochement with the USSR could reduce the Bucharest regime's internal viability in a period of maximum weakness. Gorbachev may appear attractive in juxtaposition to Ceauşescu, but he is a Russian, and once Ceauşescu leaves the scene, fears of Russian domination are likely to reappear. There is also little indication that the Gorbachev politburo would wish to pay the economic price of bailing Romania out of its difficulties. Romania needs the USSR as a source of raw materials and a market for Romanian exports, but the relationship has been mutually beneficial in economic terms. Gorbachev has his own internal problems, and he will look for the cheapest possible solution for Romania. He would probably be content with Romanian autonomy after Ceauşescu if the new leaders could improve the economic situation and maintain internal stability without tremendous Soviet subsidies. Most probably, the new Romanian leaders would attempt to present the Soviets with a fait accompli as in 1965—by quickly electing new officials—and would reassure Moscow of their ultimate loyalty to WTO and CMEA. Simultaneously, they would appeal to the Romanian population for support, and implicit in this appeal would be the fear that disorder might lead to Soviet intervention. The regime thus would continue to walk the fence between the Soviet leaders and the Romanian population.

## The New Era

What aspects of the Ceauşescu era will remain as permanent features of Romanian politics after the post-Ceauşescu transition period? First, although the commitments to Marxism and the Soviet alliance are departures from pre-1945 Romanian traditions, no change in either is likely without a basic restructuring of the overall international environment. Second, nationalism is likely to remain a feature of Romanian politics. The Soviets accepted the compromise achieved by Gheorghiu-Dej and Ceauşescu and are unlikely to pay the economic and military price of forcing conformity on the Romanians as long as those in Bucharest accept the limitations on their autonomy implicit in WTO and CMEA membership. If Moscow does not take steps to eliminate nationalism from Romanian politics, the RCP is unlikely to abandon its nationalist postures voluntarily. The regime needs every shred of legitimacy it can muster to maintain itself in power and to achieve its economic goals, and nationalism is its most potent source of popular acceptance. Nationalism has been a feature of Romanian politics for over a century and, like Marxism, is likely to outlive Ceauşescu in Romania.

Personalized power has been just as constant a feature of Romanian politics as nationalism, and under Ceauşescu the two have been mutually supportive: Ceauşescu's political strength has made national autonomy possible, just as nationalism has contributed to the personal power of Ceauşescu. This close connection between nationalism and personalized power in Ceauşescu's Romania is indicative of a more general relationship between national autonomy and personal rule. Cults of personality in communist systems tend to appear in states that are striving for or have achieved national independence. Lenin, Mao, and Tito were simultaneously symbols of revolution and nationalism. In contrast, for almost two decades after 1944 the Romanian Communist Party and its leaders were regarded by most Romanians as antithetical to the interests of the Romanian nation since they were perceived as instruments of the USSR, one of Romania's major enemies. Ironically enough, the problem of legitimacy and the consequent need for a cult did not arise for the RCP before the 1960s because the party simply had no chance for legitimacy. Only as the quarrel developed with the Soviet leaders did internal legitimacy become both possible and necessary for the Romanian communist regime.

The distinction among socialist states between loyal Moscow allies and regimes seeking autonomy or total independence helps to explain the absence of a cult in Bulgaria and Hungary, and its presence in China, Yugoslavia, and Romania. In the "national" communist state, the local communist party cannot rely on support from Moscow and so must seek domestic legitimacy in the eyes of its own population. Nationalism is often the major factor stimulating such legitimacy, but the local regime will be further strengthened if it can produce a national hero on whom to focus the newly established anti-Soviet allegiance. Even the creation of mass loyalty to an individual is not sufficient; if possible, the local party must replace the ideological authority of Moscow among its own members with a national interpreter of Marxism. A charismatic leader with revolutionary credentials can serve these functions for the masses and for party loyalists.[31]

Other factors are, of course, important in producing or preventing the emergence of a cult. Choices made by individual leaders, systemic factors such as history, social structure, and culture, as well as bilateral relations with Moscow have all played a role in the various countries. But it is striking that the most successful and pervasive cults in communist systems have appeared only in the "national" communist states where Soviet support no longer is available—forcing the local party to find indigenous acceptance—and where, moreover, that party and its members must substitute the personal authority of the national leader for the ideological authority of the CPSU as an organization.

The combination of nationalized and personalized power in Ceauşescu's case, therefore, results from general attributes of communist political systems as well as from factors specific to Ceauşescu and to Romania. As a result, personalized power is likely to continue in a Romania that is both Marxist and nationalist with or without Ceauşescu. That personalized power need not, however, include nepotism or a cult; in fact, the post-Ceauşescu era in Romania is likely to have less obvious nepotism and no cult, at least at first while the new leader who emerges from the transition process rejects any techniques reminiscent of the unpopular Ceauşescu. Thus, an initial emphasis on compromise and collective leadership should eventually produce a new leader; this new leader (or perhaps even earlier, the collective leadership) will turn away from Ceauşescu and eventually denounce him much more vehemently than he criticized Gheorghiu-Dej.

After the transition period, regime policies will depend on the priorities of the new leader who may initiate a new cult, or find more institutionalized methods acceptable to himself, the party, and the population. That new leader may also choose new methods of economic management that will enable Romania to achieve a transition to consumer-oriented development strategies. We can take hope from the knowledge that the new leader will not be a first-generation revolutionary and will probably have a better education than Ceauşescu. But we must also remember that the new leader will have lived for many years in Ceauşescu's Romania and will probably have gained the top position through success in applying Ceauşescu's methods.

# PROJECTIONS
*Robert R. King*

No significant historical ties link the United States with Romania as they do the United States and some of the other East European countries.[32] Furthermore, no large ethnic Romanian community in America lobbies for federal government support of the Romanian people as is true with other countries of Eastern Europe.[33] Nevertheless, U.S. relations with Romania in the late 1960s and early 1970s were probably better than with any other country of Eastern Europe. Over the last decade relations cooled because of changes in the international environment and repressive domestic policies in Romania. The decade of the 1990s, however, should bring a change in leadership to Romania, and this may provide new opportunities for an improved and more productive relationship.

## Original Basis of U.S.-Romania Relations: Friendly Ties as a Reward for Independence from Moscow

Following completion of negotiations for a treaty of peace with Romania in 1947, U.S. interest remained limited. Establishment of totalitarian communist party rule and the full integration of Romania into the Soviet system by 1949 left American-Romania relations as simply a function of Soviet-America relations. In the 1960s the United States warmed noticeably toward Romania, in contrast to relations with most other countries of Eastern Europe. The reason for the change was the assertion of greater autonomy by Romania vis-à-vis the Soviet Union.[34]

During the administration of President Lyndon Johnson (1963–1969), the United States began the policy of "building bridges" to Eastern Europe. This was an American effort to encourage countries that were members of the Warsaw Pact to act independently of the Soviet Union. In this era of continued Cold War confrontation, Moscow followed a policy that mirrored that of the United States. It sought to encourage the countries of Western Europe to distance themselves from the NATO alliance. At the same time that Moscow was seeking to cultivate good relations with Paris to encourage French independence and dissent within NATO, the United States was extending political friendship and trade benefits to Bucharest as the reward for Romania's demonstrative autonomy from the Soviet Union. Romania's positive actions (from the American perspective) covered the whole range of foreign policy: defiance of Moscow in the United Nations; refusal to participate in joint Warsaw Pact military maneuvers; the only Warsaw Pact state refusing to follow the Soviet lead in breaking diplomatic relations with Israel after the June 1967 war; establishing full diplomatic relations with West Germany without coordination and approval of the Soviet Union and East Germany in 1967; and most important, the vigorous Romanian condemnation of the Soviet-led invasion of Czechoslovakia in August 1968.

This policy of seeking to encourage independent action by Soviet client states was the basis of the favorable U.S. relationship with Romania in the 1960s and 1970s. During the administration of President Richard Nixon (1969–1974), Henry Kissinger explained, "We attempted a more differentiated policy to encourage the countries of Eastern Europe to act more independently within their possibilities . . . We would reward those with a more independent foreign policy and stay aloof where a nation, by necessity or choice, slavishly followed the Soviet line.[35] In keeping with the policy of demonstrating American approval for such independence from the Soviet Union, Nixon became the first U.S. president to stop at a Warsaw Pact capital, when he made an official visit to Bucharest in August 1969. The following year, Romanian President Nicolae Ceauşescu accepted an invitation to pay a state visit to the United States, and U.S. Secretary of State William Rogers visited Bucharest again in 1972.

## Human Rights and Domestic Liberalization: Problem Areas

Whereas independence from the Soviet Union continued to be an important criterion in U.S. relations with Eastern Europe, and the basis for a continuing good relationship between Washington and Bucharest, a second important element began to affect relations during the early 1970s; the United States government increasingly gave greater emphasis to human rights as a factor in its foreign policy. This became a major issue in the context of Jewish emigration from the Soviet Union in the early 1970s when free emigration, which Washington wanted, was linked with trade liberalization, which Moscow sought. At about the same time, negotiations preceding the Conference on Security and Cooperation in Europe (CSCE) gave much greater impetus and importance to human rights.

The administration of President Jimmy Carter (1977–1981) followed a similar policy of giving preference to countries that were relatively more independent of the Soviet Union, but the Carter administration also gave greater emphasis and importance to human rights. In relations with Eastern Europe, the new attitude toward human rights was made explicit by also giving preference in U.S. policy to those countries that were more liberal internally.[36] The Carter policy continued to keep U.S.-East European relations subsidiary to the overarching American relationship with the USSR—countries that were independent of the Soviet Union in domestic or foreign policy were favored. This policy continued to benefit Romania because of its international policy, but it expanded the list of favored countries to include Poland and Hungary. Romania was rewarded during the Carter years with another state visit by Ceauşescu to Washington in the spring of 1978.

The Reagan administration followed this same fundamental policy toward Eastern Europe. As Secretary of State George P. Shultz explained: "We differentiate among them [the countries of Eastern Europe], and between them and the Soviet Union, to encourage more independent foreign policies, greater respect for human rights, and economic and social reforms. Governments that show such positive trends receive our reinforcing acknowledgement.[37]

Although during the 1970s and the 1980s independence of foreign policy remained an important criterion in differentiating U.S. policy toward the countries of Eastern Europe, changes in the international environment and in Soviet-American relations have resulted in that factor being a less important foreign policy priority for the United States. The Soviet invasion of Czechoslovakia and Soviet handling of other crises in Eastern Europe emphasized the limits of Moscow's tolerance for independent foreign policy action by its client states. It also became increasingly evident to U.S. policymakers that there was no alternative to direct cooperation with the USSR in key areas such as arms control and the limitation of regional conflicts. The Nixon/Kissinger policy of détente was the result of these changes. In the context of improving direct relations with the Soviet Union, encouraging independence by Soviet client states is not only less important, but it can also be counterproductive. Fostering East European independence could increase Soviet doubts about ultimate American intentions, and this could be harmful to more important foreign policy goals such as arms control or the reduction of tensions in other critical regions, such as the Middle East.

At the same time, with the greater emphasis on human rights and domestic liberalization, Romania's repressive policies began to cause increasing problems in its relations with Washington. Jewish emigration was not the problem for Romania that it was for the Soviet Union. Through a cynical and calculating policy, Romania permitted its Jews to emigrate to Israel in return for ransom payments in hard currency. Israel and the

Jewish community were willing to live with that unsavory policy, because it was successful in permitting Jewish immigration; hence there were few problems for the United States on this issue. The CSCE process, which gained momentum after the Helsinki conference in 1975, focused increased international attention on basic human rights, such as freedom of speech, press, religion, protection of the rights of ethnic minorities, and intellectual dissent. As attention focused on these issues, repressive domestic conditions for all Romanians became a factor that hampered relations with the United States.

In the 1980s American and international concern with human rights violations in Romania has increased the strain on U.S.-Romanian relations. Fundamentalist Christians in the United States have become increasingly active in domestic American politics, and a top item on their international agenda is the assurance of religious freedom for fundamentalist Christians around the world. Ceauşescu's policy of repressing non-cooperative religious groups has made Romania a prime target of American fundamentalists. Furthermore, Bucharest's treatment of its non-Romanian population—particularly the Hungarian and German minorities—has come in for increasing international criticism. In the United States, Hungarian-Americans have successfully lobbied Congress and the administration against Romania's nationality policies. Even "the fraternal socialist ally" Hungary has been outspokenly critical of the treatment of the Hungarian minority in Transylvania. Such criticism in private meetings between leaders of the two countries has been frequent in the past, but in recent years Hungary's harsh criticism of Romania has taken place in the controlled Hungarian press and the open Western media, as well as in such international forums as the CSCE follow-up conferences.

The result of these human rights problems has been the revocation by the United States of a number of economic benefits that were important for Romania. In January 1987 the U.S. government removed Romania from the duty-free generalized system of preferences (GSP) because of that country's disregard for the rights of its workers. In 1987 and 1988 bipartisan congressional majorities voted to suspend MFN (Most-Favored-Nation) status for Romania for six months and possibly longer because of human rights violations.[38] After both House and Senate had approved this legislation, but before the president had either signed or vetoed the bill, the Romanian government renounced MFN status to avoid the embarrassment of having it stripped away. Also during 1988 the U.S. Congress, in renewing the charter for the Overseas Private Investment Corporation (OPIC), removed Romania from the list of countries eligible to participate in this program of U.S. government guarantees and insurance for trade and international economic cooperation.[39]

The cost of these actions to Romania in purely economic terms will be substantial. It was estimated by U.S. government officials that the loss of exports to the United States for Romania as a result of its removal from GSP in the first year alone could be as high as $150 million in lost exports to the United States. Estimates of the cost in lost exports to Romania from the revocation of MFN status were placed as high as $300 million a year. Trade between the two countries in 1986 gave Romania a surplus of $588 million, with U.S. imports from Romania of $839 million and exports to Romania of only $251 million.[40]

## The Impact of the Gorbachev Era: *Glasnost', Perestroika,* and Romanian-American Relations

There is no question that the most important factor in U.S.-East European relations has been and continues to be the American relationship with the Soviet Union. The Gorbachev era has not only begun an important transformation in America-Soviet relations, but it has also amplified the effects of those two elements that have contributed to the significant weakening of the U.S.-Romanian relationship over the last decade.

First, even before Gorbachev's accession to power, the Soviet Union and the United States had begun the process of moving toward a more cooperative relationship. The hiatus in progress on arms negotiations during the early 1980s was principally the result of the Soviet leadership stagnation, caused by Brezhnev's advanced age and the inability of the Politburo to resolve the leadership vacuum. Gorbachev's selection as leader gave the process of improving relations with the United States a new momentum and impetus. By the late 1970s U.S. policy was less interested in encouraging independence from Moscow than in reducing tensions through direct dealings with Moscow. Gorbachev's policies have given greater emphasis to that trend, thus making Romanian autonomy from the Soviet Union even less important a goal for the United States now than before.

Second, internal reforms in the USSR under Gorbachev have highlighted the human rights abuses inside Romania. Soviet efforts to enhance real political participation, to move toward a freer press, to grant greater rights to national minorities, increased Jewish emigration, the lifting of many restrictions on political dissidents and intellectuals, relaxation of some restrictions on the free exercise of religion, and efforts to improve the availability, quality, and variety of food and consumer goods, have all served to highlight the continued repression practiced by the Ceauşescu regime in Romania.[41] Furthermore, the poor Romanian record on human rights and domestic liberalization has been highlighted by the contrast with the Soviet record on each occasion when Gorbachev has met with Ceauşescu, because the USSR leader has been openly critical of Romania's record.

Thus the effect of the Gorbachev era has been to give greater emphasis to those very problems that have resulted in the weakening of Romanian-American relations over the last decade. It should be emphasized, however, that the Gorbachev reforms in Soviet domestic and international policy are certainly not irreversible or permanent thus far. Strong opposition to Gorbachev is evident with the communist party apparatus and other segments of the Soviet leadership. The ability of Gorbachev to maintain power and to continue his reform program will be tested in the future, and it is by no means certain that he will prevail. If Gorbachev fails and is removed from power, a conservative reaction will most likely follow, which could result in a reversion to the more repressive internal policies and more confrontational international policies that marked the Soviet Union in the past. Such a conservative reaction could have the opposite effect on Romanian-American relations. Encouraging independence from the USSR could again become more important and domestic Soviet repression would ease the pressure on Romania in the area of human rights.

## Prospects for Romanian-American Relations in the 1990s

In making projections about the course Romanian-American relations may take over the next decade, clearly the single most important factor "will be the longevity of the powerful and idiosyncratic Romanian President Nicolae Ceauşescu," in the words of Mary Ellen Fischer. Any options matrix on future U.S. policy toward Romania must have as two of its major categories "with Ceauşescu" and "without Ceauşescu."

*"With Ceauşescu."* If Ceauşescu remains the dominant force in the Romanian political equation, the key word will be continuity. Although earlier in his career he has exhibited some flexibility in adapting to realities, his longevity in power and his autocratic style of leadership have left him increasingly rigid and inflexible. If he continues to lead Romania in the next decade, major changes in either domestic or international policies are not likely.

Romania's policy of autonomy from the Soviet Union will change little so long as Ceauşescu remains in power. He has been clearly identified with this policy during the almost quarter-century he has held the reins. This nationalistic foreign policy, carefully carried out within limits the USSR will tolerate (though not always happily), is an important source of what legitimacy Ceauşescu and his regime have achieved, and he is unlikely to alter it. Romania has long since probed the outer limits of Soviet toleration. There is little to be gained for Romania to seek to expand those limits and thus provoke a confrontation with Moscow. In fact, if there are shifts in one direction or another, economic realities could draw Romania closer to the USSR and the other East European countries. Trade benefits and credits from Western Europe and the United States will not be forthcoming, because of the weak domestic economy and Romania's human rights record.

In the area of domestic economic reform and human rights, there is little in Ceauşescu policies to indicate change in directions that will help improve relations with the United States. Whereas the Romanian leader has been willing to make a few limited and temporary accommodations in the case of violent worker unrest, these improvements have not resulted in fundamental policy changes. He has shown little flexibility with regard to the Hungarian ethnic community or treatment of fundamentalist Christians.

Increasingly, Ceauşescu's reaction to adversity is to "hunker down" and resist accommodation. In some cases, he has used foreign criticism as the basis to rally Romanian nationalist sentiment to withstand pressure for change in his policies. This "bunker mentality" was clearly shown in 1988 when Congress adopted the legislation to deny Romania MFN status for a six-month period. The U.S. Department of State, although certainly critical of Ceauşescu's human rights record, did not favor denial of MFN status and urged a policy of working with the Romanians to seek improvements that would not result in suspension of MFN. Any sign of concessions from Romania would have given the U.S. administration grounds to argue in favor of continuing MFN status for Romania. Rather than make concessions, however, Ceauşescu renounced MFN status before the U.S. administration had time to act.

*"Without Ceauşescu."* Professor Fischer has identified various possibilities for a post-Ceauşescu leadership in Romania. Whereas it is fruitless to speculate on possible changes that would result from specific individuals assuming the leadership, in general terms it is possible to identify general aspects of the current political situation that will form the param-

eters within which any new leaders will have to operate. The Romanian Communist Party will continue to be the dominant force in the country, and the preeminence of the party apparatus in conjunction with the political leadership of the security and military forces will play the key role in determining Ceauşescu's successor. Most important, for the foreseeable future the Soviet Union will remain the dominant factor in Romania's international environment.

Under these conditions, there is no reason to expect a new Romanian leadership to move away from Ceauşescu's policy of autonomy from the USSR. This policy has long been a source of international prestige for Romania, as well as an important source of domestic legitimacy for Ceauşescu personally and for the Romanian Communist Party. This autonomous foreign policy has been a significant element in the Romanian nationalism that Ceauşescu and the party have fostered and manipulated. Continuity in this important aspect of Romanian policy will help with the establishment of a new leadership.

A new leadership will be preoccupied with its domestic power base and will focus on internal party matters and internal political issues until it is firmly established. During at least the first two years of any new regime, this will be true. If there is a transitional leadership (as was the case in the Soviet Union during the period between the death of Leonid Brezhnev and the selection of Gorbachev as head of the communist party), this quiet period of restrained international activity could last even longer. A new leadership is unlikely to provoke a confrontation with the USSR; hence, the period will be a quiet one in terms of Romanian foreign policy autonomy.

From the perspective of the United States, a new leadership will not fundamentally alter the basis for Romanian-American relations. The key question is whether there will be a fundamental change in Romanian domestic policy that will minimize the human rights problems that are now a key factor in the deterioration of friendly relations. It is difficult to predict whether a new leadership will be willing to make domestic changes that will improve the Romanian record. Some domestic improvements, at least in the short run, would seem to be necessary to win a degree of popular support and allow the regime time to consolidate its position. It is impossible to tell whether such improvements would translate into permanent improvements in the area of human rights and domestic policies.

Once the new leadership in Romania is firmly established and begins to play a more active international role, it is likely to be less bound by precedents set during the Ceauşescu regime in the area of foreign policy.

This does not mean, however, that a new leadership will embark on a radically different foreign policy. The general *strategy* of Romanian foreign policy has been followed for well over a quarter of a century and has broad support within the party and among the population generally, but a new leadership will be less bound to specific *tactics* of the previous regime. Thus it should exhibit a greater degree of flexibility and a greater willingness to accommodate to new conditions and circumstances. This should be helpful in working out problems between Washington and Bucharest.

With a leadership change in Romania, there are policies the United States could pursue to encourage those positive developments in Romanian policy that will contribute to improved relations. Positive steps in Romanian domestic and human rights policies should be welcomed by the United States with gestures of political and economic support. Political gestures—high-level visits, statements of support—can be extended with relative ease by the executive branch. Economic support is both more meaningful and more difficult to extend. The most useful economic aid— MFN status and OPIC eligibility—requires congressional action. Such congressional action requires time, considerable effort, and is not always successful.

The most important factor that will influence the nature and policies of a new leadership in Romania—and this will fundamentally affect the future of Romanian-American relations—is the course of internal and external policy in the Soviet Union. The success of Mikhail Gorbachev's international policies will create new opportunities for American relations with all of Eastern Europe, including Romania. Success with his domestic policies will increase pressure upon Ceaușescu's successors to improve domestic human rights conditions, and this in turn will help remove that obstacle from the path of improved Romanian-American relations. Since 1945 the key element in American relations with Romania, and all of Eastern Europe, has been the USSR and Soviet-American relations. That will continue to be true, regardless of any change of leadership in Romania.

### Notes to Chapter 7

1. Parts of this chapter are based on my *Nicolae Ceaușescu: A Study in Political Leadership* (Boulder, CO: Lynne Rienner, 1989).

2. The terms "iconography" and "bible" as well as "gospel" and "shrine"

have been applied to the Lenin cult by Nina Tumarkin in *Lenin Lives! The Lenin Cult in Soviet Russia* (Cambridge: Harvard University Press, 1983). A series of what are essentially concordances to Ceauşescu's collected works have been published as "Documente ale Partidului Comunist Român." On ritual, see Walter M. Bacon, Jr., "The Liturgics of Ceauşescuism," paper presented at the annual meeting of the AAASS, Boston, November 1987, and RFE *Romanian SR/2* (28 January 1988), pp. 7–9. For more details on the Ceauşescu cult, see my "Idol or Leader? The Origins and Future of the Ceauşescu Cult," in Daniel N. Nelson, ed., *Romania in the 1980s* (Boulder, CO: Westview, 1981), pp. 117–141.

3. For a general study of Romanian politics, see Michael Shafir's excellent *Romania: Politics, Economics and Society* (Boulder, CO: Lynne Rienner, 1985). For a detailed discussion of Ceauşescu's political techniques, see my *Nicolae Ceauşescu: A Study in Political Leadership*. On Elena Ceauşescu, see my "Women in Romanian Politics: Elena Ceauşescu, Pronatalism, and the Promotion of Women," in Sharon L. Wolchik and Alfred G. Meyer, eds., *Women, State and Party in Eastern Europe* (Durham, NC: Duke University Press, 1985), pp. 121–137, 388–393. For comparisons with Gheorghiu-Dej, see my "Political Leadership in Rumania Under the Communists," *International Journal of Rumanian Studies*, 5, No. 1 (1987), 1–31.

4. Kenneth Jowitt, *Revolutionary Breakthroughs and National Development: The Case of Romania, 1944–1965* (Berkeley: University of California Press, 1971), p. 273. The literature on autonomy in Romania foreign policy is voluminous; see especially the following and the sources cited: Aurel Braun, *Romanian Foreign Policy Since 1965* (New York: Praeger, 1978); Robert Farlow, "Romanian Foreign Policy: A Case of Partial Alignment," *Problems of Communism*, 20, no. 6 (November–December 1971), 99–113; Ronald H. Linden, *Bear and Foxes* (Boulder, CO: East European Quarterly, 1979), and his *Communist States and International Change: Romania and Yugoslavia in Comparative Perspective* (Boston: Allen and Unwin, 1987); and Robert Weiner, *Romania at the United Nations* (New York: Praeger, 1984).

5. As William Zimmerman put it in his "Hierarchical Regional Systems and the Politics of System Boundaries," *International Organization*, 26 (Winter 1978), 32.

6. See, e.g., Christopher D. Jones, *Soviet Influence in Eastern Europe: Political Autonomy and the Warsaw Pact* (New York: Praeger, 1981).

7. For Ceauşescu's views on any subject, see his collected speeches, Nicolae Ceauşescu, *Romania on the Way . . .* (Bucharest: Meridiane, 1969–); over 20 volumes have appeared in many languages.

8. See U.S. Department of Commerce, International Trade Administration, Office of East-West Policy and Planning, "U.S.-Romanian Trade Trends, January–June 1981" (October 1981), p. 2. On Romanian autarky, see Marvin R. Jackson, "Romania," in U.S. Congress, Joint Economic Committee, *East European Economic Assessment*, Part I, *Country Studies, 1980* (Washington, DC: 97th Congress, 1st Session, 1981), especially pp. 269–270, 285, and his "Perspectives on Romania's Economic Development," in Nelson, ed., *Romania in the 1980s*, esp. p. 271.

9. On the post-1975 economic problems, see Marvin R. Jackson, "Roman-

ia's Debt Crisis: Its Causes and Consequences," U.S. Congress, Joint Economic Committee, *East European Economies: Slow Growth in the 1980s*, Vol. 3, *Country Studies on Eastern Europe and Yugoslavia* (Washington, D.C.: 99th Congress, 2nd Session, March 28, 1986), pp. 489–542; on per capita foreign debt, see p. 494. For the origins of these policies in the 1960s, see J. Michael Montias, *Economic Development in Communist Rumania* (Cambridge: MIT Press, 1967); note his perceptive warnings about the future.

10. Other factors, of course, also have worked against such an explosion. See below, especially Note 23 and the accompanying text.

11. On these issues, see Jackson, "Romania's Debt."

12. The picture is much more complicated than we can describe here; see *ibid.*, pp. 526–534.

13. Official retail prices in 1982, e.g., rose an average of 17 percent, and retail prices of agricultural goods were up by about 35 percent; *ibid.*, p. 527. Descriptions are from my own visits in May 1982 and September 1984.

14. See, e.g., the summaries of Political Executive Committee meetings in *Scînteia*, 24 July 1981 and 23 January 1982.

15. On the NEFM, see Alan Smith, "The Romanian Industrial Enterprise," in Ian Jeffries, ed., *The Industrial Enterprise in Eastern Europe* (New York: Praeger, 1981), pp. 63–83, and Jackson, *Romania's Debt*, pp. 534–538.

16. In a speech to a Central Committee working conference, *Scînteia*, 1 June 1980.

17. Jackson, *Romania's Debt*, p. 493.

18. On the *acord global*, see Jackson, *Romania's Debt*, p. 536; on 1987, see *Scînteia*, 6 October 1987, and Radio Free Europe Research, *Romanian SR/12* (6 November 1987), pp. 6–7.

19. *Scînteia*, 21 November 1981, and 22–25 November 1986.

20. For succinct descriptions, see Michael Shafir, "The Historical Background to Rural Resettlement," and Dan Ionescu, "Bucharest's Hinterland: A Test Ground for Rural Resettlement," in Radio Free Europe Research, *Romanian SR/10* (23 August 1988), pp. 3–15.

21. For evaluations of the military and police, see William Crowther, "'Ceauşescuism' and Civil-Military Relations in Romania," *Armed Forces and Society*, 15 (Winter 1989), pp. 202–25; Alex Alexiev, "Party-Military Relations in Eastern Europe: The Case of Romania," in Roman Kolkowicz and Andrzej Korbonski, eds., *Soldiers, Peasants, and Bureaucrats: Civil-Military Relations in Communist and Modernizing Societies* (London: George Allen and Unwin, 1982), pp. 199–227; Walter M. Bacon Jr., "Civil-Military Relations in Romania," *Studies in Comparative Communism*, 11 (Autumn 1978), pp. 237–249, and his "Romanian Secret Police," in Jonathan R. Adelman, ed., *Terror and Communist Politics: The Role of the Secret Police in Communist States* (Boulder, CO: Westview, 1984), pp. 135–154.

22. On Olteanu, see also Michael Shafir, "Former Defense Minister Appointed Ideological Chief," Radio Free Europe Research, *Romanian SR/8* (23 June 1988), pp. 3–5.

23. Both Michael Shafir and Steven Sampson have provided perceptive anal-

yses of political quiescence in Romania; see Shafir, *Romania,* ch. 9, and his "Political Culture, Intellectual Dissent, and Intellectual Concent: The Case of Romania," *Orbis,* 27 (Summer 1983), 393–420; Sampson, "Muddling Through in Romania (Or Why the Mamaliga Doesn't Explode)," paper delivered at the Second International Conference of Romanian Studies, Avignon, October 1983, "Is Romania the Next Poland?" *Critique* (Glasgow), 16 (1983), 139–144, and "Regime and Society in Rumania," *International Journal of Rumanian Studies,* 5, no. 1 (1987), 41–51.

24. It is often impossible to tell the difference until the individual's next career move.

25. *Scînteia,* 28 April 1968.

26. As the term is used by George W. Breslauer in *Khrushchev and Brezhnev As Leaders: Building Authority in Soviet Politics* (London: George Allen and Unwin, 1982).

27. On Romanian historiography and the use of history by Ceauşescu, see Robert R. King, *History of the Romanian Communist Party* (Stanford: Hoover, 1980), especially the Introduction.

28. Particularly good on the plight of Romanian historians and the flights of fancy is Vlad Georgescu, *Politică şi istorie: cazul comuniştilor români 1944– 1977* (Munich: Ion Dumitru Verlag, 1981).

29. *Scînteia,* 23 August 1968.

30. I spent the second half of 1974 in Romania and heard such remarks many times.

31. On this point, see Jeremy T. Paltiel, "The Cult of Personality: Some Comparative Reflections on Political Culture in Leninist Regimes," *Studies in Comparative Communism,* 16 (Spring/Summer 1983), 49–50.

32. For example, Czechoslovakia's founding statesman Thomas Masaryk visited the United States on a number of occasions, was married to an American, and his ideas of democracy were very much influenced by American concepts of liberty and democracy.

33. The substantial Polish-American population—which is vocal, organized, and politically active in the United States—is an important factor in U.S. government interest in and attention to Poland. An indication of the lack of such support for Romanian-American relations are the figures on individual Americans who claimed a single ethnic ancestry in the 1980 census: Polish–8,228,037; Czech–1,892,456; Hungarian–1,776,902; Slovak–776,806; and Romanian– 315,238. U.S. Bureau of the Census, *Supplementary Report: Ancestry of the Population by State, 1980* (Washington, DC, 1983), p. 20.

34. Romania's autonomous foreign policy has been the subject of a great deal of description and analysis. A discussion of that policy and the reasons for it are beyond the scope of this chapter. The following are some of the most thoughtful works: R. L. Braham, "Rumania, On to the Separate Path," *Problems of Communism,* 13, No. 3 (May–June 1964), 14–24; J. F. Brown, "Rumania Steps Out of Line," *Survey,* No. 49 (October 1963), pp. 19–34; R. V. Burks, "The Rumanian National Deviation: An Accounting," in Kurt London, ed., *Eastern Eu-*

*rope in Transition* (Baltimore: Johns Hopkins Press, 1966); Robert Farlow, "Romanian Foreign Policy: A Case of Partial Alignment," *Problems of Communism*, 20, No. 6 (November–December 1971), 54–63; Stephen Fischer-Galati, *The New Rumania: From People's Democracy to Socialist Republic* (Cambridge: MIT Press, 1967); David Floyd, *Rumania: Russia's Dissident Ally* (New York: Praeger, 1965); Graeme J. Gill, "Rumania's Background to Autonomy," *Survey*, No. 87 (Summer 1967), pp. 94–113; George Gross, "Rumania: Fruits of Autonomy," *Problems of Communism*, 15, No. 1 (January–February 1966), 16–28; and Kenneth Jowitt, *Revolutionary Breakthroughs and National Development: The Case of Romania, 1944–1965* (Berkeley: University of California Press, 1971), pp. 198–272. For my own analysis of Romanian foreign policy autonomy, see *History of the Romanian Communist Party* (Stanford: Hoover, 1980), pp. 135–149; "Autonomy and Detente: The Problems of Rumanian Foreign Policy," *Survey*, No. 91–92 (Spring–Summer 1974), pp. 105–120; "Romania's Struggle for an Autonomous Foreign Policy," *The World Today*, 35, No. 8 (July 1979), 340–348.

35. Henry Kissinger, *The White House Years* (Boston: Little, Brown, 1979), p. 156.

36. For a discussion of the background to the Carter administration's policy statement on Eastern Europe, see Zbigniew Brzezinski, *Power and Principle: Memoirs of the National Security Adviser, 1977–1981* (New York: Farrar, Straus and Giroux, 1983), pp. 296–297.

37. Quoted in William G. Hyland, Karl Kaiser, and Kiroshi Kimura, *Prospects for East-West Relations*, Triangle Papers, No. 31 (New York, Tokyo, and Paris: The Trilateral Commission, 1986), p. 33.

38. U.S. Congress, House of Representatives, Committee on Foreign Affairs, *United States-Romanian Relations and Most-Favored-Nation [MFN] Status for Romania* (Washington, DC: Government Printing Office, 30 July 1987).

39. See U.S. Congress, House of Representatives, *Miscellaneous International Affairs Authorization Act of 1988* (Washington, DC: May 3, 1988), 100th Congress, 2nd Session, Report 100-594, p. 7.

40. *New York Times*, 27 June 1987.

41. This is not to imply an uncritical acceptance of developments in that the Soviet Union Human Rights conditions are significantly improved over what they have been in the past; nevertheless, Soviet human rights conditions still do not meet Western standards, and there is room for a great deal of improvement. Progress thus far has been dramatic in view of past Soviet practice, however.

# Chapter 8

# BULGARIA

## UNEASY IN THE 1990s?

*John D. Bell*

Since establishment of the communist regime, Bulgaria's leaders have stressed the close relationship between their country and the Soviet Union. In Todor Zhivkov's imagery, Bulgaria and the USSR share a "single circulatory system" and "the Bulgarian watch runs on Moscow time." And such hyperbole has a solid foundation in reality. Alone among the communist-ruled states of Eastern Europe, Bulgaria has never experienced a crisis in its relations with the USSR. The Bulgarian and Soviet economies are tightly linked; USSR universities and higher institutes train the country's elite; and Bulgaria's military security rests on its membership in the Warsaw Pact. Zhivkov, whose climb to power depended heavily on the backing of Khrushchev, has ever been an acute Kremlinologist, sensitive to shifts in Soviet policy, and ready to adjust course in Bulgaria accordingly. Consequently, it was to be expected that the ideas associated with *perestroika, glasnost'*, and "new thinking" would have a major impact on Bulgarian public life. Indeed, they have, but Bulgaria has not adjusted easily to the new situation. No consensus has emerged on how to apply the Soviet experience to the Bulgarian context. Zhivkov has blown hot and cold on issues of reform, and there is at least some evidence that he has not been fully in control of the situation. Outside the government, elements in the population have seized the moment to exhibit a degree of independence unprecedented in the country. The party leadership appears divided, and the role of the USSR in shaping events, and even its attitude toward Bulgarian developments, is far from clear. Under these

circumstances, it is difficult to predict the course of events in the immediate future, but an examination of developments to the present time
does allow the identification of factors that should to be influential over
the long term.

## The Initial Phase

Changes in the USSR were reflected in Bulgaria almost immediately after
the death of Brezhnev. In its traditional, almost mechanical way, the government inaugurated campaigns against alcohol abuse, corruption, and
bureaucratic formalism that echoed the measures adopted by Andropov.
There were rumors that Zhivkov was relieved by Andropov's death and
the selection of Chernenko, which promised a reprise of the Brezhnev
era.[1] Mikhail Gorbachev's succession, however, created a new environment marked by direct Soviet criticism of Bulgarian performance, particularly in the economic sphere. The progress of Gorbachev's domestic
reforms, particularly the lifting of censorship on frank discussion of the
reality and legacy of Stalinism, had a deeply unsettling effect in Sofia.

Bulgaria initially responded to the new situation with modest moves in
the reorganization of economic administration and legalization of private
enterprise in the service sector.[2] But at the Bulgarian Communist party
(BCP) Central Committee plenum in July 1987, Zhivkov dramatically
embraced *perestroika* and appeared to position himself at the head of a
movement for radical reform. The achievements of Bulgarian socialism
have been immense, he said in his opening address, but the present system "has exhausted itself" and the time has come for a "180 degree change
of course." Declaring war on "bureaucratization and social deforma-
tions," he announced that Bulgaria had entered a period of transition from
"power on behalf of the people to power through the people." To implement this new program, he outlined sweeping changes in economic
and political administration that included major structural reforms and the
adoption of the principle of multiple candidacies for elective office at
every level.[3]

Within the next two months the government scrapped the system of
economic administration that had been set up only one year before, creating in its place a new Ministry of the Economy and Planning with extensive powers over the economic sphere. It was placed in the hands of
Stoian Ovcharov, a 45-year-old specialist in biotechnology who, at the
time of his appointment, was not even a candidate member of the BCP
Central Committee.[4] In August 1987 the National Assembly rapidly pushed

through a major reform of territorial organization, replacing the 28 districts with nine *oblasti* (provinces) governments. Although this consolidation was supposed to take place gradually over the course of a year, in what amounted to a virtual coup d'état directed against the district leaderships, the Politburo proceeded to implement the reform at once and appointed "temporary" *oblast'* party committees and people's councils. Only about one-third of the local government officials received appointments at the *oblast'* level, and the rest were urged to find work at lower administrative levels or in economic enterprises.

Zhivkov also struck at what he called "pomposity, megalomania, and needless extravagance" by reforming state rituals and doing away with the slogans, billboards, and portraits customarily placed on buildings and along roadways, approving the removal of his own statue from his native Pravets. These cosmetic changes were accompanied by the more significant promise that in the future state decorations would be awarded only for merit rather than age or length of service. Because such awards carry direct financial benefits to the recipients and give preference in admission to desirable programs of study for their children, they have constituted an important mechanism by which members of the elite pass on their privileges to their progeny, and they were deeply resented by citizens who are not so well connected.

Outside of official circles, *glasnost'* and *perestroika* stimulated a more vigorous press and other public initiatives. Several newspapers, particularly the trade union daily *Trud,* exposed cases of high-level corruption, and the press in general became more open in its reporting on economic shortcomings, crime, and other social problems. Some members of the intelligentsia, clearly impressed by the assault by Soviet intellectuals on Stalinism, called for a similar openness in dealing with the Bulgarian past. The English-language *Sofia News* inaugurated a series, "Remembrance," devoted to examining "the fate of Bulgarian political emigrés in the USSR and of the functionaries of the international communist and worker's movement who were repressed during the years of the personality cult." It began with the memoirs of Krustiu (Christian) Rakovsky's niece, who recounted her uncle's arrest in 1938 and called on historians to discover the truth about his death.[5] The well-known writer Evtim Evtimov, editor of *Literaturen front,* called upon the party to publish the complete stenographic record of the April 1956 plenum that began Bulgaria's de-Stalinization process, the complete records of the investigation and trial of Traicho Kostov in 1949, and the records of the 1942 interrogation of Anton Ivanov by Bulgarian authorities. Each of these events is surrounded by a cloud of myth in party tradition, and the first two involved party leaders, including Zhivkov himself, who are still on the scene.[6]

It would soon be proven that such manifestations of *glasnost'* far exceeded the limits that the party leadership would be willing to accept. But what probably seemed even more threatening was the appearance of "voluntary associations." These were first noticeable among young people, who ignored Komsomol activities in favor of spontaneously forming clubs devoted to Western rock stars of fashion. A small but open dissident movement also surfaced, calling the attention of the Western press to human rights abuses.[7] Far more striking, because of the breadth of its support, was the emergence of an ecological movement focused around the city of Russe.[8]

In 1982 a Soviet-built chlorine and sodium combine was opened at Giurgiu on the Romanian side of the Danube River. Owing to methods of operation and to prevailing winds, it immediately created a major health problem for the approximately 200,000 inhabitants of Russe, Bulgaria's fourth largest city, where the incidence of lung disease and birth defects rose to catastrophic levels. The Sofia government, asserting its close, fraternal relations with Bucharest, maintained that the problem would be resolved in a cooperative spirit, but apparently has been completely unable to persuade the Romanians to reduce the level of pollution or even to accept responsibility.[9] Spontaneous demonstrations reportedly broke out in Russe during the fall of 1987, and these were followed by the formation of a committee for defense of the city that gained broad support from the country's intelligentsia. Although the full membership of the committee cannot be determined, some of its participants included prominent members of Bulgaria's artistic and scientific elite and even important party figures. Among its leaders, it is possible to identify Neshka Robeva, the coach of Bulgaria's world championship rhythmic gymnastics team. She is a native of Russe, who had earlier become the first deputy ever to vote against a government-sponsored bill in the National Assembly when she opposed the downgrading of Russe's status in the territorial reorganization; the artist Svetlin Rusev, director of the National Gallery of Fine Arts; and the wife of Politburo-member Stanko Todorov, Sonia Bakish-Todorova, who had been dismissed as editor of the women's journal *Zhenata dnes* for her liberal views in 1981. The committee also clearly had the support of the journals *Literaturen front* and *Narodna kultura* and of many representatives in the medical community, including Evgeni Nazarov, chief physician at Russe's municipal hospital.

In December 1987 and January 1988 the committee held an art exhibition in Russe, called "Ecology—Russe '87," displaying the works of local painters, sculptors, and engravers depicting in the most striking terms the suffering of the region and its people. The exhibit included displays of scientific charts and graphs showing the levels of chlorine pollution in the air and on land, and the rising incidence of lung disease and birth defects. The exhibit was described by *Narodna kultura,* which also reprinted the statistical evidence. Soon afterward, the Union of Bulgarian Artists published an appeal to the country's intellectuals to take action to save a city living "in a state of chemical warfare" and warned of a "loss of faith" in the government's ability to improve the situation. It also quoted letters from Russe mothers comparing the city to Chernobyl in the USSR or Bhopal in India and pleading with authorities to "save the lives of their children." Several days before a scheduled meeting of Bulgarian and Romanian prime ministers on 20 February 1988, a mass demonstration was held in Russe that occasioned a strongly worded article in *Literaturen front,* the organ of the Bulgarian Writers' Union, attributing the unrest in the city to the suffering of its population and to censorship that "did not permit even a small outlet to relieve the people's souls from all the accumulated pain."

## Retrenchment

Although critical of the government's lack of action, those involved in the Russe protest movement committed no overt act that could reasonably be described as critical of the communist system. Nevertheless, the unprecedented level of independent and spontaneous activity led to a major crackdown during the spring and summer of 1988. Signs of the party leadership's wavering commitment to reform had already begun to appear in the fall of 1987. There were rumors then of widespread discontent among officials displaced by the territorial reform. Nor, apparently, was there unity at the highest level in the party. On at least two occasions, high-ranking officials complained in print that the public positions in favor of change taken by some party leaders masked skepticism and outright opposition which were expressed openly in meetings behind closed doors.[10]

In October 1987 Zhivkov had been suddenly summoned to Moscow for consultations with Gorbachev. Although their meeting went unreported in the Bulgarian press, TASS stated that the Soviet leader had emphasized the importance of maintaining the leading role of the party during the reform process. There was speculation that Gorbachev was disturbed by the chaotic character of Bulgarian restructuring. In his speeches to a Central Committee plenum in November 1987 and at the party conference in January 1988, Zhivkov took positions far more restrained than those he had advocated the preceding July.

Much had been expected from the party conference, which Zhivkov suggested would concretize and implement his July proposals. In any event, the conference took no action at all. Zhivkov proposed that fundamental party reforms be deferred to the 14th BCP Congress in 1991. The documents and resolutions presented to the conference included an explicit recognition of the right of citizens to form independent groups and associations, but only insofar as they eschewed "anarchy, chaos, and demagoguery."[11]

The March 1988 elections for regional and municipal peoples' councils were supposed to have been the first fulfillment of Zhivkov's pledge of multiple candidacies in every electoral contest. However, when they were held, more than one candidate appeared on the ballot in only one-fifth of the cases. In the rest, local election commissions disqualified all but a single nominee.[12]

Further signs of retrenchment came later that same month, with a series of purges in the intellectual community.[13] Damian Obreskov, editor-in-chief of *Trud,* was removed from his post after the publication of a hard-hitting series of articles on local corruption. Their author, journalist Georgi Tambuev, was also fired and subsequently expelled from the party. Evtim Evtimov was forced to resign as editor of *Literaturen front* amid charges that he had committed "literary-sociological demogoguery." Svetlin Rusev was dismissed as director of the National Gallery of Fine Arts. It was also reported, in the Chinese press, that Stanko Todorov's wife had been expelled from the party because of her involvement in the Russe events and for other activities.[14]

These purges were followed by the announcement that a Central Committee plenum would be held to discuss restructuring in intellectual life. At the end of April 1988, Zhivkov issued his "Considerations" of this problem, defining some clear limits on permissible activities.[15] According to this document, problems now receiving public attention "in some socialist countries" had long ago been dealt with in Bulgaria, specifically at the famous April 1956 plenum. Some elements among the Bulgarian intelligentsia, Zhivkov continued, had fallen under the misapprehension that the experience of restructuring in other states would automatically be transferred to Bulgaria. This was especially true regarding certain "sensational" aspects of the past that were being revealed in the USSR. But, he continued, restructuring must proceed in accordance with specific conditions prevailing in each country, so that despite Bulgaria's tradition of looking to Soviet experience, there was no need to repeat specific USSR measures. The Bulgarian media should understand that openness and restructuring mean "to support the new" and that the country does not need "complaints, moaning, and groaning which form an incorrect attitude toward restructuring."

On the issue of independent associations, Zhivkov stated that Bulgaria welcomed the idea of "socialist pluralism," but that it had to be *socialist* pluralism based on "our principles, ethics and ideals." Any other course would endanger the socialist way of life and invite anarchy, which "we will not tolerate." Zhivkov was particularly severe in his criticism of the Union of Bulgarian Artists, whose governing board "took 'fateful decisions' outside the agenda and without any preliminary discussion, concerning the relations between Bulgaria and another state," adding that "restructuring in these conditions is impossible."

Zhivkov called on the party to direct "socialist pluralism," stating that it was "a time-honored tradition of our party that communists be the initiators of various voluntary organizations." Moreover, he criticized the primary BCP organizations in the cultural unions for allowing the situation to get out of hand. Central Committee secretary Stoian Mikhailov, in charge of ideological affairs, was condemned by name for his failure to ensure party leadership in this sphere. In conclusion, Zhivkov, declared that the BCP welcomed and encouraged the growing activization of public consciousness, leading to creative discussion and dialogues. "But the tone is set by the party, by the Central Committee."

Apparently, Zhivkov's hard line did not have unanimous support in the BCP leadership, because the plenum was delayed for more than a month. When it did meet, in addition to the expected dismissals of Mikhailov from the secretariat and Svetlin Rusev from the Central Committee, it removed Stanko Todorov from the Politburo and Chudomir Alexandrov from both the Politburo and the Secretariat. A second plenum in December added to the disgrace of Alexandrov and Mikhailov by removing them from the Central Committee "for reasons of expediency." It also appointed two full members of the Politburo: Ivan Panev, head of the Sofia party organization, and Colonel General Dimitŭr Stoianov, minister of internal affairs since 1973. Stoianov was given responsibility for party cadres and was replaced at the interior ministry by Georgi Tanev, who made his mark as a ruthless administrator while head of the Kurdzhali party organization when forced Bulgarianization was imposed on the region's ethnic Turks.[16] These appointments seemed to indicate Zhivkov's determination to follow a hard line.

The government also inspired the formation of two new "independent" national oganizations: a Committee on the Rights of Citizens and a Committee on the Environment, both led by the usual reliable luminaries. These "company unions" seemed clearly intended to put the human rights and environmental movements under official direction.

In the past, Bulgaria's intellectuals have been easily cowed by demonstrations of party anger. This time, however, they did not retreat into passivity. In November 1988, 110 individuals from literary, scientific, and artistic fields, including many of the most prominent figures in Bulgarian culture, met at Sofia University to form a "Club for the Support of *Perestroika* and *Glasnost'* in Bulgaria." Declaring their intention to act openly and in complete accord with the Bulgarian constitution, they asserted their intention to remain independent of all outside authority while advancing discussion of economic and environmental problems and issues of human rights and civil liberties at this "crucial stage in the democratization of our country."[17] The government had issued no official reaction at the time of this writing, although it was reported that some members of the club had been subjected to police harassment.

## Prospects

Whereas at the time of this writing the regime seems to be engaged in a holding action against the further impact of *perestroika* and *glasnost'*, significant factors exist in the Bulgarian environment that favor their continuation. The most important, of course, is the unfolding of the reform process in the USSR. Soviet publications on the USSR's history, visiting Soviet intellectuals, and Moscow television reports on the struggle for reform have already had a profound effect on the Bulgarian public and undoubtedly will continue to do so even if the USSR makes no direct effort to dislodge Zhivkov and his coterie. Bulgaria's economic problems and the environmental crisis in Russe will not disappear by themselves and cannot be ignored.

At the same time Bulgaria is under pressure from the East, it must take increasing account of attitudes in the West. In order to carry through its program of economic modernization, Bulgaria has made strenuous efforts to improve its economic relations with Western Europe and the United States. During 1988 Bulgaria began negotiations to join GATT and to work toward a relationship with the EEC. In these circumstances, it has become more difficult for the Bulgarian regime to ignore Western pressure in the field of human rights, and there is ample evidence that the attention of the Western press and statements of concern by Western leaders have provided some constraint on the government in its handling of its critics.

Changes in the international environment are not the only factors at work in Bulgaria. The country's long period of political stability and Zhivkov's extraordinary tenure have obscured significant changes in Bulgarian society that have occurred since the communist regime was established. The BCP leadership was committed to a program of modernization, at least in the sense of fostering industrial development and of participating in the "scientific-technological revolution." To be sure, this was only one side of its activity. The goal of consolidating political power and liquidating class enemies brought a degree of economic disruption and struck at artisan and manufacturing groups whose knowledge and skills had been the backbone of the prewar nonagricultural economy. Extensive reliance on Soviet experience led to the adoption of organizational forms and investment priorities that were not always suited to Bulgarian conditions. Still, despite great human and material cost, communist Bulgaria undertook the process of constructing the foundations of a modern industrial economy, attainment of which would become its proudest achievement and chief claim to legitimacy.

An American economist has estimated that Bulgaria's growth in national income between 1951 and 1967 averaged 9.6 percent annually, and between 1967 and 1974 about 7.5 percent. This was accompanied by substantial structural change; the share of industry in national income rose from 37 percent in 1950 to 51 percent in 1972. By 1979 it had reached 58 percent. The late 1970s saw worldwide economic retrenchment, but the Bulgarian economy continued to grow, although at a slower rate of between 4 and 5 percent.[18] Bulgaria is no longer the primitive, agrarian state that it was when Zhivkov came to power. It is predominantly an industrial and urbanized nation.

The drive for economic modernization demanded creation of a class of people with scientific, technical, and managerial skills to operate and develop a modern economy. This led the regime to place a heavy emphasis on education. Whereas many skilled teachers and professionals were purged during the party's consolidation of power, in the long run this factor was more than offset by the sheer physical expansion of the educational system. At the end of the 1970s, with 86 percent of the eligible population group enrolled in secondary schools, Bulgaria was in seventh place among the world's nations in this category, just behind France and ahead of the United States. With 22 percent of the population between the ages of 20 and 24 studying at institutions of higher education, Bulgaria ranked ninth in the world, just ahead of Sweden. At the end of the 1970s, it was eleventh in terms of scientific and engineering personnel on a per capital basis (230 per 10,000).[19] The contribution of the USSR to this educational development was not inconsiderable. In 1980 it was reported that more than 8,500 Bulgarian citizens had received a higher education in the Soviet Union and that more than 1,250 had defended doctoral and candidate-level dissertations.[20]

The point here is that Bulgaria has produced in the generation born after World War II a significant element that is both more skilled and more sophisticated in its outlook and ambitions. It is, for the most part, neither alienated nor unpatriotic; indeed, its members show considerable pride in what "tiny Bulgaria" has accomplished, particularly in comparison with Yugoslavia, Romania, Greece, and Turkey, which provide the standards against which Bulgarians usually measure themselves. However, many of these same individuals are increasingly inclined to view the rigid "Marxist fundamentalism" of the older generation and the bureaucratic control over society that it exercises as irrelevant to contemporary life or even an obstacle to further progress.

Whereas the greater sophistication of the generation now coming to maturity is difficult to measure precisely, it can certainly be felt. In recent years Sofia has seen the opening of an aerobic dance center, its first Chinese restaurant, and the transformation of Vitosha Boulevard into a "Balkan Via Veneto" with numerous outlets for Western fashion (including one for hush puppies, which received considerable attention in the national press). In Freedom Park fashionably dressed younger citizens can be seen playing tennis or walking well-groomed dogs, unmistakable signs of an emerging *embourgeoisement*. Members of this class aspire to a better and fuller life, a desire that has both material and nonmaterial dimensions. The present regime has taken some steps to satisfy the former. In the mid-1970s, when the press debated the legitimacy of a desire for "luxury" goods, Zhivkov weighed in on the side of luxury. The current salary reform has approximately doubled the wages of technical and managerial specialists in comparison with other categories, like industrial workers. But it remains to be seen whether it can satisfy its desires for greater freedom in such areas as access to information and entertainment or for greater autonomy in personal and professional life.

Another factor, whose impact is difficult to measure precisely, is the growing influence of women in the generation that has been raised under the communist regime. After World War II, Marxist ideology regarding the equality of women and economic necessity combined to oppose traditional values inherited from the centuries of Ottoman domination. The principle of legal equality for women was included in the Dimitrov constitution, and in subsequent years the government introduced a network of measures (including the legalization of abortion, institutional child care, legislation protecting the employment rights of pregnant women and new mothers) to adapt to and to encourage the changing position of women in Bulgarian society.

The impact of the evolving role of Bulgarian women has so far been small at the highest political levels. Only two women, Tsola Dragoicheva and Liudmila Zhivkova, have sat on the Politburo, and only 12 of the 195 full members of the Central Committee elected in 1986 were females. But in other areas of life, particularly in the professions, change has been much more visible. At the end of the 1970s, some 53 percent of Bulgaria's university students were women. This was the third highest percentage in the world, behind only Kuwait and the Philippines.[21] The extent to which a "gender gap" may exist in the political attitudes of Bulgarian men and women is difficult to measure. There is some evidence, based on a reading of the Bulgarian press and on personal observation, that professional women tend to be highly oriented toward practical issues and less "ideological" than their male counterparts.

Bulgarian women, such as the writer Blaga Dimitrova, Neshka Robeva and Sonia Bakish-Todorova, have been very prominent among the activists for change. To a considerable degree, Liudmila Zhivkova may be seen as an advocate of *perestroika* even before the end of the Brezhnev era. Born in 1942, Zhivkova specialized in history at Sofia University during the late 1960s and spent a year at Oxford in 1970. After completion of her dissertation in 1971 and the death of her mother, she assumed the role of Bulgaria's "first lady" and became increasingly prominent in public life. She was particularly active in intellectual affairs, organizing the Committee on Culture with power over education, publishing, and international cultural relations, as well as traditional cultural fields. She became a full member of the Central Committee in 1976 and three years later, at age 36, she was made a full member of the Politburo, the first of her generation to be so honored. As Bulgaria's chief cultural official, she devoted more material and political support to scholarly and intellectual enterprises than they had ever received before, loosened censorship, and vastly expanded Bulgaria's cultural ties with the West. As a devotee of Eastern religions and certain forms of mysticism, she gave little more than lip service to traditional ideology, and she encouraged both the cultural avant-garde and the exploration of traditional nationalist themes. Moreover, she furthered the careers of numerous cultural liberals, many of whom were purged after her untimely death in 1981. Although initially derided as a "princess" who exploited her father's position, Zhivkova won immense popularity among Bulgaria's younger generation, and her death was sincerely mourned. Her outlook and policies may provide some preview of the course Bulgaria is likely to follow, as the next generation of Bulgarian men and women move into positions of power.

## PROJECTIONS

### Jack R. Perry

At the close of the 1980s, with a new president in Washington, a strong leader in Moscow facing the discouraging facts of life beyond the slogans, and the senior leader of the Communist world apparently in lasting control at Sofia, what are the challenges and opportunities in the American-Bulgarian relationship? Those who know how surprising Bulgaria can be will find the question more interesting than some might expect.

Let us consider, first, Bulgaria's situation today; second, its condition within the Soviet sphere of interest; and third, its relationship with the United States.

### Bulgaria Today

Scholars, and people who come from those countries lying between the Gulf of Finland and the Aegean and Adriatic seas, dislike the term "Eastern Europe," which somehow manages to imply that the 140 million people to the west of the Russians and Belorussians and Ukrainians are part of Eastern Slavdom. These same people should also dislike any analysis of Bulgaria that places it with Hungary and Romania in the so-called southern tier, as if the ideological division of Europe was of primary importance. I must confess that during my two years in Sofia, I found Bulgaria to be more Balkan than Communist. And I believe that the realistic way to look at Bulgaria, considering its geography, history, and the outlook of its people, is as part of the Balkans, part of southeastern Europe. My framework of hope in this section is that over the next few years we shall see a diminution of the Soviet hold over its neighbors, a movement toward the *l'Europe des patries* of which De Gaulle spoke, progress toward erasing artificial lines across the map of Europe. This hope, of course, brings with it difficulties and fears as well. The consolidation of the European communities by the end of 1992 poses a particular challenge to the desire in the East to statesmanship—and concern for Eastern neighbors—ought to be able to meet even this challenge.

If we are to begin within the postwar framework and look at Bulgaria as being east of the Iron Curtain, remaining a loyal member of the Warsaw Pact, then we should also keep in mind that Bulgaria is the only Pact member non-contiguous to the Soviet Union. If we consider Bulgaria as part of "the southern tier," then viewed from Moscow, its strategic position is sensitive, for if it were to defect, unreliable Romania would become the southern flank, and the situation of the Soviet Union as regards Yugoslavia and Greece and Turkey would be much changed. Those geographic ideas are still important, but becoming less significant, I believe, in the Gorbachev era.

Historically, Bulgaria has enmities with the Turks, and with the Yugoslavs and Greeks. Newcomers to the area sometimes forget these by focusing totally on the Bulgarian-Soviet relationship. But people in the Balkans have long memories. The first words Todor Zhivkov said to a new West German ambassador in the late 1970s were, "We fought together in two world wars, and it was disastrous." Zhivkov is keenly aware not only that the Soviet Union put the regime he heads into power, but also that the *pax Sovietica* has provided shelter for Bulgaria from potential enemies on its borders. Like other Bulgarian Communists, he refers to the tsarist Russian role in the liberation from the Turks as well. He may well know that this debt must be exaggerated in their propaganda, for the popular feeling toward the Russians has slipped into something like apathy if not dislike.

Zhivkov also realizes that the economic progress Bulgaria has made since World War II was helped enormously by the Soviet Union. There is little doubt that Bulgaria received more benefits from the Soviet relationship than any other country in Eastern Europe. If he looks around at the economic ailments of Romania or Yugoslavia, Zhivkov must feel some pride in what Bulgaria has accomplished in industrialization and urbanization since the 1940s. The price was of course high, politically. But the accomplishments were real.

U.S. Department of State analysts today call Bulgaria "the most stable country in Eastern Europe." This is partly because the pot is boiling in most countries—perhaps only Hungary and East Germany can also be considered relatively stable. It is also because Zhivkov, at age 77, has been in power for a long, long time, and provides—with his ability to keep potential rivals out of his way—a continuity that may be depressing to some but is certainly solid. His talent for picking clever lieutenants with economic experience and ability also pays off for the country.

A word about popular attitudes and expectations. First, of all the European countries, none suffers more from slanted stereotypes than Bulgaria. The popular American image of a grim place looking like an imitation Russia, shackled by Stalinist policies, is wildly wrong. After serving in Moscow and Prague, and traveling in every East European country except Albania, I found the Bulgarians refreshingly well educated, sophisticated, independent-minded, and Western oriented. Their old gratitude to Russia, the bond of the shared orthodox tradition and the anti-Ottoman history, even the loudly proclaimed communist allegiance to Moscow—these did not alter the fact of Bulgaria's healthy pride in its own national identity. Or its leaders' ability to discern true national interests along with the personal benefits of allegiance to Moscow. (I remember Zhivkov telling a group of U.S. congressmen that he would switch allegiances if we in the West would give him a better deal than the Soviets gave. It was a joke, but can one picture Jaruzelski or Jakeš making that joke?)

From my own time in Sofia, I think of Liudmila Zhivkova, the daughter of Todor Zhivkov, as a kind of dramatic symbol of Bulgarian identity, with all the strains and stresses that identity puts upon its ties to Moscow. Zhivkova was the tsarina of culture when I was in Bulgaria, a very powerful person politically, a controversial figure within the leadership and among the populace. Many Bulgarians resented her unorthodox ways, her attachment to yoga, her intense intellectualism that came close to a kind of spiritualism. Some may also have resented, but many applauded silently—and supported her demonstrative affirmation of Bulgaria's cultural orientation toward the West. Having done graduate work in England, she found it easy to be at home with Western culture, and not so easy to be at home with local communists. In her invitation of foreign guests, in the exhibits and other events she sponsored, her pro-Western outlook became increasingly clear in the late 1970s. Zhivkova was plainly the guiding spirit behind planning for a grand celebration in 1981 of Bulgaria's 1,300th year of statehood—the oldest continually existing nation in Europe, she and her supporters liked to boast—and to those of us watching the preparations it was also plain that the Soviets were having much trouble accepting her plans. Tension over these anniversary preparations went much deeper, we diplomats felt, than could be proved on the surface. In any event, Zhivkova's untimely death in 1981 was a shock, and clearly so to her father, who withdrew from public life for some time, and had to be pushed back into activity by his colleagues. There were rumors in Sofia that the stresses caused by Zhivkova's Western orientation—and the opposition to it in Moscow and by Moscow loyalists in Bulgaria—played a role in Liudmila Zhivkova's demise. No doubt we will never know. But the drama of her life and death underlined the drama of Bulgaria's tension between East and West, and the fundamental fact that Sofia is not a suburb of Moscow.

## Bulgaria and the Soviet Sphere

What is Bulgaria's condition within the Soviet sphere of interest? For, after all, in the present moment the tie with Moscow still comes first, whatever the future may bring, whatever the sympathies of the populace.

As we know, the position of the communist party leaders in Eastern Europe has become more complex since Gorbachev began his program of change in 1985 under the slogans of *glasnost'* and *perestroika*. Raising popular hopes for greater independence is dangerous for any emperor.

As the Soviet economic problems worsened in recent years, it has become harder for Zhivkov to obtain the subsidies and favors he apparently received in the past. Why Bulgaria did so well in its share of Soviet largesse for so long is a good question—because of its delicate, non-contiguous geographical position? Because of its utter loyalty to Moscow? Because its needs were relatively modest, and Zhivkov was clever at presenting them as being in the Soviet interest? One part of it was certainly careful cultivation of USSR leaders. Zhivkov was particularly successful with Brezhnev. When Andropov came to power for his brief term, Moscow-Sofia relations soured, and interestingly enough, Bulgarian overtures to Washington warmed up. Then came the also brief Chernenko episode, and again Zhivkov was a favorite son in the Kremlin. But then came Gorbachev, and signs have emerged that Zhivkov no longer has favored status.

And, of course, Zhivkov had to cope with the new challenges presented by *glasnost'* and *perestroika*.

*Glasnost'* has had some impact in Bulgaria, but an impact that so far the regime has controlled without undue difficulty. Zhivkov used to deny that there were any "dissidents" among the Bulgarians, and now presumably he would have to admit that a few avowed dissidents have surfaced under the supposedly more liberal atmosphere of *glasnost'* (although a Western diplomat has said that the true dissidents could be counted on both hands and one foot). Still, the pressures among the intellectuals for a Western opening—so aptly symbolized by Liudmila Zhivkova—have found fresh excuses for expression, and presumably fresh concern from the Soviet watchers of the Bulgarian scene.

Thinking of the Greens in Western Europe, it is perhaps not surprising that the environment provided a primary focus for the dissident stirrings. The dire chemical pollution of the Danube city of Russe by the factory that Ceauşescu erected there, right across the Bulgarian border, generated much public outcry and became such a focus of discontent that the Bulgarian authorities had to crack down. Similarly, the stirrings within the literary community—always a strong center of Western tendencies in the cultural sense—led to the dismissal of one of the chief literary figures in the country. And there have been other incidents within the Bulgarian intellectual community—including at Sofia University—which showed increased willingness of Bulgarians to stand up to the authorities on behalf of a more open system. My personal estimate, from this considerable distance, is that the stirrings of *glasnost'* inside Bulgaria can be contained, so as not to constitute any kind of serious political challenge, but that they continue to represent the westward-leaning orientation of Bulgarians which will undermine the bond with the Soviet Union. And which may lead eventually to liberalization of the system of rule in Bulgaria.

The harsh treatment of Bulgaria's large Turkish minority remains of concern to the West. Whatever the current line in Sofia, the fact is that until a few years ago the existence of a Turkish minority of some 10 percent of the population was acknowledged. Now it is not. The human rights violations have been disturbing. Why did Sofia decide to "make its Turks disappear"? To convert their names and identities to Bulgarian? One official told me, I think frankly, that given a huge Turkey looming on the Bulgarian border, for security reasons it was no longer acceptable to have a large and growing minority which might owe primary allegiance to that neighbor. So, within a certain Balkan tradition, the problem was solved by "merger." The treatment of this minority is an irritant to U.S.-

Bulgarian relations, but at this point one does not see any easy reversal of the situation.

*Perestroika* is the heart of the matter. After hearing the first, glorious promises about *perestroika* in the Soviet Union, Zhivkov began making enthusiastic noises and promises even more daring than those in Moscow. He went too far. Whether sincerely or not, Zhivkov allowed talk about diminishing the role of the communist party. Summoned to Moscow, he was apparently lectured by Gorbachev and told to rein in his rhetoric and his declared plans for *perestroistvo,* the Bulgarian model of *perestroika.* So at the party conference in Bulgaria, instead of dramatic new developments, there was retrenchment and a retreat behind slogans. Was the rhetoric about reducing the party's role a mere cover for getting at the party bureaucracy? Was it a ploy by Zhivkov to consolidate his own power? How did it relate to Gorbachev's own reforms? These answers are not clear, but it *is* clear that no dramatic change is taking place in the Bulgarian status quo as yet.

The word used by the Soviets and others, including TASS, to describe the Bulgarian *perestroika* situation was "confusion." The Bulgarians did not appreciate the word, since what confusion there was had been caused, as they saw it, by confusing signals out of the USSR. Of course, as in Moscow, Sofia had an ample supply of bureaucrats who, as one diplomat put it, "resisted taking responsibility along with authority." Those officials who wanted to press ahead too fast, who got out of phase with the new cautious line, were given the axe, including Chudomir Alexandrov, who had been in a leading position. Wily as always, Zhivkov saw the line from Moscow, in the final analysis, as dictating lip service to *perestroika*—but no risky adventures. Admittedly there are younger officials who are probably ready to move ahead more adventurously when Zhivkov finally relinquishes power, but who knows when that might be?

Another word heard often to describe the Bulgarian economic situation is "interesting." This means that the record of the economy is more innovative than many suppose, and the prospects for growth more promising than in longer-industrialized countries to the north. There are some very able people, like Andrei Lukanov, with plans and ideas for pushing Bulgaria forward economically, once the green light is given. My own feeling after two years in Bulgaria is that given the high level of education and talent among the people, Bulgaria may surprise many of us in the future, once some restraints are lifted.

For the present, however, given the stresses and uncertainties that *perestroika* is creating within the USSR, and given the strained situation among the CMEA partners, Bulgaria faces large economic challenges. In recent months Bulgarians have been fairly frank in talking about the strains within CMEA, acknowledging that Soviet attempts at closer coordination among the national economies are being resisted, as well as USSR changes in pricing within CMEA. With economic sympathies and prospects increasingly leaning toward the West, the CMEA members, including Bulgaria, chafe at what is in effect a Soviet attempt to give less and get more out of the relationship. It is said that recently the USSR has in effect stopped a subsidy to Bulgaria of three billion rubles a year, used in the past as compensation for disadvantages to Bulgaria in the pricing within CMEA of manufactured goods. Adjusting, without this huge subsidy, will obviously create problems.

Yet overall, and especially if you compare Bulgaria with its neighbors, the economic situation does not look too dark. Whereas dramatic changes will probably not take place until after Zhivkov's departure from the scene, the groundwork in effect has been laid. In its modest way, Bulgaria looks to the economic future with some hope.

## U.S. Relations

"God is in his heaven, America is far away, and we Europeans are here on the continent together." That, or words to that effect, was uttered by Todor Zhivkov during my service in Bulgaria. I found the phrase rather apt. One of the things an American diplomat learns in Sofia is that Washington is a lot farther away than is Moscow or Bonn. Compared to Czechoslovakia, where the presence of the United States in history and consciousness was undeniable, in Bulgaria the United States is merely part of the world scene. Yet trade and culture—and to some extent the existence of Washington as a certain counter-balance to Moscow—mean that the Bulgarian leaders will always be keenly attentive to the American relationship.

We do not know yet if we are going too far in taking up Paul Kennedy's thesis about "the rise and fall of Great Powers" and tending to assume that the Soviet Union is "the Sick Man of Europe" at the end of the twentieth century just as the Ottoman Empire was at the end of the nineteenth. We may be bitterly disappointed that the feeling of optimism in the air about greater independence for all the non-Russian nationalities of Eastern and East Central Europe, on both sides of the Soviet border, may be overdrawn, or may invoke a Russian reaction, or may lead to a change of leadership in the Kremlin. Yet just now, based not only on Gorbachev's words but also on what we believe are his real needs and real interests, we think we can see a loosening of old bonds, a fading of old lines, a rationalization and liberalization of the European and the world scene. Let us hope that we are not misled in this optimism, that we shall not see again the reaction from an 1848—or 1956 or 1968.

For the moment, Gorbachev is in power, and he is talking emphatically about *perestroika* and *glasnost'*. And the leaders of Eastern Europe, one eye on Moscow and one on their resentful populations, wonder how far all this will go and what it will do to them. Meanwhile we Americans want to say to the Bulgarians and others in Eastern Europe, "Why aren't *you* instituting changes like the Soviets?" And I am told the Bulgarians, at least the ones at the embassy in Washington, respond: "You have always criticized us for slavishly following the Soviet line. New look—we are no longer puppets!" (This line has also been attributed to Czechs. It would come naturally to many East European communists.)

In plain truth, it is a terribly uncertain time for American *and* Soviet *and* local national policies in Eastern Europe. I risk being accused of standing for the old Department of State position when I say our interest lies in "evolution, not revolution," but I am compelled to say that an explosion in Eastern Europe could endanger a great many things. The promise for Eastern Europe is great, now. We do not want to endanger it. For those yearning for the downfall of the Soviet hegemonial position, mine are hard words. But I repeat what I have heard hundreds of times during six years of service in Moscow and Prague and Sofia: "History is on our side." On the side of the *peoples* of that part of the world. The yearning of the Bulgarians to be themselves, of all the peoples of Europe to be themselves, is a potent force, and one that is growing. American policy, during every administration since Franklin D. Roosevelt's, has asserted its support for the true independence of the nations of Eastern Europe. At times that sounded like whistling in the dark, even like hypocrisy. But we meant it. And the Soviets know we still mean it. And the policy is right. It is not American policy that is bringing these vast changes in Eastern Europe. But we are a part of the process.

In the coming years, the U.S. relationship with the USSR—within which our attitude toward the countries of Eastern Europe is a major component—will be critical in shaping the next phase in world history. The emergence of Eastern Europe from the Soviet shadow, without in any way threatening Moscow's security, is fundamental in our global strategy. As part of that picture, the normalization of the American relationship with Bulgaria is well worth pursuring, and is attainable. In my opinion, it is a time for optimism as we look at the map of Europe.

## Notes to Chapter 8

1. It is perhaps significant that at this time Bulgaria launched its campaign to denationalize its Turkish minority.

2. To a considerable extent, the latter measure simply legitimized an existing underground economy.

3. *Rabotnichesko delo,* 29 July 1987.

4. In December 1988, Ovcharov was made a candidate member of the Politburo. *Sofia News,* 21 December 1988.

5. *Sofia News,* 13 January 1988. Although published in English, this paper is widely read by educated Bulgarians both for language practice and for its reporting. Kurstiu (Christian) Rakovsky was active in the founding of both the Bulgarian and Romanian socialist parties, but is best known for his career in the Soviet Union, where he held several important administrative and diplomatic positions before his purge as a Trotskyite in 1938. A new, highly adulatory biography of Rakovsky was published in April 1988. It may be that authorities anticipate that new revelations about the Stalinist era will tear the reputation of Georgi Dimitrov, so that a new hero will be needed.

6. *Literaturen front,* 15 October 1987. Anton Ivanov became a member of the BCP Politburo in 1940 and fell into the hands of the police in 1942. It is generally believed that despite the official legend of his heroism under torture, he provided information that allowed the police to roll up the party underground. Traicho Kostov, who organized the party's consolidation of power in Bulgaria after World War II, was purged in 1947. On the role that Zhivkov may have played in Kostov's downfall, see John D. Bell, *The Bulgarian Communist Party from Blagoev to Zhivkov* (Stanford: Hoover, 1987), p. 105.

7. In the spring of 1987, French television and the newspaper *Le Quotidien de Paris* devoted considerable attention to Bulgarian political dissidents.

8. *Radio Free Europe Research,* 11 February 1988, 8 March 1988, 27 May 1988.

9. Later in 1988 Bulgarian and Romanian authorities agreed jointly to investigate the problem and to monitor the release of chlorine into the air at the Giurgiu plant.

10. *Rabotnichesko delo,* 30 January 1988; *Sofia News,* 23 March 1988.

11. *Rabotnichesko delo,* 26 January 1988.

12. *Sofia News,* 2 March 1988.

13. It is suggestive that the crackdown came shortly after the publication of the "Nina Andreeva" letter in *Pravda* (Moscow).

14. *Radio Free Europe Research,* 27 May 1988.

15. *Sofia News*, 4 May 1988.

16. *Sofia News*, 21 December 1988.

17. *Free Bulgarian Center Newsletter*, No. 1, January 1989.

18. George Feiwel, *Growth and Reform in Centrally Planned Economies: The Lessons of the Bulgarian Experience* (New York: Praeger, 1977), pp. 270, 276.

19. George T. Kurian, *The Book of World Rankings* (New York: Facts on File, 1979).

20. E. Shevchenko, "Sovietsko-bolgarskoe sotrudnichestvo v oblasti vysshego obrazovaniia, 1966–1980 gg.," in Pantelei Zarev et al., eds., *Razvitie na naukata i obrazovanieto v Bulgariia* (Sofia, 1982), p. 608.

21. Kurian, *World Rankings*.

# Chapter 9

# HUNGARY

## THE "HALFWAY HOUSE" IN THE 1990s
*Peter A. Toma*

In order to understand the complex factors and variables responsible for the present development of Hungarian society, it would be necessary to construct an extensive index characteristic of that society and by means of a thorough analysis of class structure and attitudinal responses to sensitive political, economic, social, and cultural issues search for an answer to the question, what makes Hungarians tick?[1] Since such an under-taking is not in the purview of this chapter, we must condense, abridge, and oversimplify the rich, colorful, and at times tragic historical developments of the Hungarian political culture by accentuating the background to recent developments. Our major aim is to identify the key political and economic issues affecting contemporary society and, where appropriate, to make projections with an intent to analyze the implications of the proposed changes for individual autonomy and citizenship.

By October 1956 the party authorities had learned from past experience that the attempted destruction of the traditional hierarchical structures and the replacement of the latter by strict ideological conformity ended in complete failure and, therefore, that they had no choice but to initiate a policy of cooperation with the populace rather than coercion. Prior to that time, Hungary suffered from a high rate of alcoholism, suicide, and divorce—coupled with such contributing factors leading to the decline of the population as the catastrophic lack of housing, the aging population, fewer marriages, more frequent abortions, stillbirths, and the rising cost of living. The choice for the crippled party leadership was either a return to the Rákosiite-type of dictatorship—laced with terror—or to seek stabilization through accommodation. By 1962 the conditions were ripe for the party leader, János Kádár, to formulate his famous slogan: "Whereas the Rákosiites used to say that those who are not with us are against us, we say those who are not against us are with us."[2] The same year Kádár's "alliance policy," promising gradual liberalization for the future, received the highest accolade from the Hungarian Socialist Workers' Party (HSWP) 8th Congress.[3] Amnesties were granted to "counterrevolutionaries;" nonparty technocrats were recruited for leadership positions in the state and economic apparatus: and Kádár was seeking reconciliation with the people who had condemned him as a traitor in 1956. At the same time, the party leadership had decided that political problems had an economic solution and, therefore, it had become more and more obvious that the traditional command economy could not be used for solving Hungary's economic problems. Thus, in December 1963, the HSWP Central Committee authorized then Minister of Finance Rezsö Nyers, to prepare a program for economic reform.

With a thorough preparation and endorsement from the party, on 1 January 1968, Hungary launched its New Economic Mechanism (NEM). During the first three years, significant progress was achieved. The foreign trade balance turned positive and a booming agriculture and consumer production raised the morale of the Hungarian people. This "economic miracle," however, created new problems. Whereas some shortages on consumer markets were gradually eliminated, others remained. Whereas enterprises were given a wider scope for decision making, nevertheless their relationship with central authorities retained many of the rigidities to be found in centrally planned economies. The investment and consumption expansion led to excessive imports of Western technology and consumer goods, and the volume of unfulfilled investments continued to grow. At the same time, sharp differentials in the income structure triggered widespread criticism from the lower income groups. By 1972 the party leadership had been split into pro- and antireformist supporters. Those in the "center," which incuded Kádár and some of his followers, could not be persuaded by the pro-reformists (Rezsö Nyers, György Aczél, Jenö Fock, and Lajos Fehér) to support further economic reform. Later that year, the center finally opted to halt the reform temporarily. Nyers disapproved of this compromise and was removed from leadership—as was Jenö Fock a short time later.[4] According to an interview on 4 May 1988 over Radio Budapest, called "Question Mark," Nyers blamed the Soviet leaders for stalling the Hungarian reforms during 1972–1973 because they

failed to understand the international changes, the resilience of capitalism, the technological revolution, and economic reality. The reform, still
only confined to the economic sphere, was relaunched once more in a
piecemeal fashion during 1979 and 1980. However, the measure did not
bring expected results and the Hungarian economy, artificially propped
up for years by means of large foreign loans, entered a period of stagnation and decline, with a short and deceptive respite during 1983 and
1984.

In 1985 several elements of the Hungarian economic management system was modified in the light of previous experience and changes in national priorities. The changes in the central control and supervision over
state enterprises and some new forms of enterprise management were supposed to further increase the independence of enterprise decision making.
In addition to the establishment of enterprise councils, there were changes
in the tax system, new wage regulations, and a shift away from the so-
called competitive price scheme. Even so, Hungarian enterprises did not
respond to market signals but to a web of ever-changing regulations and
interventions. Without effective competition in both the domestic and international economies, these changes proved to be inadequate to reverse
the downward trend of the Hungarian economy. By the end of 1986, it
had become obvious that Hungary was in the midst of a serious economic
and socio-political crisis for which János Kádár, secretary general of the
HSWP since its 13th Congress in March 1985,[5] was being increasingly
blamed both outside and inside the party. Suddenly the perception of
Kádár—the major guarantor of the reform—had changed to make him
look like an impediment to the radical changes urgently needed. In June
1987 during party reshuffle, Kádár, in an effort to preserve his own prestige and to get rid of his enemies in the newly revamped Politburo and
Secretariat, succeeded in appointment of Károly Grósz as prime minister,
with the unenviable mission of salvaging Hungary's economy. Kádár's
plot to discredit Grósz as well as his minimizing of the crisis situation in
Hungary actually backfired on him because by March 1988 the HSWP
Central Committee was duly aware that the economic situation was a
grave one and required immediate attention.

Since 1968 when the NEM was introduced, political authority has remained at least formally as a separate sphere from economic activity,
especially in the second economy (which includes small-scale farming,
private workshops, retail trading, and regular or occasional work done
on the black market—all influenced by the market place). Only in recent
years was the economic sphere given a slightly greater degree of self-

regulation through the means of private initiative. The reasons for this were not demands created by market forces but specific goals set by the party leaders to achieve social change and technological modernization of the country, while moving toward an improved standard of living, social stratification, and political stability.

Despite the changes in strategy and tactics of the party under the Kádár regime to transform the structure of Hungarian society from conflictual to a more consensual one, today there are still not one, but two, societies in Hungary—each characterized by different structural properties. Officially, there are only three friendly classes (workers, peasants, and intelligentsia) cooperating in the process of socialist production. Unofficially, however, there are not only competing but conflicting interests and differentiations among several stratified groups in today's Hungarian society.

There is a general disenchantment with Marxism-Leninism and a movement toward religion among youth. Many young Hungarians have no political convictions; they have a "secondary [everyday] ideology" characterized by abstention from politics. The young people of Hungary favor individualism and independence and reject collectivism imposed from above. The overwhelming majority of university students are dissatisfied with the teachings of Marxism-Leninism; they condemn materialism, selfishness, corruption, and the inflated bureaucracy. Most of them disagree with the official allegation that public life in Hungary has become more democratic.

Other disenchantment and criticism are noticeable in contemporary Hungarian society by groups and individuals who were victims of the "new types of inequalities." They can be found in the material living conditions among the unskilled group, administrative workers, subordinate professionals, and skilled workers, whose financial situation is extremely differentiated. The differences in material living conditions are particularly noticeable between the smaller group of high income entrepreneurs in the second economy and the large segment of the low income populations. The visible differences between rich and poor are one of the main concerns of Hungarian policymakers today. The party's "alliance policy" acts as a safety valve to permit the disgruntled elements of Hungarian society to lodge their dissatisfaction through a channel of command to be heard at the very top of the political structure. The price, however, for this "social pluralism" is the creation of a new party that has become socialized and has embraced many "old" values. Thus some of the questions raised today by concerned citizens are the following: (1) Who should create the new system of values in the stage of building a socialist democracy? (2) How many interests can exist in a "one-class" socialist state, and how should they be prioritized? (3) How to democratize power and enable citizens to share in it? (4) How can the party retain the "leading role" and at the same time abandon its "monopoly of power?"

In the economic area, there are several dilemmas facing Hungary's policymakers today. The questions frequently being asked include: (1) Will the authorities opt for continued equity in income distribution, even if it means reducing workers' incentives and productivity? (2) Will they opt for continued guarantees of full employment, which may reduce competition, and call for increased subsidies for enterprises that are deficient and unprofitable? (3) Will they opt for a further decentralization of the economic system, stability of the policy environment, greater control over resources by the enterprises, and their greater accountability for the use of resources? In other words, will the reforms bring about technological change that could make Hungary more competitive in the international markets of the future, or will they be half-measures manipulated from above in order to satisfy the interests of the ruling élite rather than the people at large?

## Party Leadership and Authority in Crisis: The National Party Conference

What had been only rumored after the 13th HSWP Congress of March 1985 became a reality during the third HSWP national conference held at Budapest from 20 to 22 May 1988. Economic conditions of the country continued to deteriorate without visible hope for a turnaround; discontent and apathy of the work force was growing at an alarming rate, and party policy was subjected to criticism not only outside but within the party itself. Past shortcomings were no longer discussed in terms of failure to implement policy decisions, but whether or not they were the correct policy decisions and who should take the blame for them. Suddenly the focus of attention was on the leadership and the authority of the party, headed by János Kádár and a majority of his handpicked loyalists. In his keynote address, opening the meeting on 20 May, Kádár admitted that the national conference had been convened because of the economic problems that had developed after the 13th HSWP Congress, whose decisions had been ill-founded and poorly implemented. He also admitted that the Hungarian people at large were dissatisfied and losing their trust in the party and its leaders, that the standard of living had stagnated and even dropped, and that the present political system was inadequate.[6]

Even during this crisis situation, however, the party leadership was seeking an oversimplified solution to the problem. On 23–24 March 1988 the HSWP Central Committee approved a draft position paper that was submitted to the basic party organizations for a three-week debate prior to its endorsement at the HSWP national conference.[7] The draft statement, according to the critics, was too general, too formal, sketchy, and flawed. The rank-and-file placed the blame for past mistakes squarely on the party leadership and not the party membership as a whole. The views submitted to the Central Committee by the various county party committees have shown that party members were strongly critical of the draft on a wide range of issues and that they were unwilling to settle for less than a major change in party leadership;[8] the Central Committee had thus been compelled to revise the document before submitting it to the national conference.

The criticism waged by conference participants about past economic and political mistakes of the party can be summarized under the following headings.[9]

Economic mistakes:

1. Success with economic reforms, before the 13th HSWP Congress, led to complacency.
2. Economic reforms were delayed because of a stagnant party leadership, which needs regeneration.
3. The economic situation had failed to improve, the hard-currency debt had continued to grow, inflation had risen, and the standard of living had dropped, creating growing social tension and public dissatisfaction.
4. State subsidies for unproductive enterprises (200 billion forint in 1987) were the consequence of a full employment policy. It was a mistake to guarantee the right of full employment, because the right of full employment and state subsidies for unproductive enterprises lead to lack of discipline, poor work ethics, and low productivity.
5. The disproportionately large unemployment of young people, the shortage of housing, low starting salaries, and cuts in state subsidies for families with children (a reduction of 20 percent since 1980) had caused alienation toward party and government leadership among the young people. (The proportion of young people in white collar

managerial positions had declined from 1970 to 1987 by 20 percent and 60 percent respectively.)

Political Mistakes:

1. The party was encrusted with ideological prejudices, secrecy, and isolationism—it lacked flexibility by not allowing different views to be heard, and thus encouraged a movement toward a multiparty system.
2. Lack of competition for holding high government and party posts resulted in stagnation.
3. Lack of constitutional guarantees and protection of the right to hold minority views led to public apathy toward the party and government because of arbitrary "legal" actions against dissent.
4. Lack of democratic decision making in cultural and ideological matters created false unity, and thus alienated intellectuals and rank-and-file members in the party and government, because different views were not heard.
5. Alienation of young people through "administrative methods" caused scrutiny and then rejection of party ideology because of the great discrepancies between theory and practice.
6. Unclear policies left people confused and indifferent, apathetic, or incensed.
7. Exclusion or expulsion of party members who disagreed with party policy caused division, loss of confidence, and disunity in party ranks.

When the national conference adopted on 22 May the final policy statement, the new Central Committee was instructed to set up two working groups, one to draw up a long-range program for the "building of socialism" and the other to rewrite the party statutes.[10] Since then, on 23 June 1988, the Central Committee created three more working groups, one to analyze the "past decades" of Hungary's society and economy, another to review the party conference's policy statement, and the third to establish a system of advisory units. According to Politburo member and Central Committee secretary János Berecz, the schedule of operations adopted by the Central Committee contained 29 points that had to be completed before the 14th HSWP Congress in 1990.[11] Two days later, party leader and prime minister, Károly Grósz, in a speech to the Patriotic People's Front national presidium, pointed out that the next Central Com-

mittee meeting would set up yet more working groups to draft a paper
on long-term economic policy and to prepare amendments to Hungary's
constitution. Hence, it is appropriate to ask the question: What were the
changes and accomplishments by the critics who voiced their dissatisfaction before and during the party's national conference in May 1988?

Clearly, the reformists were victorious, but they did not have their way
in all of their demands. There were 986 delegates to the party's third
national conference—one per 1,000 party members, plus 106 Central
Committee and 25 Central Control Committee members. Delegates had
been selected by the then ruling party group rather than by the party base.[12]
The conference was empowered to elect a new Central Committee, which
in turn resulted in a new Politburo and Secretariat. The new 108-member
Central Committee included 70 reelected members. Five of the eight
members who were removed from the Politburo (Gáspár, Lázár, Károly
Németh, Óvári, and Havasi) were also dropped from the Central Committee, as were other prominent old-guard members, such as Apró, Czi-
nege, Méhes, Kornidész, Péter, and Rényi. On the other hand, the former
prime minister and a strong proponent of economic reforms, Jenö Fock,
who lost his membership in 1975 was now re-elected to the Central Committee. It is interesting to note that there were 113 people nominated for
the Central Committee but only 108 elected to membership.

The greatest change took place in the Politburo and Secretariat. The
size of the former was reduced from 13 to 11 members and the average
dropped from roughly 60 to 52 years of age. In response to the party
membership's vocal demands to establish personal and collective responsibility for past mistakes, the new Central Committee removed eight of
its longest-serving members (Kádár, Gáspár, Aczél, Lázár, K. Németh,
Óvari, Maróthy, and Havasi) and reelected only the five newer incumbents (Grósz, Szabó, Hámori, Berecz, and Csehák) who had been appointed at the 13th HSWP Congress in March 1985 or during the June
1987 reshuffling of the party leadership. The six new members elected
to the Politburo were Rezsö Nyers, the so-called father of Hungary's economic reform whose political career came to a standstill in 1975 when
he was removed from the Politburo; Imre Pozsgay, the former secretary
of the Patriotic People's Front since 1982 and one of the most outspoken
proponents of political and social reforms; Ilona Tatai who is considered
the new expert on management because she distinguished herself by using
advanced managerial techniques to make the Taurus Rubber Works the
shining star of Hungary's chemical industry; János Lukács who had been
a Central Committee secretary since 1987; Miklós Németh, also a sec-

retary in charge of economic policy since 1987; and Pál Iványi, an engineer by profession, formerly head of the economic policy section for the Budapest HSWP Committee and chairman (or mayor) of the Budapest municipal council since December 1986.[13]

The appointment of Lukács and Miklos Németh to the Politburo has increased the number of secretaries, who are also Politburo members from one (Berecz) to three. Only Miklós Óvári, a secretary since 1970, and György Lázár, deputy general secretary, were removed from the Secretariat. All the other incumbents (Berecz, Fejti, Lukács, Németh, Pál, and Szürös) were retained. János Kádár was elevated from general secretary to chairman, a new position whose duties at that time had not been made clear. What is revealing, however, according to János Lukács (who headed the national conference's nominating committee) is that it was János Kádár who had proposed Károly Grósz for general secretary and the nominees for both the Politburo and the Secretariat. As Lukács stated in an interview on 29 May 1988 over Budapest television, the nominations were then put to a secret vote without any comment or debate and were unanimously approved. An argument could be made that this election process resembled a well-staged act, where the participants fulfilled their roles according to a script calling for rejuvenation of the party leadership and the promise of building socialism through mass support and party unity.[14]

Since some of the leading critics during the national conference gained popular recognition and were elected to key positions of authority, for example, Pozsgay, Hámori, Nyers, and Grósz, it is fair to ask whether or not their criticisms were meaningful enough to bring about the sought-after economic, political, and social changes. As it becomes evident throughout this chapter, the revolutionary rejuvenation of party leadership meant only timid reflections of rejuvenating party programs. Those critics who demanded *glasnost'* in party affairs received only a faint hope of halfway compromises. For example, the demand for legalization of minority (opposition) views was rejected, for it would have come very close to allowing a plurality of opinion and consequently a multiparty system. As Károly Grósz, Hungary's prime minister and new HSWP general secretary, emphasized during his visit to the United States in July 1988, he was personally opposed to a multiparty system in Hungary during his lifetime.[15] He mentioned a number of goals of the new Hungarian leadership, including the need to bring the constitution in line with current and future requirements, to continue to develop the electoral system, to increase the role of the legislature, and to regulate the political and economic spheres by means of law rather than arbitrary decisions. Whereas dissidents could also play a role in the decision-making process, Grósz made it clear that there were constitutional and legal limits to individual freedom. In other words, as long as the fundamental law makes the HSWP the leading and guiding force of Hungarian society and the nucleus of the political system, there can be no pluralism or democratic decision making in Hungary the way we know it in the West. Therefore, what the post-Kádárist leadership seeks is an institutionalized consensus derived from (an unequal) participation of the party, government, parliament, the courts, as well as the autonomous interest groups—but only those groups that endorse the principles of socialism and accept the leading role of the party. The main objective of the new reformists of the old reforms is to stimulate and reenergize the movement from below, that is, the grass roots of society so that the party can again regain the trust and respect of the people. However, in order to accomplish this goal, the new leadership will most likely try to reduce the ubiquity of communist values in the management of society. In practice, this could mean a partial withdrawal by the party from much of the decision making, especially in the economy;[16] the creation of new institutions such as in the parliament, the Patriotic People's Front, that can promote a variety of interests, and the cooperation by the party with the budding citizen groups organized outside the establishment. It could also mean that the Central Committee would be more involved in formulating policy, and as a result, the Politburo would take over from the Secretariat a greater responsibility in overseeing the implementation of decisions. If such a change in the decision-making process should take place, which according to Grósz is inevitable, the Central Committee and Politburo would not only cease to decide governmental (state, executive) issues but transform the three-tiered system of decision making into a two-tiered one.[17]

All of these changes—designed more for greater efficiency than substantive reforms—will have to occur among a burgeoning of private enterprises and an expanded Western influence on plans to improve economic efficiency. Such ideological constraints as the guaranteed right of full employment and state subsidies for unproductive enterprises, which the old-guard reformists considered taboo, will now have to be discarded in order to make the economic reform effective again. The commitment to move forward with the reforms, regardless of what happens to Gorbachev's *perestroika,* will force the new leadership to formulate policies that will seek to regain the trust and respect of the Hungarian people and thus invigorate the creative and productive forces of the workers resembling the situation in the late 1970s. Should the reforms again turn out to be only half measures, the rejuvenated leadership could run the risk of facing a distrustful and more apathetic ¯opulace, which could force it into admission that the reforms have failed. The more gloomy scenario, after admitting failure, would be to find a pretext for a return to pre-1956 rigid rule, which most certainly would trigger another confrontation and catastrophe.

## Reforming the Political Reforms: Is It for Real?

There are early indications that the promised political reforms and turn-about in Hungary's economy are proving slow to materialize and that the general mood of the public has failed to improve—in some quarters it has even deteriorated. One survey, conducted by the Public Opinion Research Institute, asked respondents to evaluate some of their conditions on a scale of minus to plus 100. The respondents' personal financial conditions were rated at minus 77.7 in March and minus 75.6 in June 1988. On the question of Hungary's economic problems, 65 percent of the respondents viewed them as considerable and 52 percent as permanent. Residents with the highest income tended to give the worst evaluations of the country's economy.[18] This skepticism was also underscored by several reform-minded political leaders. According to the newly appointed minister of state, Imre Pozsgay, conditions for the birth of "active, sovereign citizens were still lacking."[19] Csaba Hámori, first secretary of the communist Youth League, also revealed his disenchantment with the lack of any "real" change since Károly Grósz took over the country's leadership when he said that "I am not sure that a new period has started."[20]

Several months after the national party conference, it appears that the Grósz coalition is not as open and harmonious as it was expected by the rank-and-file when the new Central Committee elected the rejuvenated party leadership. Just as the old Kádárist coalition, the new Grósz coalition is a secret one lacking cohesion and popular support because differences among party leaders are still not allowed to be aired publicly. There are major differences between Grósz and Pozsgay on such important issues as pluralism and the role and status of a multiparty system, between Grósz and Berecz on whether or not to combine top party and government positions, between Grósz and Hámori on how to deal with the problems faced by young Hungarians, between Grósz and Szürös on minority issues, and between Grósz and Nyers on wages and pricing policies. These differences in policies were not revealed through public information—as the draft position paper and the final document of the na-

tional conference called for—but through piecing together conflicting
pronouncements by individual members of the Politburo on occasions other
than their meetings for decision making. The only change in this regard
is the Central Committee decision of 23 June 1988, according to which
Politburo meetings should be followed by announcements and, in the case
of topics of special importance (determined by the Politburo), a spokesman should provide appropriate information to the press. The Central
Committee comminqué further stated that the party's key recommendations had to be submitted in advance to the various party bodies and members for comment. Once decisions had been made, the leading party bodies then had to inform the territorial and institutional party organizations
as well as those in workplaces of the decisions that had been made, thereby
ensuring that the entire membership was informed. In order to keep the
nonparty public informed, important proposals for Central Committee
meetings should also be reported in advance in *Népszabadság* and its
sessions by all the media.[21] Whereas this procedure may appear to be
perfectly democratic, there is a caveat. According to the new rules, internal Central Committee decisions—including those of the Politburo—
will be announced by a seven-member ad hoc drafting committee (and
not the Politburo or the Secretariat), but only after they had been made
and not before. Thus it would seem that the new Grósz coalition is just
as unable to resolve the issue of practicing "pluralism" within a one-party
system as the reformist leadership had been under János Kádár.

In accordance with the 23 June Central Committee decision, on 9 July
1988, for the first time the party daily *Népszabadság* published in advance
of the plenum a draft proposal for legislation to regulate freedom of assembly and association. In addition to economic difficulties, the legal
regulation on the rights of assembly and association are considered the
most pressing problems the new party leadership is facing. The Central
Committee could no longer postpone addressing the issue in view of increasing political activism among various segments of the population and
the proliferation of citizens' gatherings, demonstrations, and the establishment of a variety of independent associations. All this has taken place
in the absence of any clear-cut legislation, something that Hungary's op-
postion has been demanding for a number of years.

Among some 50 organizations and movements at least five major independent political groups advocating radical reform have been set up in
Hungary. A group of populist writers, reform economists, and intellectuals founded the *Hungarian Democratic Forum* (HDF) in Lakitelek in
the fall of 1987. Other new groups have followed their example by claim-

ing that their activities were protected by the constitution. They include the *New March Front* (NMF), founded in December 1987, named after a short-lived reform movement launched on 15 March 1937, and consisting mostly of party members who seek to create "democratic socialism" through the constant monitoring of political power by society and guarantees of individual and collective rights; the *Federation of Young Democrats* (FIDESZ), established on 30 March 1988 and committed to founding a new independent social alliance that would group together politically active, radically reform-minded youth groups and individuals; the *Network of Free Initiatives* (NFI), an umbrella organization of diverse dissident environmental, church, and other organizations, formed on 1 May 1988 at the Hagi Restaurant in Budapest; and the new *Democratic Union of Scientific and Academic Workers* (TDDSZ), the first free labor union in Eastern Europe since Solidarity in Poland, which was initiated on 14 May 1986 by historians at the Hungarian Academy of Sciences to protest the official labor union's (SZOT) failure to represent researchers' interests.

Because lack of adequate laws on associations seemed to have led to confusion among party and government officials about how to deal with the perceived threat to the one-party system, these independent political organizations have been intimidated, harassed, threatened, and hindered by the authorities from carrying out their normal activities. Since the groups maintained that they were not associations, they posed a constitutional problem for the authorities, that is, whether or not they had the right to assemble or form social organizations—a right guaranteed by the Hungarian constitution. Thus on 14 July 1988 the HSWP Central Committee unanimously approved a proposal to draft legislation regulating the rights of assembly and association in Hungary.[22] This was an attempt to provide a legal framework for dissent while at the same time protecting the party's own interests and power.

On 27 August the draft versions of the laws on assembly and association were published in all Budapest dailies. They dealt with the organization and holding of assemblies, with regulations governing the establishment of public organizations, including mass organizations, mass movements, and associations, but excluding "political parties" and trade unions. These draft laws were submitted in September 1988 to a nationwide "public debate" organized by the Patriotic People's Front. There were more than 400 discussion meetings, and the response was overwhelmingly negative. Two opposition groups, the Network of Free Initiatives and the Association of Young Democrats, argued that the rights of assembly and association were intended to limit the state's power and should not be regarded as a gift from the authorities. On 21 October 1988 the Presidium of the PPF National Council debated and accepted a report by its own legal committee and concluded that the freedoms involved were not gifts from the state but inalienable rights. During the debate Presidium member István Sarlós (also an HSWP Politburo member until 1987), observed that the one-party system will cease to exist sooner or later and parties will be formed. Therefore, the law cannot contain a rule that hinders the formation of parties. The final version of the proposed laws was then submitted to the government for approval. On 10 November 1988 the Hungarian Council of Ministers approved the revised draft laws that will allow the establishment of political parties and trade unions. However, before any new political parties could legally become operational, their role and status in society would first have to be determined by another piece of legislation specifically applying to them, which would be ready for open public discussion and presentation to the National Assembly by 1 August 1989. This became known on 11 January 1989 when the assembly passed the two laws by an overwhelming majority (only two opposing votes and sixteen abstentions on the law on assembly and six votes against and twenty-four abstentions on the law on association). Whereas the first law guarantees citizens of socialist Hungary the right to assemble (demonstrate), the second one permits them to form associations, including independent political parties.

The acceptance of the principle of a multiparty system raises further questions about the future relations between the HSWP and any new political parties and the "leading role" of the HSWP under "socialist pluralism." When Grósz replaced Kádár, the assumption was that the party, as the key player, would set up consultative groups and advisory bodies to provide a forum under the auspices of the Patriotic People's Front, for debates and evaluation of various views. All this would call for "good intentions" and "goodwill" on both sides in order to achieve a constructive environment for consensus building. Because the regime feels that there is very limited actual hostility toward socialism in Hungary, it believes it can afford to encourage dissenting views to come into the open and then seek cooperation rather than confrontation. Without the opportunity of having autonomous citizens' activities, according to the present party leaders, the feeling of helplessness, indifference, and passivity among the populace would continue, and thus the reforms would be doomed to failure. To play it safe, however, the Grósz leadership, like the Kádár leadership before the national party conference, has made it clear that the people at large will have to observe the law and that the laws are intended above everything else to protect the interests of socialism. It is clear that before 11 January 1989 the proposed new laws regulating the rights of assembly and association were flexible enough to allow the authorities different interpretations of their application. For example, they were applied on 16 June 1988 to brutally suppress a demonstration commemorating the thirtieth anniversary of Prime Minister Imre Nagy's execution,[23] and on 27 June 1988 to authorize a mass demonstration condemning Romanian policies toward the Hungarian national minority in Transylvania.[24]

As it now stands, the gray area between what is legal and illegal is still too great in the existing laws to prevent future confusion, apathy, and indifference among the general public. For the time being, however, the Grósz leadership is counseling patience and no misuse of the situation by the new organization before the new constitution and legislation dealing with political parties are approved. This is particularly true with regard to the Béla Kovács Association established on 28 October 1988 at Budapest whose aim is to revive the postwar Smallholders' party—Hungary's largest democratic party before it was suppressed (not outlawed) by the Rákosi regime. After all, the party leadership needs the noncommunity participation more than its influence and, to that end, it will go a long way to encourage and promote the emergence of citizens' organizations "from below," which would be willing to acknowledge the legitimacy of the new party leadership in the decision-making process. This has been the role of the people's fronts in the past and this is the role today—what has changed is only the form and not the substance. Nevertheless, the legitimization of a multiparty system in Hungary represents an incremental change that can appropriately be termed part of the political reform. The question that remains to be answered is: Will the HSWP continue to enjoy a monopoly of power and thus treat the mushrooming party organizations and associations as people's fronts, or will it share its power with the newly created organizations and parties which do not aspire to socialism on the basis of equality?

As noted above, there are several proposals dealing with political reforms currently pending before the National Assembly. It is important to ask what kind of a legislative body the National Assembly is, and what type of legislation can be expected from it. The 244 new deputies elected to the 387-member body in 1985 are 90 percent party and only 10 percent nonparty voters' nominees. Despite the electoral reforms in 1983, the proportion of party members rose from 71.6 percent to 75.1 percent.[25]

As the former general secretary of the Patriotic People's Front stated, the National Assembly not only has lacked legal and political guarantees of representation for special interests but acted as a rubber stamp for government proposals without any genuine debate.[26] The National Assembly's law-making role has been minimal over the last 40 years; until 1948 it passed 60 to 80 laws annually, but since 1950 the average has decreased to only three per year.[27] Even so, the legislative function of the National Assembly has been considerably curtailed by the Presidential Council and the Council of Ministers. Although in the winter of 1987 the National Assembly attempted to correct this problem by adopting a new law regulating matters that are strictly under parliament's jurisdiction, the Presidential Council still has the authority to adopt, modify, and invalidate virtually all laws by issuing legal decrees without the consent of the National Assembly. Since the Council of Ministers—under the party's direction—dominates the decision making at the state's highest level, and because it meets more often than the other two bodies,[28] it is actually the most powerful lawmaker in the country. It drafts the bills that are put before the other two bodies for approval with little if any change.

The National Assembly is only one of the many Hungarian political institutions that needs thorough overhauling in order to achieve "modernization" or a transformation from a monopolistic to a hegemonic political power structure—not to speak of democracy.[29] To that end, on 11 January 1989 the National Assembly approved modified standing orders designed to democratize the procedures of the assembly. According to the new rules, no deputy can be arrested or prosecuted without the consent of the National Assembly; only the assembly can remove a duly elected official from its body. Deputies are now entitled to receive 40 days off from work a year in order to take care of public business, and 50 instead of 30 deputies are now needed to request a closed National Assembly session. Another important change in the rules permits the setting up of parliamentary factions, such as the "Group of Independent Deputies," consisting of 51 of the 97 deputies who do not belong to the HSWP. In spite of these changes in standing orders, however, the primary function of the National Assembly is still to serve the interests of the party rather than the members of the electorate (about 7,500,000 Hungarian citizens). The reason for this can be found in the election laws of Hungary. The electoral reform of 1983, according to some critics, could become useful only if far-reaching organizational changes were implemented. They would like to see not only candidates nominated by the electorate (instead of the party or its auxiliary organizations) but such candidates to have complete freedom in formulating their own political programs, instead of the one laid down by the Patriotic People's Front as it now stands. They would also like to see the deputies more accountable to their constituencies, rather than to the power structure of the National Assembly.[30] Whereas the Central Committee concurred that, in order to strengthen and broaden democracy in Hungary, the electoral system would require further modification. It recommended a set of proposals to be submitted to a nationwide debate organized by the Patriotic People's Front and asked the Council of Ministers to draw up in the light of these debates the relevant legislation for submission to the National Assembly.[31] Again, it would appear that there will be plenty of fora and debates, but the final formulation of the legislative proposal will be done by the party (the Council of Ministers) and the enactment of this proposal into law by the National Assembly, which is nothing more than permitting free discussion to arrive at a predetermined conclusion. There is, however, some comfort for the critics in knowing that the new leadership in the government is much more pro-reform minded than the old one.

The most significant changes so far are the new government posts (ministers of state): one created for Imre Pozsgay and the other one for Rezsö Nyers as well as the appointment of Miklós Németh as prime minister—replacing Károly Grósz—and the appointments of Kálmán Kulcsár and Tibor Czibere as ministers of justice-culture and education, respectively. The changes in the Presidental Council and the National Assembly are of lesser significance, because these bodies exercise very little control over the Council of Ministers. It is interesting to note that only two of the 20 members of the Council of Ministers were replaced by others; one was old and in poor health seeking retirement (Béla Köpeczi) and the other a technocrat with no influential position in the party (László Medve). For all practical purposes, the new Council of Ministers resembles more the personal choice of its former prime minister, Károly Grósz, than a real shake-up based on party philosophy. This, however, cannot be said about the Presidential Council. The displacement of both Károly Németh and Sándor Gáspár from the leadership position of the Presidential Council expresses more of a substantive rather than a pro forma change. Gáspár and Németh were both on the HSWP politburo and Central Committee at the May 1988 national party conference. The new head of state, Bruno F. Straub, age 74, is a non-communist Academy of Sciences member and a symbol of Hungary's intelligentsia.

Other reforms required to achieve modernization in the Hungarian political system also include the revision of the constitution, which has remained virtually unchanged since 1949, in spite of some social and economic changes that had occurred since 1956. Although there is general agreement on the need for changing the "Stalinist-type" constitution, there is no agreement on the extent of constitutional modification. Judging from the current debate, the most important changes will most likely affect the constitutional status of the entire system of political institutions, including the role of the HSWP and other party organizations and associations, the types of ownership, judicial procedures, and guarantees of human rights.[32] Because it is very unlikely that the writing of a final draft, enactment, and implementation of constitutional changes will take place before 1990, on 10 January 1989 the National Assembly by a vote of 345 (88%) endorsed a two-page government proposal to amend Hungary's Constitution. Before 1990, the Hungarian authorities will probably prefer to experiment with new laws and regulations resembling what they call "socialist pluralism." After all, it is much easier for them to bring about the modernization of the state's administrative practices and procedures than the deletion from the constitution of frequent references to the communist party's leading role.

## Economic Halfway House: Neither Central Planning Nor Effective Market

It is common knowledge that had the NEM satisfactorily worked and the objectives of the economic plans been met, all the above mentioned proposals for political reforms would not have been necessary. In a socialist system it is incumbent upon the leadership to apply the scientific formulae of Marxism-Leninism to make the economic element of the system work as well, if not better, as in a capitalist system. Hungary learned the hard way that a centrally planned economy—combined with political terror— that was imposed on the Hungarian people before October 1956 led to catastrophic consequences. Therefore, as a subterfuge for the survival of the system, the leadership had no choice but to embark on economic reforms, which also necessitated political reforms. As in the past, today the aims and priorities of the Hungarian authorities are on economic stability, modernization, and growth. However, the failure to achieve these goals has impelled the leadership to constant reexamination, tinkering, intervention, and regulation of economic policies. So far the experiment of economic reforms has not measured up to expectations because, according to the critics, the past leaders were not bold enough to let the market forces come into play and because they were deceiving themselves by adopting only half measures in anticipation that they would perform miracles. Not until the national party conference in May 1988 did the party admit that economic targets had not been met and blamed the decline in living standards and the increase in the foreign debt and inflation squarely on "internal reasons and mistakes . . . [committed] by the Central Committee and the government because [they] erroneously judged developments in the international economy."[33]

Just how serious are these economic problems in Hungary today, and how are the "reformed" economic and financial systems coping with these problems? The budgetary deficit for 1988 was scheduled to be 20.3 billion forint ($422,000,000), but already by midyear the treasury's shortfall had reached about 30 billion forint.[34] The unrealistic estimates of only a 10 billion forint deficit for the entire year were revised when the figures for the first two quarters of 1988 showed a 25 percent increase in convertible-currency trade and a 5.4 percent decline in imports. The government had been unable to slow down the state's support for enterprises and, as a result, one out of every two firms still received state subsidies. Therefore, in order to reduce the deficit, the outlook is for more price increases.

As far as Hungary's industrial performance is concerned, that, too, is in an ailing condition. Industrial production advanced by only a token 0.9 percent in the first quarter of 1988, whereas inflation grew by 17.7 percent (or much higher unofficially) in the first four months, calling into question the 15 percent growth in inflation that had been projected for the year. Hungarian goods had been increasingly unable to compete on the world market. According to the new minister of industry, Frigyes Berecz, only 3 percent of all firms were capable of producing world-class products; at the same time more than one-third of them could not survive without state subsidies. As a result, Hungary's share of the world market had significantly diminished during the past years.

The prospects for reducing Hungary's foreign debt are just as gloomy. In addition to the $1.5 billion in loans taken out during the first half of 1988, according to Hungarian National Bank (HNB) officials, the country needed another 2.5 billion in new loans during 1988 to continue paying its maturing loans, to finance the $500 million deficit in the balance of payments, to provide enterprises with $5 billion for import purposes, and to keep currency reserves at the present level. Hungary is the leading socialist country among the per capita debtor nations. Over the past 13 years the nation's convertible currency gross debt rose from $1.9 billion to $18.5 billion.

The problems in Hungary's economy are persistent, in spite of the many changes in its regulation system since 1968.[35] The most logical explanation for this is the fact that Hungary is a halfway house, lying somewhere between a typical Soviet-type centrally planned economy and a typical West European market system. Many of the current signs of economic crisis are, directly or indirectly, related to this syndrome: neither central planning nor an effective market. There seems to be a void in the Hungarian economy today regarding the economic system of management (what the Hungarians call "coordination mechanism"). Central planning has been seriously weakened and dismantled to a large (and probably irreversible) extent, but effective market forces have not yet been created. Past party leaders were of the naive opinion that by removing the mechanisms of central planning Hungary could automatically create room for effective market forces that would guide enterprise decisions toward better resource allocation, higher quality of products, and supply-demand equilibrium.

A good example of such a folly is the financial system. In January 1987 Hungary undertook to restructure its financial system with the introduction of a two-tiered banking system. The Hungarian National Bank now acts as a central bank; it has retained its monopoly over foreign exchange and printing of the forint and acts as a central clearing bank. The second tier, consisting of five new commercial banks and 10 specialized development banks (housed at the existing branches of HNB), became relatively independent and theoretically speaking more commercialy oriented.

Hungary's decentralization in banking, however, should not be equated with "deregulation" in finance. The Hungarian National Bank has been reluctant to provide the second tier with an adequate supply of money that was needed during the initial stage; and the independent banks have lost potential customers through their inability to finance large-scale and long-term investment projects. Nor have the new banks been allowed to refuse to do business with (subsidized) unprofitable enterprises. In other words, the banks are not in a position to demand profitability from state-owned enterprises, whose key investment decisions continue to be made by central authorities and not by their management according to market conditions. Perhaps one of the reasons why Hungary's devaluation in banking retained considerable central control is its ability to borrow money from abroad. In 1982 Hungary was admitted to membership in the International Monetary Fund (IMF) and the World Bank (WB). Consequently, loans from these organizations saved the country from insolvency and from having to reschedule its debt. Since new loans with the same terms will be more difficult for Hungary to obtain, it is most likely that the new leadership will have to be more flexible in furthering economic reforms to guarantee confidence in its financial reliability.

Since Hungary has already reached the critical point at which it cannot speed up economic growth without increasing the rate of borrowing much needed hard currency, the final document of the national party conference cited the need to "intensify private activities" to improve economic performance and to address the problems of foreign debt, the domestic balance of payments, unemployment, and the standard of living. The final policy statement also pointed out that the public should be encouraged not only to save but to invest; and that the consequences of industrial restructuring, such as reorganization of the metallurgical and mining industries and the planned reduction of state subsidies, should be accepted. The final document omitted a reference contained in the draft version making the role of state and cooperative ownership determinative. Instead the policy statement called for the formulation of a new law on business organization, which, according to the new minister of justice, Kálmán Kulcsár, goes into effect in January 1989 and includes the following features: foreigners will be allowed up to full ownership of enterprises; Hungarians will be allowed to trade shares in private companies and employ up to 500 fellow citizens for private profit; joint ventures with less than 50 percent foreign participation will require no official registration; dividends paid on investments for the sake of modernizing the economy as well as greater disparity of individual incomes will be acceptable. The new law will largely abolish a number of rules governing state and private enterprises, leaving regulation mainly to financial means.[36] As Miklós Németh, the new prime minister and Central Committee secretary in charge of the economy, pointed out, the party and the state are convinced that the economy requires fundamental change because of low productivity, the antiquated infrastructure, and lack of capital markets and because the authorities' plan for a market-oriented system was still not in place.[37]

On 13 and 14 July 1988, the 108-member Central Committee overwhelmingly accepted the need to act swiftly and even brutally to bring about a long-term improvement and restructuring of the Hungarian economy. Two distinct proposals were advanced: a more drastic plan A and a moderate plan B. The more radical plan A envisioned fundamental industrial restructuring, in which enterprises capable of adapting to meet the country's economic needs would be encouraged and inefficient enterprises would be abolished, causing unemployment to go as high as

80,000 to 100,000 in 1989—about 2 percent of the labor force, or an increase over the current level of 30,000 without work. Plan A also called for currency devaluation in addition to a loosening of regulations on foreign trade, particularly restrictions on imports. Under plan A, inflation in 1989 would be expected to exceed the 1988 level.

Plan B placed more emphasis on continuation rather than a break with economic policy. Under plan B, unemployment expected to reach only 30,000 to 50,000 in 1989 and inflation would be lower than in 1988. Plan B would also fit in more easily with Council for Mutual Economic Assistance (CMEA) commitments. However, its measures would not be extensive enough to reach the "critical mass" needed to bring about a genuine economic transformation and, therefore, contained "the danger of reversal." Accordingly, the Central Committee endorsed plan A with only three dissenting votes and one abstention.[38] The detailed version of the plan, however, was to have been decided at the 1 and 2 November 1988 meeting of the HSWP Central Committee. Whereas the statement issued after the session again endorsed plan A, the nation's highest political body failed to give the country the much-needed economic direction.

The initial response to the endorsement of plan A reforms was cautiously optimistic. Miklós Németh, in his keynote address, listed four essential steps for economic recovery that resembled the IMF's requirements. First, small enterprises should be expanded; real commodity, money, capital, and labor markets established; and the domestic market linked with foreign commodity and capital markets. Second, regulations for enterprises should be changed so that they could use their own resources independently. Third, there should be a strict monetary, financial, and budgetary policy leading to a more efficient use of resources. Fourth, state intervention in enterprise affairs should be indirect and only corresponding with laws and regulations. Now that Németh is heading the government, it is feasible that most, if not all, of the above state conditions will become part of the macroeconomic program endorsed in plan A.

In accordance with the Central Committee proposals, on 19 July 1988, the forint was devalued by 6 percent; interest rates on private loans for apartment buyers and builders were raised up to 15 percent; interest rates on other loans were raised by an average of 2 to 3 percentage points; maturities were shortened by an average of five years; and proposals for restructuring the pension system were postponed until 1989. Although it is not certain that the party leadership will have the courage to match deeds with words, these proposed economic changes could in the near future place such a severe strain on the public that it might induce the authorities to search for a scapegoat. Could it become the IMF and finance capitalism, or perhaps some of the newly created political groups, for example, the HDF, NFI, or FIDESZ?

It may seem that the decisions to implement plan A are entirely an internal problem for the Hungarian leaders. A closer scrutiny, however, will reveal that outside influences also will have a bearing on the extent and speed with which these reforms can be made operational. One such influential player is CMEA. Whether or not Hungary's new economic reform will prove to be successful depends, to a large extent, on the environment within CMEA for the expansion of trade with the West and for the promotion of competition in the world market, specialization, and technological progress. Budapest's trade with the developed market economies is of vital importance, because it permits acquisition of technology not available from CMEA partners. However, it is trade with the latter that constitutes the bulk of Hungary's commercial exchange. In 1987 some 52.5 percent of all imports were from CMEA countries and 41.3 percent from developed market economies; exports amounted to 54.9 percent to CMEA countries and 36.7 percent to developed market economies.[39] The Soviet Union is the most significant trading partner accounting for 28.5 percent imports and 32.7 percent of exports.[40] Although Hungary's trade arrangements with the USSR and other CMEA countries (because of surpluses) may appear to be advantageous, in reality they are not. During 1987, for example, trade with CMEA countries resulted in a loss to Hungary of 12.8 billion forint. About two-thirds of the support subsidies allotted to about four dozen or so of the largest Hungarian enterprises went for exports of food and light industrial products.[41] The fact remains that these subsidized enterprises are also the least competitive and most backward, because they have a guaranteed clientele. Since the Soviets had previously expressed the wish to eliminate these chronic trade deficits and earlier in 1988 had concluded negotiations for reducing deliveries to the USSR, it was relatively easy for the Hungarian party leadership to depart from the previous practice of secrecy. On 1 July 1988 it made public the reduction of state subsidies for trade with CMEA member countries, particularly the Soviet Union. Whereas staunch reformists hailed this decision, the managers and workers of these enterprises, afraid of losing their influence and power under the new rules, were vehemently opposed to it.

A less important outside influence affecting the future of Hungary's

economy is the European [Economic] Community (EC). In 1987 the EC
countries accounted for some 24.4 percent of Hungary's total imports and
19.9 percent of its exports.[42] From 1979 to 1986 alone, the chronic surplus of EC exports vs. imports resulted in a deficit of more than $5 billion
in Hungary's balance of trade. This is not only because these exports are
unable to compete with Western products in quality and selection but also
because they are subject to very restrictive trade regulations by the EC.
On 30 June 1988, after several years of negotiation, Hungary and the EC
reached an agreement on trade and economic cooperation.[43] It is estimated
that the new agreement with the EC would increase Hungary's export
sales by 25 to 50 million dollars a year, or between 0.5 and 1 percent of
its total convertible-currency trade. The agreement is an expression of
West European confidence in Hungary's economic reforms; it is valid for
10 years and can be automatically renewed for another 10 years. After
the agreement was announced, Hungary immediately asked for diplomatic relations with the EC, following similar requests by the Soviet Union,
the GDR, Czechoslovakia, and Bulgaria.

Although the United States is its eighth largest trading partner, U.S.-
Hungarian trade amounts to only 2.75 percent of Hungary's total trade
turnover. Exports to the U.S. amounted to only 3 percent of total exports;
and imports from the U.S. made up only 2.5 percent of Hungary's total
imports. American exports to Hungary amounted to 0.07 percent of total
U.S. exports. The first trade agreement between the U.S. and Hungary
was signed in 1978, and it had an automatic renewal clause effective
every three years. The U.S.-Hungarian Business Council is responsible
for promoting joint venture operations. There are 10 such joint ventures
in Hungary and four in the United States.[44] The total amount of American
capital invested in Hungary is a negligible $58 million. It is understand-
able that Hungary would like to see this amount greatly increased. It
would also like to see the most-favored-nation (MFN) status renewed every
three years, instead of every year. They would also appreciate an easing
of restrictions set by the Coordinating Committee for Multilateral Export
Controls (CoCom) on the sale of certain high technology goods. Since it
is well known that whatever Hungary acquires in these products or information is automatically shared with the Soviet Union, the easing of
CoCom restrictions is a very sensitive subject.

The main reason for the poor penetration of the huge American market
by Hungarian products is the same that applies to the potential market in
Western Europe—their low quality. However, with the anticipated higher

U.S. tariffs on imports from Southeast Asia, Hungarian goods might become more competitive in the near future.[45]

## Conclusions

For the past decade or so, we have seen a trend developing where the "military-political world" has been challenged by the "trade world" for the global leadership role. Simultaneously, the world has witnessed an ever widening gap between the economies of countries with "socialist" models and the developed market economies of the major industrial states in the West. For example, the ratio of Soviet GNP to the combined GNP figure of the West decreased from 28 percent in 1960 to 12 percent in 1986. As the director of the Hungarian Academy of Sciences Institute for World Economics, József Bognár, said at an international economic conference held during 18–22 March 1988, in Györ, Hungary, the socialist economies were in a crisis because they had not kept pace with capitalism. Capitalism, rather than being in a crisis as had been predicted by all Soviet leaders from Lenin to Brezhnev, was instead developing and spreading to other countries, by giving rise to the technological revolution and displaying new vitality unparalleled in its rate of growth and scope. Socialist economies, according to Bognár, had no choice but to modernize and to make the necessary adjustments in their own economies. Should they fail to do so, socialist countries could lose the foundation of their legitimacy and thus revert to administrative and oppressive measures, which would make economic progress impossible. The Hungarian leaders, during the final phase of the October 1956 upheaval, made a commitment to overcome the impediments of socialist stagnation and rigidities inherited from Stalinist times; thus in 1968 Hungary embarked on economic reforms called NEM. The country had changed considerably since that time. Economically it became more prosperous, socially and culturally more discerning, and politically more liberal than other socialist countries with the Soviet bloc.

Hungary's economic structure had three major aspects: planning, regulation, and organization. It has done away with mandatory planning, in which the state directly assigns production quotes to enterprises. Apart from some strategic tasks that are prescribed by the state (e.g., capital construction projects, national defense, and cooperative projects with CMEA), production and management activities are determined by the enterprises themselves. Enterprises also make their own production plans, which need not be submitted to higher authorities. But central planning has not yet been eliminated, because the targets and priorities for economic development are stipulated by the state. Therefore, planning is still the basis of the party and government leadership. In case of contradictions between the state plan and the enterprise plan, the two sides search for a consensus through the economic means of the regulation system.

Hungary's regulation system has undergone substantial changes. The centralized system of allocation was replaced by a trading system. Enterprises now purchase from the market the means of production that they need. They can also sell their products for the domestic market directly to shops or run shops themselves. Finally, they also have the authority to conduct foreign trade. As a result, pricing has become more flexible; enterprises must turn over a portion of their revenues and profits to the state, and they can keep the rest. Wages and salaries are differentiated from enterprise to enterprise, based on the productivity and profitability of the firms.

Managers of enterprises are chosen in three ways. First, in the large enterprises belonging to the state, managers are appointed by the party goverment. Second, other large and middle-size enterprises establish their own enterprise committees consisting of a director and leading cadres from the workshops, party organizations, and trade unions. It is this committee that elects the factory director. Third, factory directors of smaller enterprises are elected by a staff and workers' assembly, which has the right to recall the directors.

The economic reform also served as an impetus to initiate structural political reforms. At the beginning of the 1980s, an administrative reorganization was introduced so as to further extend the rights of village congresses and party committees to act independently on local issues. In 1986 the HSWP Central Committee passed a resolution, according to which party and government leaders cannot serve more than two terms in the same post. Even so, during the past three years, Hungary experienced the most severe economic and political crises since 1968, when NEM was launched.

As discussed throughout this chapter, the political and economic issues are many and complex. The seriousness of these issues led to crisis situations that brought about a drastic change in the party leadership and a commitment to pursue political reforms vigorously in order to make the future economic reform a success. Because time is of the essence, the new leaders are aware of the fact that they must act swiftly, resolutely, and even brutally if they want to turn the prevailing conditions around. Recent data released by the Central Statistical Office speak for themselves: 1.5 to three million Hungarians fall within the official definition of "socially poor"; from 40 to 50 percent of all pensioners, roughly one-half of all families with two children, and 70 to 90 percent of all families with three or more children are officially defined as having low incomes. According to the same source, 24 percent of Hungary's population of 10,604,000 had incomes below the "social minimum" of 4,010 forint per month as of 1987. Beggars and homeless people have become an everyday sight on the streets of Budapest. Families with children are streaming into the capital from provinces in search of work.[46] Those individuals and families who are unable to cope financially cite the recent price increases and the new taxes as reasons for the deteriorating living standards.

Hungary's welfare system is too small and underfunded to deal adequately with the problems of the poor. It is not surprising, therefore, that the new leadership has offered legislation to deal with this and similar problems expeditiously. Presumably the leaders are well aware of the past mistakes committed by their predecessors, that is, that economic reforms move in tandem with political reforms and that one is meaningless without the other. Therefore, half measures, window dressing, or just sheer cosmetics for an approach to reforms has run its course. It will depend a great deal on the honestly and not the promises to implement the radical reforms. The key to future success of the Hungarian economic reform—in addition to creating the necessary political conditions, which alone will not accomplish the turnabout—lies in the creation of effective market mechanisms that would put genuine competitive performance pressure on enterprises. Import competition is a major prerequisite, and in this connection it would be crucial for the authorities to remove the present contradiction that exists between the macro-openness and micro-closeness of the Hungarian economy.

Should boldness of the party leaders prevail in forging ahead toward unrestricted reforms, there is a likelihood that fear of political unrest, corruption, and poverty will gradually be transformed into a new prosperity, harmony, and trust. If for any reason the present party leaders should default on their commitments to pursue all-out reforms vigorously, it is more than likely that the pent-up emotions of the Hungarian populace could reach a point of no return and thus compel the leadership to resort to forceful measures that would put an end not only to reforms but to confidence-building and socialist development.

---

# PROJECTIONS

*Martin J. Hillenbrand*

## U.S. Foreign Policy Options

Rather than commenting on the details of Professor Toma's excellent survey in the first part of this chapter, with whose analysis and conclusions I largely agree, I focus here on U.S. foreign policy options with respect to Hungary during the 1990s. It is obviously clear that the Hungarian system is in a transitional state and that how it emerges will largely depend on whether a successful resolution can be found to the current dichotomous state of the economy stressed in this chapter. Unless the country can move beyond its present economic halfway house, caught between a largely dismantled central planning mechanism and an only partly achieved market system, the threat remains of a return to the old, oppressive kind of political system and rigid economic central planning that antedated attempts at reform. Not that central planning bureaucracies have ever proved even moderately successful in maintaining reasonable economic growth, efficiency in production, competitiveness of manufactures, and satisfaction of consumer wants. But they are the inevitable institutional result of political reaction within a Marxist framework.

One may note that the Soviet Union will inevitably face the same problem of transition and that Gorbachev's retention of power may well depend on his ability to find a bridge into a workable market system without great delay.

American policy toward Hungary cannot, of course, be developed in isolation, but only within the broader context of policy toward Eastern Europe as a whole, including the Soviet Union. We can, if the situation so warrants, give preferential treatment to one or another Eastern European country, such as Hungary, but our ability to do so will be limited by the restraint that too much favoritism, if indeed it is accepted at all, may ultimately be damaging to the recipient if it provokes the wrath of Moscow or recriminations from other less-favored Eastern European countries.

This is perhaps all too obvious. What may not be so obvious to an American government accustomed to playing a leading role in the formulation of Western policy in the postwar period is that the United States is not in a position to play an independently decisive role with respect to the future of Eastern Europe. As I have written elsewhere, "The slow process of favorable change which many Europeans hope for will either take place, or be frustrated. Wise policy will recognize this, leaving to the Europeans, especially the [West] Germans, the influencing of change at a pace not likely to precipitate Soviet repression. Such awareness in Washington will not only permit Soviet-American relations in other fields to develop at their own pace, but is also most likely to be conducive to the achievement of our objectives in Eastern Europe."[47]

Recognition of this reality and of the new reality that, in the formulation of his economic goals, Gorbachev seems to be moving faster than other European countries (with, of course, the exception of Hungary) could open the way to a healthy reassessment of American policy options with respect to the Soviet Union and Eastern Europe. It is clear that the superpower relationship will remain dominant at the level of nuclear weaponry and within their respective alliance systems, but beyond that we are likewise entering a fluid period during which the shape of East-West political and economic relations for the last portion of this century will take form.

One can postulate a number of scenarios, each of which would demand the choice of a different policy by the United States. One might be that Gorbachev will succeed in revising the Soviet economy, with the Hungarian leadership achieving similar success. One might ask, as U.S. Secretary of Defense Frank Carlucci did in 1988, whether an economically stronger Soviet Union with continuing hostile intent will not be a greater threat to the United States and its allies. Alternately, one might argue that the kind of economic change that Gorbachev and the Hungarian leadership are seeking is bound to bring with it significant political and social change of a kind that will alter the alignments of the post-World War II era. We obviously cannot have complete certainty, should economic reform succeed, about which of these alternatives represents the future. The implications for U.S. policy options would be clear if we could be sure. In the absence of certainty, the most sensible policy would appear to be to encourage those actions that seem best calculated to move toward both economic and political liberalization, while recognizing the clear limits on American ability to exercise decisive influence.

Another, and certainly the least desirable, scenario would envisage the eventual complete breakdown of economic and political reform, and the reversion to the kind of closed system that had previously been characteristic of both the Soviet Union, and at an earlier point, Hungary. It is difficult to see what advantage the United States would obtain from a development likely to result in a revival of the Cold War.

If it is true that the determining economic influence in Eastern Europe will inevitably come from the members of the European Community (EC), American diplomacy would seem to have an interest in encouraging our European friends to do those things best calculated to assist the process of reform and change in Hungary and the Soviet Union. Washington did not react positively in 1988 to the extension of some six billion dollars of private credit to the USSR, expressing our position in the slogan that one should "encourage reform but not finance it." European willingness to heed our advice on this point appears negligible, and we need to take a hard, new look at both our traditional credit and trade policies with respect to Eastern Europe. Continuing U.S. current account deficits and the resulting constraints on aid and credit flow will in any event limit our capacity to act on the same scale as the Europeans, or the Japanese for that matter, should such a review lead to a shift in U.S. policy. Should we decide on a relaxation of controls over so-called dual use (International List I) goods, for example, it would at least mitigate what has been a continuing source of contention with our European allies and permit a more unified approach to the problem of Eastern Europe's future, and how we can best influence developments there in a direction favorable to our interests.

To reiterate, an examination of our foreign poplicy options with respect to Hungary must, therefore, take place within the broader context of policy toward Eastern Europe as a whole, including the Soviet Union. Any idea that we could play off one country against the other simply does not seem relevant under present circumstances, nor would pronounced favoritism toward any one country in the absence of more general progress.

## Notes to Chapter 9

1. For such a study examining the Hungarian social character, see Peter A. Toma, *Socialist Authority: The Hungarian Experience* (New York: Praeger, 1988).

2. *Népszabadság,* 21 January, 1962.

3. See *A MSZMP VIII kongresszusának jegyzökönyve* (Protocols of the 8th HSWP Congress) (Budapest, 20–24 November, 1962).

4. Only very recently has it been revealed that Kádár offered to resign as party first secretary in 1972 but that his offer was not accepted by the HSWP Central Committee.

5. After much negotiations behind the scene, Kádár refused to accept the token position of president of the state; he did agree to a change of title from first secretary to secretary general, so that a new position of deputy secretary general could be created.

6. *Népszabadság,* 21 May, 1988.

7. The draft statement was published in a supplement to *ibid.,* 31 March 1988.

8. For a summary of the party debates, see *ibid.* and *Magyar hírlap,* 25 April 1988.

9. For speeches by critics of party policies, see *Magyar hírlap, Népszabadság, Magyar nemzet,* and *Népszava,* 21, 22, 23 May 1988.

10. For the revision to the final document, see supplement to the party daily *Népszabadság,* 23 May 1988.

11. *Ibid.,* 25 June 1988.

12. *Magyarország,* 8 April 1988.

13. It is interesting to note that Iványi was the favored candidate nominated to run against Mihály Jassó for the position of first secretary of the Budapest Municipal party committee, a post vacated by Ferenc Havasi who failed to gain reelection to the HSWP CC in May 1988, but after three rounds of secret ballotting, Iványi lost to Jassó. See *Esti hírlap,* 28 June 1988.

14. See Politburo member and secretary János Berecz's statement before an international press conference in *Népszabadság,* 23 May 1988.

15. *Los Angeles Times,* 23 July 1988.

16. See Károly Grósz's radio and television interview immediately after the party conference in which he said that although the move to separate the party and the state was not incompatible, with the top state and party posts being held by the same person (which was not standard practice in Hungary), the two functions would have to be separated again in the not too distant future. *Népszabadság,* 23 May 1988.

17. See interview with Károly Grósz in *Magyar hírlap,* 23 May 1988.

18. *Népszabadság,* 13 August 1988.

19. *Magyar nemzet,* 17 August 1988.

20. "Talking about Today's and Yesterday's Politics," *Új tükör,* 31 July 1988, pp. 6–7.

21. See *Népszabadság,* 25 June 1988.

22. *Ibid.,* 15 July 1988.

23. *New York Times,* 27 June 1988.

24. It should be pointed out, however, that before the authorities endorsed this policy, they were pressured by dissident groups.

25. See István Soltész, "The Important Experiences of the General and Local Elections of 1985," *Állam és Igazgatás,* no. 4 (1988), pp. 290–299.

26. See "Pointing Ahead: An Interview with Imre Pozsgay," *Heti világgazdaság,* 24 October 1987.

27. See "Reform and Democracy: Conversation with Péter Schmidt," *Új tükör*, 4 October 1987.

28. From 1980 to 1985 there were 20 sessions of the National Assembly, totaling only 32 days. See *Népszabadság*, 25 November 1987.

29. See Attilla Ágh, "Alternative Forms of Political Reform," *Tiszatáj* (June 1988), pp. 78–90.

30. See *Új tükör*, 11 October 1987.

31. *Népszabadság*, 25 June 1988.

32. András Deák, "Search for a Constitution," *Magyarország*, 5 February 1988, p. 24; "What Should the New Constitution Be Like? Interview with Professor Péter Schmidt," *Népszava*, 10 February 1988; and *Magyar nemzet*, 27 May 1988.

33. See *Népszabadság*, 23 May 1988.

34. *Heti világgazdaság*, 25 June 1988.

35. For a review of accomplishments and shortcomings of NEM before June 1985, see Josef C. Brada and István Dobozi, eds., *The Hungarian Economy in the 1980s: Reforming the System and Adjusting to External Shocks* (Greenwich, CT: JAI Press, 1988).

36. *New York Times*, 6 October 1988.

37. *Népszabadság*, 22 May 1988 and *Magyar hírlap*, 28 May 1988.

38. MTI-ECONEWS, 13 July 1988.

39. See Központi Statisztikai Hivatal, *Magyar Statisztikai Zsebkönyv 1987* (Budapest: Statisztikai Kiadó Vállalat, 1988), p. 192.

40. One of the major problems for Hungary has been the chronic trade surplus with the USSR, based on a post-World War II bilateral agreement committing Hungary to make large deliveries of food stuffs and consumer goods at deflated prices of the 1950s until the end of this century.

41. See *Heti világgazdság*, 6 August 1988. Total subsidies to enterprises in 1987 amounted to about 38 billion forint. *Népszabadság*, 18 December 1987.

42. *Statisztikai havi közlemények*, no. 1 (1988), p. 5.

43. *Magyar hírlap*, 5 July 1988.

44. In Hungary they include Corning International, ALM Holding, American Supply, Computerworld International Communication, City Bank Overseas Investment, Truflex, Bechtel, Levi Strauss, and MacDonald's International.

45. See *Heti világgazdaság*, 21 May 1988.

46. *Ibid.*, 4 June 1988 and *Képes*, 4 June 1988.

47. Martin J. Hillenbrand, "U.S.-Soviet Political Interaction," in Andrew J. Goodpaster, Walter J. Stoessel, Jr., and Robert Kennedy, eds., *U.S. Policy Toward the Soviet Union: A Long-Term Western Perspective 1987–2000* (Lanham, MD: University Press of America, 1988), p. 75.

# Part IV

# Non-WTO Members

# Chapter 10

# YUGOSLAVIA

## COMPROMISE OR ADJUSTMENT TO POLITICAL AND ECONOMIC CRISIS?

*Susan L. Woodward*

The 1980s have seen hard times in Yugoslavia. They began with the death of Marshal Tito. They are ending with a flare of Serbian nationalism. Price inflation rose steadily from 60 percent to more than 200 percent a year. Unemployment is officially over 15 percent, surpassing the million-person mark in 1985. The austerity policies of the long-term stabilization program begun in 1982 have reduced living standards to levels of the mid-1960s. Workers angered at the steep decline in their real incomes for almost a decade have increasingly resorted to the strike since 1985; in 1987 some 1,570 work stoppages involving 365,000 workers were officially reported. By the fall of 1988 massive delegations from factories in Croatia, Vojvodina, and Serbia walked their protest to the doors of parliament in Belgrade. The political struggle for republic status by the Albanian population of Kosovo province turned increasingly violent and led authorities twice in the decade to impose martial law. The return to proposals for economic reform have been joined, as in the past, with demands for political and constitutional reform, but voices raised against the failure of the 1974 constitution have become increasingly strident, turning in some cases openly critical of the entire postwar order in ways unimaginable even a few years earlier.

The decade also began and ended, however, with substantial financial expression of Western support for Yugoslav independence in the form of reprogramming the foreign debt and new commercial and public lending.

International Monetary Fund standby credits have been secured three times, and World Bank lending has continued. In 1988 the Nonalignment Movement turned back to Yugoslavia for leaders as if they were elder statesmen who act as a respected presence against a more radical choice. They played this role as well by organizing a Balkan conference that was the first to bring together officials from all six countries in more than 50 years.

Which image is more true: the apparent economic and political crisis at home, or the confidence in Yugoslavia shown by foreign banks and governments? Is the country on the brink of disintegration? Must the Balkans always threaten balkanization? Or is the long crisis of the 1980s reaching its climax, with resolution in renewal and reform? Is Yugoslavia politically unstable or stable?

The answer to such questions depends on the international environment. Far more than many recognize, the policies of the federal government and leadership have been addressed throughout the postwar period to their face with the external world—their international reputation, the opportunities for foreign economic assistance and trade, the state of their balance of payments, and their concern for national security and the deterrent of a strong defense. This lends an element of uncertainty to any Yugoslav future, whatever the point of measurement.

Within that uncertain frame, however, the pattern of domestic adjustment and response has very definite characteristics. That pattern is the result of a series of compromises on which both Yugoslavia's international reputation and domestic political stability rest. This chapter attempts to set out those compromises and their domestic consequences, concluding with an interpretation of the current political struggles over reform.

## The Faustian Bargain: Compromise I

The dominant struggle during the first decade of communist party leadership in Yugoslavia was to create the bases for national sovereignty with a strong, independent military. Establishment of the Partisan army was the party's contribution to the Allied war effort and the basis for its victory in the civil war, but attempts to gain British, Soviet, and American material support for that army and leadership embroiled them in numerous quarrels during wartime. These only became more intense after the war. Conflicts with Britain and especially the United States over Allied Military Liaison aid, Lend-Lease, UNRRA, Trieste and Zone A, U.S. penetration of Yugoslav airspace and the shooting down of those American planes, aid to the Democratic Army of Greece in the civil war, the strategic embargo (CoCom accords) against the East and against Yugoslav negotiations in particular with American companies and banks to purchase equipment needed for the army and defense industries dominated the period between 1943–1948. They faded in public perception only because the Truman Doctrine and the growing conflict with the USSR over the same issues shifted attention to the East. Between 1947–1949 the so-called Tito-Stalin dispute also involved military doctrine, the independence of the Yugoslav Army from Soviet plans for an integrated command, Belgrade's insistence on peaceful coexistence, Yugoslav aid to Greece and armed presence in Albania, and numerous disputes over defense-related aid from the Cominform countries to Yugoslavia.

To insist on a strong and independent military as the necessary basis of national sovereignty was the key preoccupation of Marshal Josip Broz-Tito throughout his lifetime. He and Edvard Kardelj supplemented that military deterrence with other tactics—the nonalignment movement, the Balkan Pact, trilateral (East-West-Third World) trade relations, nurturing their reputation as an independent third force in international forums, especially the United Nations, organizing frequent international conferences on Yugoslav soil, and constant diplomatic activity to maintain that external presence. Although this activity grew out of a genuine dedication to the creation of a different world order, its basis was always national defense and Yugoslav sovereignty.

This policy is a compromise, however, whose benefits entail numerous costs as well. The Yugoslav leaders' response to their conflicts with both East and West in 1941–1949 was to reject what one might consider their "natural" alliance as a communist party—the Eastern bloc and even more so, in the language of that period, integration into a Soviet-centered political and economic community (socialist internationalism). They remained outside the Warsaw Pact but were also excluded (unhappily) from CMEA. The domestic debate over such allegiances was not resolved until 1966–1969 (and some wonder whether it can ever be fully resolved). In its wake, there were significant purges from 1947 on.

A particularly heavy price has been paid in two ways, primarily during 1948–1953 but continuing ever since, for an impressive domestic defensive capability. The first was the other side of the 1949 resolution, the receipt of U.S. and American-negotiated allied military and economic assistance—U.S. Export-Import Bank credits, World Bank loans, International Monetary Fund financing, military and food aid, and reduced restrictions on the strategic embargo from the West. Such aid was particularly useful in the 1950s, but it also set up a relationship between the federal government and Western financing that by 1961 became ever more defined by debt, reprogramming, and IMF conditionality for transitional loans. Since 1979–1982 this has become apparent to all. Moreover, while the West gained not only a propaganda advantage against the Soviet Union but also a friend (if not a formal ally) in the strategically delicate Balkans and eastern Mediterranean, it also demands in return political stability for its continued support. As the relationship has moved increasingly from military to financial assistance, the nature of that political stability has simply shifted emphasis, from peaceful relations with neighbors to effective implementation of austerity measures to repay the debt without a political explosion at home.

The other price of this compromise was the method of resolving the ideological tension between communist party rule and national independence. Neutrality—remaining outside Western as well as Eastern economic and military alliances—was essential to domestic legitimacy, Western tolerance of the internal order, and international strength in spite of actual weakness in global terms. Although an associate member of CMEA and the OECD, with special ties to the European Community and to the EFTA, Yugoslavia has chosen therefore to live with the unpredictable barriers against its goods in Western markets and the difficulty of balancing through domestic policy the different relations with different trade blocs (e.g., the prerequisites of GATT membership and the obligations of government-negotiated or guaranteed bilateral trade treaties). Although it gains in some cases with close ties to Third World countries (e.g., in the early days of oil price rises), it cannot afford to antagonize such friends by calling in unpaid bills too quickly.

This position of neutrality has also meant a continuing commitment to the domestic bases for a strong defense. The first five-year plan for industrialization (1947–1952) keyed the industrial structure and industrial location to the needs of defense. An entire subeconomy continues to operate for military needs. The withdrawal in 1949 into an interior security zone (Bosnia, western Serbia, Kosovo, eastern Croatia) reinforced with economic interests the traditional conflict between outwardly oriented trading regions, such as Slovenia, Dalmatia, and parts of Macedonia, and domestically oriented production and military occupations. Government protection for security interests within agriculture, energy, and transport is inevitable under periods of a perceived security threat, while the dominant presence of a military in federal decisions such as the Federal Office for Trade in Special Goods is a fact of political life. The one-third rule for military equipment and armaments (one-third eastern, one-third western, and one-third domestic production) insures that domestic production for defense and the conflicts arising therefrom over the use of resources will always be present.

## Withering Away of the State but Not the Nation: Compromise II

The Yugoslav communist party was formed in the heat of the battle over the national question, and its struggles throughout the interwar period to choose a position on that question left an indelible imprint. The choice of federalism and constitutional guarantees of national equality and autonomy may have been necessary to win popular support after the period of Serbian rule (as many argue), but it was an outcome ensured by the dominance within the party leadership after 1937 of a national autonomist tendency—above all among Slovenes. The importance of regional economic self-sufficiency and national equality to men like Edvard Kardelj was interpreted through a Marxist lens. The program of the national autonomists, therefore, became an attack on the exploitation of any central state power and the necessity of denying to a socialist state (the federal government in the Yugoslav case) the economic basis for interfering with the right of "direct producers" (enterprises or "organizations of associated labor") to determine the use and allocation of their surplus value (or value added in realized production and capital).

Creating a weak center and strong republics and enterprises was inevitably in conflict with the prerequisites for a united defense and an overall policy of development for a poor country. Kardelj's solution to this tension was the party—a strong, united Leninist organization that would set policy and supervise all societal functions to ensure that policy prevailed.

The tension within the government was then institutionalized by a division of labor. The federal government is responsible for defense, foreign affairs, and broad developmental questions. The republics are responsible for their own economies and for welfare (education, health, and so forth, which they actually share with communes). Central policy is set by the federal party leadership and the federal government, but those decisions are made in consultation with representatives of the republic party and governmental leaderships.

The evolution of this system established in 1946 has been consistently in the direction of Kardelj's intention: a progressive reduction in the authority of the federal government and the transfer of responsibilities as well as powers to the republics. Education, transportation, energy, agriculture, and labor were republic responsibilities from the beginning, affirmed by the decentralizations of 1950–1952 and the 1953 constitutional law. Developmental policy became a republic responsibility in 1958, and the commitment to national equality became subject to fiscal redistribution rather than ex ante planning principles. Federal transfers for development are only one part of the country's tax and transfer system; they are outweighed by transfers that benefit the richer regions; and because they are managed by representatives of all the republics and provinces, they are the subject of constant disagreement and negotiation. Defense policy, finally, became shared with the republics and localities—the territorial, "all-people's" defense alongside the central command of the Yugoslav People's Army (YPA)—by the mid–1960s. By 1987 some 67 percent of the federal budget was allocated for the YPA, and military employees were the largest category of federal employees; the remaining third went mostly for veterans' pensions and benefits and to aid the less developed republics.

The tension between central authority and republic authority is built into federal systems everywhere. In Yugoslavia, too, it is primarily a struggle over central rules vs. local control and over the allocation of resources from some tax authorities to others in support of central preferences. These struggles are played out over specific policies and over more general reform. Because republic governments participate in making federal policy and because it is they who share ownership rights with firms, not the federal government, federal policy is subject to the bargaining tactics and economic resources of the respective federal units.

The only consistent player is Slovenia, which, as the wealthiest and most economically developed republic, always prefers policies that benefit republic discretion over political questions (control over the courts, the military and police, education, and fiscal regulations) and either market allocation of economic resources or republic control of governmental allocations. The poorer republics—Montenegro, Macedonia, and usually Bosnia-Herzegovnia—and the province of Kosovo always prefer central allocation of economic resources because their less-developed economies need assistance. They vary, however, on their preferences over political questions. Serbia and Croatia, the two largest republics and the most internally heterogeneous, choose different preferences depending on which faction of their republic parties is dominant and what their current perception of their economic interests is. Although the Serbs tend to prefer

central political rules and the Croats tend to be staunch national autonomists, these preferences do not always transfer to economic issues.

Whatever the bargaining positions among the republics and provinces,
however, the role that the party is meant to play reveals the basic tensions
within the system. In creating a united front and integrating the separate
"communities" of Yugoslavia into one country, the party leadership con-
fronts republic party leaderships who have different interests. Any particular conflict may be resolved in one of two ways: by the fiat of central
leaders, or by a bargained compromise among the republics. Even a central fiat must find a way to prevent serious alienation among the losers
in that instance, however. Thus all decisions result in some compromise.

As long as Marshal Tito was alive, his priority on defense (both the
army and their international reputation) and on maintaining his personal
dominance provided two clear principles for decision making. His political skill assured those priorities when he chose to assert them. With that
gone, compromises become ever more subject to the bargaining resources
among negotiating parties. Although this drags out negotiations and makes
the bargaining far more transparent to outsiders, the first compromise
maintains its power over the party leadership. International position, although it may be variously defined, dominates federal governmental policy. Domestic political peace takes second priority—between party leaders because their acquiescence is essential to party rule, and in the population
at large because of the implicit contract with their international supporters.

## Socialist Commodity Production: Compromise III

The third compromise that shaped the Yugoslav system was to combine
the economic institutions of free enterprise with those of socialist ownership and values. Called socialist commodity production by the Yugoslavs, and occasionally market socialism by others, this system grew out
of the decisions taken above: the extensive use of Western financing for
defense and development, with the obligations that entails; and limits on
the economic power of the central government, and therefore on central
planning or the administrative allocation of resources.

According to the system architects, especially Boris Kidrič, the law of
value (balancing supply and demand) would continue to rule economies
during the early stages of development and socialism. Production was the
basis on which all else rested, and consumption had to adjust to its limits.
The best incentive to increasing productivity was, however, the expec-

tation of greater reward, and the closer to the act of laboring and production decisions that this was, the more effective it would be. The primary role of the central government was in turn to ensure that macrobalances prevailed, using information and investment guidelines to keep the relations between industry and agriculture, money demand and goods supply, and exports and imports in balance.

Enterprises are, therefore, operationally autonomous and expected to produce for profit (primarily through cost reductions, but in fact through all the methods found in other market economies). They are managed by the entire work collective, which sets production plans and decides on internal allocations in accordance with the law of value—in effect, in response to information in prices and financial instruments and with the obligation to keep incomes and other consumption within the limits of earnings. Moreover, the economy is open to the world economy, and enterprises are supposed to compete in the world market as an incentive to maximal efficiency. Because of the nearly insatiable interest in Western technology among Yugoslav firms, and the country's need for certain strategic raw materials, this openness is also meant as an incentive to the export earnings that are necessary to keep the balance of payments in line. Because the trade account is nearly always in deficit, particularly with hard currency countries, the government is under a virtually constant search for ways to attract foreign exchange to the country—permitting Yugoslavs to work in Western Europe and encouraging them to send remittances home, liberalizing once cautious restrictions on foreign investment and joint ventures, and permitting enterprises to seek suppliers' credits and foreign loans, and so forth.

Although the principles of market behavior are expected to govern decisions at the micro level, above all to stimulate efficiency and productivity, and the economy is not centrally planned, the institutions for the economy as a whole are not those of a market. The system is characterized primarily by social ownership, and the government is committed to socialist values. This means that it attempts to use public policy to prevent the nonegalitarian outcomes of a capitalist economy by placing limits on the sale and maximum holdings of private property, by regulating the distribution of wealth in favor of relatively egalitarian distribution, and by rules to ensure that the return on effort is according to labor invested (rather than, e.g., market advantage or speculation). It accepts the responsibility, in principle if not always in practice, to assist weaker members of the community. It influences the allocation of economic resources (through credit policies of the banks, rules on foreign exchange, taxation, and regulations on wages, prices, and accounting practices in enterprises and other social institutions) to achieve social preferences, such as overall development of the economy or defense.

Thus neither capital nor labor moves freely in response to the rules of the market. For example, to aid final producers and consumers, the government for a long time regulated the prices of raw materials and intermediate goods. When inflation is high or balance of payments deficits must be reduced, it imposes temporary price or wage freezes. Worker self-management is meant to bind employed persons to their workplace— a "socialist community"—for a long period. The property rights and economic authority of the republics encourages protectionist policies (among other things to increase their own tax revenues) that also limit the free flow of labor, capital, and goods within republic boundaries. Redistribution for the purposes of developing the poorer regions and through solidarity funds to protect the minimum wage for workers in the socialist sector are constitutional principles. Although retail markets, relations within the private sector (most of agriculture and a large part of petty services), and domestic-foreign economic relations all operate more or less in a regulated market economy, relations within the socialized sector of industry, mining, and transport are more often in terms of negotiated contracts (either bilateral or multilateral). Moreover, the industrial structure is highly concentrated, with little entry of new firms and institutionalized cartels (the economic chambers) alongside powerful oligopolistic pressures in the operation of the economy.

## Political Conflict over Federal Policy and the World of Second Best

Each of these compromises was an attempt to reconcile incompatible objectives of the different players in Yugoslavia's early postwar period. They were the basis on which political peace among those players was achieved and a political order was built. The system has evolved over time, but its primary conflicts remain those defined by these three compromises. But political stability also demands that these conflicts be managed so that the system does not disintegrate. The task of management lies with the federal party leadership and government.

The choice of international strategy, the first compromise, is never debated publicly (and one suspects rarely behind the scenes since the mid– 1960s). Priority to international reputation and to a balancing act among blocs translates, however, into priority in federal policy to preventing international default and maintaining good trading relations. In other words, the balance of payments has priority over all domestic policy. Policies to reduce a trade deficit or protect reserves or repay debts must take precedence over other values. Moreover, this necessarily grants substantial influence to outside forces over which they have no control—movement in their terms of trade, policies of central banks in the countries of the primary international currencies (the United States, West Germany, and Japan), domestic difficulties that lead other countries to delay payment of their obligations to Yugoslav firms (as the effect of the Iran-Iraq war on Yugoslav construction companies), the demands of their foreign creditors (such as the IMF and commercial banks), and changes in the strategic policy of regional and global powers. Domestic policy follows cycles of adjustment to shifts in their foreign economic and security environment.

These policy shifts affect both macroeconomic policy to reduce the balance of payments deficit and the revenues and expenditures of the federal budget. The Yugoslav government always approaches a balance of payments deficit with contractionary policies—to cut domestic demand and expand exports. But it cannot at the same time forego other objectives. These deflationary policies are as a result followed by compensations of various kinds. For example, a devaluation to stimulate exports and cut import demand also reduces the revenues of enterprises overnight and not as a result of labor, but of changed price relations in its external environment. To retain the principle that return should be according to labor *and* to retain the incentives to higher productivity of potential wage rises, a devaluation is frequently accompanied by tax cuts to permit an enterprise to retain a greater portion of its earnings. Across-the-board changes in monetary values may hurt seasonal industries (e.g., tourism) or industries with long production periods (e.g., shipbuilding); in this case, particular subsidies or tax relief might be offered as compensation. If export incentives or restrictive monetary policy harm essential strategic industries, compensating protections or monies will likely follow.

As most of these policies simultaneously cut the revenues and raise the expenditures of governmental budgets, they are followed by a search for alternative revenue—new taxes, a demand for federal subsidies of lower governments, restraints on trade to keep revenue bases within a territory. Although a major objective of the policies they choose to use to reduce trade deficits is to cut federal expenditures, the federal budget is also responsible primarily for foreign obligations—above all defense. A budget deficit in this case is usually resolved by governmental "borrowing" from the National Bank (because there is no capital market, this means the federal executive council tells the Bank to monetize its debts and so expand the money supply).

Such policies naturally led as well to debates over federal expenditures and therefore to disagreements over its jurisdictions: over monies for defense, for veterans' pensions, and for transfers to the less-developed republics. These substantive debates also feed into the conflict of the second compromise. The relation between republic and federal economic authority is played out primarily in the relation between their budgets. Republics can refuse to pay their federal taxes or can be without the resources to fulfill essential obligations, such as ensuring that workers receive their minimum wage in poorer localities or that projects crucial to federal goals be completed. Moreover, firms that suffer under macroeconomic policies, such as enterprises that produce essential materials for domestic manufacturers and thus earn little or no foreign currency but that also depend on critical imported materials for their production, will plead with their republics for assistance. That republic will take their case to policy discussions at the federal level.

The conflicts among different economic interests lead, in other words, to debates at two levels: over the allocation of monies for conflicting purposes, and over the jurisdiction of those who have authority over allocation—governments, enterprises, and banks. At the first level choices are made, but they are also compensated. Above all, the combination of deflationary macro policies to reduce the balance of payments and the accommodating adjustments to protect crucial domestic interests that would otherwise be harmed creates serious inflation. This invites renewed deflationary policies and as real incomes and revenues are cut by the price rises and tax cuts, workers strike for increased wages or the removal of the wage freeze and governments adjust budgets upward. Cycles of restriction and compensation result. The attempt to compensate for this "soft budget constraint" with a hard budget constraint on the enterprise leads to growing unemployment as enterprises rationalize on labor and to declining workers' wages in loss-making firms. And although federal subsidies for the less-developed regions and for defense-related industries appear to some to be the source of the "irrationalities" of the soft budget constraint, the overall effect of restrictive policies on budgets and enterprises together with the specific incentives to export industries is to increase the inequalities between rich and poor and to burden the less-developed republics and provinces with the costs of adjustment.

One could hardly say that these outcomes were intended by policymakers. The Theorem of Second Best tells us that in the real world of imperfect markets, there is no best solution but necessarily a choice among several "second-best" alternatives. Economic theory also gives no guidance over which choice is "best." At moments of liberalization toward the foreign sector, because balance of payments deficits or foreign debt are so high that leaders perceive no choice, then the conflicts contained within the three compromises appear in particularly stark relief. Then the sacrifice of economic performance to political stability becomes ever less acceptable to many. Pressures for reform intensify, and they are seconded from the sources of external assistance.

Conflicts at this second level, over jurisdictions to allocate monies, follow lines that are always present because of the three compromises but that only produce pressures for reform under certain circumstances. These are conflicts over: the foreign exchange regime, monetary policy, fiscal policy, and the instruments of political control (the criminal law and the courts, the police, the party). All economic reformers seek ways to increase financial discipline and make the restrictive policies effective. They come of two kinds, however.

The market reformers, which always includes the Slovene government and most Slovene economists, want foreign exchange to be allocated by the commercial banks on a fully operating market, thus with full convertibility. In their view this would make available foreign exchange (i.e., the means to buy imports) to those who earned it, but because they would deposit those earnings in banks, it would also make hard currency available to those holding dinars only (perhaps because they do not produce exports) at the price set in the foreign exchange market. In addition, these reformers want to separate monetary and fiscal policy by making the National Bank into a true central bank independent of pressures from the government (the federal executive council) to accommodate its needs by printing more money. Their objective is to make deflationary monetary policy effective and prevent the accommodating pressures from spending ministries. Third, these reformers object to a centralized, uniform tax and transfer regime, arguing that this deprives republics of the necessary authority to adjust their fiscal policy to the needs of their particular economies. And on similar grounds, fourth, they insist on republic control over implementaton of the criminal law—again, to adjust to local circumstances (including language) and to protect against federal statutes with which they disagree.

The "unified market" reformers also wish to make the macroeconomic policies of the federal government more effective and to harden financial discipline. In their analysis, however, this requires enhanced federal powers against the overdecentralization to republics. The National Bank should allocate foreign exchange, and criteria should be set by the federal executive council to ensure that economic priorities rather than political patronage networks in localities and republics have sway. Monetary and fiscal policy should be separated, but fiscal policy should also be uniform and centralized. The federal government should have greater revenue sources within the country so that monetary emission is not necessary to cover its expenditures, categories that are to them necessary. A uniform tax and transfer system would also reduce regional inequalities in their view. Federal statutes should have priority over republic statutes so that political control is more effective countrywide (and so that the majority in parliament wins the day). This means that the system of bloc voting and the effective regional veto in parliament must be eliminated, while majority rule rather than consensus must become the principle in the National Bank, federal executive council, and similar federal bodies.

The reformers agree, however, on labor and capital. To reduce the waste and improve the efficiency in the allocation of scarce resources, consistently loss-making enterprises should go bankrupt. Their assets and labor should be redeployed. Moreover, the protections against dismissal and layoff in the Law on Associated Labor should be removed. Labor mobility and wage flexibility, in their view, must be increased. Solidarity funds in the communes to protect workers' minimum wages must go. Moreover, the limits on property holdings in the private sector, for example, on agricultural land and in tourism, must be removed. Foreign investment and joint ventures need to be encouraged as well. All this should increase investment and with it employment as well as production.

## The Political Struggle in the Late 1980s

The current period in Yugoslavia has been dominated by policies to repay the country's foreign debt. This phase began in 1979 with the decision of NATO forces to increase their defense allocations, the second oil price shock, the rise in U.S. dollar interest rates, the increasing foreign debt of the country (both public and enterprise debt, but for which the government is ultimately guarantor), the resumption of an IMF credit and conditionality (followed by a three-year standby in 1982), and the decline in Western commercial bank lending to Eastern Europe (including Yugoslavia). The burden on the federal budget was massive; declining resources increased conflicts over their allocation; and foreign illiquidity threatened a serious crisis. The fact that so many other countries were in similar straits made it politically possible to refer to crisis. The death of Tito in early 1980 enabled federal leaders to rally the country to a show of unity against adversity. Two years later a long-term stabilization program was being negotiated, first with the IMF, and then with ad hoc policy commissions and with the parliament. This program included a commitment to economic reform. Because constitutions in Yugoslavia specify the basic rules of the economic system and of property rights, this meant necessarily a constitutional reform as well. As the global recession worsened, the need for austerity and budget cuts increased, and the voices for economic reform were strengthened.

The political momentum of austerity and reform politics has been remarkably similar to the previous period in the 1960s. Strikes have mounted, financial corruption increased, scandals unveiled, nationalist sentiment intensifed, and student activism reemerged. At the same time political jockeying for bargaining room among party and government leaders led, by 1987–1988, to outright mobilization of popular discontent by certain party leaders. The players have changed roles, and many of the issues have changed. The dynamic, however, is eerily similar. Now the Slovene students are in the vanguard. Their concerns are the environment, nuclear power, conscientious objection against military service, and press freedom. Now the leader of Serbia, an economic reformer but political hardliner, is mobilizing national sentiment. But the Slovenes still want a market for foreign exchange and the Serbs still want centralized allocation. Kosovo is only continuing its postwar cycle of protest. The military is under threat, not directly but because of declining federal revenues. Like the Serbs, the Croats are also led by economic reformers who are hardliners (whereas in the 1960s they were led by liberals as well as economic reformers).

The public side of constitutional reform began in 1986. It consists of three separate agendas: an economic reform of 43 constitutional amendments, a political reform of the judicial and electoral systems, and a party reform over which there is substantial disagreement. The Slovenes are insisting that economic reform come first. The reelection of Prime Minister Branko Mikulić in the spring of 1988 (against Ante Marković, from Croatia) ensured the government would proceed with the Slovene and IMF proposals. Since midyear, a market for foreign exchange has been in effect. The bankruptcy law of 1 July has been implemented in Montenegro, closing enterprises with a total of 3,500 workers, but there is resistance in other republics. Foreign investors, as of 1989, will be permitted to own up to 100 percent of joint ventures in direct proportion to their initial investment; the restrictions on exported profits will end. Free trade zones have been established at Belgrade, Koper, Rijeka, and Bar. Limits on property holdings in agriculture and tourism have already been lifted in Croatia. In the meantime the economic chambers are fighting for a constitution without property statutes at all so that reform can continue at the legislative level. At the same time the federal government has increased its powers—with a new federal value-added tax and continuation of import licensing alongside liberalized imports in other categories.

A primary objective of the economic reformers, in their many changes to effect financial discipline, is to force political leaders to make the choices that this system is designed to avoid. If political stability cannot be upheld by financial concessions and accommodating monetary policy, by buying the allegiance of competing interests, how then will it be maintained? Memories from the 1960s reforms, when unemployment and income inequalities increased significantly and mass demonstrations among workers, students, and nationalists threatened disintegration, are easily drawn on. Already arrests and court sentences against counterrevolutionaries with "foreign ties" and others prosecutable under Article 133 have been numerous in the 1980s. The military has reacted strongly to the growing attacks on its budget, its honor, and the draft. Military districts have already been reorganized to cut across republic lines and reduce their number (and the number of commands). The state presidency (responsible for external and internal security of the "constitutional order") has been given greater powers to appoint and dismiss high officials, though with parliamentary confirmation, in the case of an emergency. The secretary of defense not surprisingly is seeking transfer of the military budget into an independent fund in order to protect it from parliamentary wrangling over its size; a separate revenue base in the federal value-added tax has already been voted for that purpose.

Even without such memories, however, politicians know that they need to enhance their political resources. Although liberals reign in Slovenia, political conservatives hold Croatia and Serbia. Milošević's tactics, to mobilize popular nationalism in Serbia as a bargaining tool within the leadership and regain political powers over the courts and police, lost to Vojvodina and Kosovo in the 1960s, have been successful. Slovene concessions on some fiscal recentralization may well have been bargained with an eye to the equally crucial republic control over the judiciary.

Croat silence reflects satisfaction with this outcome: the Slovenes are making their economic and judicial arguments, the Serbs their political ones. After all, Milošević is only playing the role Stipe Šuvar demanded of Serbs in 1984. Nonetheless, it is difficult to imagine that political reformers will concede to the Slovenes' and popular desire for competitive and direct elections—the end of the delegate system proposed in the constitutional amendments—with Serbian nationalism now openly mobilized.

This rise of political conservatism as a necessary component of economic reform in the 1980s is also a pattern in other parts of the region and the world. In Yugoslavia it would be difficult to separate it from the IMF's implicit pressures for some time. In budgetary terms, however, this emphasis on "land and order" does not bode well for the economic reform. Nor does the emphasis on restrengthening the party suggest much room for its reform. Although the new independent body for human rights, established under grass-roots pressure, underlines the significant changes that seem to be taking place in the sphere of the civil and criminal law and the judiciary, the widespread resignations and removals of liberals and moderates from the press are more in line with the times. The problem of Kosovo continues to appear intractable. The evidence lies plainly in the government's recent response: to increase federal investment grants while imposing emergency security measures under the federal police.

## Conclusion

The argument of this chapter, however, is that the outcome of domestic policy will be within the framework of its external environment. That environment is undergoing potentially radical change with the financial and trade integration of the European Community by 1992, the Soviet reform process and its influence over foreign trade and security policy, and changing East-West relations. New monies to help Yugoslavia reschedule its debt may assist the reform process, but what are the prospects for improved trade? In the uncertainty over political reforms currently being debated there is room for much interest, but those reforms will take a long time to secure roots. Without an improved economic soil, the proponents of law and order will have the upper hand. The dominant proposals for that improvement deny the compromises that have prevented polarization from escalating too far in the past. They also give little promise against the harsh pain of adjustment that many individual Yugoslavs have been suffering for some time.

# PROJECTIONS
*Richard E. Johnson*

The United States rushed to provide economic and military aid to Tito immediately after his 1948 break with Stalin, intent on helping preserve the country's independence and territorial integrity in the face of what was then seen as a serious threat from the USSR. That threat is less immediate nowadays, and Yugoslavia's one-time symbolic importance as a socialist heretic vanished as the countries of the Soviet bloc moved to liberalize their own economic systems. With Tito's death the country's role in international affairs has become less prominent and, in recent years, Belgrade has commanded less attention among Washington policymakers. But although not taking the lead, the United States has continued to be supportive of efforts to resolve Yugoslavia's pressing economic problems. We still view it as important that this piece of geography be free of Soviet interference as well as of conflict, and that its people be reasonably well disposed toward the United States.

Yugoslavia is now experiencing problems, both economic and political, as critical as any it has encountered since World War II. It is logical for us to ask where the interests of the United States lie in the present situation. What if anything should we do? What *can* we do? These questions provide the central theme for this part of Chapter 10.

## Principal Elements of U.S. Policy

American policy toward Yugoslavia is unique for its consistency. Since Tito's break with Stalin, four decades ago, we have unwaveringly supported the country's independence, unity, and territorial integrity.

When initially adopted, this policy was designed to block threatened Soviet moves into the Balkans and toward the Adriatic. Through the years, our defense of Yugoslavia's independent status has been reiterated often in public statements. We have continued to seek a unified, strong country, friendly to the United States if not supportive of our policies. Maintaining the status quo in Yugoslavia has been and remains to this day our primary goal.

In the pursuit of this goal we have sought to develop a close and active relationship involving a wide variety of ties, in the political and cultural sectors as well as the economic. There have been high-level visits and meetings, the frequency depending largely on the availability of Washington dignitaries to spare the time for a stopover. Yugoslavia is the only communist-ruled country in which we have an independent Fulbright commission, with free and open competition for grants. There is a very active jointly financed technological exchange program, which funds research, mostly in Yugoslav institutions. The depth of our interest in cultural ties is evidenced by the fact that we have USIS libraries, with American officers assigned, in the capitals of each of the six republics, including the city of Titograd, with a 1981 population of only 132,000.

A strong Yugoslavia implies an economically viable country, and our economic support has been continuous. Economic and military assistance was terminated in the 1950s, partly at Tito's request, but "trade not aid" assistance has been generous. Yugoslavia is one of the Export-Import Bank's major borrowers, has benefited regularly from Department of Agriculture CCC credits, and has received favorable consideration for investment assistance furnished by the Overseas Private Investment Corporation. Most-favored-nation (MFN) treatment and eligibility under the Generalized System of Preferences are other ways in which we have sought to promote trade.

When in 1983 Yugoslavia requested the first debt rescheduling, the United States was the leader in convening the "friends of Yugoslavia" group. Since then we have not been anxious to play a leadership role but have gone along with the others in the group. This is a reflection of our discouragement and frustration over the continuing inability of the Yugoslav government to come to grips with mounting internal economic problems, but it also suggests that the country's political and strategic importance in U.S. eyes has lessened. The threat of Soviet interference seems to have dwindled. With Tito's demise, the country's more muted role in world affairs has made it less interesting to U.S. policymakers. The Congress, and with it the executive branch, is not anxious nowadays to find new ways to be generous. But we still adhere, officially and publicly, to our time-honored stand of support. We have put money in the hat when it was passed. In 1988 this meant supporting the Paris Club rescheduling agreement plus an extended bridge loan, arranged in concert with the Bank for International Settlements, and an additional $50 million in CCC (agricultural export) credits.

Although generally consistent, the relationship has not always been devoid of friction points. As a leading spokesman for the nonaligned movement, Tito felt it necessary to express publicly strong criticism of alleged U.S. imperialism in Southeast Asia and elsewhere in the developing world. These often gratuitous outbursts brought occasional angry U.S. government reactions. For its part, the Yugoslav government professed to resent deeply what is termed interference in the country's internal affairs when, for example, Congress debated that country's commitment to communist goals or its ties with the Soviet Union is considering its eligibility for most-favored-nation treatment. Other rough spots in the relationship were caused by our inability to control incidents of Croatian terrorism against Yugoslav offices in the United States, and the introduction of bills in the House of Representatives excoriating Yugoslavia for harboring terrorists or for human rights violations against national minorities, and demanding withdrawal of MFN status.

But these flare-ups were always short-lived. Adjusting gradually to the idea of Yugoslavia's nonalignment, we came to accept public criticism of U.S. policy as a part of that stance. We were even prepared to overlook the fact that "nonaligned" criticism of the USSR was very rare. After Tito's death in 1980, Yugoslavia's profile in the nonaligned movement became much lower and its foreign policy pronouncements less aggressive and shrill. As for Yugoslav criticism of our alleged interference, there seems to be grudging understanding, if not acceptance, of the fact that our Congress speaks with many voices. The Yugoslavs know that a single representative's statement does not constitute policy, nor does a bill that is opposed by the executive branch and eventually tabled without action. Our representations on human rights questions have been discreet and, although not welcomed, tolerated.

## Current Challenges

The decades since Tito's break with Stalin have generally been devoid of internal social or political crises. In the face of deteriorating economic conditions, the Yugolsavs have been patient and long suffering. Until this year they have refrained from taking to the streets (one must expect the outburst of Croatian nationalism in the 1970s, which Tito quickly dealt with). The Yugoslavs have believed that their condition was at least more fortunate than that of their neighbors in the Soviet bloc, and that boat-rocking could have dangerous results in terms of outside interference. For its part, the United States was comfortable with its policy of broad support for the status quo, and saw no need to consider future contingencies.

This situation has altered recently. A reduction in real wages has brought strikes, increasing in frequency and duration over the past two years. And since June 1988 we have seen a resurgence of Serbian nationalism, orchestrated by Serbian communist party chief Slobodan Milošević. Crowds in the tens of thousands have surged through cities and towns in the republic of Serbia, including the two autonomous provinces, and in Montenegro. Their basic demand has been for the protection of brother Serbs and Montenegrins in Kosovo from alleged persecution at the hands of the Albanian majority. However, slogans have gone beyond this immediate objective and urge Serbs to regain full control of their homeland. Milošević is a folk hero.

Undoubtedly, discontent with the continuing decline in real wages is a partial motive for these outbreaks. Although tensions between the Yugoslav nationalities are long-standing, economic problems are at the root of the immediate crisis. Were the Yugoslav government somehow to get a grip on the deteriorating internal economic situation, the zeal for demonstrating would lessen. But there is no indication as yet that the IMF stand-by agreement signed in the spring of 1988 is working insofar as it concerns the domestic economy. Inflation continues to mount, presently well over 250 percent. Production is stagnating. Unemployment stands at about 15 percent and is much higher in the poorer southern areas.

The political situation is fluid and fast-changing, and it is difficult to reach assumptions concerning future trends on which to base policy decisions. Matters seem to have calmed—at least temporarily. The 19 October Central Committee plenum of the League of Communists of Yugoslavia (LCY) had been initially expected to result in polarization and increased interrepublic tension. Instead, it seems to have had a defusing effect. There have been few mass demonstrations since then. The plenum proved unmistakeably to Milošević that the Western republics could not be bowled over, and led to a majority vote of no confidence in one of the two Serbian members of the Central Committee. However, in the interest of avoiding a deepening split, the LCY leadership stoutly disputed allegations that Serbia had "lost" the plenum. The plenum also brought forth statements by ranking military leaders supportive of Yugoslavia's federal structure, dispelling concern that the military establishment would remain totally apart from a threat to the country's unity.

It was fortunate indeed that Yugoslavia already had at hand a step that would accommodate the immediate objective of Milošević and his Serbian following. Included in the constitutional amendments then in draft form was a provision for change in the statutes for Kosovo and Vojvodina, which would restore to the Serbian Republic authority over the crucial sectors of the courts and police. Shortly after the plenum the Federal Assembly gave its approval to these amendments.

Optimists claim that the political situation has been calmed for an indefinite period. Milošević, they state, has seen that he cannot take on the rest of the country. He has achieved his immediate objective in any event. The entire affair, it is argued, has brought the LCY, and with it the country, closer together and rendered central authority more effective. A new prime minister, Ante Marković, has been named who appears to have broader support than his predecessor.

It is wrong to assume, however, that Milošević has been completely chastened. A politician ambitious and determined enough to call tens of thousands into the street at a time of widespread tension among workers is not likely to accept a reprimand passively. Milošević may consider it his manifest destiny to regain for the Serbs their historically dominant position in the Balkans. The best guess is that he is considering his options and that we will hear more from him before very long.

The problem, of course, involves far more than the rights of the Albanian majority in Kosovo (or of the Hungarian in Vojvodina). Slovenes and Croats have a traditional fear of resurgent Serbian nationalism. The Slovene authorities have already expressed their concern publicly. The result of continued activity by the Serbs could well be a dangerous rise in tensions and a weakening of the ties that bind the federation.

## Considerations for U.S. Policy

Obviously it would be a mistake for the United States to intervene in this situation. This is a Yugoslav domestic problem, and our potential influence in its settlement is marginal in any case. But the United States should nonetheless be prepared to use what influence it has in the pursuit of its interests, whatever they may be.

A number of policy considerations are involved, some of them conflicting.

Commenting publicly on the current Yugoslav situation, a U.S. government spokesman has said that we would not like to see the nationalist ambitions of one group satisfied at the expense of another. This implied defense of the cause of the Albanians in Kosovo coincides with strong feelings coming from a small group in the U.S. Congress, as well as our supposedly consistent worldwide stand in favor of self-determination. Some fear that to abandon the Albanians in Yugoslavia would impair our right to continue to speak out for the Estonians in the USSR, for example.

On the other hand, we cannot afford to become identified with forces blocking Serbian ambitions, thereby closing off access to Milošević and his backers. He is the only Yugoslav politician able to command mass personal support. He is not likely to vanish from the scene, in the near future anyway, and will in all likelihood be a part of any political modus vivendi that emerges. We will want to remain on decent terms with him.

There are favorable aspects of the recent ferment that we should not overlook. It brought more openness to the country's political life, more participation than has been seen in recent memory. The demonstrations themselves represent a direct form of political self-expression. The remarks during the 17th plenum were frank and lively, even at times scurrilous, a sharp contrast to the usual generalities, platitudes, and broad exhortations. The press published them in detail, and editorials in the various organs of the republics have taken sides. The federation's decentralization has contributed to emboldening youth journals, among others, to speak out in the interests of broader democracy, touching on formerly taboo subjects, and there has been no effort to avoid washing dirty linen.

It is important to note that the demonstrations to date have been devoid of violence, tame in comparison with those, for example, in South Korea. No shots are fired, no bricks thrown, no cars overturned. There has been little pushing and shoving, and only one reported injury. Only one case of the use of teargas by police was reported, and it caused such an outcry locally that it was a factor in the resignation of the Montenegrin leadership. These gatherings might more fittingly be described as "political rallies."

But if the situation exacerbates we will not want to watch Yugoslavia drifting into prolonged civil strife, with the end result a loosening of ties that bind the federation. It is in our interest now as it was in the late 1940s to preserve an independent and stable Yugoslavia rather than see the emergence of a Balkan battleground in that part of the world. It is even more in the interests of the nearby West European countries. We would like to see a stronger central government emerge from the present critical economic and political crisis, a government that can take public demonstration in stride without allowing them to be manipulated, and that posesses the authority and support to launch reform measures necessary to pull the economy out of its present morass.

There are those who argue that the present system renders effective government an impossibility. Each republic has the authority to veto effectively any action that might impinge on its interests, and any efforts to diminish this authority and strengthen the federal government are doomed before they start. But Yugoslavia has no alternative but to live with such an arrangement, working out differences by negotiation and coming up with halfway measures that are better than none. National differences and separate economic interests are not going to disappear. Recent developments in Serbia proper, Kosovo, Slovenia, and earlier in Croatia suggest that they have diminished little, if at all, since World War II, despite Tito's unifying presence until 1980.

Nor is it correct to say that the Yugoslav government has proven totally incapable of forthright, effective measures to deal with the country's current problems. The "three liberalizations" introduced during May 1988 regarding prices, imports, and foreign exchange were put in place without friction or prolonged debate. To be sure, these steps were taken following promises made to the IMF, but the acceptance of an IMF stand-by arrangement was in itself a major step by the government (many Yugoslav officials, incuding the finance minister, predicted in 1987 that the country would have trouble swallowing a retreat to another IMF stand-by). The LCY plenum in October 1988 and the consensus on the constitutional amendments, embodying far-reaching reforms, are more recent examples of a readiness to pull together at times in the face of crises.

These outcomes involve dialogue and compromise. They require extreme patience on the part of the LCY and government leadership, and forbearance and understanding on the part of Yugoslavia's foreign friends. The Yugoslavs must work out these compromises alone, and signs of impatience from the outside will not help.

Milošević will have to accept some accommodation with the other republics. His positions on economic issues, including opening Yugoslavia more to outside trade, investment, and technology, are apparently on the "liberal" side. If so, they would probably accord in some respects with those of Slovenia and Croatia. Such a powerful trio would afford promise of more effective handling of Yugoslavia's economic problems in future years.

## The U.S. Stance

If preserving Yugoslavia's independence, territorial integrity, and unity remains our cardinal objective, what, if anything, should we be prepared to do now, or later if the situation worsens? Granted that the problems are basically Yugoslav internal matters and as such not within our province and that patience and forebearance are required on our part, is there any contribution we can make to move economic and political problems toward a satisfactory outcome?

It goes without saying that we should continue our close and continuous dialogue with the Yugoslavs. In the present situation, we should avoid evidencing the jitters over political events, even recognize as favorable the increasing openness of the present debate and indicate confidence in the ability of the Yugoslav government to handle the situation. In our dialogue, the United States has already done its bit for the Albanians in Kosovo by expressing to the Yugoslav authorities our hope that the situation will be resolved "in a way that protects the rights of all Yugoslav citizens" (having given them this advice, we hastened to add that it is exclusively their problem).

It will be desirable on occasion to reaffirm our stand in support of Yugoslavia's unity, independence, and nonalignment publicly, but we should stay clear of the issue of Serbian nationalism. We should give high priority to maintaining an open channel of communication with Milošević and avoid giving him the impression that we are out to block his path.

In the economic sphere, we can give the government credit publicly for having reaffirmed its commitment to the market economy concept. But as the actual program develops, we should freely criticize its inadequacies. As financial backers of Yugoslavia's economic recovery, we have that right. U.S. comments on the Yugoslav economic reform program have in fact been invited. Not to comment frankly concerning the economic situation and the government's program for dealing with it suggests that we are confident Yugoslavia is well on the road to recovery, a misleading impression under present circumstances and one we would not wish to convey. Whereas the constitutional amendments are hailed as clearing the way for a market-oriented economy and the more efficient functioning of the workers' self-management system, drafts of some of the legislation to follow are still the subject of strong debate between reformers and traditionalists. If they are watered down extensively, economic reform will be modest in its scope. Deep surgery is needed.

Disavowal by the Yugoslavs of socialist workers' self-management, the country's trademark and part of Tito's legacy, is not in the cards. However, it should be critically examined, setting ideological preconceptions aside. Workers' councils can serve to shackle entrepreneurial initiative in the management of Yugoslav enterprises, fostering a laissez-faire attitude in the face of repeated years of operating in the red. The system is inherently inflationary, since it brings pressures for wage increases not matched by improvements in productivity. Second, a "market economy" where there is no means of access to the market by new producers is a contradiction in terms. Most sectors of production have been dominated for years by a handful of enterprises. They raise prices in lockstep to cover costs and a healthy profit, confident that no one will undercut their prices and steal customers away. Means should be found to capitalize start-ups by independent entrepreneurs who see a market niche for themselves. Acknowledging the absence of price competition among Yugoslav enterprises, the government has decided to set hundreds of millions of dollars aside for the import of consumer goods that Yugoslavia itself produces. The authorities reason that, if and when these goods come on the market, competition will force the prices of domestic producers down. It is interesting and somewhat ominous that to date few Yugoslav foreign trading firms have seen fit to utilize this import opportunity.

We should take appropriate occasions to remind the Yugoslav authorities that a genuine commitment to a market economy necessarily involves these and other adjustments. They will be difficult to come by, since many older hands in the LCY and government will argue that they are inconsistent with the country's socialist path.

The Department of State may shrink at times from becoming too deeply involved in the solution of Yugoslavia's economic problems. In such a case, it can rely increasingly on the U.S.-Yugoslav Economic Council, speaking on behalf of American companies in business with Yugoslavia, to get the points across.

A question logically arises as to whether the United States should push once more for increased financial assistance to Yugoslavia, as a means of helping the authorities to deal with the twin problems of inflation and lagging productivity. There is an argument for credits tied to imports of new technology.

The commercial banks, the Paris Club, and the IMF and the World Bank contributed $1.4 bilion in financial assistance during 1988, a sum that the Yugoslavs themselves considered adequate under the circumstances. For their part, the latter have achieved surprising success in improving their balance of payments with the hard currency countries. Their current account with these countries recorded a 1988 surplus of over one billion dollars. The precipitous drop in the value of the dinar has increased not only exports but also central bank receipts from tourism. The black market now has less attraction for visitors to Yugoslavia. This situation is likely to last for a while, unless and until the government decides to abandon its free market stance in favor of a return to controls.

To slam down our Export-Import Bank loan window at this point, because of the murkiness of the domestic economic picture, would be a bad symbol expressing lack of confidence in the country and indifference to its problems. The rates of interest charged by the bank have recently been adjusted upward to take account of the risks inherent in the domestic economic situation, as seen by the bank's economists. With these rates, on top of the high rates charged by the major New York banks, we have already pushed many U.S. manufacturers out of the Yugoslav market. West European banks and firms are increasingly moving in. Given this situation and the continuing accumulation by Yugoslavia of hard currency balances, it is hard to see why the bank would feel it imprudent to continue case-by-case lending for safe projects.

But in these circumstances it is equally hard to justify major new infusions of Western credit. Some of the credits already extended are not being used. Now that the foreign exchange market is open and functioning well, some domestic enterprises prefer to borrow dinars and buy dollars within Yugoslavia instead of utilizing the foreign credits that are on the books.

Nor is there at present a good argument for the extension by the United States and other governments of new credits tied to economic reforms, such as those described above. The IMF with its stand-by commitments and the World Bank with its credits for structural reform are already in this business, although without signal successes. At this point to base the extension of credits on major economic policy moves by Yugoslavia would involve the United States more in the domestic economic muddle than we would consider healthy. It would be certain to cause deep resentments within the country.

The Yugoslavs are well aware of the need to reform their system. They have given it a decent trial for over 35 years; its inherent inefficiencies have become increasingly apparent. They have amended their constitution to increase the independence of producing units, to sharpen the role of market forces in the decision-making process, and to give private economic activity improved status and opportunity. New legislation will open the country more to foreign trade and investment.

Indications are that the recently enacted legislation and that currently in draft form will fall short. More will have to be done to make the economy productive. But the Yugoslavs seem to be prepared to make adjustments and to be moving in the right direction. The United States should offer encouragement, but not gloss over shortcomings. We should be interested, supportive as necessary, as they seek to work out their economic problems. On the political side, we should demonstrate confidence that they will succeed, as they have for decades, in adjusting their complex differences.

# Chapter 11
# ALBANIA

## "ODD MAN OUT" IN THE 1990s
*Elez Biberaj\**

With a remarkable history of dogged resistance to foreign domination, interference, and influence, Albania, the smallest nation in the ever volatile Balkans, enters the last decade of the twentieth century with uncertainty and ill-prepared to meet the great challenges of the next century. With its maverick domestic and foreign policies, Albania at the end of the 1980s found itself in the position of being the odd man out in the loosely defined international communist system. Whereas its former successive communist patrons—Yugoslavia, the Soviet Union, and China—as well as most East European countries had initiated significant reforms, which if fully implemented would likely challenge the dominant position of their ruling communist parties, tiny Albania remained what a leading expert on its affairs described as "the last bastion of Stalinism."[1] Tiranë was perhaps the most outspoken and constant critic of post-Stalin developments in the Soviet bloc, accusing Kremlin leaders and their allies in Eastern Europe of having "betrayed" Marxism-Leninism and having allowed the restoration of capitalism in their countries. The same charges were also leveled against China. Self-styled as the world's only truly socialist state, Albania strongly denounced Soviet leader Mikhail Gorbachev's *perestroika* and *glasnost'* policies.

Enver Hoxha, who ruled "the sons of the eagle" with an iron hand over four decades, left his hand-picked successor Ramiz Alia an author-

---

*The views expressed in this section represent those of the author and do not necessarily represent the official position of the U.S. government.

itarian system that had stunted the political growth and freedom of the Albanian people, stifled individual initiative, and distorted economic development. Upon his accession to power in 1985, Alia faced an array of interrelated and seemingly inextricably intertwined problems. The rigid centralized economic system had led to a sluggish economic performance, further widening the gap between Albania and its neighbors. The standard of living had stagnated, mainly as a result of the cessation of foreign assistance from China in 1978, and opportunities for social mobility had declined. After four decades in power, the communist regime was unable to meet the population's basic material needs. Social malaise had become pervasive and significant segments of the population seemed bent on rejecting established regime values. But perhaps more important, the political and economic institutions, fashioned after the Stalinist model, were not functioning well and were in dire need of change. Alia faced increasing internal pressures to reinvigorate the economy, brighten the drab world in which Albanians lived, and loosen some of the ruling party's severe controls over society. Moreover, Albania, although not a member of the Warsaw Treaty Organization (WTO) or the Council for Mutual Economic Assistance (CMEA), was not immune to developments in the Soviet bloc. Tiranë could not escape the reverberations of Gorbachev's *perestroika* and *glasnost'*.

Alia had to grapple with the poisoned legacy of his mentor and faced a gargantuan task of reversing the effects of decades of economic mismanagement, stagnation, and repression. In the years ahead, Albania will likely find itself at a critical juncture. In charting a domestic and foreign policy course that will lead the country into the next century, the leadership will be confronted with a difficult task in sorting through the political and economic choices, at a time when the population's patience with the highly centralized leadership is likely to wear thin. Ever since it came to power, the ruling Albanian Party of Labor (APL) had sought to boost the living standards of the population in return for political obedience. The standard of living had increased dramatically compared with the past, but so did popular aspirations for a freer and more abundant life. At the same time, however, the ability of the government to meet these aspirations had declined considerably. Economic difficulties as well as adverse social trends, most dramatically reflected in the increasing disintegration of social controls and self-discipline, which pointed to the waning hold of the official ideology, were beginning to undermine the social contract that had kept the Albanians politically quiescent throughout the post-1945 era.

Albania's rigidly centralized system, characterized by an absence of initiative and motivation, appeared uniquely unsuited to tackle the country's growing problems. It was doubtful Alia would be able to extricate Albania from its lingering political, social, and economic difficulties without repudiating some of the very policies he was hand-picked by Hoxha to preserve. Reform, a nonexisting word in the political lexicon during Hoxha's era, appeared to be the only way out of Albania's impasse. Unless the government took radical measures to redress some of the most damaging aspects of Hoxha's rule, there was a high probability that in the 1990s Albania would be confronted with political, social, and economic upheavals. At the minimum, the failure to institute meaningful reforms would likely cause Albania to sink to the developmental level of poor Third World countries.

Alia's first four years as party leader produced few tangible changes. He conveyed a sense of continuity and stability, and the name of Hoxha maintained its sacred status. At all levels of the Albanian society, Hoxha remained the necessary icon, the historical hero, the ideological gyroscope. Alia would countenance no criticism of his predecessor and, as a result, there was no public reexamination of the past. Subjects such as the sordid history of party purges, crimes committed by the secret police (*Sigurimi*), forced labor camps, the abolition of religion, and collectivization remained taboo. Like his predecessor, Alia did not appear particularly prone to accepting risks or initiating bold reforms. But although there was no evidence to indicate the Alia government would in the near future dismantle the most damaging elements of the country's rigid political and economic system, he gradually distanced himself from Hoxha's idological policy and self-imposed constraints, moving instead cautiously toward moderation in both domestic and foreign policies. Alia appeared committed to promoting economic reinvigoration and ending his country's international isolation, especially by promoting a policy of bridge-building and cooperation with neighbors and Western Europe.

## The Alia Leadership

Alia's political experience closely resembled that of Hoxha, and his world outlook did not seem to differ much from that of his mentor. Born in 1925 in the northern town of Shkodër, Alia had joined the communist-led National Liberation Movement as a teenager, becoming a party member in 1943. At the age of 19, he was appointed political commissar, with the rank of lieutenant colonel, of the fifth combat division. Immediately after the war, Alia occupied leadership posts in the youth organization and in the office of propaganda and agitation of the APL Central Committee. He moved through party ranks at a time of great domestic upheaval and party factionalism. At the 1st APL Congress in 1948, he was elected a member of the Central Committee. After completing advanced studies in 1954 in the Soviet Union, he rose rapidly under Hoxha's patronage, serving as minister of education (1955–1958) and becoming a candidate member of the Politburo in 1956. He joined the Hoxha leadership's inner circle in 1961, when at the 4th APL Congress he became a full member of the Politburo and a member of the Secretariat. Throughout the 1960s and the 1970s, Alia acquired extensive experience in party affairs as well as in the cultural and ideological sectors. He played a prominent role in Tiranë's ideological campaign against Soviet, Yugoslav, and later Chinese "revisionism."

In his public pronouncements, Alia invariably echoed Hoxha's ideas on key foreign and domestic policy issues. In a major speech on the occasion of the centenary of Stalin's birth, in December 1979, he offered a tempestuous defense of the APL's Stalinist policies, which had come under increased criticism both at home and abroad. Noting that the APL was the only ruling communist party that had not repudiated Stalinism, Alia asserted that the attitude toward Stalin represented "a clear line of demarcation between Marxist-Leninists and modern revisionists." He added:

> The enemies of communism frequently call us Albanians "Stalinists." Enslaved by their own slanders and fabrications against Stalin, they think that by describing us in this way, they are abusing and insulting us. But it is an honor for us Albanians that we uphold the teachings of Stalin, which are the teachings of Marxism-Leninism, that we are working and struggling for socialism and communism with that determination and courage with which Stalin worked and struggled. To the communists and people of Albania, Stalin was and is inseparable from the triumphant doctrine of the proletariat which has lit the way to the achievement of all our victories.[2]

Whereas Alia showed remarkable talent throughout his career for surviving the many purges that swept the top party and government echelons, he was not known as someone who publicly spoke his mind. Nonetheless, many party members and, particularly, the creative intelligentsia believed Alia exerted a moderating influence on the leadership, especially during periods of domestic convulsions.[3] Consequently, his main power base was the central party apparatus and his most loyal allies were to be found among the intelligentsia. He emerged as the chief beneficiary of extensive leadership changes that followed the demise in 1981 of Prime Minister Mehmet Shehu, reputedly the second-ranking member of the leadership. In November 1982, Alia, in addition to retaining his party posts, was named president of the presidium of the People's Assembly (the titular head of state).

In early 1983 Hoxha increasingly limited his political activity, going into semiretirement. With impeccable party credentials and with Hoxha publicly according him a proximity to himself that he had denied to other members of the ruling elite,[4] Alia assumed the day-to-day administration of the nation's affairs. The only member of the leadership to hold two top posts, he traveled extensively, took Hoxha's place on major occasions, and delivered authoritative policy statements. That the succession had been decided well in advance of Hoxha's demise was confirmed by the speed and smoothness of Alia's selection as APL first secretary on April 13, 1985, only two days after Hoxha's death and before his funeral.[5]

Although personally selected by Hoxha as his successor, Alia did not possess Hoxha's charisma and obviously wielded considerably less power and authority than his mentor. Nonetheless, he had the advantage of being more than "the first among equals" in the Politburo. During the last years of Hoxha's life, Alia had played a preeminent role in the governing of the country, which enabled him to build his authority. Only Rita Marko (born 1920) and Manush Myftiu (b. 1919) had served longer than Alia on the Politburo, both having been elected at the 3rd APL Congress in 1956. Prime Minister Adil Çarçani, who became a Politburo member at the same time Alia did, had a purely government career. Neither of the three, however, was considered a serious contender for the post of APL first secretary.

The composition of the top leadership that Alia inherited in April 1985 differed substantially from a decade earlier. Of the 15 full and candidate Politburo members, 11 had been elevated to that body after 1975, most of them owing their rise to power personally to Hoxha. Nine of them were representatives of the postwar generation of leaders and had gone through a different political experience from their senior colleagues. The majority had made their political careers after the break with the Soviet Union. Almost all full and candidate Politburo members selected after 1975 had alternated between party and government posts. In contrast to their more senior colleagues, the newcomers had a superior level of formal education, giving a strong technocratic cast to the post-Hoxha leadership. Four of the freshmen had previously headed the ministry of industry and mines and their elevation to the Politburo reflected the importance the leadership continued to give to the development of heavy industry.

Following the dismissal of high-ranking cultural, economic, and military officials in the 1970s, Hoxha had rejuvenated the leadership by naming to top positions relatively young people who had distinguished themselves as local and district administrators. In May 1975 Hekuran Isai (b. 1933) and Pali Miska (b. 1931) were selected as full Politburo members; Llambi Gegprifti (b. 1942) and Qirjako Mihali (b. 1929) as candidate Politburo members.[6] Significantly, Isai and Miska became full Politburo members without passing through the candidate stage as was normally done. Evidently, Isai caught Hoxha's attention with his good performance as first district party secretary in Librazhd and Dibër. The 7th APL Congress in 1976 confirmed the selection of the above named officials. In addition, it elected two new candidate Poliburo members: Lenka Çuko (b. 1938), an agricultural specialist who had distinguished herself as first party secretary in the Lushnje district, and Simon Stefani (b. 1929), a specialist in the oil industry and first district party secretary at Permet and later Tiranë. None of them had purely party careers, and their prior links with Alia were probably minimal.

Hoxha continued with the invigoration of the party leadership at the 8th APL Congress in 1981 with the promotion of Çuko and Stefani to full membership in the Politburo, the selection of two new full members, Muho Asllani (b. 1937) and Hajredin Çeliku (b. 1927), and three candidate members, Besnik Bekteshi (b. 1914), Foto Çami (b. 1925), and Prokop Murra (b. 1921). As in the case of Isai and Miska in 1975, Asllani and Çeliku became full Politburo members without passing through the candidate stage. Although there is no evidence of close links between Alia and Çeliku, who by profession is a mechanical engineer, Alia most likely was instrumental in the elevation to the Politburo of Asllani, Bekteshi, Çami, and Murra. The latter, with the exception of Bekteshi, had served as first district party secretaries at Shkodër, Alia's hometown. Both Asllani and Bekteshi were born in Shkodër. Alia's links with Murra were further strengthened after Murra's appointment to the APL Secretariat in 1976. Foto Çami has had a long-standing association with Alia. A prominent member of the intelligentsia and the prestigious Academy of Sciences, Çami, in contrast to his Politburo colleagues, saw his political career flourish rather belatedly. At the time of his selection as candidate Politburo member in 1981, he was 56 years old. An active participant in the partisan war, he joined the party in 1944, but did not become a member of the Central Committee until 1971. A prolific writer, he worked for many years in the Central Committee's propaganda section. He also served as first district party secretary at Krujë and Tiranë, in addition to Shkodër. In July 1985 during the first post-Hoxha leadership change, Çami was appointed to the Secretariat.

Conveying a sense of continuity and stability, Alia moved gradually but confidently to strengthen his power and build his authority. Within a short period of time, he established a dominant profile in the official media and took over all the posts held by Hoxha, with the exception of chairman of the Democratic Front, the country's largest and most important mass organization. In March 1986 Hoxha's widow was named chairperson of the Democratic Front, a post with high visibility but little power.

The 9th APL Congress, which met in November 1986, confirmed Alia as the country's undisputed leader. Changes approved by the congress suggested that Alia's supporters dominate the Politburo and Secretariat. The new Central Committee elected at the 9th Congress also reflected Alia's strength. Not surprisingly, Çami, Bekteshi, and Murra were promoted to full membership in the Politburo, thus filling the positions left vacant by the demise of Hoxha, Mehmet Shehu, and Kadri Hasbiu, former defense minister who was purged after Shehu's death. Vangjel Çërrava (b. 1941) and Pirro Kondi (b. 1932?), who in 1985 had replaced Çami as first party secretary for the Tiranë district, and Kiço Mustaqi, first deputy minister of defense and chief of the general staff, were elected candidate Politburo members. The promotion of Murra to full membership and Mustaqi to candidate membership of the Politburo restored to the military an institutional voice in the highest party organ. Despite the rejuvenation of the top leadership, at the 9th Congress the postwar generation had not yet replaced its predecessors. The Old Guard, consisting of Alia, Çarçani, Çami, Çeliku, Marko, Murra, and Myftiu was still firmly in control.

## Charting a New Course

Alia inherited a country isolated from the outside world, largely dispirited, an apathetic population, menacing economic and political problems requiring adaptive responses, and, perhaps more important, one of the most secretive and doctrinaire communist leaderships in the world. The internal political situation appeared strained amid a deepening economic crisis, an apparent growing rift between large portions of society and their rulers, and uncertainty about the future. The economy suffered from a host of problems endemic to centrally planned systems: low productivity, permanent shortages of basic foodstuffs, an ailing infrastructure, and huge subsidies. There appeared to be considerable discontent over the regime's failure to observe internationally recognized standards of human rights and its inability to meet basic human and material needs. Young people seemed to be alienated and disillusioned with the system and its ideology, and, to the consternation of party ideologues, highly susceptible to Western lifestyles, art, literature, music, and fashion.

Although confronted with home-grown problems, Alia appeared to be a true believer in the system he had helped create. There was no evidence to suggest that he or any other member of the top leadership questioned or had serious doubts about the efficacy of the system. Nevertheless, soon after his accession, it became apparent that Alia was not a prisoner of past policies and was indeed searching for new solutions to the nation's problems. He displayed a distinct political style with different priorities. Although perilously constrained by Hoxha's legacy, Alia began to put his own stamp on the country's politics, changing the tenor of both domestic and foreign policies. He indicated, however, that change would be carried out in an orderly fashion. His major dilemma appeared to be how to move away from the rigid policies of his predecessor without alienating party hardliners and unleashing pent-up forces that would pose a danger to his hold on power. While insisting that Hoxha's "teachings" remained the foundation of the general foreign and domestic policy line of Albania, Alia initiated small but potentially significant economic innovations, relaxed somewhat the party's tight grip on society, and practically ended Albania's international isolation.

Alia's domestic policies were characterized by a mixture of conservative and reformist elements. He ruled out the possibility of fundamental, systemic reforms that held out the promise of overcoming the stagnation, inertia, and backwardness caused by Hoxha's policies. Neither did he loosen the country's rigid political structure, expose Hoxha's harsh political legacy, or fill in the blank spots in Albania's turbulent post-1944 history. But Alia, whose main preoccupation appeared to be the economy, indicated that his objective was to gird the party and the masses for significant changes that would revitalize the economy. He stressed the need to face realities in the economic field. Insisting that these were "unusual times" for Albania, he called for a "great leap forward."[7] Giving a remarkably frank recitation of the various ills that plagued the economy, he summoned the country to major improvements in economic performance, giving priority to addressing the long-deferred needs of consumers and raising the population's standard of living. He urged economists to play a greater role "in order to find the optimal solutions and the most rational ways of using the country's potentials and in order to clarify prospects."[8]

At the 9th APL Congress, Alia said the problems facing Albania had become more difficult and complex and could no longer be solved by "preindustrial" methods of management. He criticized the excessively centralized economic system and called for a decentralization of the decision-making process. Alia sharply criticized "the tendency to centralize even the smaller things, to take away the competencies of the lower organs, and to transform the base into a mere executor."[9]

The Albanian leader blamed current economic difficulties on problems accrued during the last years of Hoxha's rule, allowing the inference that responsibility for many of the problems ultimately lay with Hoxha. Subtly but unmistakably, he questioned the wisdom of some past economic policies. In a speech to the party *aktiv* at Tiranë in March 1987, Alia drew a distinction between what he described as "primary" tenets of the system, which "must be preserved and developed," and "secondary" ones, which must undergo constant "change and refinement."[10] Echoing these pronouncements, Premier Çarçani said there was a need for a new approach, insisting that party cadres should "not remain slaves of practices and methods which have been overtaken by time."[11]

Much of the criticism that permeated official statements and media reports on economic affairs was directed at overcentralization, economic mismanagement, low labor productivity, the inability to unleash the initiative of all sections of production and management, and the failure of the centralized planning system to deliver the goods. Foto Çami, who emerged as the leadership's point man in advocating change, displayed a novel style, going futher than both Alia and Çarçani in stressing the need for "new solutions." In what appeared to be a radical proposal in Albania's context, Çami asserted that as long as the country's freedom and independence were protected and the social order preserved, "other things can and must be changed when necessary, suffice that they do not affect the foundations of our socialist system, but serve them."[12] In a major address during October 1987, Çami said that Marxism-Leninism provides only basic guidelines and that "it would be wrong and naive to demand from it schemes and ready-made recipes for all the specific issues which arise in the course of social practice." Everything must be subjected to the test of practice, he said, adding that "things, which are not questions of principle and do not run counter to the foundations of our socialist system, can and must be changed when the time demands it, and when it is made necessary by the needs of the development of the country, and the interests of the homeland and of socialism." Reflecting the leadership's growing impatience with economists, theoreticians, and ideologues who had lagged behind practical developments instead of taking the lead in formulating new ideas that would have practical impact, he chastised officials and cadres who wait for instructions and orders from above. Çami added:

> There is a dominant way of thinking among many cadres that I would call metaphysical. They see themselves more as channels and simple performers of instructions led from above, wanting the leadership to say or demand everything, hesitating or not exerting their brains to raise problems and offer suggestions for creative solutions, changes, and refinements that must be introduced into our past practice, and so on. Such a spirit and attitude leads to dogmatism and conservatism, to becoming a slave to habits and old forms and methods that are unsuitable or which have been superseded by time. As the 9th APL Congress pointed out, it even leads to the creation of a social type who is frightened of everything that is new, of all kinds of change, and who becomes an obstacle to futher progress.[13]

The government instituted a series of measures designed to improve the system's efficiency and meet the population's basic needs. These measures did not threaten the foundation of the Albanian system and therefore were not politically risky for Alia, although some of them represented a departure from Hoxha's approach. Alia moved toward a partial decentralization of state economic management, a selective reform of prices, and took other steps designed to increase economic performance. He appeared distressed with worker alienation and low labor productivity, caused by wage leveling, overstaffing, the lack of work incentives, and the absence of workplace democracy. His proposed solution was to give managers and workers more responsibility. In some enterprises, workers' wages were linked to the enterprises' profits and their own performance. Although not reversing Hoxha's policy on the abolition of private plots, Alia recognized the importance these plots played in increasing food supplies. Peasants were urged to raise more livestock and plant more vegetables on their private plots for delivery to the market. To encourage farmers to increase output, the government raised the purchasing prices for agricultural and livestock products. In a marked departure from past policies, Alia changed the practice of having only the cooperatives raise livestock. He instituted a new system that permitted production teams, or brigades, to raise small herds. In addition, with the formation of a State Control Commission, stringent quality controls were introduced.

Available evidence indicated that Alia did not share Hoxha's ruthlessness and paranoia. He stressed the use of persuasion rather than coercion in dealing with socio-political problems confronting his regime. Alia lifted slightly the excessive restraints and controls on the population. Foreign travel restrictions were eased, with growing numbers of Albanians being permitted to visit their relatives abroad, mainly in Greece, Yugoslavia, and certain West European countires. A general amnesty announced in January 1986, on the occasion of the 40th anniversary of the proclamation of the Albanian People's Republic, reportedly resulted in the release of many long-term prisoners. Increasing numbers of tourists visited Albania from abroad. Foreign journalists reported a relaxed atmosphere, with most official and nonofficial Albanian interlocutors willing to engage in wide-ranging discussions. But despite the apparent relaxation of restrictions and the increase in tourism, Albania's contacts with the outside world remained strictly controlled because of the fear that such interaction would expose the country to foreign, particularly Western, liberal ideals and eventually political leverage.

In the sphere of human rights and cultural policy, Alia displayed a degree of openness and toleration, but took no meaningful measures to allow greater political freedom or to liberalize intellectual and artistic life. Whereas repression was not applied indiscriminately and on a massive scale, as during Hoxha's era, the persecution of political opponents continued. The Albanian government, although sensitive to outside criticism, continued to display an intransigent position on the issue of human rights. Political participation remained limited, with nonparty groups having practically no chance to participate in the country's affairs, and the ruling elite's monopoly on power unshaken. The government appeared as determined as ever to suppress any signs of dissent.

Although censorship was not eased, Alia encouraged public discussion of cultural, economic, and social problems. At a meeting with writers and artists in Korçë, during August 1985, Alia called for a new standard of literature, sparking a lively debate and a plea for freedom of expression. In a marked departure from past practice, Alia also advocated an Albanian-style *glasnost'* campaign, insisting that "people should always be talked to openly, whether about their complaints or about difficulties and shortcomings."[14] In a message of greetings to the editorial board of the party daily *Zëri i popullit*, on its 45th anniversary, Alia sharply criticized the role of the press in Albania. He called for a struggle "against

hollow phrases which seek to conceal poverty of thought, against over-
blown euphoria which seeks to replace the analysis of facts, against stereotypes and schematicism which illustrate poverty of imagination, and
which unfortunately are not uncommonly encountered in some press articles and in radio and television programs."[15] Meanwhile, Çami, in a
wholesale attack during October 1987 on the media's failure to provide
timely, objective, and comprehensive information to the masses, asserted
paradoxically that, "the strength of our propaganda lies in its truth." He
added:

> The more frank we are with the masses, the more openly we talk, and the
> more honest we are with them, the better we present problems before the
> people and discuss them, the more responsible they then become for tasks
> that emerge and the stronger the ties between party and people grow. Let
> us give people more information both on domestic and foreign problems.[16]

Controversial articles appeared in the official media, which during
Hoxha's era would have been unthinkable. Hamit Beqja, a prominent
sociologist, called for an intensification of the "free debate," maintaining
that debate "stimulates, democratizes, and revolutionizes the country's
entire life" and serves as a guarantee against "fruitless doctrinaire thinking and blind conformism."[17] Other scholars, echoing Alia's encouragement of public debate, called for an expansion of cultural ties with other
countries, and rejected the use of "administrative" (i.e., repressive) methods in dealing with social, particularly youth, problems.[18]

Alia received mixed responses from intellectuals, workers, and up-
wardly mobile professionals to his calls for reinvigoration of Albanian
society. His program of economic change rested on a narrow popular
base. The intellectuals appeared most supportive of Alia. Workers were
generally apathetic because of Alia's inability to offer them immediate
and visible improvements in their daily lives. Alia's discipline campaign
resulted in workers having to work harder while being paid less because
of recently established quality controls. Moreover, Alia indicated he favored giving managers the authority to fire workers and take administrative measures against employees who steal or misappropriate state property, including denial of housing and material benefits. The elderly,
especially party ideologues, appeared uneasy about Alia's policy, and the
young largely indifferent. But perhaps more important, many bureau-

cratic middlemen and party functionaries, fearing that their power and privileged positions were being undermined, resisted the proposed changes. Alia indicated there were serious problems in changing the authoritarian style of party officials and managers.[19]

Although official pronouncements reflected strong rhetoric on the need for change, the Alia leadership did not offer a blueprint nor did it create an institutionalized base for fundamental reforms. The economy continued to be managed in a cumbersome way, with a perverse system of economic incentives and planning. In order to reinvigorate the economy, Alia would have to undo four decades of Stalinist central planning and overcome tremendous resistance based as much on Hoxha's legacy as on the country's conservative culture. The regime, however, feared that economic liberalization and encouragement of individual initiative would lead to political liberalization and uncontrollable consequences, thus threatening the party's hold on power. Implementing meaningful reforms involved trading current job security for greater future opportunity and posed, at least in the short run, serious political risks. Shutting down outmoded industries was politically unacceptable and would lead to unemployment and bankruptcy, which remained extraordinarily sensitive issues. Workers had been told their job security was one of the superior aspects of Albania's communist system. Officials bristled at the possibility of unemployment. Removing subsidies and increasing prices would lead to inflation, consumer panic, and a significant cost of living increase. Moreover, strong conservative elements within the APL and the government opposed measures that threatened to loosen the party's ideological controls.

With such strong impediments to change, radical reforms seemed highly unlikely. But the alternative to reform, a prolonged period of economic stagnation and decline that posed the risk of political ferment, was analogously unacceptable to Alia. As a result, he opted for partial reforms and tried to tackle economic problems without tampering with the fundamental features of the system he inherited from Hoxha. Although the long-term success of his limited reforms remained uncertain, Alia started a slow process of economic change and held out the promise that more significant reforms were forthcoming. But no economic reforms were likely to succeed if they were not backed up with similar political changes and a more responsible use of power by the governing elite. But whereas the winds of change seemed to be blowing in Albania, too, their direction and ultimate effects remained uncertain. Reform, especially in the political field, was therefore likely to be difficult, risky and contentious.

## Foreign Policy Pragmatism

Upon Ramiz Alia's accession to power, Albania faced a relatively favorable external environment, with most Western and East European countries, including the two superpowers, having adopted a benevolent attitude toward Tiranë. Although adherence to a rigid Stalinist ideology had made Albania the most politically repressive regime in Eastern Europe, Tiranë found other governments quite receptive to its initiatives for improvement of relations. Since the early 1960s, West European countries had become appreciative of the benefits of Albania's independence from the Soviet bloc. Tiranë's break with Moscow had contributed significantly to Western interests in the Balkans. As in the case of Yugoslavia, West European capitals downplayed the question of human rights violations in their overtures to Albania, giving precedence to that country's strategic importance. Similarly, the United States, beginning in 1973, expressed willingness to resume ties with Albania. It was in the U.S. interest that Albania pursue an independent foreign policy and not reestablish close relations, especially military ties, with the Soviet Union. A revival of the alliance would give the USSR military access to the Adriatic, increase potential Soviet pressure on Yugoslavia and Greece, and heighten the threat to NATO's southern flank. An independent, nonaligned Albania was thus important for Western policy in the volatile Balkans. After Hoxha's death, senior American officials reiterated the United States view that "should Albania indicate an interest in resuming relations with us, we would be prepared to respond."[20]

Soviet bloc policy toward Albania also had undergone significant changes. In the early 1960s the USSR, distressed with Albania having taken the Chinese side in the Sino-Soviet conflict, cut all relations with Tiranë, resorted to political and economic pressures, attempted to incite popular dissatisfaction against Hoxha's regime, and excluded Albania from the Warsaw Pact and CMEA. As Albania proceeded with its own model of communist development, Hoxha in the mid- and late 1960s took measures to eradicate signs of Soviet influence and legacy from all fields of Albanian society. After Nikita S. Khrushchev's downfall in 1964, Moscow expressed willingness to normalize relations. Tiranë, however, insisted that the USSR first apologize publicly for its decision to break diplomatic relations with Albania in 1961, a condition the Kremlin refused to accept. During the last phase, and after disintegration of the Albanian-Chinese alliance, the Soviets adopted a friendly attitude toward Albania. At a minimum, they hoped to reestablish diplomatic relations with Tiranë and prevent Albania from joining Western political and military organizations. But Moscow's long-term objective remained the full reintegration of Albania into the Soviet bloc. In addition to the obvious military importance for the Warsaw Pact, a reintegrated Albania could serve as a model for other "defectors" and as a reminder to restless East European countries that socialist regimes cannot succeed outside the bloc.

With Hoxha's death in April 1985, a reassessment of Albania's foreign policy had become indispensable. Adverse economic consequences, caused primarily by a long period of isolation and reflected most dramatically in the nonfulfillment of economic targets and chronic shortages, made it imperative that Albania interact more with the outside world. The Albanians realized that the technological modernization of economy could not be achieved without such interaction. Sofokli Lazri, member of the APL Central Committee and director of the influential Foreign Affairs Institute, disclosed at the 9th Party Congress in November 1986 that Albania, although abiding by its policy of self-reliance, would significantly expand trade exchanges with other countries, importing factories, equipment, and various kinds of modern technology.[21] The Albanian government evidently hoped that the introduction of more advanced technology would alleviate the country's economic difficulties. However, limited hard currency reserves and constitutional restrictions on foreign loans and credits continued to limit Tiranë's imports of technology. Moreover, with the shortage of qualified experts, Albania experienced difficulty absorbing and fully utilizing new technology.

Whereas this opening up was undoubtedly motivated by economic necessity, political considerations were also important. Alia apparently realized that Hoxha's isolationist policy, which had deprived the country of the political and economic advantages of greater interaction with the outside world, was not viable in the long run. Moreover, with the exasperation of the ethnic conflict in Kosovë in the wake of Belgrade's failure to meet Kosovar demands for establishment of an Albanian republic within the federation, Yugoslavia had resorted to economic, military, and political pressures on Albania. A major objective of Albanian diplomacy became the prevention of the establishment of an anti-Albanian coalition in the Balkans directed by Belgrade. This required stabilization and strengthening of relations with other countries, particularly neighboring Greece, Italy, and Bulgaria.

One of the main characteristics of Hoxha's foreign policy had been the view that Albania's immediate neighbors—individually or collectively—represented the main sources of external threat. This perception accounted for the fact that Albania refused to join neighboring states in attempts at multilateral cooperation. Hoxha had warned repeatedly that the superpowers represented the main threat to stability in the Balkans and had called on Greece and Turkey as well as Bulgaria and Romania to withdraw from NATO and the Warsaw Pact, respectively. He also had urged Yugoslavia to deny Soviet and American navies access to its ports and facilities.

Soon after Alia's accession significant changes became evident in Albanian perceptions about international politics, signaling that Alia would inject a new flexibility into his country's foreign policy and do away with the most damaging self-imposed constraints that had limited the country's foreign policy options. Tiranë moved away from some of the old stereotypes propagated by the official media for decades. The outside world was no longer portrayed in black-and-white terms. Albania now appeared willing to take advantage of disagreements among its immediate neighbors, pursuing a policy of differentiation toward them. Neighboring countries were no longer characterized collectively as sources of an external threat, although Yugoslavia continued to be cast in the role of a country essentially hostile to Albanian national goals and objectives.

In public statements, Alia indicated that his foreign policy would focus less on the regime's Marxist-Leninist ideology and more on political and economic realities confronting Albania. In a speech at the 4th plenum of the Central Committee in July 1987, Alia declared:

> The tactics followed in the field of our international relations change, since problems change and evolve in the ebb and flow of revolutionary national liberation movements, new issues arise requiring fresh consideration, and so on. What does not change is the general line of the party, the preservation of total political and economic independence, national defense, complete irreconcilability with imperialism and revisionism, proletarian internationalism and solidarity with the peoples, who are against war, in favor of peace and the progress of mankind.[22]

On the occasion of the 75th anniversary of Albania's independence, Alia said, "We do not intend to stand aside from the rest of the world, or to live in isolation. We do not hesitate to cooperate with others and we do not fear their power and wealth. On the contrary, we seek such cooperation since we consider it a factor that will contribute to our internal development . . ."[23]

Albania's foreign policy pragmatism in the post-Hoxha era was perhaps best dramatized by its participation in the Balkan Foreign Ministers' Conference, held at Belgrade during February 1988. This represented a clear departure from Hoxha's policy of shunning multilateral meetings. At the conference, Foreign Minister Reis Malile said that Albania "is for the independent development and stability of each Balkan country. We are aware that destabilization of any of our countries is to the detriment of each of us and of peace and security in general." He called for the reactivation of Balkan committees on trade, transportation, and other issues. "Not only do we not hesitate to cooperate with others but, on the contrary, we want this cooperation and consider it a factor which contributes to our internal development too," he said. Without mentioning the thorny issue of Kosovë, which had complicated Tiranë-Belgrade relations, Malile declared that minorities

> should be turned into a factor of cohesion and stability within the country and a bridge for relations of cooperation with the neighboring countries. Our times are not those of colonializations, of the oppression of the minorities and the suppression of their rights which are recognized by international law and the Charter of the United Nations.[24]

Albania's participation in the Balkan conference represented an important departure from Hoxha's policies. It marked the beginning of a new phase in Albania's foreign policy and the clearest indication of Alia's determination to return his country to the mainstream of international politics. With participation in the Balkan Conference, Alia for all practical purposes ended Albania's isolation. He accelerated the process of diversifying Tiranë's external relations, concentrating on stabilizing and strengthening relations with Greece, Italy, and Turkey, finding a modus vivendi with Yugoslavia and containing the adverse effects of the ethnic conflict in Kosovë on Tiranë-Belgrade relations, and expanding ties with other European and Third World countries, simultaneously maintaining a hostile attitude toward the two superpowers. Albania embarked on a more pragmatic and active foreign policy. It established ties with West Germany and upgraded its relations to the ambassadorial level with several East European countries. The Albanian leadership apparently recognized the fact that Hoxha's isolationist policies had caused the country considerable political damage. Alia's policy of returning Albania to the mainstream of international politics was also motivated by economic considerations. Whereas Hoxha had exploited tensions with other countries, especially by fostering an atmosphere of a besieged fortress and mobilizing the population around the theme of an alleged threat to the country's independence to implement his orthodox domestic policies, Alia saw the expansion of external interactions as a means of helping Tiranë tackle its economic difficulties.

The most likely scenario for Albania's foreign policy in the 1990s appears to be a gradual but steady expansion of relations with both East and West. Although fanatically preserving its foreign policy independence, Albania will most likely reassess its policy of self-reliance. West Germany and Italy are likely to become Albania's primary foreign partners. With the passage of time, the issues that in the past prevented Albania from restoring ties with the United States and the USSR are likely to become less salient, thus opening the way for the normalization of these relations. Although the Kremlin has been persistent in its efforts to woo Albania back into the fold, Tiranë is not likely to reintegrate itself with the Soviet bloc. Ties with Yugoslavia are likely to remain strained, since there appear to be few prospects for a solution of the Kosovë problem.

Western policymakers would be well advised to pay greater attention to Albania. Developments in that tiny country are likely to have implications far beyond its borders. The United States and its NATO allies have a high stake in the Balkans. Instability in Albania, coupled with the exasperation of the ethnic conflict and the economic crisis in Yugoslavia, could adversely affect the delicate balance of power in the volatile Balkans, long known as the "powder keg" of Europe. Western policy should take advantage of Albania's apparent opening to the outside world and domestic changes. Positive political, economic, and human rights developments ought to be rewarded with economic ties and support. In addition to opposing the restoration of Soviet influence in Albania, one of the main Western objectives should be the promotion of greater pluralism and better human rights performances through expansion and broadening of dialogue and contacts with both the Albanian government and society.

# PROJECTIONS
## *Nathaniel Davis**

The author of the first section of this chapter, Elez Biberaj, is a key figure in the official community of the United States dealing with Albania. As head of the Albanian service for the Voice of America, he probably commands more man-hours of dedicated, available personnel to work on Albanian analysis and commentary than any other U.S. government official. Moreover, the Voice of America is not jammed, and its influence is great. Also, Dr. Biberaj is widely connected among Albanian emigré circles in the United States and Western Europe and is among the best-informed of the observers of the Albanian scene in America. So his observations should be viewed with respect and attention.

I was struck by the similarity between Dr. Biberaj's analysis of leadership struggles in Albanian politics over the past few years and the "Kremlinology" that all veterans in the Soviet field are familiar with from the 1940s and 1950s. There are the same sort of careful gleanings from the Albanian press, tracking of politicians' careers on the basis of propinquity to leading figures, published job shifts between party and government posts, and so on. This reflects the evident fact that Albania is still "unreconstructed," and still a society closed to ready contact and free interchange of people and ideas. Glints of insight must still be gained from the visible tip of a mostly submerged iceberg.

In a somewhat ironic twist to Albania's isolation, that country was the only nation in Europe in early 1985 *not* to have reported a single case of AIDS.[25]

The phenomena just described are beginning to change. More Albanians are going abroad; more Americans of Albanian descent are visiting Albania; more Western diplomats are living and working in Tiranë as foreign embassies in the Albanian capital multiply, and, as Dr. Biberaj points out, Albanians are talking more freely. So we may have more sources of information in the future than we have had in the past. It will be a relief to see the 75 or more volumes of Enver Hoxha's speeches and memoirs loom a bit less prominently than they once did in the corpus of contemporary Albanian published works.

---

*In working out the comments in this section, I am particularly indebted to Professor Nicholas C. Pano of Western Illinois University, John A. Cloud of the Office of Eastern European and Yugoslav Affairs in the U.S. Department of State, Adrian J. Harmata in the Office of Analysis for the Soviet Union and Eastern Europe of the State Department, and several CIA analysts. The insights and information provided by these experts were crucial in the preparation of this commentary.

## Perestroika

Albania has been called the most centralized planned economy in the world; however, things are changing a little. Although *perestroika* is publicly denounced, it is grudgingly emulated—cautiously, gradually, but inexorably. The economic situation in the country is terrible, and the relatively pragmatic Ramiz Alia knows he has to do something. Local people's councils are exhorted to become more involved; managers are encouraged to take initiative; limited wage reforms are bringing increased differentiation of wages, with the productive workers earning more than the slothful ones. Moreover, differentiation in the quality and price of consumer goods promises the industrious laborer better things to buy. Whereas in the past Albanian bicycle models were standard, and depressingly so, there are now "deluxe" models of these and other products. Changes in the labor code make it a bit easier for a worker to change jobs. The safety of workers in the mines and shops is a little better ensured. Alia seems genuinely attempting to reduce the alienation of the labor force and raise workers' output. The quality of food and services appears a trifle improved. Perhaps this is not much, but it is something.

In agriculture, Albania is working resolutely toward the condition of the USSR *before* Gorbachev's reforms—or perhaps even before Khrushchev. Hoxha's goal had been to abolish peasants' private plots altogether. In 1987 garden plots were again permitted; and in late 1988 a congress of agricultural cooperatives declared that peasants could sell their privately grown produce at farmers' markets for the prices the market would bear—as in the collective farm markets in the USSR. Peasants are permitted to keep a few animals of their own.

## Religion

Under Enver Hoxha, Albania had in 1967 become the premier atheist state in the world, the first so pronounced by legal action. All of the churches, mosques, and other religious institutions were closed, and religious practice was supposedly eliminated altogether. In a move reminiscent of Peter the Great's "modernizing" and antireligiously traditionalist sentiments, the Albanians outlawed beards, even giving foreigners entering the country involuntary clean shaves at the border.[26] To mention only one poignant example of religious suppression, the son of an orthodox mother and a Jewish father escaped to Greece in 1986. This young man of 31 years, Samuel Matathia, reported that he "knew no prayer," had never seen a Jewish text or had "heard a Hebrew word." The only religious acts he had ever known were "secret gatherings" at which traditional Sephardic Jewish sweets were "eaten in memory of the dead."[27] As Biberaj notes, however, the "abolition of religion" has not been entirely successful.

Hoxha's policies have not been reversed by Alia, nor have the churches and mosques been allowed to reopen, but a few slight evidences of change have become apparent. The forced clean shaves at the border are gone. Albanian newspapers and journals occasionally mention, albeit with disapproval, observances of religious holy days, baptisms, and visits by the populace to the sites of former churches and mosques. Formerly, mention of the subject of religion had been virtually taboo, as Dr. Biberaj has noted. The general amnesty of 1986 did result in some long-imprisoned clerics being released. This past summer, American orthodox and Roman Catholic priests, some Muslim clergy, and one or two other American clerics were allowed to visit Albania and, in a few cases, were even allowed to appear in public in clerical garb. A museum of atheism and antireligion in Shkodër has been closed. Western observers have seen a few Muslims performing their prayers in public. These are modest changes, but there is a bit more toleration of religious practice in homes, in rural byways, and even in the towns.

## Foreign Relations

Albania's relations with its Balkan neighbors have been improving significantly. In January of 1989 Albania hosted the deputy foreign ministers of the Balkan states at Tiranë, and it is slated to be the site of the next regularly scheduled ministerial-level meeting in 1990. As Biberaj notes, the Albanian foreign minister attended the Balkan ministerial meeting at Belgrade in February 1988. Reportedly, he made a forthcoming impression and commented responsively and moderately on Yugoslav ties, notwithstanding the Kosovë problem. The press reported at the time that Yugoslavia and Albania had agreed to resume scientific, technical, and cultural exchanges, permit local border traffic, and establish a 220 kw transmission line linking the power grids of the two countries.[28]

As for other Eastern European neighbors, such as Hungary and Czechoslovakia, Albania's hope for barter arrangements and increased economic ties provides a stimulus to improved relations. Eastern European stirrings in the direction of increased freedom from the political and economic grip of Moscow also appear to provide some encouragement to the Albanians.

Relations between Albania and Western Europe, including states that are members of NATO, have also improved. As a consequence of relations established with the Federal Republic of Germany, Foreign Minister Hans-Dietrich Genscher visited Albania. So have the Greek and Turkish foreign ministers. An increased number of Greek tourists have been able to visit the country, and ethnic Greek Albanians have been able to visit Greece.[29] Relations have also been opened with Canada, Australia, and Spain.[30] The Federal Republic of Germany already may have replaced Czechoslovakia as Albania's largest trading partner.

So far as the U.S.-Albanian relationship is concerned, starting in 1973 the United States offered through a number of channels to discuss the normalization of relations with Albania. The Albanians never responded, probably for two reasons. The first is their desire to remain equidistant from the two superpowers, condemning the "hegemonic" pretensions of both. Dr. Biberaj, with whom I discussed the matter, believes that this factor is receding in importance. In the first place, defiance of the superpowers was a very personal crusade of Enver Hoxha himself, and Ramiz Alia has less of a personal stake in ideological intransigence. It is interesting in this regard that references to "equidistance" between the superpowers have more or less been dropped from standard pronouncements in the Albanian press. Moreover, the old Hoxha position had always been that the Soviets would have to apologize for the events of 1960–1961 before Albania would consider resuming relations. In a way, the USSR has now done so. At least *Pravda* has publicly stated that the Soviet action with respect to Albania was a mistake on Khrushchev's part. The USSR also publicly indicated in late 1986 that Soviet-Albanian relations are not "normal" and steps should be taken to make them so.[31] In addition a dispatch from Vienna a few months ago, in connection with the restoration of full diplomatic ties between Hungary and Albania, intimated that Albania was willing to consider relations with any country respectful of Albania's position. That sort of intimation could open a door to either the USSR or the United States. So Dr. Biberaj does see the possibility of Soviet-Albanian ties some time in the future, and perhaps even U.S.-Albanian ties in the next three to five years.

There is a second impediment to U.S.-Albanian ties in the near future. That is the fact that the Albanians have relatively little to gain, as they do not have much to offer the United States in trade, little hope of substantial American economic help, and modest possibilities of tangible benefit in other areas. A tripartite U.S.-U.K.-French commission sits on a small hoard of sequestered royal Albanian gold, and some settlement of American citizens' claims over confiscated and nationalized properties in Albania would no doubt be the price of a truly normalized relationship, as it has been elsewhere in Eastern Europe. Still, there have been a few signs of progress, and prospects for U.S.-Albanian trade are becoming a little better.

The Albanians were helpful when a private American yacht was stranded in Albanian waters in June of 1987. In Hoxha's time, the Albanians might have found a way to seize or sink it. In this case, they rescued the yacht in a storm, sheltered its passengers for three days, and sent it on its way when the weather improved. They sent a note from their Belgrade embassy to the American embassy there advising the U.S. government about the episode and their actions, something Hoxha would not have dreamed of doing. They even were prepared to receive and accept an answering note of thanks from the U.S. embassy.[32]

An NBC camera crew was allowed into Albania a few months ago, although the network commentator was Canadian and others in the crew were not American citizens. The number of emigrés in the United States allowed to visit relatives and former homes has increased a little. Also, the Albanian community in the United States exerts a modest influence on both the Albanian and U.S. governments in the direction of some normalization of relations.

With respect to Dr. Biberaj's analysis, the following observation seems particularly interesting: "Instability in Albania . . . could adversely affect the delicate balance of power in the volatile Balkans . . ." This statement provides an echo of the famous "Sonnenfeldt Doctrine" during the 1976 presidential campaign. What Dr. Biberaj seems to be suggesting is that stability is better than instability, because instability would probably not bring democracy and freedom to the Albanians but would more likely open the door to renewed Soviet dominance. It implies that the status quo, or very gradual change to a more open regime, is the West's best hope as well as the Albanians' best hope. This is difficult judgment; perhaps Dr. Biberaj is right.

Elez Biberaj is relatively optimistic—as well he should be in his position—and hopeful that "economic ties and support" from the West may promote or accelerate change and a better Albanian human rights performance. As already noted, he also believes that the passage of time may reduce the importance of U.S.-Albanian differences and open the way to a normalization of relations. Biberaj may be correct in this view, since the realities of Eastern Europe are changing with such speed as to make the pessimists wise in being cautious about saying what will not happen. It seems, however, that American ability to stimulate or induce change in Albania remains small. Some external shock or internal upheaval in Albania may alter its government's attitudes quickly and radically, but it is doubtful that the United States can bring about that result by means of U.S. policy alone. American influence and leverage remain marginal, and the limited resources and diverse priorities competing for U.S. attention and commitment make a massive American effort to change Albanian realities somewhat unlikely.

## Notes to Chapter 11

1. Nicholas C. Pano, "Albania: The Last Bastion of Stalinism," in Milorad M. Drachkovitch, ed., *East Central Europe: Yesterday, Today, Tomorrow* (Stanford: Hoover, 1982), pp. 187–218.

2. Ramiz Alia, *Stalin and his Work—A Banner of Struggle for all Revolutionaries* (Tiranë: "8 Nëntori," 1979), pp. 6–8, 55–56.

3. Louis Zanga, "Albania Begins the Post-Hoxha Era," RAD Background Report/33 (Eastern Europe), *Radio Free Europe Research*, 18 April 1985, p. 2.

4. In a speech in September 1982, Hoxha referred to Alia as "one of my outstanding cofighters." *Zëri i popullit*, 16 September 1982. An article published in the same paper shortly before Hoxha's death characterized Alia as "one of Comrade Enver's most distinguished cofighters." *Ibid.*, 19 January 1985.

5. *Ibid.*, 14 April 1985.

6. Enver Hoxha, *Vepra*, 56 (Tiranë: "8 Nëntori," 1987), 470–473.

7. Ramiz Alia, *Fjalime e Biseda 1986*, 2 (Tiranë: "8 Nëntori," 1987), 13, 29.

8. *Zëri i popullit*, 4 November 1986.

9. *Ibid.*

10. Ramiz Alia, *Fjalime e Biseda*, 4 (Tiranë: "8 Nëntori," 1988), 203–204.

11. *Zëri i popullit*, 11 April 1987, pp. 1–2.

12. Foto Çami, "Our Science Should Competently Confront the Great Tasks Set Out by the Ninth APL Congress," *Rruga e partisë*, no. 4 (April 1987), p. 12.

13. *Zëri i popullit*, 9 October 1987, pp. 1–3.

14. *Ibid.*, 4 November 1986.

15. *Ibid.*, 25 August 1987, p. 1.

16. *Ibid.*, 9 October 1987, pp. 1–3.

17. Hamit Beqja, "Kindling Further Debate," *Zëri i popullit*, 27 February 1987, pp. 3–4.

18. *Ibid.*, 9 October, 12 December, and 25 December 1986.

19. Alia, *Fjalime e biseda*, 4:11–12, 309–310, 366–367.

20. U.S. House of Representatives, Committee on Foreign Affairs, *U.S. Policy Toward Eastern Europe, 1985* (Washington, DC: U.S. Government Printing Office, 1986), p. 6.

21. *Zëri i popullit*, 8 November 1986.

22. *Ibid.*, 12 July 1987.

23. *Ibid.*, 29 November 1987.

24. *Ibid.*, 25 February 1988.

25. *The Times* (London), 1 April 1985, p. 10.

26. Alan Cowell, "A Hint of Change in the Albanian Air," *New York Times*, 30 August 1986, p. 2.

27. Henry Kamm, "An Albanian Jew Flees, with Grim Tale to Tell," *New York Times*, 30 August 1986, p. 2.

28. David Binder, "Rivalry Aside, Six Balkan Lands Meets and Agree," *New York Times*, 6 March 1988, p. 8.

29. See *New York Times*, 13 April 1986, and 29 August 1987, p. 3.

30. Cowell, "A Hint of Change in the Albanian Air," *New York Times*, 20 June 1988, p. 3.

31. *New York Times*, 30 November 1986, p. 4.

32. Kamm, "Albanian Aid to U.S. Yacht Hints of Slight Thaw," *New York Times*, 13 September 1987, p. 6.

# Index

# About the Contributors

**NICHOLAS G. ANDREWS** (Chapter 4), Princeton (A.B.), retired from the U.S. Foreign Service after serving as deputy chief of mission in Warsaw. He is author of *Poland 1980–81: Solidarity versus the Party* (1985).

**JOHN D. BELL** (Chapter 8), Princeton (Ph.D.), is an associate professor of history at the University of Maryland in Baltimore. His latest book, *The Bulgarian Communist Party: From Blagoev to Zhivkov*, appeared in 1986.

**ELEZ BIBERAJ** (Chapter 11), Columbia (Ph.D.), directs the Albanian radio service for the Voice of America. He is the author of *Albania and China: A Study of an Unequal Alliance* (1986).

**JOSEF C. BRADA** (Chapter 2), Minnesota (Ph.D.), is professor of economics at Arizona State University. The most recent among his six books, *The Hungarian Economy in the 1980's*, was published in 1988.

**NATHANIEL DAVIS** (Chapter 11), Fletcher School of Law and Diplomacy (Ph.D.), is a former envoy extraordinary and minister plenipotentiary to Bulgaria and senior National Security Council advisor for Soviet and Eastern European affairs to President Lyndon B. Johnson. Retired from the U.S. Foreign Service, he currently is the Alexander and Adelaide Hixon Professor of Humanities at Harvey Mudd College in Claremont, California.

**MARY ELLEN FISCHER** (Chapter 7), Harvard (Ph.D.), was a visiting scholar at the Russian Research Center of that university during 1988–1989. She is the Joseph C. Palamountain, Jr., Professor of Government at Skidmore College, and chairs the department. Her book, entitled *Nicolae Ceauşescu: A Study in Political Leadership*, will be published in 1989.

**JOHN P. HARDT** (Chapter 2), Columbia (Ph.D.), is the associate director for research coordination and senior specialist in Soviet economics for the Congressional Research Service as well as an adjunct professor at George Washington and Georgetown universities. He has contributed to many volumes on the economies of communist-ruled states, published by the Joint Economic Committee of the U.S. Congress, and most recently coedited *Planned Economies: Confronting the Challenges of the 1980's*, which was published in 1988.

**MARTIN J. HILLENBRAND** (Chapter 9), Columbia (Ph.D.), retired from the U.S. Foreign Service after being ambassador to Hungary and to West Germany, and assistant secretary of state for European affairs. He is currently the Dean Rusk Professor of International Relations and codirector of the Center for East-West Policy Studies at the University of Georgia. He is the author or editor of five books.

**ROBERT L. HUTCHINGS** (Chapter 1), Virginia (Ph.D.), currently serves as assistant national intelligence officer with the National Intelligence Council and professorial lecturer in Soviet studies at The Johns Hopkins University School for Advanced International Studies. He is the author of *Soviet-East European Relations: Consolidation and Conflict* (1983; rev. pb ed., 1987) and *Foreign and Security Policy Coordination in the Warsaw Pact* (1985).

**RICHARD E. JOHNSON** (Chapter 10), Georgetown (M.A.), served as chargé d'affaires and deputy chief of mission in Belgrade for a total of five years on two assignments; other postings included Warsaw and Sofia. Retired from the U.S. Foreign Service, he is currently president of the U.S.-Yugoslav Economic Council in Washington, D.C.

**CHRISTOPHER D. JONES** (Chapter 3), Harvard (Ph.D.), is an associate professor in the Henry M. Jackson School of International Studies at the University of Washington. He has published *Soviet Influence in Eastern Europe* (1981) and coauthored *The Warsaw Pact: The Question of Cohesion* (1984–1986) in four volumes.

**ROBERT R. KING** (Chapter 7), Fletcher School of Law and Diplomacy (Ph.D.), formerly on the National Security Council staff, now works as administrative aide to a U.S. congressman. Among his several books is *The History of the Romanian Communist Party* (1980), which will be published in a revised edition.

**NELSON C. LEDSKY** (Chapter 5), Columbia University (M.A.), is a former special assistant to the President and senior director for Europe on the National Security Council Staff. A career Foreign Service Officer, he previously served as chief of mission in West Berlin, with the rank of minister.

**ROBERT GERALD LIVINGSTON** (Chapter 5), Harvard (Ph.D.), directs the American Institute for Contemporary German Studies at The Johns Hopkins University in Washington, D.C. He was previously president of the German Marshall Fund of the United States. He has coauthored and edited *The Federal Republic of Germany in the 1980s: Foreign Policies and Domestic Changes* (1983) and *West German Political Parties* (1986).

**JACK R. PERRY** (Chapter 8), Columbia (Ph.D.), is director of the Dean Rusk Program in International Studies at Davidson College. A former career foreign service officer, he served as the U.S. ambassador to Bulgaria.

**ARTHUR R. RACHWALD** (Chapter 4), University of California at Santa Barbara (Ph.D.), is an associate professor in the department of political science at the U.S. Naval Academy. His most recent book, *Poland Between the Superpowers*, appeared in 1983.

**CARL W. SCHMIDT** (Chapter 6), Fletcher School of Law and Diplomacy (M.A.), is a U.S. Foreign Service Officer whose assignments have included deputy chief of mission in Prague (1985–1988) and director of the Office of Eastern European Affairs (1978–1980). He is currently attached to the Center for the Study of Foreign Affairs, U.S. Department of State.

**RICHARD F. STAAR** (Introduction), Michigan (Ph.D.), is coordinator of the international studies program for the Hoover Institution on War, Revolution and Peace at Stanford University. He served as U.S. ambassador to the Mutual and Balanced Force Reduction negotiations in Vienna, Austria (1981–1983).

**ZDENEK L. SUDA** (Chapter 6), Charles University (Ph.D.), is professor emeritus of sociology and senior associate of the Center for International Studies at the University of Pittsburgh. One of his books, entitled *Zealots and Rebels: A History of the Communist Party of Czechoslovakia* (1980), will soon be revised.

**PETER A. TOMA** (Chapter 9), University of Southern California (Ph.D.), is professor of political science and international relations at the University of Arizona and former director of the Europe and USSR area program at the National War College. He has authored or coauthored eight books, including most recently *Socialist Authority: The Hungarian Experience* (1988) and *Introduction to International Relations* with Robert Gorman (forthcoming).

**SUSAN L. WOODWARD** (Chapter 10), Princeton (Ph.D.), is an associate professor of political science at Yale University. Her next book, *Liberal Socialism and Unemployment: Reducing Labor Power in Yugoslavia, 1950–85*, will be published this year.

# Books by Richard F. Staar

*Arms Control: Myth versus Reality* (editor)
Aspects of Modern Communism (editor)
*Communist Regimes in Eastern Europe*
*Future Information Revolution in the USSR* (editor)
*Long-Range Environmental Study of the Northern Tier of Eastern Europe in 1990–
    2000*
*Poland 1944–1962: Sovietization of a Captive People*
*Public Diplomacy: USA versus USSR* (editor)
*Soviet Military Policies Since World War Two* (coauthor)
*United States-East European Relations in the 1990s* (editor)
*USSR Foreign Policies After Detente*
*Yearbook on International Communist Affairs* (editor)